THE JUDGMENT OF MARVELL

THE JUDGMENT
OF MARVELL

CHRISTINE REES

Pinter Publishers, London and New York

First published in Great Britain in 1989 by
Pinter Publishers Limited
25 Floral Street, London WC2E 9DS

British Library Cataloguing in Publication Data
A CIP catalogue record for this book is available from the
British Library
ISBN 0 86187 805 1

Library of Congress Cataloging-in-Publication Data
Rees, Christine.
    The judgment of Marvell/Christine Rees.
        p.   cm.
    Includes bibliographical references.
    ISBN 0-86178-805-1
    1. Marvell, Andrew, 1621-1678—Criticism and interpretation.
    I. Title.
    PR3546.R44   1989
    821'.4—dc20   89-39048
    CIP
                                                            CIP

Typeset by GCS, Leighton Buzzard, Beds.
Printed and bound in Great Britain by Biddles Ltd.,
Guildford and King's Lynn.

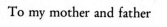

To my mother and father

Contents

Acknowledgements

My debts to those who have made this book possible are more than purely scholarly ones: they extend over a lifetime, beginning with the one acknowledged in the dedication. And I have been very fortunate at every stage of my education to have enjoyed inspired teaching both in English and in classical literature, which made reading a source of pleasure as well as contemplation.

Among those I should especially like to thank in connection with my work on Marvell are the supervisor of my first research, Miss Rosemary Syfret, and the examiners who scrutinised and commented helpfully on the results, Mrs E.E. Duncan-Jones and Professor Alastair Fowler; Professor Roger Sharrock, who read an early draft, and whose wide and profound knowledge of seventeenth-century literature and culture has been a constant benefit and stimulus; and all the Marvellian scholars and critics who have continued to throw fresh light on the poetry, especially those among my academic colleagues and students in the University of London and elsewhere: in particular, Dr Warren Chernaik, Dr Gareth Roberts, and Dr Jerry Sokol, who generously shared their own insights and knowledge. I am grateful also for institutional support: the award of a Carnegie Scholarship, and of a Mary Ewart Junior Research Fellowship at Somerville College, Oxford, at the outset of my career, and since then the opportunities provided in the congenial environment of King's College, London. My warmest thanks go to my present and former colleagues in the English Department at King's, for their encouragement when it was needed and their tact in not enquiring too frequently about the progress of a book that at times threatened to resemble Marvell's own 'vegetable Love'.

Finally, my deepest and most enduring debt is also a tribute to a choice of life that could not have been happier or more fulfilling: to my husband, Roger.

Introduction

Marvell and the Choice of Life

Contemplative and bookish men, must of necessitie be more quarrelsome than others, because they contend not about matter of fact, nor can determine their controversies by any certaine witnesses, nor judges. But as long as they goe towards peace, that is Truth, it is no matter which way.

John Donne, Preface to *Biathanatos.*

Undertaking a critical commentary on Marvell's poetry is like undertaking some legendary task without any magical shortcuts: the commentator has to sort out seeds like Psyche, or cut a way through the thorny subtleties that have sprung up in the last hundred years to choke the lyrics. Though Marvell critics are not necessarily more quarrelsome than others, it is not certain that they all make for peace, or truth, by their devious routes. Partly this is because 'matter of fact' in Marvell's case is in relatively short supply. In spite of the increase in knowledge brought about by the devoted efforts of Marvell scholars, important facts, including the chronology of poetic composition, remain matter of conjecture. But it is also partly because many twentieth-century critics have chosen circuitous and difficult routes to the truth of the poetry, finding it excitingly resistant in its very guardedness. They have preferred hidden meanings to explicit ones, since these provide more challenge to exegesis. So, as the Middle Ages and Renaissance had their Ovid *moralisé*, we have our Marvell *moralisé*. Up to a point, this treatment has served the lyrics well, bringing their fine detail to the hard light of critical scrutiny. But the light *is* hard, and sometimes throws as many shadows as it dispels. For all their claims to accuracy, the laser beam of structuralist or post-structuralist critics may prove even more difficult to operate as a means towards the reader's understanding of the poetry. What is gained in formal terms may be lost in terms of that human interest so dear to Dr Johnson and the 'common reader'. But these emphases need not be mutually exclusive. In this commentary on the lyrics I hope to do justice to exegetical subtleties, but also to recover an idea of Marvell as a poet who can be judged by Johnsonian standards.

The framework and rationale of the commentary is essentially that of the first half of the 1681 Folio of Marvell's *Miscellaneous Poems,*[1] with minimal changes: the insertion of *A Dialogue (between Thyrsis and Dorinda)* between two other dialogues, *Clorinda and Damon* and *A Dialogue between the Soul and Body*; the transposition of *The Picture of little T.C. in a Prospect of Flowers* and *The Match*; and the omission of *Tom May's Death*, which seems to have been misplaced. Marvell's modern editors have examined, and surmised about, the status and bibliographical peculiarities of the Folio text, a posthumous publication surrounded by mysterious circumstances.[2] The self-styled Mary Marvell's guarantee that the poems 'are Printed according to the exact Copies of my late dear Husband, under his own Hand-Writing, being found since his Death among his other Papers' is only as trustworthy as the guarantor. In the absence of documentary proof of a marriage between Marvell and his housekeeper, Mary Palmer, her claim has been discredited more often than defended.[3] Yet even if her credibility is accepted, we are still very ill-informed about the poems themselves: if and how they were selected, whether they were originally in some sort of order, who put them together.

The order of poems in the Folio is especially interesting since, judging from those that can be dated, it is clearly not based on chronology. Nor does it appear to be random: I have become convinced that a principle of organisation is at work, even if not always consistently applied, and that its rationale is connected less with form and genre than with subject-matter. Although the subjects are 'miscellaneous', readers and critics alike notice how interrelated Marvell's ideas and images actually are, how one poem comments upon another. For a long time, the cohesiveness of the lyric poetry has been attributed primarily to Marvell's wit, regarded both as a function of style and as a quality of mind which, in the often-quoted words of T.S. Eliot, 'implies a constant inspection and criticism of experience' and 'involves, probably, a recognition, implicit in the expression of every experience, of other kinds of experience which are possible'.[4] But in the general admiration for the wit of Marvell, the judgment of Marvell—in the seventeenth-century sense—should not be obscured. Judgment selects, separates out, classifies experiences in order to evaluate them.[5] Marvell's poetry implies not only the kinds of experience which are possible but also, finally, the kinds of experience which are desirable—and those which are inescapable.

What Marvell chooses to write about is often choice itself, or the impossibility of choosing. Those critics who have written on his politics and religion have usually acknowledged this as central. In writing about the lyric poetry however, it may seem more valid to concentrate on literary choices rather than values, especially in the current critical climate. Yet for a Renaissance writer, and for writers who inherit the Renaissance belief in man as a choosing being, these are not dissociated categories. Like the earlier Jonson and the later Johnson, and like Milton, Marvell cannot rid himself of the problem of choice. It is perhaps Samuel Johnson, a century later, who carves out the most powerful and simple phrases for an ancient idea: the choice of life and the choice of eternity. No one knew better than Johnson what complexity lies behind the phrases, how individual choices are frequently if not invariably limited and conditioned by circumstance and haunted by doubt. Out of this knowledge he wrote his fable, *Rasselas*, to expose the illusions of choice and yet maintain the dignity of choosing, even or especially when all that we are free to choose is an attitude of mind. Out of the same knowledge Marvell wrote his lyric poetry, which also confronts the choice of life and the choice of eternity with its equally idiosyncratic ironies. It seems scarcely fortuitous that the poem placed first in the Folio, *A Dialogue between the Resolved Soul and Created Pleasure*, precisely schematises the rival claims on man that underlie so much of Marvell's verse.

Two of these claims have long been recognised and studied by Marvell critics, the claims of the active and the contemplative life. But though contemplation and action have proved useful terms for analysing Marvellian dialectic, and indeed for interpreting his career, the application of the 'choice of life' scheme has been incompletely realised. An influential Renaissance version classifies the choice of life under three heads rather than just two: the *vita contemplativa*, the *vita activa*, and the third, the *vita voluptuosa*, or life of pleasure. The corresponding myth in Renaissance iconography is the Judgment of Paris, allegorised by the Neoplatonist, Ficino, popularised by poets and painters, and said to be the key to one of the major Renaissance mythographies, that of Natalis Comes. Ficino gives his interpretation in a letter to Lorenzo de Medici: he identifies each of the three deities competing for the golden apple, Minerva, Juno, and Venus, with the corresponding mode of life, contemplation, action, and pleasure; contemplation is then subdivided into learning and religious retreat, action into military and civil power, and pleasure into the delights of the five senses and respite from cares and labour.[7] A similar scheme may be traced in *A Dialogue between the Resolved Soul and Created Pleasure*. But the Resolved Soul adopts an attitude which is the reverse of Ficino's. Ficino argues that the choice of any one of the three is imperfect because it restricts human potential: to favour one deity is to invite catastrophe, for the rejected deities will take their revenge. His ideal is their union in the *triplex vita*, the threefold life which is true fulfilment, and he diplomatically praises Lorenzo for keeping in the good graces of all three deities. In contrast, Marvell's Resolved Soul totally rejects all three options, not only sensual pleasure and worldly power but the life of the intellect as well. Yet if the first poem in the collection turns its back on the *triplex vita*, the greater poem at its centre redresses the balance. *The Garden* is prepared to embrace life's richness, at least on its own metamorphic terms. And the majority of Marvell's *Miscellaneous Poems* move between these polarities.

I am far from claiming that Marvell himself would have systematised his poems according to this or any other scheme (though it is interesting that Milton, for instance, retrospectively classifying his prose works, finds it natural to adopt a threefold scheme of a different kind).[8] I do not believe that allegory is the key to his poetry, nor even that Neoplatonism is as central to an understanding of his work as has sometimes been assumed. When he did once make overt use of the Judgment of Paris myth, it was in an occasional Latin poem called *A Letter to Doctor Ingelo*. Nevertheless, the whole range of his lyrics is attuned on a deeper level to the theme of which this myth is a paradigm (indeed it is a classical analogue of the Fall of Man, since, in awarding the golden apple to Venus, Paris started the landslide of human error that swept away the towers of Troy). Because he is writing lyrics, not narrative, Marvell does not need to devise a single shaping myth for related ideas: the treatment can be small-scale, provisional, individual. If there is a recurrent myth, it is surely that of the Fall itself, in his lyric versions of paradise lost and paradise regained.[9] These are expanded in *Upon Appleton House*, Marvell's longest poem, which also takes as its theme the choice of life and the choice of eternity. But *Upon Appleton House* mediates the judgment of Marvell through the judgment of Fairfax, and unlike most of the lyrics it is rooted in an identifiable place and time. It belongs to the second half of the Folio where the poems diversify, becoming more obviously topical and more of a commentary on the active life, its personalities and events. (Even the private poems are more occasional.) By retiring to Appleton House, the Lord General Fairfax, former commander-in-chief of the Parliamentary forces, made a choice of life which he believed to be also a choice of eternity; yet he did not, or could not, divest himself and his environment of reminders of war. The values of contemplation and pleasure have to stand the test of such reminders, for both the general and his poet-in-residence.

In all his lyrics from *A Dialogue between the Resolved Soul and Created Pleasure* to *The Garden* (which may have been written at Appleton House), Marvell puts these same values to the test so that, for all their variety, these poems are strung on a continuing thread. Without resorting to an arcane reading of the Folio arrangement, it is possible to observe that these lyrics are grouped in an order that makes imaginative sense. The judgment of Marvell, like the judgment of Paris, is challenged by three rival claims: the claim of contemplative truth, the claim of sexual pleasure, and the claim of active power. Up to and including *The Garden* the active life is peripheral to the poetry's concerns, often perceived as hostile and so either evaded or rendered harmless. But the claims of contemplation and pleasure are continually defined and redefined, adjusted and readjusted. *A Dialogue between the Resolved Soul and Created Pleasure* introduces a sequence of poems which are generically differentiated as dialogues, emblem derivations, pastorals, devotional lyrics, but which are all slanted towards a religious or philosophical view of human existence. Not surprisingly the choice of eternity tends to supersede the choice of life, since contemplation as a value is already assumed—and also since a basic premise of these poems is that the condition of being a soul in a body, a fallen consciousness in a fallen world, is not a matter of choice. No human soul asks to be born. Yet the soul's reaction to its state *is* a matter of choice, whether struggle or resignation or cooperation. Developed further this becomes a choice of life. In the most 'mythic' poems of this group, *Bermudas* and *The Nymph complaining for the death of her Faun*, Marvell's protagonists move towards a choice of eternity through a choice of life which can reconcile contemplation and pleasure, given that it is pleasure of the right kind: the right sort of banquet in *Bermudas*, the right sort of love between the nymph and her fawn. Yet it is a forced choice in both instances, brought about by the inimical pressures of the world of political and military power, and in the nymph's story by the prior experience of the wrong sort of love, the sexual love that hurts and betrays. The Sylvio episode in *A Nymph complaining for the death of her Faun* introduces an erotic motif which heralds the next major grouping of the Folio, the love lyrics.

Or, lyrics about love and 'pleasure': if the word 'love' in this connection almost requires inverted commas, 'pleasure' certainly does. Although love and pleasure are traditionally identified in the *vita voluptuosa*—the life of pleasure is, after all, in the gift of Venus—Marvell does his best to drive a wedge between them. His lovers experience their choice of life as predominantly painful, and again there is a real question of how far they are free to choose at all. While there *are* pleasures to be had, the pleasures of the senses (touch in *To his Coy Mistress*, sight in *The Gallery*, hearing in *The Fair Singer*) are a snare if not a delusion. Sight, hearing, taste and smell are all gratified in *The Unfortunate Lover* but not for the lover himself, whose sacrifice provides the gratification. The pain/pleasure equation in love is a literary truism, but Marvell uses it to sharpen judgment as well as wit. It is necessary to distinguish true pleasure from the specious pleasure of sex, to take the measure of the choices available in severely limited circumstances: even in this world there are alternatives which the obsessed lover wantonly destroys, as Damon does in the Mower poems. As for the next world, the choice of eternity acquires a new irony in *To his Coy Mistress* and *The Definition of Love* where singularly bleak eternities are on offer.

Up to this point in *Miscellaneous Poems* no poem, with the possible exception of *Bermudas*, has fully ratified its choices judged against the rest. The Resolved Soul and Created Pleasure have not called a truce, and the victories of the former have conceivably turned out to be Pyrrhic. But in the two lyrics, *Musicks Empire* and *The Garden*, which are, as it were, isolated at the very heart of Marvell's poetry, we reach a point of rare equilibrium. Out of music and a garden, a threefold harmony is born: contemplation and pleasure assume their true forms as modes of experience which reconcile human beings to earth and also initiate them into eternity; even sex and militarism are transformed into innocence and order when their power is symbolically invested in musical notes and trees. Of course a number of readers will deny that these poems in any way represent a more considered judgment of Marvell than do the other lyrics, and certainly his wit is as active and elusive as ever. Nevertheless, I should wish to argue that here the theme of choice does appear at its most complete, even if the completeness is perhaps illusory and at best transitory. For *Musicks Empire* and *The Garden* conclude nothing. The poet has to return to his own Abyssinia like Johnson's characters at the end of *Rasselas*—but not the Happy Valley. Much of the rest of the Folio, with its greater bulk and less cohesion, records the creative detritus of an active life spent travelling, tutoring, looking for a job in public service and ultimately settling for professional politics as MP for Hull. The logical direction of most of these subsequent poems is out into the public domain, and more than one modern editor has found it expedient to extend the text of *Miscellaneous Poems* into the more treacherous and uncertain territory of the Restoration satires.

So the broad pattern of the Folio, obscured and interrupted in a few places, defies chronology to produce a discernible and overlapping thematic concern with the values of the *vita contemplativa*, the *vita voluptuosa*, and the *vita activa*. As, coincidentally, does the pattern of Marvell's biography. Had

Johnson written a Life of Marvell for *Lives of the Poets*,[10] he would presumably have found much to censure in his subject's choices but he would surely have recognised their relevance to his work. In the earliest stages, his father's calling as a minister, and Marvell's own student years in the Cambridge of the pre-war 1630s presented him with versions of the contemplative life—at least of a nominal kind—that he might have chosen to follow;[11] his extended European travels in the 1640s exposed him to the *vita voluptuosa* in its most seductive forms—wine, sun, paintings, music, gardens—and possibly (we are unlikely ever to know) gave him a sentimental education as well; and his varied experiences of England in the 1650s, which intensified his political awareness but also his awareness of other gentler values at Nunappleton, may at a guess have brought to a head for him the conflicting claims of the *triplex vita*. If his final decision was for the world of action, it was a choice of life made perhaps under constraint but in full knowledge of the alternatives.

'"Very few", said the poet, "live by choice. Every man is placed in his present condition by causes which acted without his foresight, and with which he did not always willingly co-operate"' (*Rasselas*, I.xvi). This was especially true of Englishmen of Marvell's generation, caught up in the condition of civil war and its aftermath. Did Marvell, like some others, compromise—or feel that he had compromised—his choice of eternity in his choice of life? Or did he concede to himself the extenuation of circumstance? As Johnson puts it 'The causes of good and evil...are so various and uncertain, so often entangled with each other, so diversified by various relations, and so much subject to accidents which cannot be foreseen, that he who would fix his condition upon incontestable reasons of preference, must live and die inquiring and deliberating' (ibid.). In a sense, Marvell did 'live and die inquiring and deliberating', while occasionally acknowledging the futility of inquiry.[12] It is clear from his post-Restoration prose works that the issues at stake continued to engage him deeply: some of the passages in *The Rehearsal Transpros'd* and its second part seem uncannily to anticipate Johnson. Without more certain evidence and insight than we possess, we should be wary of judging Marvell on his choices as a man. But we can attempt to judge his choices as a poet: and it is the poetry that rehearses most imaginatively and wittily the judgment of Marvell. Of the *Miscellaneous Poems* it can be said, as the editor of Natalis Comes said in his preface to the 1627 edition of the great *Mythologie*—'De ces trois façons de viure il est amplement traitté dans cette Oeuure . . .'.

Part I

The Contemplative Life

Set your affection on things above, not on things on the earth.

Colossians 3: 2

It could be argued that all Marvell's poetry (even the satire) is essentially contemplative, in the root meaning of the word. Etymologically it derives from the Latin *contemplare*, which has as its centre *templum*, 'an open place for observation, marked out by the augur with his staff' (*OED*, 'contemple'). Marvell's poems make or find open places for observation, with the poet himself playing the augur. He characteristically draws the reader's attention to an object, or more frequently to a manner of doing something: 'See how the Orient Dew'; 'See with what simplicity'; 'See how the arched Earth does here': 'See how loose Nature, in respect'; 'Heark how the Mower *Damon* Sung'.[1] But to attend is not enough, without thinking, interpreting, feeling, or wondering. With wonder, contemplation shades into religious experience: we see how things are, in order to feel the mystery that they are. With regard to the Creator, wonder is 'broken knowledge', in Bacon's phrase. But 'all knowledge and wonder (which is the seed of knowledge) is an impression of pleasure in itself'. Contemplation is the proper function of both soul and mind.[2]

While the practice of contemplation is in the very grain of Marvellian lyric, it is the poems early in the sequence which concentrate more immediately on recognisable contemplative subjects and techniques. Elsewhere in his poetry Marvell makes use of the contemplative life as a theme, but here he also uses formal means such as emblems to practise contemplation in a narrower, more specialised sense. Before a choice of life can be made, the individual has to confront the fundamental conditions that determine human existence. These lyrics are addressed precisely to the problem of spiritual survival in, and response to, an earthly environment. Consequently the poet invades the territory of moral philosopher and theologian, and in particular he appropriates one of their favourite domains, the study of the soul.

How much of an 'easie Philosopher' could Marvell claim to be? Certainly in the seventeenth century no educated man was completely untrai matters. Unlike a number of religious metaphysical poets, Mar himself in orders: nor was he an academic philosopher. But even ap classical and religious education, while still a very young man l exposed to at least three influences which could shape and colour perceptions: his Calvinistically inclined father; the powerful currents of Platonism and Puritanism swirling through Cambridge when Marvell was up as an undergraduate (though his own college, Trinity, was not in the mainstream of either); and the counterforce, briefly experienced, of Jesuit teaching, which apparently swept him out of Cambridge to London where he was 'rescued' by his parent. On a personal level, this paternal influence was probably the deepest and most long-lasting, as *The Rehearsal Transpros'd* seems to indicate.[3] But in relation to his poetry it is the sheer range of intellectual choice that is suggestive. How eclectic is Marvell in drawing on these different traditions—Calvinist, Platonist, Catholic—for his lyric imagining of the soul?

The contemplative life may be historically associated with Catholicism rather than Protestantism for a variety of reasons: but through modern scholarship it has become possible to understand, on the one hand how accessible and sympathetic Catholic habits and techniques of devotional exercise could be to seventeenth-century Protestants, even when they opposed Catholic dogma, and on the other hand how a distinctively Protestant meditative mode could develop.[4] It is hardly surprising that Protestants should value and practise religious meditation, without necessarily equating it with the contemplative life as such. Even if one discounts the need for some form of meditation to nourish spiritual being, the Protestant and especially the Puritan emphasis on inwardness, on unmediated communion between the soul and God, encourages withdrawal into prayerful and directed thought. Puritanism fosters an introspective preoccupation with the state and destiny of the soul; for the most precise Calvinists, the doctrine of the elect intensified this soul-searching. Yet Calvin himself did not limit meditation to the hard line of self-interrogation designed to bring to light the soul's innate depravity. He recognised the power and reach of thought directed positively towards the heavenly life, and endorsed Paul's words 'Set your affection on things above' (Colossians 3: 2). Marvell's contemporary, Richard Baxter, exactly demonstrates this 'Heavenly Meditation' in *The Saints' Everlasting Rest* (1650), setting other objects of contemplation in relation to their chief end:

> Meditation hath a large field to walk in, and hath as many objects work upon, as there are matters, and lines, and words in the Scripture, as there are known Creatures in the whole Creation, and as there are particular discernable passages of Providence...through the world: But the Meditation that I now direct you in, is onely of the end of all these, and of these as they refer to that end.[5]

Marvell's *Dialogue between the Resolved Soul and Created Pleasure* is in the tradition of Puritan contemplation as Baxter defines it. It is fascinating to watch Baxter confronting Created Pleasure with a rhetorical strategy similar to that of the Resolved Soul (and incidentally betraying his own lively sense of that pleasure):

Compare also the delights above, with the lawfull delights of moderated senses . . .
. . . .
How delightful are pleasant odors to our smel? how delightful is perfect musick to
the ear? how delightful are beauteous sights to the eye? . . . . O then think every time
thou seest or remembrest these, what a fragrant smell hath the pretious ointment
which is poured on the head of our glorified Saviour, and which must be poured on
the heads of all his Saints? . . . how delightful is the musick of the heavenly host?
how pleasing will be those real beauties above?

He goes on to compare the delights of 'natural knowledg' with those above,
and concludes that just as they surpass sensual beauty and pleasure so they in
turn are surpassed by the beauty of God. If the strategy resembles that of the
Resolved Soul, it is not however identical with it: where Baxter compares,
Marvell contrasts, making hardly any concessions to 'the lawfull delights of
moderated senses' or of 'natural knowledg'. Nor is the Resolved Soul so
specific in describing the sounds and scents of heaven. While averting his gaze
from this world, he does not fix it so precisely on things above, perhaps wiser
in this than those contemplatives who make heaven into too close an image of
earth's glories.

For Marvell's equivalent of Baxter's Puritan pleasures, we have to turn to
Bermudas. This island paradise is not the saints' everlasting rest, but it is their
refuge from persecution, created and sustained (we are asked to believe) by a
predestinating deity for the joy and contemplation of his elect. In the view of
some readers it is a flawed paradise; but there is no indication that their song
of praise is unacceptable to the God they address. What happens when a song
is unacceptable is bleakly adumbrated in *The Coronet*, perhaps the most
Puritan of Marvell's contemplative poems in its formal soul-searching and its
Calvinist theology of innate depravity and arbitrary grace. *A Dialogue
between the Resolved Soul and Created Pleasure*, *The Coronet*, and *Bermudas*
could be said to represent three points on a spectrum of Puritan thinking
about the possibility of spiritual choice.

But there are other ways of looking at the soul's dilemma. Interspersed
among these Puritan poems are lyrics reflecting a different philosophy. In the
course of his intellectual development Marvell had absorbed a mental
colouring which could camouflage him as he moved delicately through the
thickets of seventeenth-century doctrine. He could think like a Calvinist or a
Platonist, choosing whether to reconcile or accentuate—or leave ambiguous—traditional teachings about the soul.

Marvell's contact with contemporary Platonism is less determinate than his
contact with Puritanism, but while he was up at university he might well have
been exposed to the ideas of the scholarly group of Cambridge Platonists who
were shaping pre-war Cambridge in the image of ancient Athens and
Renaissance Florence. Ideas are contagious in an academic society, and it
seems unlikely that Marvell would be insensitive to the strongly idealistic
atmosphere radiating from men like Benjamin Whichcote (whose sermons
Marvell would have had the opportunity of hearing).[7] The Cambridge
Platonists exemplified how the choice of the contemplative life, as opposed to
the life of worldly ambition, could be its own justification and fulfilment. Yet

they did not divorce thought from action, or truth from beauty. 'There is an inward beauty, life and loveliness in Divine Truth, which cannot be known but onely then when it is digested into life and practice', affirms John Smith—a principle supported by Ralph Cudworth and Benjamin Whichcote, who coined the aphorism 'God expects Man should *Do*; as He makes him capable'. The intellect is given its due, since 'true Knowledge' is 'so noble and gallant a perfection of the mind' (Cudworth).[8] In short, pleasure and action fall into place as by-products of contemplation: the threefold life is a real possibility.

This is where Cambridge Platonism diverges from strict Calvinism. Perhaps the simplest reason for the difference is that Cambridge Platonists hold a much higher opinion of the human soul. In their language, it is '*the Candle of the Lord;* Lighted *by* God, and Lighting us *to* God'; their message is '*intra te quaere Deum*, seek for God within thine own soul'.[9] Because the human soul can still be regarded as deiform, as in the original Neoplatonic system, self-contemplation (so harrowing an experience for the Calvinist) becomes inseparable from the serene contemplation of the divine. Whereas Calvin in his commentary on the soul constantly emphasises its present depravity as a result of the Fall—'although we grant that the image of God was not utterly effaced and destroyed in him, it was, however, so corrupted, that any thing which remains is fearful deformity'[10]—the Cambridge Platonists in a beautiful communal image derived from Macrobius's *Commentary* envisage the soul as a sleeping musician, who needs only to be awakened to a few phrases from a remembered song to reconstruct the whole piece.[11] Plato is ultimately responsible for this theory of innate ideas. Even Calvin, it is worth noting, although dismissive of moral philosophy in general—'it were vain to seek a definition of the soul from philosophers'—makes an exception of Plato, as the one ancient philosopher who maintains the immortality of the soul and regards it as an image of God.[12] In Calvin's view, philosophers are not only wrong about the nature of the soul, but also about freedom of choice:

> The principle they set out with was, that man could not be a rational animal unless he had a free choice of good and evil. They also imagined that the distinction between virtue and vice was destroyed, if man did not of his own counsel arrange his life. So far well, had there been no change in man. This being unknown to them, it is not surprising that they throw everything into confusion. But those who, while they profess to be the disciples of Christ, still seek for free-will in man, notwithstanding of his being lost and drowned in spiritual destruction, labour under manifold delusion, making a heterogeneous mixture of inspired doctrine and philosophical opinions, and so erring as to both.
>
> (*Institutes*, I.xv.8.)[13]

'A heterogeneous mixture of inspired doctrine and philosophical opinions': the opponents of Cambridge Platonism might well have savoured and applied such a phrase. But metaphysical poets are not dismayed by heterogeneous mixtures, and, on all the evidence, Platonism of any kind has more to offer the poetic imagination than Calvinism. As a moral and artistic being, man needs to believe in choice, no matter how hedged about that choice may be. Once the possibility of choice is assumed, the poet-philosopher is free to investigate the soul's reactions to its fallen existence—a subject that clearly fascinates Marvell.

Further, the dignity of the soul seems to depend, in some measure at least, on a dualistic habit of thinking that separates it from mortal matter. But Christian theology resists *moral* dualism. The biblical imagery of flesh warring against spirit should not be simply equated with a conflict between body and soul, since corruption is located in the human will (which again raises the problem of choice). For Neoplatonists, the relation of the soul to matter can be seen both positively and negatively. On one hand, the soul functions constructively and creatively, as indispensable mediator between the divine intelligence and the world of matter; on the other hand, it is, as it were, an alien transplant, always in danger of being attacked, contaminated or rejected while in the body.[14]

And from the soul's viewpoint, the world of matter is most intimately represented by, and experienced in, its own body. Marvell images this truism in the uneasy contact of dewdrop and flower in On a Drop of Dew, a poem which seems to owe something to Neoplatonism, and exploits it in the witty Cartesian Dialogue between the Soul and Body, in which both parties make a futile unilateral declaration of independence. By extension from its body, the soul finds itself in relation to the rest of the physical world: it can derive pleasure from it, act upon it, and—most important, because it is a unique source of power—contemplate it. It follows that the soul can hardly remain neutral, but must accept, tolerate, or reject what it sees. Plato and Plotinus, Augustine and Calvin, all have much to say on this subject. From these intellectual tensions it is possible to harness more than enough imaginative energy to generate poetry, and this is precisely what Marvell does.

Whatever the differences among theorists of the soul, there is substantial agreement on one point: for the contemplative soul, the creation is a means, not an end. Both Platonists and Puritans distinguish between an inferior and a superior good, though the latter take a gloomier view of the soul's capacity to utilise the means without being led astray into creating and worshipping false gods. The beauty of the created world can be used or abused even by the contemplative, since it either draws the soul towards, or distracts it from, the higher relationship with divinity that is the ultimate goal. This issue, rather than the inherent goodness of matter, is Marvell's primary concern in his contemplative poems.

Finally, although Marvell's supposed Catholic conversion was short-lived, the experience may have contributed something permanent to his art. Jesuit literature offered him not only a further emphasis on choice, but also a methodology, a way of organising his contemplation and giving it formal expression. If Puritanism and Platonism could concentrate the mind on the soul and its connection with the senses, Catholic art could embody ideas in creative forms which Calvinists in particular—because of their distrust of the human faculties—were reluctant to develop. Marvell's liking for such forms (shared by other non-Catholic English poets) leads him to experiment with a well-known subgenre in *Eyes and Tears*, and to adapt a Jesuit source in *A Dialogue between the Soul and Body*.[15] Possibly this literary taste had its origins in some quality of temperament that accounts for his early response to Catholicism. Does his later witty and vehement rejection of 'Popery' in all its forms derive part of its force from a repressed attraction? Whether or not that is the case, his attack is not made in ignorance, and is not wholly political. His main objection to the Catholic version of the contemplative life seems to be that it becomes a travesty: the *vita contemplativa* is confounded in the *vita voluptuosa*. Certainly this is true of the convent sequence in *Upon Appleton House* which—since in this poem Marvell's foreign reminiscences surface surprisingly often—may owe something to impressions gained from his extensive travels in Catholic Europe. Yet if his judgment found against the Catholic tradition on account of its power of illusion and sensuality, the artist in him engages with these same powers. Contemplation and pleasure are not so easily separated, even in the contemplative lyrics. From *A Dialogue between the Resolved Soul and Created Pleasure* to *The Nymph complaining for the death of her Faun* imagination and judgment contest their territory, putting the final onus of choice on Marvell's readers.

(i) The Choice of Eternity: A Dialogue between the Resolved Soul and Created Pleasure

The poem which introduces the reader to the 1681 *Miscellaneous Poems* has received less attention than its position might warrant, perhaps because it appears neither sufficiently difficult nor sufficiently imposing.[1] But it is salutary to remember that Marvell himself expresses elsewhere a preference for humble gateways, praising

> that more sober Age and Mind,
> When larger sized Men did stoop
> To enter at a narrow loop;
> As practising, in doors so strait,
> To strain themselves through *Heavens Gate.*
>
> (*Upon Appleton House,* iv, 28–32)

However quizzical in tone, this sentiment with its biblical allusion[2] fits *A Dialogue between the Resolved Soul and Created Pleasure* very neatly. If the larger size of critic finds it embarrassingly 'strait', the reader may come to feel that it serves adequately to frame the wider landscape of Marvellian lyric. As befits a gateway, it is Janus-faced, looking in two directions: it is, after all, a dialogue. Yet it does not face both ways quite in the sense of what we usually mean when we speak of Marvell's 'ambiguity', and the dialogue's 'ballance' is not even. It turns out to be less about choice in the making than about a choice well made. This trial by combat is effectively a staged demonstration of fighting skills ('shew' . . . 'shew'). The poet—himself, incidentally, Spanish-trained—is rehearsing his soul in the martial art of self-defence.[3]

> Courage my Soul, now learn to wield
> The weight of thine immortal Shield.
> Close on thy Head thy Helmet bright.
> Ballance thy Sword against the Fight.
> See where an Army, strong as fair
> With silken Banners spreads the air.
> Now, if thou bee'st that thing Divine,
> In this day's Combat let it shine:
> And shew that Nature wants an Art
> To conquer one resolved Heart.
>
> (ll. 1–10)

At the outset, the poem presents its Puritan credentials: not only does the imagery recall biblical sources, in particular Ephesians 6:13-17, and perhaps, out of context, the magnificent phrase 'terrible as an army with banners' (Canticles 6: 4); the idea of the warfaring Christian was also an especially vital and pervasive one in Puritan literature. One sentence from the Dedicatory

Epistle to John Downame's *Christian Warfare*, 1604, which ran into a number of seventeenth-century editions, can stand as representative:

> We are besieged with forraine forces, the world and the divell; and we nourish in us secret traytors, even the flesh, with whole legions of the lusts thereof, which are continually readie to open the gates of our soules, even our senses of seeing, hearing, touching, tasting, smelling, whereby whole troupes of temptations enter and surprize us.[4]

Downame counts off the senses, as it were, on his fingers, and this, combined with his military metaphor, anticipates Marvell's development of a similar scheme for the first part of his dialogue. But Created Pleasure is no mere purveyor of sensual delights. Like other subtle tempters, conspicuously Milton's,[5] he presents the Resolved Soul with an image of itself in relation to its environment, an image all the more dangerous because it is not altogether false. When he first greets the objects of his seduction as 'the Creations Guest,/Lord of Earth, and Heavens Heir', he is expressing a received doctrine regarding the original status of unfallen man, a doctrine which for most Christians other than the strictest Calvinists still coloured fallen man's religious response to nature's beauty and generosity. As George Herbert puts it in his poems *Man* and *Providence*—

> The whole is, either our cupboard of *food*,
> 　Or cabinet of *pleasure*.
>
> (Man, ll. 29–30)
>
> Thy creatures leap not, but expresse a feast,
> Where all the guests sit close, and nothing wants.
>
> (Providence, ll. 133–4)[6]

But what are we to make of Created Pleasure's version of this banquet?

> Where the Souls of fruits and flow'rs
> Stand prepar'd to heighten yours.
>
> (ll. 15–16)

This is no ordinary temptation of taste. Whether or not a precise theory of how fruit and flowers participate in soul underlies Marvell's lines, the imaginative effect is the opposite of Herbert's—the creatures *do* 'leap', with a resulting snarl in the chain of being which entangles and degrades the human soul. It should not need its powers heightened by means that suggest intoxication rather than true spirituality. For this experience the Resolved Soul substitutes a heavenly hospitality, briefly hinting at the consummation celebrated in Herbert's greatest 'feast' poem, *Love (III):*

> I sup above, and cannot stay
> To bait so long upon the way.
>
> (ll. 17–18)

A number of critics have noted how the metrical contrast between Created Pleasure's trochaic rhythms and the Resolved Soul's octosyllabic couplets contributes to their characterisation.[7] With his wordplay on 'bait', the Resolved Soul assumes the dual Puritan roles of wayfaring and warfaring Christian, and also proves that the sword he balances is a weapon of wit.

Against this weapon Created Pleasure attacks with his own brand of eloquence. Like a skilled advertiser of this world's wares, he offers fantasies rather than material objects as such. In this opening sequence he sets out his properties, fruit, flowers, perfumes, music, to conjure up a special kind of life, that *vita voluptuosa* brought to a fine art in pagan and neo-pagan cultures.

> On these downy Pillows lye,
> Whose soft Plumes will thither fly:
> On these Roses strow'd so plain
> Lest one Leaf thy Side should strain.
>
> (ll. 19–22):

The Sybaritic bed of roses may have been taken directly from its Senecan source, but Marvell would also be familiar with its erotically inviting aspect in Elizabethan and libertine verse. Spenser's Acrasia lies on a bed of roses, and Marlowe's passionate shepherd and Thomas Carew both entice their loves with the prospect of similar beds.[8] In passing, it seems not altogether unlikely that Marvell might have had Marlowe's famous lyric singing in his head when he was composing Created Pleasure's side of the dialogue, for although he chooses a different metre, the imagery has more than a hint of Marlovian pastoral: in particular, the stanza allotted to Music (ll. 37–40) faintly recalls the enchantment of 'shallow rivers, to whose falls/ Melodious birds sing madrigals'. But to return to the bed of roses, clearly the Resolved Soul has heeded such warnings as that of Francis Quarles—'And he repents in Thornes, that sleeps in Beds of Roses'[9]—for he retorts

> My gentler Rest is on a Thought,
> Conscious of doing what I ought.
>
> (ll. 23–4)

The play on 'Rest', 'which includes the idea not only of *repose* but of *choice* ... and also more remotely that of *support*'[10] is worthy of Herbert; but the tone might betray a possible weakness in the Soul's defences, a tendency to self-sufficiency, if not spiritual pride. At any rate, his opponent immediately addresses himself to this possibility.

The succeeding temptations are targeted precisely on the consciousness of self. Perfume is valued less for its sweetness than for its symbolism: it will make the Soul appear 'Like another God below' ('ye shall be as gods' said the serpent to Eve).[11] The Resolved Soul readily identifies the trap, but Created Pleasure continues with the idea of substituting self for godhead more covertly in the stanza directed at the sense of sight:

> Every thing does seem to vie
> Which should first attract thine Eye:
> But since none deserves that grace,
> In this Crystal view *thy* face.
>
> (ll. 31–4)

This is the first occurrence in the Folio text of an image that continually intrigues Marvell, the mirror image. He makes use of it in different contexts as an analogy for the problematic relationship between the mind and external reality—particularly the natural world, the *speculum mundi*—or, in a more complicated fashion, for the mind's consciousness of itself.[12] The twentieth-century philosopher, Gilbert Ryle, in *The Concept of Mind*, gives an elegant and hostile account of how this analogy developed in the seventeenth century, concluding that 'the myth of consciousness is a piece of para-optics.'[13] In Marvell's dialogue consciousness is not a myth, but through the optical image the Resolved Soul is being tempted to the wrong kind of 'reflection'. He has to be alert not only to the danger of narcissism but also to that of blasphemy, for the creation reflects God, not man, and the grace is His alone. Salluste du Bartas had so described the unfallen world: in the words of his translator, Josuah Sylvester—

> It glads me much to view this Frame; wherein,
> As in a Glasse God's glorious face is seene . . .[14]

This is the orthodox view of the original creation. A less orthodox account of creation and fall, found in the Hermetic writings, comes closer to what Created Pleasure is suggesting. In this version, the human soul falls in love with nature as a reflection of its own beauty: in the words of Everard's 1657 translation of *Hermes Mercurius Trismegistus, his Divine Pymander*, 'seeing in the Water a shape, a shape like unto himself, in himself he loved it' (ii,24);[15] and the consequence is the soul's descent into matter. But Marvell's Resolved Soul proves himself capable of the crucial discrimination between Creator and created, and penetrates the 'Earth disguis'd' (ll. 35–6).

Created Pleasure then resorts to the most potent of the temptations aimed against the senses: even gods and nature succumb to the Orphic power of music:

> Heark how Musick then prepares
> For thy Stay these charming Aires;
> Which the posting Winds recall,
> And suspend the Rivers Fall.
>
> (ll. 37–40)

Unfortunately, it was not only Orpheus who could claim such powers in the ancient world. Thessalian witches had a similar prerogative which could be used for sinister purposes (as Marvell could have learnt from Lucan).[16] It is in character that Created Pleasure should evoke pagan associations of an ambiguous kind. But these could be countered positively in a Christian context. Indeed from a Puritan viewpoint, there is a Scriptural case to be made for music as solace and recreation: David displaces Orpheus as the archetypal sweet singer. In spite of the controversy over Church music, eminent Puritans such as Cromwell and Milton shared a passion for music in their personal lives.[17] Moreover, the primacy of hearing over sight in Marvell's arrangement, which is the less usual form of sense hierarchy, is true to the values of Puritanism, or at least the reformed tradition.[18] By his own standards this is the severest test of the Resolved Soul, and nowhere does he reveal greater spiritual effort in maintaining his freedom of mind, and resisting a beauty which, had he but world enough and time, would absorb his total attention:

> Had I but any time to lose,
> On this I would it all dispose.
> Cease Tempter. None can chain a mind
> Whom this sweet Chordage cannot bind.
>
> (ll. 41-4)

The pun on 'Chordage' is both arrestingly simple and an erudite conceit. John Hollander observes that 'a pun on *chorda* ("string") and *cor, cordis* ("heart"), possibly first introduced by Cassiodorus, became so deeply embedded in habitual thinking that the very origins of the word "concord" ... often even today are mistaken for being musical.'[19] The notion of heart-strings lent itself to emblems: hence the punning motto, *Chorda trahit corda*. Frank Kermode makes another learned connection with the words of St Augustine: 'voluptates aurium tenacius me implicaverant et subiugaverant', 'the pleasures of the ear had more firmly entangled and subdued me' than those of the other senses (*Confessions*, x.ii et seq.).[20] The weight of allusion makes this perhaps the most interesting and imaginative of the Resolved Soul's answers. But what is also interesting is that he departs from the established pattern in one important respect. Given the previous answers, where the Resolved Soul offers a spiritual counterpart to earthly pleasures—the divine feast, the 'gentler Rest', the perfume of humility, the Creator's art—we might expect that he would substitute the music of heaven for the Orphic music that magically controls the winds and waters of the lower world. But he does not, although such an answer would be in line with an accepted procedure of Puritan meditation.[21] Joseph Hall, in *The Arte of Divine Meditation* (1607), gives as an example of the right response to hearing sweet music the cry 'What Musicke may we thinke there is in heauen?' (pp. 14–15), and Baxter's similar instance has already been noticed (see above, Part I, 'The Contemplative Life'). The Resolved Soul is more puritanical than his possible mentors: perhaps because any alternative would be too great a concession to music's power over the mind.

Paradoxically, the whole form of *A Dialogue between the Resolved Soul and Created Pleasure* seems to cry out for a musical setting. 'Acting in song, especially in dialogues, hath an extreme good grace', says Bacon in his essay, *Of Masques and Triumphs*.[22] Certainly the Chorus show no inhibitions about expressing themselves musically, and their intervention, separating the two temptation sequences, audaciously appeals to both eye and ear:

> *Earth cannot shew so brave a Sight*
> *As when a single Soul does fence*
> *The Batteries of alluring Sense,*
> *And Heaven views it with delight.*
> *Then persevere: for still new Charges sound:*
> *And if thou overcom'st thou shalt be crown'd.*

((ll. 45–50)

'Brave' is a doubly appropriate epithet, since it applies not only to the Soul's courage, but also to the quality of the spectacle *as* spectacle. Like the Unfortunate Lover, whose struggle also evokes masque, the Resolved Soul has the most august audience in the universe. Here Marvell blends classical and Christian allusion, Seneca's *De Providentia*[23] and the promises of the New Testament (see, for example, 2 Timothy 2: 3–5 and 4: 7–8).

If the poem is analogous to a miniature masque or triumph, some kind of structuring mythological device would be in order, and as the dialogue progresses into its second sequence interesting possibilities present themselves. Frank Kermode has made a convincing case for associating Marvell's entire scheme with the Christianised myth of the Choice of Hercules, the Prodician Choice.[24] A parallel myth, not cited by Kermode, is the Judgment of Paris, which in later antiquity was associated with the Hercules Story and its meaning:

> the Judgement of Paris, as told in poetry by the writers of an older time, is really a *trial of pleasure against virtue* [my italics]. Aphrodite, for example—and she represents pleasure—was given the preference, and so everything was thrown into turmoil. I think, too, that our noble Xenophon invented the story of Heracles and Virtue with the same motive.
>
> (Athenaeus, *Deipnosophistae*, XII, 510c)[25]

The trial of virtue against pleasure is a common motif in masques. And in the second, more generalised, temptation sequence of *A Dialogue between the Resolved Soul and Created Pleasure* there are clues which suggest that Marvell might indeed be using a 'choice of life' schema, centred on the question of what man should live for—pleasure, power, or the life of the mind.

The first of these temptations is of special interest:

> All this fair, and soft, and sweet,
>   Which scatteringly doth shine,
> Shall within one Beauty meet,
> And she be only thine.

(ll. 51–4)

In the Judgment of Paris myth, the life of pleasure is symbolised by the possession of the one perfect beauty, a Helen among women. Kermode glosses these lines with a reference to Zeuxis the painter, mentioned in Cicero's *De Inventione*, who 'believing that in nature all possible beauties could not be found in one body (*uno in corpore*...) used many models for his painting of Helen.'[26] The motif is a favourite one with Renaissance poets, so that by the seventeenth century there are many such Helens gracing English lyrics, making the idea of beauty's unique epitome self-defeatingly commonplace. Apparently Marvell had not far to seek for his phrasing. Margoliouth based his emendation of the Folio reading, 'cost', to 'soft' on the grounds of comparison with the following lines from Abraham Cowley's poem *The Soul* (published in *The Mistress*, 1647):

> If all things that in *Nature* are
> Either soft, or sweet, or fair,
> Be not in Thee so' Epitomiz'd
>
> (ll. 17–19)[27]

There is at least one other poem, *A Letter to his Mistresse*, printed in Abraham Wright's *Parnassus Biceps* (1656), that uses the same formula:

> The glory of the chiefest day,
> The morning aire perfum'd in *May:*
> The first-borne Rose of all the spring,
> The down beneath the Turtles wing;
> A Lute just reaching to the eare,
> What ere is soft is sweet is faire,
> Are but her shreds, who fills the place
> And summe of every single grace.
>
> (pp. 39–40)

Although this catalogue of created pleasures is charming, the conceit improves with conciseness: Marvell's conjunction of 'scatteringly' and 'shine'—possibly with a half-recollection of Donne's 'scatt'ring bright' in *Aire and Angels*—is wittier and more alluring. Even briefer is a variant by Richard Lovelace (a friend of Marvell's) which substitutes the epithet 'bright' and introduces the metaphor of heaven:

> Her selfe the Heav'n in which did meet
> The *All* of bright, of faire and sweet.
> (*Amyntor's Grove*, ll. 11–12)[28]

But for the Resolved Soul the name of heaven is not to be taken in vain:

> If things of Sight such Heavens be,
> What Heavens are those we cannot see?
>
> (ll. 55–6)

Marvell's emphasis on *sight* as the crucial sense for the life of pleasure, which appears to contradict his original sense of hierarchy, also has a parallel in the Judgment of Paris. Several sixteenth- and seventeenth-century versions of the story stress that Paris was seduced through his highest sense, his sight, and in one instance—a fairly undistinguished *Apologie for Paris* (1649) attributed to Robert Baron—the author exploits the familiar topos, that sight takes precedence over hearing.[29] In his reply the Resolved Soul reverts to his successful strategy of substitution of the spiritual for the physical, and bears witness to his faith, 'the evidence of things not seen' (Hebrews 11:1). Created Pleasure, on the other hand, has been forced to alter his tactics, and verse-form.

The second sequence, like the first, is constructed hierarchically, and is in fact more orthodox. Traditionally on the 'choice of life' scale, pleasure occupies the lowest level, and contemplation is the highest good. Action, the middle factor, is the most variable, since the active life may take a number of forms: power can be exercised through money or force, in time of peace or in time of war. It is not therefore surprising that Created Pleasure needs two stanzas to set up his options:

> Where so e're thy Foot shall go
>   The minted Gold shall lie;
> Till thou purchase all below,
>   And want new Worlds to buy.
>   . . . .
> Wilt thou all the Glory have
>   That War or Peace commend?
> Half the World shall be thy Slave
>   The other half thy Friend.

(ll. 57–60, 63–6)

Yet these seem curiously disappointing, regarded as imaginative temptations. The flat symmetries of the second stanza in particular lack the enchantment that Created Pleasure could bring to music or sex. If in theory the sequence is an ascending one, in poetic practice it evidently declines. The test is the ultimate temptation, which corresponds to the contemplative life and which should be the climax on both Platonic and Christian scales: the temptation to acquire the supreme power, the power of (forbidden) knowledge. This is another possible application of the Judgment of Paris myth, as well as being relevant to the Fall. Montemayor's prose romance, *Diana*, which Marvell very likely knew, includes a debate on the Judgment of Paris in which a case is made for Pallas's claim to the apple inscribed 'To the fairest', on the grounds that she represents the higher beauty of the mind.[30] Yet the lines given to Created Pleasure pale in the light of that beauty, leaving its potential poetry largely untapped:

> Thou shalt know each hidden Cause;
>   And see the future Time:

> Try what depth the Centre draws;
> And then to Heaven climb.
>
> (ll. 69–72)

It would be possible to invoke Faust here, or, say, Alexander for the previous temptation: but such presences remain shadowy at best.[31] Even the Virgilian allusion, 'Felix qui potuit rerum cognoscere causas',[32] scarcely irradiates the verse. The temptation to become a magus is—relatively—unmagical.

Perhaps one explanation is that Marvell is trying to achieve two slightly contradictory effects with his second scheme. He uses the 'choice of life' format which dictates a rising pattern, but he is really writing about the choice of eternity which annihilates these distinctions. When salvation is at stake, it matters little whether it is pleasure or knowledge that costs man his soul. The wisdom of the Resolved Soul contrasts implicitly not only with the foolishness of the sensual Paris but with the wisdom of this world, sought after by the Greeks and cherished by Renaissance humanists. His retorts have lost none of their crispness: the dry distinction between 'price' and 'value' in the rejection of wealth (11. 61–2) is of the epigrammatic calibre we have come to expect. But his attitude has become almost too disengaged, too stoical in the precise sense:

> What Friends, if to my self untrue?
> What Slaves, unless I captive you?
>
> (ll. 67–8)

It could be said that the Soul's personality is coming to resemble more and more closely that of Milton's Christ in *Paradise Regained*. His final triumph is through the paradox of a humility which alone can scale the heights of heaven (ll. 73–4).

The Resolved Soul's Pauline victory—his choice of eternity—is applauded by the Chorus in unequivocal terms:

> *Triumph, triumph, victorious Soul:*
> *The World has not one Pleasure more:*
> *The rest does lie beyond the Pole,*
> *And is thine everlasting Store.*
>
> (ll. 75–8)

Yet the question remains, do the choice of life and the choice of eternity actually belong to the Resolved Soul at all? On the one hand, there is the view that the soul is morally responsible and that earthly choices have consequences hereafter, a view summed up in Henry Vaughan's lines—

> His choice in life concerns the Chooser much:
> For when he dyes, his good or ill (just such
> As here it was) goes with him hence, and staies
> Still by him, his strict Judge in the last dayes.[35]

On the other hand, according to Calvinist logic, there is only one Chooser: God. The Soul either is, or is not, already one of His elect. *A Dialogue between the Resolved Soul and Created Pleasure* would then demonstrate that he is,[34] corresponding to the later stages of the regenerate soul's progress. The early stages, vocation, conviction of sin, repentance, play no part in the poem itself. What we see is the justified soul experiencing sanctification (that is, perseverance in a holy life by God's grace), and anticipating glorification.

Yet the Calvinist reading is not entirely satisfying. The notion of free will stubbornly persists, reinforced by the original injunction 'now learn' ... Like Milton, Marvell is interested in education as a process of learning how to choose, and although the Resolved Soul knows the theory, so to speak, he has to be given the responsibility of putting it into practice. As more than one commentator has observed, he is almost a textbook illustration of the warfaring/wayfaring Christian so impressively defined by Milton in *Areopagitica:* 'He that can apprehend and consider vice with all her baits and seeming pleasures, and yet abstain, and yet distinguish, and yet prefer that which is truly better, he is the true warfaring Christian.'[35] But 'that which is truly better' has earthly as well as heavenly connotations. Many of the poems which are to follow *A Dialogue between the Resolved Soul and Created Pleasure* in the Folio will be concerned in more complicated and worldly ways with the art of making distinctions. Perhaps *A Dialogue* sacrifices something in its schematic and uncompromising manner of presenting the whole cycle of choice: nevertheless, it sets the Marvellian stamp on *Miscellaneous Poems* in both form and content.

(ii) Ars contemplativa: on a Drop of Dew, The Coronet, Eyes and Tears

On a Drop of Dew

From the soul as warrior to the soul as a drop of dew is, on the face of it, an odd metempsychosis. Between the first and second poems in the Folio the sense of active engagement diminishes abruptly: dialogue gives way to emblem. Instead of addressing his own soul at the outset, the speaker stands alongside the reader and requires him to contemplate—to look hard and closely at—a precisely visualised image:

> See how the Orient Dew,
> Shed from the Bosom of the Morn
>   Into the blowing Roses,
> Yet careless of its Mansion new;
> For the clear Region where 'twas born
>   Round in its self incloses:
> And in its little Globes Extent,
> Frames as it can its native Element.
>   How it the purple flow'r does slight,
>   Scarce touching where it lyes,
>   But gazing back upon the Skies,
>   Shines with a mournful Light;
>   Like its own Tear,
> Because so long divided from the Sphear.
>   Restless it roules and unsecure,
>   Trembling lest it grow impure:
> Till the warm Sun pitty it's Pain,
> And to the Skies exhale it back again.
>
> (ll. 1–18)

The poem is not, however, as transparent as its central image. *On a Drop of Dew* does in a sense mirror its subject perfectly: it is limpid, self-contained, apparently symmetrical—and liable to vaporise beneath the burning-glass of critical scrutiny. As Marvell's own line, transposed, would describe it, 'Bright above, but dark beneath'. The brilliant reflexive use of syntax and imagery creates a slippery surface off which the mind glances, unable to engage with something which seems to be *all* reflection.[1] Yet if the poem is to succeed as a contemplative poem, it is natural to ask what is being reflected. Among the answers to this question some familiar ideas come to light. Commentators have found reflections of Plotinus, of Augustine, of the Bible, of other poets, all more or less illuminating and by no means mutually exclusive.[2] But in the beginning is the image itself, that which reflects, Marvell's drop of dew.

    The description quoted above constitutes almost half the poem, which is self-mirroring in its very structure. The second part beginning 'So the

Soul...' explains point for point the special appropriateness of the
dewdrop/soul analogy. But the emotional parallel precedes the logical. The
analogy will only work if the reader is already disposed to see the subject in a
particular way. To this end, Marvell slants his language emotively—careless,
mournful, restless, unsecure, trembling—to make the reader feel how
vulnerable the drop of dew is, how precarious and perfect its beauty, how
pitiable its plight. There is something of the protectiveness voiced in the
Emperor Hadrian's address to his departing soul:

> Animula vagula, blandula,
> Hospes comésque corporis,
> Quae nunc abibis in loca?
> Pallidula, querula, nudula,
> Nec, ut soles, dabis jocos.

> *My soul, my pleasant soul and witty,*
> *The guest and consort of my body,*
> *Into what place now all alone*
> *Naked and sad wilt thou be gone?*
> *No mirth, no wit, as heretofore,*
> *Nor Jests wilt thou afford me more.*[3]

What is striking, in view of the shared poignancy, is the total contrast of
circumstances: Hadrian's soul is a convivial guest whose departure from the
body's hospitality is cause for grief; if Marvell's dewdrop-soul is a guest, it is a
very reluctant one. In *Ros*, the Latin counterpart of *On a Drop of Dew*, this
role is made explicit. Indeed it is as though the use of Latin verse releases a
more powerful sense of the *vita voluptuosa* as an active principle. To begin
with, the temptations of pleasure take an active rather than passive form: the
flowers 'strive to entice with their leaves' (ll. 3–4).[4] Then the virginal nature
of the dewdrop-soul is defined within a delicate sexuality: it is compared to an
inexperienced and fearful girl returning home unaccompanied after nightfall
(ll. 17–18). And, interestingly, the banquet motif recurs, requiring this
shrinking soul to enact with surprising force the classical choice already
observed in *A Dialogue between the Resolved Soul and Created Pleasure*:

> Haec quoque natalis meditans convivia coeli,
>   Evertit calices, purpureosque thoros.

(ll. 25–6)

> It too, thinking of the feasts of its native heaven,
>   Overturns the drinking cups and purple banquet couches.

In contrast, the English poem is so reticent that the reader is scarcely aware of
the soul as having, let alone making, a deliberate choice. The dewdrop slights
'the purple flow'r' simply because it is not 'its native Element' (ll. 8–9). From
the very first line, the emblem is literally exotic, 'the Orient Dew', owing its

allegiance to the East and Him whose name is Oriens or Rising.[5]

Of course the idea that the soul has an otherworldly source and destiny is a theological and philosophical commonplace. The dew emblem, both precious and commonplace, seems a perfect correlative. But is it? Marvell's skill in handling the image can camouflage certain important contradictions. One way of gauging these is to compare alternative associations. For obvious reasons, dew is often an emblem of transience, and so might more appropriately be contrasted with the Christian soul—as it is in this funeral sermon, printed in 1640:

> The world is transitorie like the dew of the morning, it fades as the grasse, and as the flower of the field; whereas on the contrarie, the soule of man is the subject of immortalitie, capable of an exceeding, surpassing, eternall weight of glory.[6]

Yet in another funeral sermon, Donne applies the dewdrop image, in an allusion to the Song of Songs, as a symbol of hope in immortality:

> I am a drop of that *dew*, that *dew* that lay upon
> the *head* of Christ... this Dew of heaven, [is]
> not Dust...[7]

Usually, however, the evanescent dew reminds man of his mortality rather than his immortality.[8] And it can also intensify the beauty of this world. The dew emblem most often set beside Marvell's is that from *Partheneia Sacra* (1633), a Jesuit work by Henry Hawkins.[9] Quoting Pliny's observation 'that the *Deaw* takes the qualitie of the thing it lights on', Hawkins embellishes it with rich detail, like a monk working on an illuminated manuscript:

> It is the *Deaw*, that covers the rose with scarlet, that clothes the lillie with innocencie, the violets with purple, which embroders the marygold with gold, and enriches al the flowers with gold, silk, and pearls... it is even the *Protheus* and *Chamaeleon* of creatures...

(p. 63)

Such promiscuous colour is totally alien to Marvell's dewdrop, which absorbs as little as possible. For colour is created by darkness adulterating light, as contemporary scientific theory affirms. Abraham Cowley notes on a passage in his *Davideis* (II. 91) that colours 'are nothing but the several mixtures of *Light* with *Darkness* in the superficies of opacous bodies; as for example, *Yellow* is the mixture of *Light* with a little darkness; *Green* with a little more; *Red* with more yet.'[10] If light, darkness, and colour are translated into moral terms, then Marvell's dewdrop denotes purity, scarcely even tinctured with original sin. Hawkins's emblem proves that this symbolism is a matter of choice and emphasis, not inherent.

This is not merely a distinction between Catholic and Protestant viewpoints, though these may be a contributory factor. It is more complicated than that. Marvell is not following a specifically Protestant interpretation either, in so insisting upon the dewdrop's purity. This is made clear by a comparison with Mildmay Fane's dew emblem, which actually reverses Marvell's in one important respect. Fane also invites us to contemplate dew dissolving in the sun, but he interprets this as the Sun of Righteousness burning off original sin:

> When we behold the Morning Dew
> Dissolve ith' rising Sun: What would it shew?
>   But that a Sun to us did rise,
> Our Fathers hoary sin to Atomise.
>   (*Contemplatio Diurna*, (ll. 1-4)[11]

Marvell's dewdrop-soul knows grief rather than guilt, as a result of its involuntary separation from the source of its being. It is 'restless' like another lost soul, Herrick's—

> When once the Soule has lost her way,
> O then, how restlesse do's she stray!
> And having not her God for light,
> How do's she erre in endlesse night!
>   (*The Soule*)[12]

But unlike Herrick's soul it is not truly lost, nor is it accused of wilful erring. It is still capable of, and wholly directed towards, heavenly contemplation. If a parallel is required, it has a closer resemblance to the picture of the ideal mind by Herrick's master, Ben Jonson, a mind

> So polished, perfect, round, and even,
> As it slid moulded off from heaven.
>   (*The Mind*, (ll. 55-6).[13]

So how essentially Christian are the premises of Marvell's poem? Unlike other users of the dew emblem, as we have seen, Marvell does not initially avail himself of a doctrinal context. On the evidence of lines 1 to 18, it is easy to argue that this is more a Neoplatonic dewdrop than a Protestant or Catholic one. Not only is it pure and barely incarnate, shunning the world of matter and turning back to the One, but it exists as part of a cyclic process, an idea more important in Platonism than in historically orientated Christianity. Yet even a Neoplatonist cannot match this dewdrop's simplicity. According to Plotinus, the soul responds ambivalently to the sensible world, for while it may long to be reunited with the One, it is a creative principle in its own right, which has a responsibility to that world and to its own body.[14] Marvell's dewdrop is innocent of such responsibility, contemplating only 'its native Element' (l.8). The beauty of the world, instead of being a means to a spiritual end, leaves it literally blank. Also, its relation with the One does not conform entirely to the Neoplatonic model. Perhaps the most important hint of Christian feeling occurs in the penultimate line (17), 'Till the warm Sun pitty it's Pain', both because of the traditional identification of Sun and Son, and because the Christian God shows compassion for His creatures, whereas the nature of Plotinus's absolute is an unmoved abstraction.

In the second part of *On a Drop of Dew* the enfolded hints open out into full-blown analogy:

> So the Soul, that Drop, that Ray
> Of the clear Fountain of Eternal Day,
> Could it within the humane flow'r be seen,
> Remembring still its former height,
> Shuns the sweat leaves and blossoms green;
> And, recollecting its own Light,
> Does, in its pure and circling thoughts, express
> The greater Heaven in an Heaven less.
> In how coy a Figure wound,
> Every way it turns away:
> So the World excluding round,
> Yet receiving in the Day.
> Dark beneath, but bright above:
> Here disdaining, there in Love.
> How loose and easie hence to go:
> How girt and ready to ascend.
> Moving but on a point below,
> It all about does upwards bend.
>
> (ll. 19–36)

The soul's behaviour imitates that of the drop of dew, but it is more purposeful, less pitiable or self-pitying. The dewdrop, in a phrase recalling Crashaw, was 'Like its own Tear' (l.13).[15] The soul, that drop of the eternal Fountain, is more strenuous and decisive, 'girt and ready to ascend' (l.34). Its contemplation is an achieved choice, not only an aspiration, without the earlier qualification 'Frames *as it can* ...' (my italics): it

> Does, in its pure and circling thoughts, express
> The greater Heaven in an Heaven less.
>
> (ll. 25–6)

This is a function of mind, not instinct, and again Jonson's *The Mind* supplies a possible parallel —

> A mind so pure, so perfect fine,
> As 'tis not radiant, but divine:
> ...
> There, high exalted in the sphere,
> As it another nature were,
> It moveth all, and makes a flight
> As circular as infinite.
>
> (ll. 25–6, 29–32)[16]

The effect on the reader is not, however, altogether positive. The description divides our sympathies, for the use of the epithet 'humane', and the lovely verdant phrase 'sweat leaves and blossoms green' are a fresh and insistent reminder that for human beings beauty is not confined to the spirit. Critics of the poem have made much of this division of sympathies, and have tried to answer the question of whether Marvell endorses or criticises the soul's purist attitude—or indeed whether he does both.[17] But of course this division reflects the philosophical division already built into the language and syntax. The soul's sense of alienation has a long ancestry: for example, the 'Here...there' distinction (l. 32) is familiar in the thought of both Plotinus and Augustine.[18] Somewhat more problematic are the terms 'Remembring' and 'recollecting' (ll. 22, 24), because they may obscure a real conceptual difference. Is Marvell talking about the pre-existence of individual souls, or the yearning of fallen humanity for a lost prelapsarian perfection? Neither possibility is excluded.[19]

But whether the distinction is phrased as one of place (here...there) or time (before and after the fall), to the soul it appears absolute. The only meaning of its existence is its return and self-immersion in 'the clear Fountain' whence it came. Its contact with this world, even with its own body, is as minimal as possible, 'a point'—possibly, it has been surmised, a glancing witty allusion to Descartes' theory that the link between body and soul is located in the tiny pineal gland.[20] This is an extreme reaction, comprehensible in certain moods, but not one that would recommend itself to many seventeenth-century Protestants. Milton, famously, rejects 'a fugitive and cloister'd vertue'.[21] Donne's view of the relation of body and soul takes many forms, but in one characteristic statement he eloquently refutes the soul's absolutism:

> Our nature is meteoric, we respect (because we partake so) both earth and heaven; for as our bodies glorified shall be capable of spiritual joy, so our souls demerged into those bodies are allowed to partake earthly pleasure. Our soul is not sent hither, only to go back again: we have some errand to do here; nor is it sent into prison because it comes innocent, and He which sent it is just.[22]

Not only does Donne use the heaven/earth analogy to prove the opposite point: he does not confine the soul to contemplation, but admits action and pleasure as lawful in the divine scheme of things. And Marvell himself elsewhere adopts a similar position. So are we to regard the dewdrop-soul's choice of a life devoted exclusively to contemplation as questionable? Like the Resolved Soul, the dewdrop performs a balancing act, but one which runs more risk of appearing unbalanced.

What finally tips the scale for some readers is the last quatrain of the poem, where the metre stabilises and the reference is reassuringly biblical:

> Such did the Manna's sacred Dew destil;
> White, and intire, though congeal'd and chill.
> Congeal'd on Earth: but does, dissolving, run

Into the Glories of th'Almighty Sun.

(ll. 39–40)

In spite of a lingering uncertainty over syntax, such readers tend to interpret this ending as a commitment to a point of view which alters the whole balance of the lyric retrospectively.[23] At last, they feel, the crypto-religious poet comes out of the closet, and shows himself as not only aware of but underlining the typological connections between dew and manna—'a small round thing, as small as the hoar frost on the ground' (Exodus 16: 14)—manna and the Eucharist, and therefore dew and Christ's Incarnation and Passion. These connections are spelt out by Henry Hawkins in the emblem already cited:

> So the humanitie of our *Saviour Christ*, as a waterie *Deaw*, being extracted from the virgin *Marie* . . . and through the Sunnie rayes of the Divinitie assumpted up to heaven in the glorious *Ascension*, through love not able to stay any longer, descends againe in the blessed *Sacrament*, to recreate and refresh us Mortals . . .
> (*Partheneia Sacra*, p. 69)

But, as has been observed, Marvell's handling of his emblem is in striking contrast to Hawkins's. Certainly the biblical reference is present in *On a Drop of Dew*, and it may even have numerological support, in view of the fact that the lyric has forty lines:[24] the Israelites spent forty years in the wilderness, where they were miraculously fed by manna, and Christ forty days, so that this number represents a complete cycle of mortal experience and temptation. Nevertheless, to argue that a difficult and subtle poem is triumphantly resolved by turning dew into an orthodox incarnational image is to push the soul/dew/manna analogy well beyond the poem's own logic. When Marvell uses the connectives 'so' or 'such' they are not always to be taken at face value. In the concluding lines there is no sign that the soul's reluctance to accept its own incarnation turns suddenly into joyous acceptance in the light of Christ's Incarnation. Although the emblem is now 'sacred' manna, rather than common or garden dew, it still sustains its purity *in spite of* its material form—'White, and intire, *though* congeal'd and chill' (l. 38), my italics). As a definition of a certain kind of holiness, the line is concise. It is not an image that lends itself readily to the humanity of the Son.

Joy, warmth and light only break through with the dissolution of earthly being which, to the end, is totally unvalued and unregretted by the soul

> Congeal'd on Earth: but does, dissolving, run
> Into the Glories of th'Almighty Sun.

(ll. 38–40)

To evoke religious ecstasy so powerfully in a mere line and a half is dazzling in its simplicity. Henry Vaughan could match it; so could Crashaw. But if these poets have comparable verses, there are also essential differences in attitude and technique, perhaps best illustrated by Marvell's tight and fastidious control of his poetic structure.[25] Although the climax of On a Drop of Dew is experienced as emotional relief after sustained tension, the contemplative discipline does not slacken. The reader is left to absorb the lesson of the emblem.

What, finally, is that lesson? Is the dewdrop-soul an example to be imitated—particularly in view of the 'happy' ending—in its purely contemplative existence? Or, on the other hand, does it represent an impossibly rarefied ideal which takes too little account of the scope of even spiritual experience? In fact, the reader, if he responds at all to the poem, is not imitating the drop of dew, because he is exercising individual sensibility upon an object of earthly beauty. And that object, by its very nature, limits the idea of the soul that he receives. The dewdrop in the flower, although more exquisite than the ghost in the machine,[26] is no less reductive as an analogy of the soul in the body, and for somewhat similar reasons. It denies the reality of commerce between the two,[27] upon which the full humanity of an individual depends. A dewdrop can scarcely represent individuality. It can only be 'soul': not the poet's soul or the reader's soul. It cannot entirely satisfy our sense of the human dignity of choice.

Perhaps this reservation puts the wrong kind of pressure on a poem whose chief attraction is its surface tension in more senses than one. There is little dispute over the almost flawless lyricism of On a Drop of Dew. Indeed its lyrical beauty can justify an ironic reading, on the grounds that the poet throughout covertly repudiates the soul's own absolutism. Such a conflict between moral asceticism and aesthetic pleasure is a familiar phenomenon. But the more subtle paradox of the poem has more to do with contemplation than with pleasure: whereas the soul contemplates the divine being directly, disdaining any means to this supreme end, the poet and reader both practise contemplation of spiritual truth *through* the observation of created beauty—doubly created, by nature's God and by human art. The latter mode is more problematic and more interesting; and the problems are scrutinised in the poem placed next in the Folio, *The Coronet*.

The Coronet

The Coronet seems to me, as it has seemed to others, a deeply Calvinist poem;[28] but its Calvinism is most evident not in the attitude to art, or the natural creation, or 'good works', but in the attitude to choice which underlies all these. If *A Dialogue between the Resolved Soul and Created Pleasure* and *On a Drop of Dew* relinquish the choice of life in favour of the choice of eternity, *The Coronet* calls into question the act of choosing itself.

It begins with an illusion of free will:

> When for the Thorns with which I long, too long,
>   With many a piercing wound,

> My Saviours head have crown'd,
>   I seek with Garlands to redress that Wrong:
>   Through every Garden, every Mead,
>   I gather flow'rs (my fruits are only flow'rs)
>   Dismantling all the fragrant Towers
> That once adorn'd my Shepherdesses head.

(ll. 1–8)

An obvious difference from the preceding poems is the direct involvement of the 'I' who chooses: he is the subject of his narrative, caught in its temporal net ('When . . . once'), so that the mental separation of self and soul collapses. Some critics argue that writer and speaker should be kept distinct, but this familiar modern procedure diminishes the poem's integrity.[29] The self-protecting idea that the poet is entirely separable from his created persona is precisely what must be sacrificed here for the poem to work. In this special case, the reader's instinct to treat the first person as the poet should be trusted. The whole point is the artist's attempt to take responsibility for his art.

At this stage, the poet's literary choices emblematise his choice of life: formerly he dedicated poetry to the life of pleasure, crowning his shepherdess with the flowers of his verse and his Saviour with the thorns of his sin; now he intends to re-dedicate his life and art to religious devotion, 'to redress that Wrong'. On the face of it, he is enacting a choice with distinguished precedents, not all by any means Puritan. In the seventeenth century, Donne is a prominent example,[30] but even the reprobate Thomas Carew had wistfully entertained the possibility that his 'restlesse soule, tyr'de with persuit/Of mortall beauty' might find what it sought in 'th'immortall Love'—but not yet. Carew also fashions appropriate wreath imagery, like a number of contemporary poets:

> Then, I no more shall court the verdant Bay,
> But the dry leavelesse Trunke on *Golgotha*;
> And rather strive to gaine from thence one Thorne,
> Then all the flourishing wreathes by Laureats worne.
> (*To my worthy friend Master Geo. Sands, on his translation of the Psalmes*)[31]

What *The Coronet* starts from is not, however, sacrificial renunciation but substitution. The poet is seeking in the expectation of finding. Yet his apparently firm initiative is already flawed. The delaying tactics and deceptiveness of the first sentence have often been observed, and such a devious structure, together with the wordplay on 'redress', signals ambiguity.[32] Regarded from a theological point of view, the poet's undertaking shows an ominous confidence in the efficacy of good intentions. If to crown his Saviour with thorns was, in some sense, to crucify Him afresh (Hebrews 6:6), then that same passage of Hebrews should warn the backslider that renewal to repentance may prove impossible: the metaphor of growing things reinforces the message—

> For the earth which drinketh in the rain that cometh oft upon it, and bringeth forth
> herbs meet for them by whom it is dressed, receiveth blessing from God: But that
> which beareth thorns and briers is rejected, and is nigh unto cursing; whose end is to
> be burned.
>
> (Hebrews 6: 7–8)

Although the author of Hebrews goes on to reassure those he addresses, the warning is plain. And the poet of *The Coronet* shows self-deprecating awareness of how far he falls short of biblical imperatives in the brilliant slipped-in parenthesis '(my fruits are only flow'rs)'. As a parenthesis, it mimics the intrusion of self-consciousness that is to vitiate his offering. At the same time, it provides a further twist in the contrast of flowers with the biblical fruits of the Spirit:[33] 'by their fruits ye shall know them' said Christ in the sermon on the mount (Matthew 7: 20). Even the modesty of the claim, its gentle self-proclaimed inadequacy, might hint at inverted pride.

The flower-gathering poet is necessarily on the defensive, for his emblematic activity is less innocuous than he makes it sound. It raises the question of the right use and value of created beauty, a question also central to *A Dialogue between the Resolved Soul and Created Pleasure* and *On a Drop of Dew*. *Carpe florem*, pluck the flower: the familiar Latin phrase condenses a classical philosophy of pleasure—defy transience by seizing the pleasure of the moment—which particularly applies to sexual experience. But verses too are flowers to be gathered and arranged. The Greek root of 'anthology' combines ἄνθος, flower, and λογία, collection (λέγω, I gather). The associations between metaphorical flower-gathering and pagan culture go very deep.

There is also a Christian iconography connected with the making of garlands, which has a bearing on the choice between the active and contemplative lives. When Michelangelo designed a papal tomb, he used the biblical figures of the two sisters, Leah and Rachel, to represent action and contemplation respectively, and he gave Leah a garland of flowers 'signifying the talents that adorn our life on earth and glorify it after death.'[34] This is positively expressed, but Leah had made a more ambiguous appearance in Dante's *Purgatorio*, gathering and arranging flowers for her own adornment, possibly to symbolise self-contemplation.[35] In a religious context, the use to which flowers are put is not the only criterion: what counts is also the motivation of the gatherer. George Herbert, with whose lyrics *The Coronet* is often compared, arranges flowers in a variety of ways, rejecting the rose of the *vita voluptuosa* (*The Quip*), cherishing the posy of the *vita contemplativa* (*Life*), commending the garland of the *vita activa* in God's service (*Employment I*). Even Herbert, however, finds on occasion that his well-meant offering of gathered flowers is superfluous to the divine recipient (*Easter*).

As for Marvell, the original purpose of *The Coronet* is, as described, an act of hubris. The anagnorisis, or moment of recognition, is prepared for by another skilfully placed parenthesis:

> And now when I have summ'd up all my store,
> Thinking (so I my self deceive)

So rich a Chaplet thence to weave
As never yet the king of Glory wore...

(ll. 9–12)

At this point he reaches the height of pride, entering into competition even with the writers of the scriptures themselves (the phrase 'king of Glory' recalls the Psalmist).[36] The verse wave rises and, inevitably, breaks:

Alas I find the Serpent old
That, twining in his speckled breast,
About the flow'rs disguis'd does fold,
With wreaths of Fame and Interest.

(ll. 13–16)

The discovery of the serpent at the poem's heart is beautifully calculated. Bruce King notes that the serpent is enthroned at 'the precise centre of the poem, a place where, knowing the Renaissance tradition of symbolic triumphal centres, we would expect "the King of Glory" crowned with the coronet.'[37] He is indeed Christ's ancient antagonist, the intruder into Eden, responsible for man's fall; and he is also the serpent coiled at the centre of the psyche, the knot of self-regard. For the religious poet in particular, he is the insidious pride of wit, the complicated weaving of self into the sense.[38]

Herbert has made the theme so much his own that it is hardly possible for any lover of seventeenth-century poetry to consider *The Coronet* in isolation from his subtle anatomising of the difficulties inherent in reclaiming art—and the poet's life—for God.[39] In the lyric closest to Marvell's in its choice of emblem, *A Wreath*, Herbert contrasts what he calls 'My crooked winding wayes, wherein I live,/Wherein I die, not live' with the clear straightness of the God-directed life, and prays 'Give me simplicitie, that I may live' (ll. 4–5, 9). It is a very inward, psychological approach to a spiritual problem. But if Marvell's problem resembles Herbert's, his diagnosis differs in being both more worldly and more fatalistic. Both poets have their eyes opened to the nature of their offerings, but Marvell's gaze suddenly and cynically narrows as he pinpoints the 'wreaths of Fame and Interest.' Although 'Interest' has been given a theological, indeed Calvinistic, gloss (grace cannot be earned through 'works' of any kind),[40] its immediate application is coloured by 'Fame': poetry can be used or abused to gain the rewards of this world as well. The serpent of self-regard grows sleek on approval and self-advancement. And the expostulation that follows in lines 17 to 18—

Ah, foolish Man, that would'st debase with them,
And mortal Glory, Heavens Diadem!—

suggests that the fame Marvell has in mind does grow on mortal soil.

This moralises the poem specifically, in a way that weakens the case for seeing the serpent in the garland of flowers as a universal emblem of Satan in the natural world.[41] If this were Spenserian allegory—and 'speckled breast' could be a Spenserian echo[42]—the serpent might represent various temptations, including the hidden sensual snare in natural beauty. But then why should he not be discovered in the flowers growing wild, rather than at the significant point when they have been gathered, 'summ'd up', turned into an art form? The dominant sin is one associated less with the senses, the life of pleasure, than with the temptations of the 'Unglorified Active and Contemplative powers of Man' in Ruskin's phrase.[43] The timing of the discovery and the explicitness of 'Fame and Interest' reinforce the Augustinian and Calvinistic teaching that evil is located not in nature but in human nature, namely the corruption of reason and will.

It follows that *The Coronet* is Calvinistic, not so much in its distrust of nature or art or works, but in its distrust of motives and choice. In theory, the writer is free to devote his skill to whatever end he chooses; but he cannot separate himself, and therefore his sin, from the act of writing or choosing. So the turning point comes when the poet relinquishes the right to choose to the only power capable of doing so, and of controlling or destroying the serpent:

> But thou who only could'st the Serpent tame,
> Either his slipp'ry knots at once untie,
> And disintangle all his winding Snare:
> Or shatter too with him my curious frame:
> And let these wither, so that he may die,
> Though set with Skill and chosen out with Care.
>
> (ll. 19–24)

Paradoxically, to relinquish choice is itself an act of choosing. Calvin, however, would attribute such an act not to free will but purely to the operation of grace: 'simply to will is the part of man, to will ill the part of corrupt nature, to will well the part of grace' (*Institutes*, II. iii. 5).[44] Grace cannot be presumed upon, and there is genuine risk as well as genuine dignity in the poet's offer of an even-handed alternative to the Lord he petitions. Does he believe in predestination of the elect? Oddly, one of the precedents proposed for the crown of flowers/crown of thorns motif is a poem by Thomas Randolph, *An Eglogue occasion'd by two Doctors disputing upon predestination* in which the barren doctrinal squabble is displaced by a hymn of heavenly love 'It gentle swaines befits of Love to sing' (l. 43).[45] But the swain of *The Coronet* knows that Love does not save indiscriminately; and he perhaps also believes that God's choice, to save or destroy, is fixed from all eternity. Yet there is a touch of special pleading, however futile, in the line 'Though set with Skill and chosen out with Care', which almost seems intended to remind the Creator of His own creation. If the logic of the poem moves towards a predestined ending—and a surprising number of critics evidently assume that they know what it is—the poet himself can still pray that the divine options should be kept open.[46]

It is not even easy to know exactly what he conceives these options to be.

The disentangling process would require all the gentleness and skill of the divine Artist, perhaps a kind of miracle, difficult to imagine in a fallen world but not impossible. But how absolute is the destruction envisaged as the alternative? The richly allusive, possibly pejorative phrase 'my curious frame' obviously signifies the poem itself ('curious Frame' is used by Sidney and Chapman as a descriptive term for allegory).[47] It is also read, in the context of *The Coronet*, as an allusion to the poet's own body. If he is indeed contemplating his death, are we to assume that it is in the assurance of his soul's salvation, or is that too left entirely to 'God's good pleasure', as Calvin would put it? Though readers may and do assume that only physical death is at stake, not eternal damnation, it is questionable how far Marvell allows us the comfort of such an assumption. The bleak uncertainty seems real enough: the violence is not as stagey as Donne's, but neither is the resignation as therapeutic as Herbert's.

The ending may be a resolution, but it is not an answer. Of the either/or alternatives, it implies that destruction is the expected outcome, but destruction which may—only may—be redeemed as an acceptable sacrifice:[48]

> That they, while Thou on both their Spoils dost tread,
> May crown thy Feet, that could not crown thy Head.
>
> (ll. 25–6)

It is possible to regard this gesture as a spiritual failure, just as the earlier attempt to substitute flowers for Christ's thorns was a failure, and for the same reason, that it is invalidated by pride. According to this view, the witty ending is 'all too clever' yet functional, designed to show that the essential condition of humility has not in fact been met.[49] But met by whom? If the *whole* lyric is a sophisticated exercise in self-deception, then the speaker is a kind of double agent whose cover can only be blown by his operator—Marvell —and the reader, working in collusion. The poet is able to wriggle off the spiritual hook at the end, and leave his pastoral persona, 'the poet', impaled upon it. This line of argument helps those who believe that the ending as it stands is unacceptably extreme, 'basically untenable (and unworkable)'.[50] But it creates other difficulties, discounting the crucial shift from 'I' to 'Thou', and rejecting the theology involved. In Calvinist logic, the ending is perfectly tenable: whether or not it works depends on God not man.

It is perhaps significant that those readers who are most critical of the conclusion of *The Coronet* tend to approach it from the direction of Herbert. Herbert's prayer in *A Wreath*, as often in his verse, implies trust in God's answer. He asks for simplicity, and from that simple request builds a sequence which culminates in the prospect of a true substitution—'For this poore wreath, give thee a crown of praise' (l. 12). Henry Vaughan's poem, *The Wreath*, is a variation on Herbert's, which explicitly avoids the error of *The Coronet*:

> The softer dressings of the Spring,

> Or Summers later store
> I will not for thy temples bring,
> Which *Thorns*, not *Roses* wore.

(ll. 5–8)[51]

His metaphoric offering is 'a twin'd wreath of *grief* and *praise*,/Praise soil'd with tears' (11. 9–10). Instead of the serpent of sin, it is tears that sully his garland, and these will be wiped away in heaven: the poem ends in joyful anticipation of

> that glad place,
> Where cloudless Quires sing without tears,
> Sing thy just praise, and see thy face.

(ll. 17–19)

Clearly this is very different in tone from Marvell's prostration under the divine feet. But another Vaughan poem, *St Mary Magdalen*, contains some beautiful lines which are closer in spirit to *The Coronet*, and have been associated with its final image:

> Dear *Soul*! thou knew'st, flowers here on earth
> At their Lords foot-stool have their birth;
> Therefore thy wither'd self in haste
> Beneath his blest feet thou didst cast,
> That at the root of this green tree
> Thy great decays restor'd might be.

(ll. 27–32)[52]

The common link is the episode in the gospels when the woman ritually crowns Christ's head or feet (the versions differ). Luke's gospel simply calls here 'a sinner' (7: 37), but she is traditionally identified with the Magdalen. In Matthew (26: 6–13) and John (12: 3–8) the story is part of the Passion Narrative, so intensifying its foreshadowing of the divine Sacrifice, and the teaching that sacrifice is not waste. By recalling this ritual at the close of *The Coronet*, Marvell frames his lyric with allusions to the Saviour's Passion, and also sets the ending in a softer, more gracious light.

Nevertheless, it remains equivocal, for the other major biblical context for this final glorification through destruction is the Day of Judgment itself, *dies irae*.[53] What we believe to be beauty will then be crushed and transcended as the Victor claims the spoils, and whether or how it is restored is beyond our knowledge. 'Spoils' is a singuarly apt word here, because it alludes not only to the warfare between Christ and Satan, but to the appropriation of pagan culture, the 'spoils of Egypt'.[54] The poet is offering up the remnants of an originally pagan art. But until that Last Judgment, Marvell's own judgment preserves the poem intact, as an act of self-contemplation which ultimately finds and submits to its true subject. Paradoxically, in yielding up his freedom of spiritual choice the poet retains artistic control. For all its proclaimed inadequacy, *The Coronet* is one of the most beautifully made of Marvell's emblems.

Eyes and Tears

Compared to the two preceding emblems, *Eyes and Tears* spreads concentration more thinly and glitteringly over a sequence of images, which ends by deconstructing the apparent duality of the title. If *On a Drop of Dew* mirrors Christian Platonism, and *The Coronet* is twined on the rigorous frame of Calvinism, *Eyes and Tears* slides gracefully into a quasi-Catholic mode of contemplation. Apparently it appealed to late seventeenth-century taste, for it was reprinted in *Poetical Recreations* (1688), in truncated form.[55] In subject and sentiment, particularly in the modish treatment of the Magdalen in stanza VIII and its Latin equivalent, the poem has affinities with European baroque. It is classified as belonging to the 'literature of tears',[56] of which Crashaw's *The Weeper* is such a prominent, not to say notorious, English example. Most detailed discussions of *Eyes and Tears* engage with its similarity to, or difference from, Crashaw's verses on the Magdalen.[57] Yet this relation may not be the *raison d'être* of the poem. As in Marvell's other contemplative poems, the true subject is the soul's choice of response to external reality, the extent to which it does or doesn't remake it in its own spiritual image.

In *Eyes and Tears* the options of created pleasure never really solidify, since the eye that contemplates them dissolves everything into its own element, to the point where, so to speak, it digests even itself in tears. Action does not seem to be an option at all. What interests Marvell is the *ars contemplativa*, and how it works. He begins by considering an argument from design, namely the way in which perceiving, interpreting, and responding are functionally related:

I

> How wisely Nature did decree,
> With the same Eyes to weep and see!
> That, having view'd the object vain,
> They might be ready to complain.

(ll. 1–4)

It is a tidy arrangement, that the structure of the eye itself should dictate the correct process of contemplation, from seeing to weeping over the vanity of the world. All that theoretically separates the two functions is a moment in time, the blink of an eye. But, as we immediately discover, the readiness is *not* all: seeing and weeping can be as separate as falsehood and truth.[58]

The second stanza brings this moral discrimination into play:

II

And, since the Self-deluding Sight,

In a false Angle takes each hight;
These Tears which better measure all,
Like wat'ry Lines and Plummets fall.

(ll. 5–8)

To see and to contemplate rightly are not the same thing, for sight is not trustworthy—a point that Marvell drives home with an analogy from the exact sciences, optics and geometry, both highly regarded in the seventeenth century.[59] It is easier to measure depths accurately with the aid of a plummet, a weighted line, than it is to gauge angle and height with the unaided and 'Self-deluding Sight': an emblem of pride and penitence. But it is an epistemological problem as well as a moral one, and it is interesting that Marvell uses geometry to define it. It has been remarked that seventeenth-century rationalists and empiricists alike 'came to realize the extraordinary utility of geometry as a tool for measuring quantitative relationships but powerless for measuring qualitative relationships'.[60] Typically, Marvell reverses this, and applies geometric metaphors as a measure of quality, both here and in *The Definition of Love*: the oblique, the 'false Angle', is imperfect, delusive; the 'Lines' are straight and true.

Geometry exemplifies 'the power of sharp distinction'[61] which is an attribute of judgment. But wit challenges conventional distinctions, and the poem proceeds to value everything according to its new weights-and-measures system—tears are the weights, eyes the balances (stanza III). Just as Henry Vaughan uses his 'paire of scales' emblem in *Regeneration* to weigh pains against pleasures,[62] so the first thing the contemplator of *Eyes and Tears* does is to test 'the true price' of pleasures, which, unsurprisingly, turns out to be grief. The notion that joy has to be paid for in tears might seem banal, were it not for the precision with which the conceit is developed. While we watch, the life of beauty and pleasure dissolves in this universal element:

IV

What in the World most fair appears,
Yea even Laughter, turns to Tears:
And all the Jewels which we prize,
Melt in these Pendants of the Eyes.

V

I have through every Garden been,
Amongst the Red, the White, the Green;
And yet, from all the flow'rs I saw,
No Hony, but these Tears could draw.

(ll. 13–20)

Laughter does literally turn to tears, flowers exude nectar or trap dew: there is a fine balancing act between literal and metaphorical, reminiscent of *A Dialogue between the Resolved Soul and Created Pleasure*, which suggests that a choice is being made between rival perceptions.

With stanza V, for the first time in the Folio, the reader encounters the Marvellian garden as a complete, independent image. In *Eyes and Tears* it is a pleasure garden, identified by its coded colours, 'the Red, the White, the Green'—colours of erotic love and hope. The speaker adopts a world-weary air, proper to one who has already exhausted the life of pleasure: 'all my Joyes' have become 'every Garden', a phrase reminiscent of *The Coronet* and with similar connotations. But instead of gathering flowers he looks at them, and, simply by looking, transforms the garden of pleasure into a garden of contemplation. These flowers yield not honey but tears: a bee image hovers, but is not actively at work as it is in *The Garden* or *Upon Appleton House*.

By the natural association of tears and dew, the poet then passes on to the great life-giving cycle presided over by the sun, which also sees and weeps:

VI

So the all-seeing Sun each day
Distills the World with Chymick Ray;
But finds the Essence only Showers,
Which straight in pity back he powers.

(ll. 21-4)

The whole world liquefies in an image neatly reversing that of *On a Drop of Dew*, since here the sun's 'pity' manifests itself in pouring moisture back to the earth after distilling it. And just as this divine alchemy signifies blessing—'He shall come down like rain upon the mown grass: as showers that water the earth' (Psalm 72: 6)—so the human behaviour that imitates it is blessed.

Tears are not simply the price to be paid for joy, they *are* true joy:

VII

Yet happy they whom Grief doth bless,
That weep the more, and see the less:
And, to preserve their Sight more true,
Bath still their Eyes in their own Dew.

(ll. 25-8)

The wise and happy are they who weep in order to purify and preserve the contemplative vision: paradoxically, weeping clears the spiritual 'Sight more true' because it obscures mere sense. The idea that a human being may have to be blinded in order to see is one of the most painful truths confronted by Shakespeare and Milton (who have both been invoked in discussions of this stanza).[63] However, Marvell's version seems more in keeping with the gentler notion of tears as eye ointment which occurs in the literature of penitence, and which eases the transition to the weeping Magdalen. For example, Henry Vaughan's *'Prayer for the grace of repentance'* in *The Mount of Olives* follows this pattern:

anoint mine Eyes with Eye-salve, that I may know and see how wretched, and miserable, and poore, and blinde, and naked I am, and may be zealous therefore and repent! O thou that . . . gavest to *Magdalen* such store of teares that she washed thy feet with them, give to me true remorse, and such a measure of repentance as may become a most miserable sinner![64]

Marvell's own portrait of the most famous weeper in Christian art is characteristically witty. He seems to have liked the effect, since he appends the Latin rendering of stanza VIII at the end of the poem:[65]

VIII

So *Magdalen*, in Tears more wise
Dissolv'd those captivating Eyes,
Whose liquid Chaines could flowing meet
To fetter her Redeemers feet.

(ll. 29–32)

By binding her Saviour's feet in 'liquid Chaines', she achieves what the poet of *The Coronet* dares only to hope. Yet the associations of her former voluptuous life cling to her. 'Those captivating Eyes', as painted by Titian for instance, heighten her sexuality while proclaiming her penitence. In Marvell's poem too, the imagery takes on an erotic colouring all the more potent for being ambiguous or denied. The following stanzas (IX and X) ask us to imagine chaste pregnancy, a 'Teeming' moon goddess, eyes that quench the source of the desire they arouse—

The sparkling Glance that shoots Desire,
Drench'd in these Waves, does lose it fire.

(ll. 37–8)

More often than not in Marvell's poetry, the sublimation of pleasure and passion is preferred to fulfilment. Desire is transferred or blocked, redirected towards natural beauty. And the most beautiful tears in this poem are not the Magdalen's, for all her lachrymose glory, but those of the universe itself.

Love poets constantly compare eyes to stars, but for Marvell

Stars shew lovely in the Night,
But as they seem the Tears of Light.

(ll. 43–4)

The effect is magical: it takes a moment to realise that it is offered as the product of illusion. In his choice of 'seem', Marvell goes against the Baconian principle that 'the truth of being and the truth of knowing are one', reflecting the stars in an enchanted glass instead.[66] The reader might conclude that the poem's reasoning breaks down at this point, since the sight is deluding itself, dazzled by imagination. The poet's vision is admittedly subjective: may he not then be suspected of taking 'a false Angle'? Does the witty strategy of turning everything into tears finally blur meaning with metaphor, not clarify it? Even judged in terms of spiritual truth, it might be urged that contemplation of the stars should produce more than a striking image. Yet if the poet stops short of explicitly proclaiming with the Psalmist that the heavens declare the glory of God,[67] the sense of wonder is still potent enough to silence criticism. In a fallen universe, the stars might well appear as tears of a divine light.

But the concluding three stanzas of the poem sharpen the critical instinct once more. The speaker makes an emotional choice, exhorting himself to weep feelingly (but for what?)

XII

Ope then mine Eyes your double Sluice,
And practise so your noblest Use.
For others too can see, or sleep;
But only humane Eyes can weep.

(ll. 45–8)

This explains the earlier 'seem' (l. 44), but at the expense of contradicting the impression of an entire grieving creation of which man is only a part. Tears are reserved as a human privilege, not *lacrimae rerum*, and the poet claims that privilege. Such self-stimulation is characteristic of the 'literature of tears'; yet here it appears forced, lacking motive and humility. Perhaps that is because the ostensible theme of penitence is not strongly and convincingly maintained.[68] What weeping is *for* is not so much for any sin or failure in the self, or even a sense of lost perfection, but more to satisfy a sense of appropriateness. Weeping to order begins to seem uncomfortably closer to Sterne than to seventheenth-century devoutness. Herbert and Vaughan (following the prophet Jeremiah) pray for tears as a gift,[69] but not so Marvell. Consequently, the contemplative impulse in *Eyes and Tears* finally turns in upon the self rather than towards God, the very danger to which *The Coronet* alerts poet and reader. And it is an aesthetic impulse also. The last stanzas are extravagant enough to rouse a suspicion that what lies behind this choice is wit rather than devotion:

XIII

Now like two Clouds dissolving, drop,
And at each Tear in distance stop:
Now like two Fountains trickle down:
Now like two floods o'return and drown.

XIIII

Thus let your Streams o'reflow your Springs,
Till Eyes and Tears be the same things:

And each the other's difference bears;
These weeping Eyes, those seeing Tears.

(ll. 49-56)

The resolution is undoubtedly witty, but it need not overturn judgment. To merge eyes and tears is not necessarily to obliterate the crucial distinctions already made between different kinds of response to the world. Seeing and weeping do not have the same value; eyes and tears are not identical, except as pure emblem. In comparison with the endings of *On a Drop of Dew* and *The Coronet*, this conclusion demands less of the reader, and is less satisfying.[70]

If, indeed, *Eyes and Tears* as a whole is technically less demanding and intellectually less satisfying than Marvell's other religious lyrics, it may be because Marvell is working within a devotional mode to which he has no complete devotional commitment. The Magdalen fires his literary inventiveness, but she does not inspire in him the kind of emotion she inspires in devotional poets such as Crashaw and Vaughan. Or can this explanation be pressed even further? Perhaps *Eyes and Tears* does not fall short of generic expectations so much as deliberately parody them? If Marvell associates this special form of contemplation primarily with Catholic or high Anglican sensibility, then he may be indirectly exposing the flaws that can result from pushing it to an extreme. The hard-won insight of the Calvinist *Coronet* does not apply in *Eyes and Tears* with its softer aesthetic and closed ending. (It has, in effect, two endings—stanza XIIII quoted above, and the self-contained Latin epigram on the Magdalen—but these do not seem to invite alternative readings.)

If the parodic interpretation stretches the poem too far in one direction, the opposite attempt to cut it down into an orthodox meditation with the Magdalen at its centre will not do either. Interestingly, the 1688 text seems to prove just this with its omission of stanzas II, III, V, IX and XI. The distinctively Marvellian images of the red, white, and green flower garden and the stars as 'Tears of Light' are lost, and with them much of the unusual quality of the poem. Nevertheless, the very fact that such mutilation does not altogether wreck the lyric structure again underlines the difference between *Eyes and Tears* and *On a Drop of Dew* or *The Coronet*. As a contemplative poem it has wit and beauty rather than the depth of spiritual insight it claims.

(iii) Contemplation in a Landscape: Bermudas, Clorinda and Damon, A Dialogue between Thyrsis and Dorinda

Bermudas

With *Bermudas*, the contemplative mood of the Folio poems enters a different phase: so radically different, that it might almost appear as a *volte-face*. Both *Bermudas* and the pastoral dialogues that follow make the natural world a central religious metaphor. But where the preceding lyrics reflect mistrust of created pleasure, they overtly celebrate the creation. The assumption that contemplation necessarily involves guilt and grief is displaced by a new sense of freedom and wonder. *Bermudas* liberates its singers from oppression, both political and psychological, and affirms their freedom to choose their historical destiny in the light of the divine guidance and blessing. Indeed, in these paradisal landscapes, choice is no longer perceived as difficult or impossible, but as a natural response of acceptance. Yet the divide from the previous contemplative poems is not absolute, since the fundamental priority is still the life of the spirit, and human experience is interpreted accordingly. And it is *shared* experience. Beside the emphasis on landscape, *Bermudas* and the pastoral dialogues represent a communal strand in the contemplative life, linked to their form, and their close association with choral music.

Bermudas is essentially a psalm of praise, which the reader has to decode—not as simple a task as it seems, for hidden hazards have split, if not shipwrecked, adventurous commentators.[1] We begin with an act of contemplation:

> Where the remote *Bermudas* ride
> In th'Oceans bosome unespy'd,
> From a small Boat, that row'd along,
> The listning Winds receiv'd this Song.
>
> (ll. 1-4)

The setting promises, and leaves, much to the imagination. In technique it is not unlike an opening film sequence, deliberately kept in long shot: the landscape, or more accurately seascape, has figures, but they are not at first identifiable—in fact, we can hardly be said to *see* them at all, only to be aware of what they are doing. Location is more important, and it is identified. There is a sense of privilege in spying on what is 'unespy'd', for the Bermudas represent an idea of remoteness, fostered by early accounts. Protected by sea storms and outlying dangerous rocks, haunted by a reputation as 'a most prodigious and inchanted place',[2] this island group seemed to be set apart even among its fellow colonies in the New World, to have a special destiny, as Lewis Hughes had claimed in 1621.[3] They 'ride' the bosom of ocean like an enchanted fleet of ships, or the mother vessel of the 'small Boat'. By a simple latent metaphor, the poet suggests something essential to the poem: the singing rowers contemplate the island landscape from an outside vantage point, but with an inside knowledge—they belong. The remote turns out to be also the familiar.

This is equally true on a literary level. The New World resonates with echoes from the Old, although, as usual, readers hear the echoes they choose to hear and tend to filter out others. On one hand, Horace's *Epode XVI* offers a potentially ironic precedent, an impossibly utopian solution to the evils of civil conflict;[4] on the other hand, Virgil's *Aeneid* provides a heroic context for colonisation, and his *Eclogues* a pastoral grace-note. In *Eclogue IX*, for example,—which treats of the bitterness of dispossession and the solace of song—the rustling breezes fall silent like Marvell's 'listning Winds':

> et nunc omne tibi stratum silet aequor et omnes,
> aspice, uentosi ceciderunt murmuris aurae.
>
> (ll. 57–8)

Dryden's version of these lines catches a quality reminiscent of *Bermudas*:

> And now the Waves roul silent to the shore;
> Hushed winds the topmost branches scarcely bend,
> As if thy tuneful song they did attend.[5]

But despite such echoes, Marvell's singers do not really inhabit the classical world of epic or pastoral. Although the early Bermudan settlers adopted a motto *Quo Fata Ferunt* from *Aeneid* III.7, 'Incerti, quo fata ferunt, ubi sistere detur', 'Not knowing where the fates bear us, where it is appointed us to settle',[6] the song of Marvell's colonists shows that they have put their faith in a known destination, and in a divine Guide who controls the Fates. Even their rowing is not precisely the voyaging of epic narrative. Some critics make heavy weather of what is going on in the poem, assuming a contradiction that needs to be resolved between the narrative line, with the colonists on the point of arrival, and the song which reports their actual experience of the islands.[7] Others feel that the ambiguity enriches the poem, hinting at a millennial rather than an imperial dream: as Philip Brockbank puts it, 'The singers have arrived, but they are still travelling hopefully.'[8]

This faith and hope are reflected in their song, which is modelled on the Psalms of David[9]—perhaps specifically, as one scholar argues, on the very popular metrical paraphrases by George Sandys.[10] Obviously psalms of thanksgiving for deliverance and praise for natural bounty are especially applicable, since they were customarily sung by Puritans in just such circumstances,[11] and they had a powerful influence on Protestant poetic. Like its biblical models, the song in *Bermudas* interweaves theology and direct human experience. But here the problems begin. How truthful are Marvell's singers in rendering and interpreting their historical experience?[12] Are they reliable narrators? The questions are as 'still-vex'd' as the 'Bermoothes' themselves, though every detail of the song has been subjected to the closest scrutiny by skilled readers.

The song actually begins with a rhetorical question:

> What should we do but sing his Praise
> That led us through the watry Maze,
> Unto an Isle so long unknown,
> And yet far kinder than our own?
> Where he the huge Sea-Monsters wracks,
> That lift the Deep upon their Backs.
> He lands us on a grassy Stage;
> Safe from the Storms, and Prelat's rage.

(ll. 5–12)

The phrase 'Prelat's rage' carries a whole political world within it. These Puritans are refugees from the violence of the active life as exemplified in Laudian England, delivered from storms that are metaphorical as well as literal. And 'the watry Maze' is also metaphorical and literal: the image recurs as a symbol of confused and futile activity at the very beginning of *The First Anniversary*. In the circumstances, it is natural that the colonists should judge their new life by the standard of the old, and find the 'so long unknown' island 'far kinder' in both climatic and political terms. Their reaction to climate is endorsed by other early voyagers who record, usually with pleasure, its temperate mildness.[13] Politically, however, the Bermudan climate could be troubled. If, as has been alleged, Marvell deliberately undermines the credibility of his Puritans by planting clues to show that they misrepresent their motives and situation, political realities provide one sort of test. There is no lack of evidence to unparadise seventeenth-century Bermuda. Nor, it seems, would Marvell have been ignorant of its existence. The allegation hangs upon an accumulation of discrepancies between the poem and facts to which Marvell would presumably have had access while staying in John Oxenbridge's house at Eton in 1653. Oxenbridge knew Bermuda at first hand, and had himself been embroiled in its religious controversies—for the colony, while being fundamentally Anglican and royalist (a point notched up by the ironists) was split and confused on certain issues.[14] To regard Bermuda unequivocally as a refuge from the conflicts of the world of action, beyond the reach of prelate's rage, might smack of wishful thinking, and is certainly a simplification. But the 'facts', as opposed to opinions, are not easy to ascertain either. The discrepancies are not just a feature of Marvell's poem, but cut deep into the island's history. One governor, a moderate Puritan, observed that 'noe great prelate will leave his pontifical pallace to take his journey to live upon a barren rock',[15] so at a stroke confirming one perception of Marvell's Bermudans and—in the phrase 'barren rock'—demolishing another, and more fundamental, one. We can only speculate about Oxenbridge's own feelings, and how far they influenced *Bermudas*. At least we know that he did not wash his hands of the colony (he became governor of the reorganised Somer Islands Company in 1655), or abandon belief in the Puritan mission to colonise and propagate the gospel.[16] Had it not been for the Oxenbridges,[17] it would probably not have occurred to Marvell to link the Puritan cause with Bermuda in particular. No doubt he is stretching a point when he implies that Bermuda can stand for Puritan idealism and liberty in the same way as Providence Island, or Massachusetts. But this would not necessarily invalidate the ideal itself. In *Bermudas* the choice of life is not just a political one. Indeed, the singers in their new environment show themselves more aware of the God of nature than the God of history. If they are held to be wrong about the nature of the Creator, that is much more damaging to the poem than any political oversimplification.

Interestingly, they begin by linking creation, preservation, and destruction. God's power in all three capacities is a repeated theme in the Old Testament: he both creates and destroys the monsters of the deep,[18] as the singers affirm—

> ...he the huge Sea-Monsters wracks,
> That lift the Deep upon their Backs.
>
> (ll. 9–10)

Influenced perhaps by an apparent allusion to Waller's *Battle of the Summer Islands*,[19] where two whales are stranded in a Bermudan bay and unsuccessfully assaulted by the island hunters, some readers have taken this couplet to be part of the catalogue of rich natural provisions. On this basis, an implicit irony may be deduced, either with respect to Waller's mock-heroic, or the historical record. Despite early optimism—'There are also great plenty of Whales, which I conceaue are very easie to be killed, for they come so vsually, and ordinarily to the shore, that we heard them oftentimes in the night a bed'[20]—whaling ventures proved unsuccessful. 'God was not so good as the singers pretend' is one possible conclusion.[21] But the poem here concentrates not so much on God's goodness as provider as on his goodness as preserver. The alternative interpretation of the great whales as an apocalyptic image signifying the final destruction of elemental evil is closer to the mark.[22]

God wrecks the whales, but lands the voyagers safely on 'a grassy Stage' that spreads before the eye a vista of earthly paradises. If in fact Bermuda did not have much grass,[23] for the purposes of Marvellian pastoral, grass is indispensable. A *locus amoenus* would be unthinkable without it. Of course the pleasures of grass may be morally suspect, but that is a separate issue from its presence or absence. Shakespeare's island in *The Tempest* provokes dissension on just this point. Gonzalo, the utopian idealist, exclaims 'How lush and lusty the grass looks! how green!', whereupon the cynics, Antonio and Sebastian, correct him mockingly 'The ground, indeed, is tawny./With an eye of green in't' (II.i.51–3).[24] Greenness is very much in the eye of the beholder.

Bermudas, like *The Tempest*, shapes its own world, under its own artistic laws, but, unlike Shakespeare, Marvell is relatively uninterested in human relations. His island is a place primarily for contemplating God and nature; the poem plays down a whole dimension of the Puritan colonial ideal, the desire to build a moral community. It is not in that sense a poem about active life. This omission has been seen as highly significant, given the evidence that the Bermudan authorities were much concerned about the moral fibre of the early colonists, and took pains to instil the work ethic and counteract the pleasure principle.[25] The serpent in their Puritan paradise was the regrettable tendency of human nature to prefer pleasure to either devotion or work. Such self-indulgent idleness, aided and abetted by beneficent Nature, is an acknowledged trap of earthly paradises in reality or fiction, and this problem too is explicitly discussed in *The Tempest* (II. i. 139–164). But not by Marvell in *Bermudas*. Yet he could not have read far in any Bermudan sources without coming across the jaundiced view that the colonists were, in the words of Antonio's gibe at Gonzalo's utopian dream, 'all idle; whores and knaves' (II. i. 162). For this, it appears, the Puritan propaganda is itself partly responsible. Writers like Lewis Hughes were almost comically torn between a desire to attract recruits by visions of a life of ease in a Golden Age environment which produced two crops annually with 'neither plowing nor harrowing', and the need to admonish them against 'loathsome lazinesse' with the threat of death from famine.[26] Reduced to the same level, *Bermudas* is almost all carrot and no stick. However, the full title of Hughes's *Relation* puts the devotional duty before the active: it is *written by way of exhortation, to stirre vp the people there to praise God*. Marvell's colonists need no stirring up to praise God, but do they bestir themselves enough with regard to nature? Latter-day Puritans think not. Fruit falls into the Bermudans' mouths, in a lyrical counterpart to the horror story, recounted with relish by both Hughes and Strachey, that the colonists ate fish or meat 'blood rawe' because they were too lazy to cook it or too greedy to wait.[27] But to see Marvell's Bermuda as a Land of Cockaigne is to isolate and coarsen the pleasure principle and ignore the strong framework of contemplation and even action that supports it. Marvell's Puritans are not, after all, lounging about open-mouthed under fig-trees, but rowing and singing the Lord's song in a strange land.

The catalogue of delights does nevertheless occupy most of the poem's centre, making a *templum* for the imagination, bright with detail:

> He gave us this eternal Spring,
> Which here enamells every thing;
> And sends the Fowl's to us in care,
> On daily Visits through the Air.
> He hangs in shades the Orange bright,
> Like golden Lamps in a green Night.
> And does in the Pomgranates close,
> Jewels more rich than *Ormus* show's.
> He makes the Figs our mouths to meet;

And throws the Melons at our feet.
But Apples plants of such a price,
No Tree could ever bear them twice.
With Cedars, chosen by his hand,
From *Lebanon*, he stores the Land.
And makes the hollow Seas, that roar,
Proclaime the Ambergris on shoar.

(ll. 13–28)

Although scholars have squeezed almost the last drop of juice from each item, the whole is greater than the sum of the parts, and retains its freshness. For underlying all the individual pleasures is something more, the restoring of man's relationship with a nature that is generous, vital, inexhaustible, constantly satisfying not only physical hunger but the hunger for meaning. As in a Renaissance painting, colour and composition express the joy of plenitude. What makes sense of the whole picture is the consistent attribution to its artist, God, and the argument from design. It is, moreover, both a completed work and a work in progress:[28] a theologically sound proposition. If the attribution is mistaken, if this is a false paradise, then Bermuda is indeed the Isle of Devils[29] in a subtle and terrible sense, a parody instead of a type.

The case for regarding the Puritan singers as self-deceived, and their earthly paradise as false, rests on evidence from natural history as well as politics. But it has to meet one major objection on literary and theological grounds, before being considered in detail. The parallel with other false paradises like Spenser's Bower of Bliss breaks down because in such places God is not directly invoked, and is certainly not the presiding presence.[30] It has been asserted that Marvell does not Christianise the pagan features of his paradise.[31] What then is God doing in the poem at all? If the island is not the kind of place the singers think it is, the corollary seems to be that God is not the kind of God they think he is either, that he is a much more ambivalent deity than the benign Creator they imagine, and has concealed some unpleasant surprises in the undergrowth. Although this might fit the idea of Marvell himself as ironist, it does not appear to fit Marvell's idea of the Christian God, so far as that is ascertainable. From a Christian viewpoint, the singers have their priorities right: as the Shorter Catechism puts it, the chief end of man is to glorify God and enjoy him for ever. Unlike the 'Suttle Nunns' of *Upon Appleton House*, who do disguise the life of pleasure as the contemplative life and who make their own art of nature, 'Still handling Natures finest Parts' (stanza XXIII), they know what true pleasure is, and acknowledge its source. If this does not fit in with our stereotype of a Puritan, the problem is with the stereotype: it is salutary to remember the beautiful interludes of relaxation, eating and drinking and making music, in the Second Part of Bunyan's *Pilgrim's Progress*.

Another accusation against Marvell's Puritans, which may also have its roots in stereotype, is that of spiritual pride. It has been alleged, for instance, that the singers 'spend relatively little time in praise, and a great deal more on the things which He has done for them'—unlike the Psalmist.[32] But this distinction is unreal: one form of praise, practised by the Psalmist, consists precisely in contemplating what God has done for you, and rejoicing in his works. The contrary hypothesis, that Marvell is using the Psalms positively to correct 'pagan' poetry like Waller's *Battle of the Summer Islands* is a more convincing explanation of the general tone and attitude of the song.[33]

Yet the reader's discrimination on the finer points of earthly paradises has still to be put to the test. A. Bartlett Giamatti has proposed one literary yardstick for the purpose: 'though not all the earthly paradises in the Renaissance poems are false or enchanted, those that are will be found wanting by some higher standard. And as a master-image of that standard, the Eden of Dante serves us well.'[34] Dante's Eden, like the song in *Bermudas*, expresses joy in the artistry of God.[35] It is a human and terrestrial joy—*beatitudo hujus vitae*—which is not the highest form of contemplation, but which is valued in, and for, itself: 'Dante's Earthly Paradise prefigures the Heavenly Paradise and eternal life precisely because it represents human life in the perfection of its self-fulfillment' writes one scholar.[36] Or, the choice of life harmonises with the choice of eternity. Coincidentally or not, *Bermudas* shares two motifs with Dante's description, and with other Renaissance descriptions of the same type: the word 'enamells' (l. 14) may conceivably trace its ancestry from Dante's 'al sommo smalto', 'the enamelled summit' (*Purgatorio*, VIII. 114);[37] and 'eternal Spring' (l. 13) is a characteristic feature of literary Edens, as well as of Ovid's Golden Age. In the brazen world of nature, eternal spring might have its disadvantages, as an often-quoted source on Bermuda, Captain John Smith's *Generall Historie*, observes.[38] But in the golden world delivered by poets, eternal spring is a transcendent season, when blossom and fruit hang on the same bough in imaginary gardens. The real Bermuda came close enough to the symbol for most seventeenth-century Englishmen to idealise it as the 'sweet Island ... that the Poet thus justly speakes on. *Hic ver perpetuum* ...'.[39] Since the gap between symbol and reality is so small, why should it be necessary to insert the wedge of irony to widen it?

The wildlife of *Bermudas* also exemplifies a biblical providence:

> And sends the Fowl's to us in care,
> On daily Visits through the Air.
>
> (ll. 15–16)

The Israelites had fed on quails in the wilderness (Exodus 16:12–13), and Elijah had been fed by ravens (I Kings 17:6). For the early Bermudan colonists, a remarkable feature of the island was the extreme tameness of the birds, in particular a nocturnal species called the cahow. In Exodus, 'at even the quails came up, and covered the camp'; in Bermuda, the cahows came out after dusk, and, according to Captain John Smith, 'if you but whoop and hollow, they will light vpon you, that with your hands you may chuse the fat and leaue the leane'.[40] Among other accounts, that of Lewis Hughes is nearest to the spirit, and almost the letter, of Marvell's lines:

> Consider also how bountifully God brought vnto
> you the Fowles of the ayre in great abundance,
> which did offer themselues to be taken by you...
> ...
> surely the tamenesse of these wilde birds, and
> their offring of themselues to be taken, is a
> manifest token of the goodnesse of God, euen of
> his loue, his care, his mercy and power working
> together, to saue this people from staruing.[41]

Of course, ecological considerations did not enter into it. As usual, man could not restrain his greed, and the cahow was nearly exterminated.[42] But Marvell seems to go out of his way not to sully his providential perspective with violence (the Elijah allusion is useful in this respect, since his fowls brought, instead of being, food). 'Daily Visits' is reassuring, and the syntax of the line allows birds as well as humans to shelter under the phrase 'in care'.[43]

Marvell shows equal tact in avoiding any obvious appeal to erotic symbolism in his catalogue of fruit. How tempting such analogies could be is borne out by Sir Richard Fanshawe's version of Camões's description of Venus's isle in *The Lusiads*. In fact, Fanshawe is more specific than his original:[44]

> A thousand gallant *Trees* to *Heav'n* up-shoot
> With *Apples*, odoriferous, and faire:
> The *Orange-tree* hath in her sightly *fruit*
> The colour DAPHNE boasted in her *Haire:*
> The *Citron-tree* bends almost to her Root
> Under the yellow burthen which she bare:
>   The goodly *Lemmons* with their *button-Caps*,
>   Hang imitating *Virgins* fragrant *Paps*.

(IX. 56)

The idea that fruit, like virgins, waits to be ravished is a commonplace in libertine idylls such as Carew's *A Rapture* or Lovelace's *Love Made in the First Age*, but it would be out of keeping with a Puritan paradise. Yet far from renouncing the appeal to the senses, Marvell outdoes his competitors, and in the poem's most famous couplet splashes a dazzling colour contrast on his canvas, worthy of a Gauguin or van Gogh:

> He hangs in shades the Orange bright,
> Like golden Lamps in a green Night.

(ll. 17–18)

As already noted, God is the original artist. If an English orchard is capable of being transformed into 'the Creators Real Poetry', as Cowley puts it, then a Bermudan orange grove is an even more spectacular revelation of his powers.[45]

But—again in Cowley's words—only 'when we with attention look/Upon the Third Dayes Volume of the Book'. The fruit of *Bermudas* offers its primary pleasure to the eye, before the touch or taste; the human eye alone can appreciate the luminosity of the oranges, or form a mental image of the hidden shining jewel-like interior of the pomegranate (ll. 19–20). But the art of God deserves more than an aesthetic response: it asks for genuine contemplation, seeing through, as well as with, the eye.

'Pulchritude' declares the Cambridge Platonist, Henry More, 'is convey'd indeed by the outward Senses unto the Soul, but a more intellectuall faculty is that which relishes it'.[46] The title of his book, *An Antidote against Atheism*, published in 1653, might well serve as an epigraph for *Bermudas* (which was probably written in 1653). More devotes a section of his argument to plants as evidence for divine Providence, giving beauty priority even before usefulness—like Marvell, it seems:

> there is that Curiosity of *forme* and *beauty* in the more noble kind of *Plants* bearing such a sutableness and harmony with the more refined sense and sagacity of the Soul of Man, that he cannot chose ... but acknowledge that some hidden Cause much a kin to his own nature, that is intellectuall, is the contriver & perfecter of these so pleasant spectacles in the world.[47]

So, plants are made to be contemplated. But they are also intended for eating, and More explains why God 'hangs' certain fruit up in trees: 'For could *Apples*, and *Oranges*, and *Grapes*, and *Apricocks*, and such like fruit be intended for *Beasts* that hold their heads downward and can scarce look up at them, much lesse know how to reach them?'[48] It is an engaging if illogical explanation. Marvell's God is less practical: although he adopts this method with his oranges, he guides figs into the colonists' mouths, and throws melons at their very feet (ll. 21–2). The melons sound hazardous, but we are not told that anyone falls over them, as the speaker does in *The Garden*—'Stumbling on Melons ... I fall on Grass' (ll. 39–40).[49]

However, there is an oblique intimation of Falling in the next couplet:

> But Apples plants of such a price,
> No Tree could ever bear them twice.
>
> (ll. 23–4)

The conjunction shifts from 'and' to 'but', so setting these apples apart from the rest of the catalogue of island fruits. For this reason, rather than because of any practical considerations,[50] it seems unlikely that they are simply to be identified with the native pineapples. It is true that Bermuda did produce excellent pineapples which prompted a contemplative reflection on the part of one Governor: 'I love to plant and preserve them and behould them in their beauty more than to munch them alone without the companie of my friends.'[51] But God's apples grow in a different garden from the Governor's pineapples.

What is stressed is their uniqueness and 'price', which associate them with the apples of Eden.[52] Perhaps, as in the allusions of *The Garden*, the purpose is to remind the sojourners in this paradise regained of another paradise lost, without compromising their innocent pleasure. Bermuda is all the more an enchanted ground because of the existence of an implied taboo; these apples excite not appetite but wonder in the presence of a mystery. And similarly with the next trees mentioned, the cedars, the emphasis is less on a purely natural resource than on their biblical provenance as 'the cedars of Lebanon, which he hath planted' (Psalm 104: 16):

> With Cedars, chosen by his hand,
> From *Lebanon*, he stores the Land.
>
> (ll. 25–6)

God selects trees, as he elects human souls. There is nothing random about this landscape, just as there is nothing random about the landfall bringing the colonists to a place already designed for them. God's choice is theirs.

After the riches of the land, the poem turns to the riches of the sea, imitating its incessant sound[53]—

> And makes the hollow Seas, that roar,
> Proclaime the Ambergris on shoar.
>
> (ll. 27–8)

Like the other items, ambergris is a commodity, a substance secreted by the sperm whale, used as a basis of perfume and as a drug with restorative properties. For those who read *Bermudas* as ironic, the mention of ambergris recalls an ugly little incident from the early days of the colony;[54] yet its associations with the life of pleasure and sensual gratification are equally, if not more, dominant. In the pagan sea-idyll in *The Gallery* (stanza V), Marvell defies geography to perfume the Mediterranean with 'a Mass of Ambergris', proclaiming the presence of Venus. In *Bermudas*, the seas proclaim the ambergris, and the ambergris proclaims God. Once more, a pleasure originally of the senses is sanctified by the imagination. Marvell's language contrasts with that of poets who do regard ambergris primarily as a material asset. Waller calculates the stuff by weight—

>   many a pound
> On the rich shore, of Amber-greece is found—

and Davenant in an earlier island poem, *Madagascar* (1638), makes it sound more like an oil-slick than anything else—

> And now I saw (what urg'd my wonder more)
> Black Suds of *Ambar-Greece* float to the shore . . .[55]

It is left to Marvell to communicate a real sense of wonder at the divine riddle, the bringing of sweetness out of the strength of the roaring seas.

Finally, God proclaims himself not only through the Book of Works but through the Word, the gospel. The last part of the song of praise shifts the frame of reference from the Old Testament to the New, beginning with a judgment on comparative values:

> He cast (of which we rather boast)
> The Gospels Pearl upon our Coast.
> And in these Rocks for us did frame
> A Temple, where to sound his Name.
> Oh let our Voice his Praise exalt,
> Till it arrive at Heavens Vault:
> Which thence (perhaps) rebounding, may
> Eccho beyond the *Mexique Bay*.
>
> (ll. 29–36)

In line 29, the force of the parenthesis lifts the couplet out of the catalogue of created pleasures. If, as one critic delightfully observes, Marvell here 'makes the best of the colonists' material disappointment'[36]—despite initial expectations, Bermuda did not yield many pearls—then he does so by a tactic worthy of the Resolved Soul, substituting a heavenly for an earthly treasure. The parable of the 'one pearl of great price', for which the merchant 'sold all that he had' (Matthew 13: 45–6), must have struck a chord with at least some of the Puritans who invested in colonial enterprises, though they obviously expected a financial return as well as the furtherance of the kingdom of heaven.[57] But the actual colonists, who are the custodians of 'the Gospels Pearl', are not boasting of their own sacrifice. Far from being arrogant, they do not attribute the casting of that pearl on the Bermudan coast to their own human agency. It is an act of God's grace, more like the legendary coming of the scriptures in a cedar casket to Bacon's fictional island, New Atlantis,[58] than a planned missionary venture.

The casket for the gospel's pearl on Bermuda is, so to speak, the rocky temple 'where to sound his Name.' St Ambrose, founder of Christian hymnody, describes in his *Hexaemeron* the sea and its islands, participating with man in a musical harmony to worship their Creator: the sea is an 'incentive to devotion'

> cum undarum leniter alluentium sono certent cantus
> psallentium, plaudant insulae tranquillo fluctuum
> sanctorum choro, hymnis sanctorum personent.
>
> (III.v.23)[59]

> so that the music of the singing of psalms contends
> with the sound of the gently flowing waves, the
> islands applaud the peaceful chorus of the holy
> waves, they resound with the hymns of the saints.

In the same spirit, Marvell's Bermudans endeavour to make the universe a sounding-board for their praise. Their temple is enclosed not only by reassuringly solid rocks, but by an equally solid sky which—'(perhaps)'—can amplify a song bounced off it.[60] Although up to this point the poem has offered the island world as a refuge from the open seas, now it launches into recognition of the claims of a world still beyond it in space and time.

In *A Seasonable Proposition of Propagating the Gospel by Christian Colonies in the Continent of Guaiana*, Oxenbridge would himself look beyond Bermuda and call for action pressing ever westward: 'If we will do any thing in this work, we must (as the Sun and Gospel do...) move forward toward the West...' (p.6). But this vision may take different forms. Among Oxenbridge's scriptural references is one to Psalm 22, where the Psalmist links his own praise with that of the nations:

> My praise shall be of thee in the great
> congregation:
>
> . . .
>
> All the ends of the world shall remember and turn
> unto the LORD: and all the kindreds of the nations
> shall worship before thee.

>   (25, 27)

To praise is to contemplate, but praise in its evangelical function is also a form of action, and subject to the same limitations as other kinds of human action. In a pre-millenarian world it is not an easy option. This particular psalm, far from being serenely confident throughout, opens with the greatest cry of desolation in the Bible—'My God, my God, why has thou forsaken me?' And the Bermudans' hymn of joy, 'chearful' as it is, makes its concession to human frailty and doubt: 'Which thence (perhaps) rebounding, may...'(l.35). Much has been made of that '(perhaps)', which can be read as scepticism or proper humility.[61] In passing, though, it should be noticed that the singers express doubt, not in God, but in the power and reach of their own art, however exalted that is, doubt of a kind already encountered in *The Coronet*. Once the song has left their lips, its destiny and efficacy are beyond their control.

Nevertheless their song *is* heard, and the final judgment is not theirs but the narrator's (and, by extension, the reader's):

> Thus sung they, in the *English* boat,
> An holy and a chearful Note,
> And all the way, to guide their Chime,
> With falling Oars they kept the time.

>   (ll. 37–40)

The narrator's distance is not necessarily that of the ironist, but it is that of the artist who contemplates, with a kind of spiritual nostalgia, a poetry more innocent and direct than his own.[62] The poem closes, as it began, with a description of an action subordinated to, and falling beautifully into the rhythm of, contemplation. In part, it is the rhythm of Arcadian pastoral, as caught by Sidney's description of 'a young shepherdess knitting and withal singing, and it seemed that her voice comforted her hands to work, and her hands kept time to her voice's music.'63 More especially, it is the rhythm of a prelapsarian world. For Marvell's account does not display the same symmetry as Sidney's: singing comes first, contemplation takes precedence of action64—and both are pleasurable.

This final image therefore completes an imaginative synthesis of pleasure, action, and contemplation. *Bermudas* celebrates a version of the threefold life, but one in which the elements are unequal. Real and tangible as it is, pleasure is valued primarily as a consequence of living in harmony with God and nature. Contemplative praise is the central activity of these islanders, and action in the usual sense is relegated to the margin of the picture, the narrative framework. As far as the reader's judgment is concerned, this framework does not cut us adrift from the central experience, but gives us a special kind of access to it.65 Whether we choose to share or reject the singers' viewpoint, or the narrator's so far as we think we know it, the situation itself has a peculiar imaginative force. These seventeenth-century Puritans have made a choice of life in a quite literal sense, and they are rewarded by no longer being forced to choose, not even between the demands of the body and the demands of the spirit. In the earthly paradise the choice of life and the choice of eternity are one, the millennium is—almost—at hand.

Clorinda and Damon and *A Dialogue between Thyrsis and Dorinda*

Although these two dialogues have much in common besides their pastoral form, they are not in fact found together in the 1681 Folio. It is the Margoliouth/Legouis edition that makes the obvious pairing, while retaining *Clorinda and Damon* in its original position immediately after *Bermudas*. On the internal evidence, this seems an eminently satisfactory solution to the problem of relocating *A Dialogue between Thyrsis and Dorinda*,66 which is grotesquely misplaced in *Miscellaneous Poems* between two poems of a very different kind, *On the Victory obtained by Blake over the Spaniards*67 and *The Character of Holland*. But the difficulties posed by *Thyrsis and Dorinda* extend further: it is not only misplaced but textually corrupt, and, in spite of its inclusion in the Folio, other external evidence casts some doubt even on its attribution. These difficulties are considered in more detail later. However, the *critical* advantages of retaining the Margoliouth/Legouis order become more, not less, apparent as interesting comparisons and contrasts between the dialogues emerge: indeed the case for claiming *Thyrsis and Dorinda* as a Marvellian lyric can only be strengthened by this conjunction. Although the following discussion does analyse them under separate headings, it also relies upon making these connections.

Clorinda and Damon

Clorinda and Damon is a slighter lyric than *Bermudas* and belongs to a more restricted and stylised genre: yet there is a kind of continuity in the concentration upon landscape and in the religious dimension. The dialogue's final question, 'Who would not in *Pan's* Praises meet?' is a pastoral echo of the opening question of the Bermudan song, 'What should we do but sing his Praise . . . ?' In order to reach that harmony, one mode of discourse, Damon's, has to dominate and displace another, Clorinda's: 'the world, as it is mans' (or, rather, woman's) gives way to 'the world, as it is Gods.'[68] Yet, unlike *Bermudas*, no change of place is involved in this choice, only a change of perception. It is still a choice of life, for although the couple share the same pastoral landscape, they have to decide whether it more truly represents the life of pleasure or the life of contemplation. This either/or, perhaps, resolves itself by the end of the poem into both/and, pleasure reconciled to virtue.[69]

In true pastoral style, Clorinda begins the dialogue with an invitation to pleasure:

> C. *Damon* come drive thy flocks this way.
> D. No: 'tis too late they went astray.
> C. I have a grassy Scutcheon spy'd,
>   Where *Flora* blazons all her pride.
>
> (ll. 1–4)

Spenser describes his Bower of Bliss, where pleasure is the only priority and *carpe florem* the only imperative, in comparable terms:

> faire grassy ground
> Mantled with greene, and goodly beautifide
> With all the ornaments of *Floraes* pride.[70]

E.K.'s gloss on 'Flora' in the March Eclogue of *The Shepheardes Calender* confirms the relevant association—'the Goddesse of flowres, but indede (as saith Tacitus) a famous harlot . . .'[71] Marvell's heraldic conceit—a 'Scutcheon' is a shield with armorial bearings—reinforces the worldliness of 'pride' and hints at an alien world of action tamed into pastoral. But such heraldry also spells death, as it does elsewhere in *The Unfortunate Lover* (stanza VIII) and *The Mower's Song* (stanza V).

Pastoral traditionally glances at greater matters, and Damon's rejection of Clorinda's pastoral invitation recalls the Anglican General Confession, 'We have erred and strayed from thy ways like lost sheep, just as later he reminds her 'Grass withers; and the Flow'rs too fade' (1.7) in the spirit of Isaiah, 'All flesh is grass . . .' (Is. 40: 6–8).[72] Clorinda for her part plays the temptress, Eve, as readers observe, to Damon's Adam.[73] Yet to interpret the dialogue as an allegory of sense versus spirit is to oversimplify. Clorinda is not incapable of a spiritualised view of nature, which makes her ripe for conversion. She is not evil but unenlightened (Marvell is inclined to be gentler with his shepherdesses than with other *femmes fatales*). Her love is genuine, expressed in offerings that are both practical and decorative:

> The Grass I aim to feast thy Sheep:
> The Flow'rs I for thy Temples keep.

(ll. 5–6)

The wordplay on 'Temples' makes the flowers into both garlands of pleasure and a pagan votive offering. Followed up by the phrase 'Love Shrine' (l.10), it shows that Clorinda has an impulse to worship but misdirects it. Her answer to mutability, that perennial shadow over beauty and pleasure, is the classic *carpe florem*, 'Seize the short Joyes then, ere they vade'(l.8).[74] And she hurries on, without giving Damon a chance to reply, to set the scene for joy's consummation.

In keeping with their creeds, the two speakers offer counter-readings of the book of nature:

> Seest thou that unfrequented Cave?
> *D.* That den? *C.* Loves Shrine. *D.* But Virtue's Grave.
> *C.* In whose cool bosome we may lye
> Safe from the Sun. *D.* not Heaven's Eye.
> *C.* Near this, a Fountaines liquid Bell
> Tinkles within the concave Shell.
> *D.* Might a Soul bath there and be clean,
> Or slake its Drought? *C.* What is't you mean?

(ll. 9–16)

On its small scale, this is an archetypal landscape of the mind, or, in Clorinda's case, of the body. For Clorinda, nature is a source of beauty and pleasure, presided over by pagan Eros: for Damon, it is a source of contemplation, and they themselves are under the constant surveillance of 'Heaven's Eye'. Clorinda will be undone by a more powerful symbolism than her own, through which her sense of beauty is made to work against her. Yet even in her own terms, the mention of the fountain is perhaps a mistake. Phallic symbol or not, the most obvious property of the fountain is to cool the fires of passion. That is why another Damon seeks the cave and fountain in vain—

> To what cool Cave shall I descend,
> Or to what gelid Fountain bend?
> (*Damon the Mower*, (ll. 27–8)

In classical verse, the same yearning for *frigus amabile*, lovely coolness, bubbles up in Virgil's *Eclogues* and in Horace's beautiful ode to the Bandusian spring.[75] Unintentionally, Clorinda has appealed to the symbol which has most power to transform the argument, and it turns out to be the most intensely lyrical and haunting image of the whole poem. It is typical of Marvell, who so often links sound and shape, to imagine a fountain like a 'liquid Bell' making Schubertian music within its concave setting. But the effect is not purely aesthetic. Like Henry Vaughan's comparable fountain, it lends 'Some use for Eares' and also awakens the spirit.[76] Damon's question comes as a spiritual shock, like the shock of cold water, touching an authentic emotion—'Might a Soul bath there and be clean...'? It is the question remembered by the anguished Consul in Lowry's *Under the Volcano*, who is 'suddenly rapt', in T. S. Eliot's phrase, 'to the image of spiritual purgation.'[77]

Clorinda is startled into the key question 'What is't you mean?' which decisively shifts the poem's centre of gravity. It is not accidental that Marvell places the two questions, Damon's rhetorical one and her real one, at the literal centre of the lyric (ll. 15–16). By asking for *meaning*, Clorinda opens her mind to contemplation, not mere enjoyment of natural beauty.

Damon begins his explanation by acknowledging pleasure but putting it firmly behind him:

> D. These once had been enticing things,
>   *Clorinda*, Pastures, Caves, and Springs.
> C. And what late change? D. The other day
>   Pan met me. C. What did great *Pan* say?
> D. Words that transcend poor Shepherds skill,
>   But He ere since my Songs does fill:
>   And his Name swells my slender Oate.
> C. Sweet must *Pan* sound in *Damons* Note.
> D. *Clorinda's* voice might make it sweet.
> C. Who would not in *Pan's* Praises meet?
>
> (ll. 17–26)

As an account of a conversion experience that itself converts the hearer, this belongs to a simpler and happier world than seventeenth-century England. No heart-searching or doubt, no agonising requirement that the singer renounce his song; only a transcendental encounter with 'great *Pan*' in person, set in a landscape close to primeval innocence, where 'still *Paradise* lay/In some green shade, or fountain.'[78] The identification of Pan with Christ by Christian humanist writers is etymologically false but poetically true. Both Spenser and Milton testify to its potency, Spenser in the May eclogue from *The Shepheardes Calender*, which E. K. glosses at length, 'Great pan is Christ, the very God of all shepheards...', and Milton in his Nativity Ode.[79] In Renaissance mythography, Pan is also the artist and creator, in love with the nymph Echo. Ralph Cudworth, the Cambridge Platonist, interprets:

> the Ancient Mythologists represented the *Nature of the Universe*, by *Pan Playing upon a Pipe* or *Harp*, and being in love with the *Nymph Eccho*; as if Nature did, by a kind of Silent Melody, make all the Parts of the Universe everywhere Daunce in measure & Proportion, it self being as it were in the mean time delighted and ravished with the Reecchoing of its own Harmony.
>
> (*The True Intellectual System of the Universe*, 1678, I.iii.37)[80]

Something of the meaning of this myth infiltrates Marvell's lyric in the echoing harmonies of its music and landscape. His Pan inspires Damon's song, which unlike the pastoral art of *The Coronet* is not condemned for moral inadequacy. It is simply raised to a level which transcends without rejecting 'poor Shepherds skill', and which can inspire others.

Although it is possible to cast doubt on the genuineness of Clorinda's conversion and Damon's response (ll. 24-5), just because it gives them the best of both worlds without seeming to cost them anything,[81] it is equally possible to accept the truth of their discovery that the divine song is all the sweeter when mediated through human music, human love. By choosing contemplation before pleasure, Pan before Eros, they do not lose but gain a world, and the final Chorus confirms that this is indeed 'the world as it is Gods', resounding in universal harmony:

Chorus

Of Pan *the flowry Pastures sing,*
Caves eccho, and the Fountains ring.
Sing then while he doth us inspire;
For all the World is our Pan's *Quire.*

(ll. 27-30)

This *benedicite* is more universal than the psalm of praise in *Bermudas*, and untroubled by any doubts concerning its echoing capacity. For those readers who would prefer doubt, tension, irony, the lyric's own imaginative capacity will seem restricted, and the choice of life a cosmetic rather than a fundamental change. Pleasure slides easily into contemplation and the pastoral continuum remains unbroken. Yet the central questions at least continue to resonate, and the answer may not be as simple as it looks: 'What is't you *mean?*'.

A Dialogue Between Thyrsis and Dorinda

Before the question of meaning even arises, with *Thyrsis and Dorinda* the first problem is to establish the text. This pastoral dialogue exists in more than one version in seventeenth-century sources, and the text included in *Miscellaneous Poems* is not only misplaced (see above, p. 55) but mutilated, 'more corrupt than that of any other poem in the book.'[82] Any critical discussion must begin from an editorial reconstruction of the text; the one adopted here is that of the Margoliouth/Legouis edition. In fact, the versions of *Thyrsis and Dorinda* prior to 1681 divide into two categories: a shorter 'original' manuscript version, whose likely date is sometime in the 1630s, and a longer 'revised' version which occurs in manuscript and print from the early 1650s to 1675.[83] It is this 'revised' version from which the Folio text evidently derives, and Margoliouth/Legouis emends accordingly.

The uncertain status of the text does, however, raise a more fundamental problem. Is *Thyrsis and Dorinda* by Marvell at all? The provenance of the earliest known version would place it unusually early in Marvell's career. Moreover, one of the relevant manuscripts is associated with Oxford, not Cambridge, and it ascribes the dialogue to an Oxford poet. On the basis of this evidence, as well as the poem's exclusion from an important Marvell source, the attribution to Marvell has been doubted or denied.[84] Although the early dating is not an insuperable difficulty—poets may be precocious, and Cowley, for instance, Marvell's contemporary, was writing publishable verse before the age of thirteen—the manuscript evidence does complicate matters. But if *Thyrsis and Dorinda* is *not* by Marvell, the opposite problem arises: how and why did this lyric limp, perhaps belatedly, into the 1681 Folio?

The existence of the two basic versions, one an extended revision of the other, suggests a tentative answer to the question. John Klause's hypothesis that Marvell might have revised and expanded an existing lyric by another hand is an attractive one for those readers who find the poem Marvellian but who accept the force of the arguments against unqualified attribution.[85] And if it is adopted as at least a working hypothesis, it opens a stimulating line of critical enquiry. What is it about this poem that makes Marvell's authorship so plausible in the first place? And how exactly do the additions—notably ll.27-30 and ll.39-48—alter our perception of the whole dialogue?

On internal evidence alone it is not difficult to guess why *Thyrsis and Dorinda* should have been accepted as Marvell's. It is more than a pretty and popular song which challenged the skill of seventeenth-century composers: it goes straight to the heart of a recurring Marvell preoccupation for which I have been borrowing Johnson's phrase 'the choice of eternity', and its relation to 'the choice of life'. In the original shorter version set by William Lawes,[86] the schema might have been tailor-made for Marvell, even if he did not invent it. A pastoral innocent, Dorinda, is asking Thyrsis one of the simplest and most profound questions about human existence: what happens next? She does not doubt that there will be an afterlife, but she wants to know where, how to reach it, and what it will be like. Thyrsis's attemps at enlightenment draw on a mixed discourse of philosophy and poetry—'Heaven is the centre of the soule' he explains, paraphrasing language used also by the Cambridge Platonists:

> It is as natural and proper for Mind and Understanding to tend towards God, as for heavy Things to tend towards their Center: For God is the Center of immortal Souls.
>
> (Benjamin Whichcote, *The Use of Reason in Matters of Religion*)[87]

(Thyrsis's line is retained almost unaltered in the Folio text, 'Heaven's the Center of the Soul'—l.18). But when he comes to describe Elysium itself, he has to fall back, like so many, on what he and Dorinda already know. What takes shape is a description of the life of innocent pleasure, a pastoral world where 'the blessings of nature [are] collected, and its evils extracted and excluded'[88]—a kind of happy valley in fact. And with this idyll, free from fear, full of lambs safely grazing in the perpetual spring sunshine, the early version concludes—though not without a hint that Thyrsis is seduced by his own vision

> Why then should we heere make delay
> Since we may bee as free as they
>
> (ll. 35-6)

This couplet is dropped from the longer version, but the hint is improved upon.

In its original form, then, the dialogue offers an easy accommodation of contemplation and pleasure, rather as *Clorinda and Damon* does, although it significantly lacks the Christian overtones of that poem. But when the longer revised version is set beside the shorter, a more subtle crossplay of choices becomes apparent, and the central relationship diverges more from the expected pattern. It does indeed begin to look like two poems stitched into one, going beyond the normal counterpointing of dialogue.

The most interesting development is in Dorinda's responses and their effect on Thyrsis. However, her first additional speech is prepared for by a change in Thyrsis's own image of Elysium. Whereas his description in the early version is all of a piece (l.21 to the end) and consistent in tone, in the later version it is split into two unequal parts (ll.21-6 and 31-8) with a marked change of emphasis. His first answer to Dorinda's question, 'But in Elizium how do they/Pass Eternity away?' (ll.19-20) is entirely in terms of contrast with earthly preoccupations. The most striking alteration from the original is in the reference to music: instead of the charming but unremarkable 'Oaten Pipes like Gold that play/A never ceasing Rowndelay', Thyrsis now tells Dorinda

> No Oat-pipe's needfull, there thine Ears
> May feast with Musick of the Spheres.
>
> (ll. 25-6)

This substitution of *musica speculativa* for *musica instrumentalis* accords with Thyrsis's previous use of Platonised language, and with his assertion 'A Chast Soul, can never mis't' (l.6), since only chaste souls can hear the music of the spheres.[89] Thyrsis captures Dorinda's imagination, as Damon does Clorinda's, by reinterpreting a powerful symbol in terms of its spiritual value. And Dorinda responds in lines added to the revised version—

> *Dorinda.* Oh sweet! oh sweet! How I my future state
> By silent thinking, Antidate:
> I prethee let us spend our time to come
> In talking of *Elizium.*
>
> (ll. 27-30)

This seems a peculiarly Marvellian touch. In particular, the relatively unusual word 'Antidate'[90] (used also in *Young Love*, l.23) points to an idea of engrossing interest to him, that is, how one can in some sense control the future by anticipating it. The method in the love poems is through pleasure. Here it is by 'silent thinking'. Dorinda is enraptured by the prospect of a life spent contemplating heaven, though she passes rather rapidly from the discipline of silent meditation to the pleasure of conversation. However, the exercise itself might be thoroughly recommended, as it is in *The Saints' Everlasting Rest:* provided, of course, that it is undertaken in the right spirit—perhaps a condition open to doubt in Dorinda's case.

Had the poem ended with this 'right' choice, it could have been claimed as a passable, if not very challenging, religious pastoral. But the revised version presses on to a much more subversive conclusion. Thyrsis's reaction shows how easily the language of contemplation slides into the purely pleasurable: ironically, at the point when Dorinda herself seems to embrace his otherworldly values, Thyrsis is betrayed by his pupil's enthusiasm into remaking Elysium more in the image of the world. 'Then I'le go on . . .' (l.31). Going on, the successful pedagogue's temptation, is his mistake.

> There, sheep are full
> Of sweetest grass, and softest wooll;
> There, birds sing Consorts, garlands grow,
> Cool winds do whisper, springs do flow.
> There, alwayes is, a rising Sun,
> And day is ever, but begun.
> Shepheards there, bear equal sway,
> And every Nimph's a Queen of *May*.
>
> (ll. 31–8)

Not even the 'rising Sun' carries the symbolic weight to distinguish this sufficiently from purely pagan pastoral. What Thyrsis offers Dorinda is what she originally wanted, a landscape of pleasure corresponding to her familiar 'home', only better. The dialogue began with a teacher-pupil relationship which seemed to make Thyrsis the dominant partner, but it is Dorinda's logic that prevails—the opposite of what happens in the sexual politics of *Clorinda and Damon.*

And Dorinda continues to raise the stakes. In her reply she changes 'Oh sweet! oh sweet!' to the even stronger 'I'm sick, I'm sick', and proposes a more startling form of antedating, putting Thyrsis to an unexpected test of action not words:

> Convince me now, that this is true;
> By bidding, with mee, all adieu.
>
> (ll. 41–2)

In comparison, Clorinda's temptation of Damon to sexual delights appears relatively harmless. Both couples, Clorinda and Damon and Thyrsis and Dorinda, have reminded readers of Milton's later Adam and Eve;[91] but the parallel holds more truly for the second pair. Giving the same reason as Milton's Adam, Thyrsis accepts Dorinda's choice, not of life but of death:

> *Thyrsis.* I cannot live, without thee, I
> Will for thee, much more with thee dye.
>
> (ll. 43–4)

Dying is associated with pleasure in the familiar pun on sexual climax. Thyrsis's careful selection of the right preposition for the circumstances makes us conscious of the difference between dying *for* and dying *with* and humorously deflates his heroic moment.

Moreover, the form of suicide pact they have in mind turns out to be distinctly unheroic and hedonistic:

> *Chorus.* Then let us give *Carillo* charge o'th Sheep,
> And thou and I'le pick poppies and them
> steep
> In wine, and drink on't even till we weep,
> So shall we smoothly pass away in sleep.
>
> (ll. 45–8)

In their way, Thyrsis and Dorinda do acknowledge the demands of the active life by the convenient arrangement of giving Carillo 'charge o'th Sheep'. Although Marvell evidently lifted the request along with the name Carillo from an earlier song, it is made there in a very different bargaining context between a herdsman and a shepherdess.[92] Marvell adapts it to reflect sympathetically on his two lovers preparing to end it all. It is the measure and also the limit of their sense of responsibility.

Apart from this touching gesture, their intention must seem spiritually irresponsible, at least by Christian standards. But should these standards be invoked? Readers divide on the question, since their own 'silent thinking' on the subject is bound to differ: the irony is all in 'what is *not* said in the poem: the all-too-real difficulties of holy living and holy dying' (Colie).[93] But there is a tendency to exonerate Dorinda at least, because of her invincibly childlike innocence. Whether Marvell himself would ever have advocated or defended suicide is beside the point:[94] he experiments with the notion in order to explore the logic of an extreme and literal choice of eternity, which turns it effectually into a parody of the *vita voluptuosa*. In the course of the dialogue a moment of equilibrium, a glimpse of holy living, is reached and lost again, toppling over into an extreme. Light, charming and lyrical as the verse is, *Thyrsis and Dorinda* is more disturbing than *Clorinda and Damon*, especially the ironically happy ending as the lovers prepare, in another eighteenth-century phrase, 'to rush unlicensed on eternity'.[95] Consequently its placing after, rather than before, *Clorinda and Damon* seems justified. Yet it might still be said that neither poem fully adjudicates the rival claims of this world and the next, matter and spirit. The next poem in the Folio, *A Dialogue between the Soul and Body*' presents a tougher intellectual proposition, abandoning pastoral convention to do so.

(iv) Self-contemplation: A Dialogue between
the Soul and Body

A Dialogue between the Soul and Body, unlike the pastoral dialogues, is an introspective analysis, a closed system. It is also a complete deadlock. The whole point of the poem is the impossibility of a free choice of life, since life itself imposes inescapable conditions.[1] Nor is there any chance of either participant in this dialogue persuading the other of his case. Indeed they virtually ignore one another until the Body rounds on the Soul in line 32.[2] Consequently there is no element of temptation either, at least in the dramatic present, although their mutual recriminations point to a past history of temptation and fall. 'Contemplative' may seem too serene an epithet for such a poem, but contemplation is exactly what the Soul and Body are engaged in, of their own navel as it were. Instead of the impulse to praise that contemplation engenders in *Bermudas* and *Clorinda and Damon*, their impulse is to complain, like the eyes of *Eyes and Tears*. But have they legitimate grounds for complaint? Are their arguments supported by theology or philosophy? Are we meant to take sides?

The number of distinguished thinkers whom the Soul and Body could call as witnesses is vast. Deciding who the principal witnesses might be—Paul or Plotinus? Augustine or Descartes?—involves critics in doctrinal quarrels of their own. To say that Marvell's poem is 'utterly undoctrinal'[3] settles nothing, for language itself is unavoidably slanted. The opening questions, never answered, could not reverberate to the same extent in a godless universe:

Soul

O who shall, from this Dungeon, raise
A Soul inslav'd so many wayes?

(11.1–2)

Body

O shall me deliver whole,
From bonds of this Tyrannic Soul?

(11.11–12)

In comparison with other body and soul dialogues, Marvell's may tilt further towards philosophy than religion—it is not a devotional poem—but the pull of theology still makes itself felt.

In the first place, Marvell builds on a Pauline foundation, like Hermann Hugo whose Latin emblem in *Pia Desideria* (Antwerp, 1624) directly influenced *A Dialogue between the Soul and Body*.[4] 'O wretched man that I am! who shall deliver me from the body of this death?' exclaims the apostle; but unlike Marvell's Soul he immediately answers his own cry 'I thank God through Jesus Christ our Lord' (Romans 7: 24–5). But for theologians it is sin, not the physical body as such, that impedes deliverance. Neither Augustine or Calvin accepted the simple attribution of guilt to the literal flesh:[5]

> For the corruption of the body, which weighs down the soul, is not the cause but the punishment of the first sin; and it was not the corruptible flesh that made the soul sinful, but the sinful soul that made the flesh corruptible.
> (Augustine, *The City of God*, XIV. iii)

Had Augustine been the judge between Marvell's Soul and Body, he could, on this premise, have found for the Body. Calvin would recognise with grim satisfaction that *both* partake of the nature of 'the flesh', which he describes as 'continually on the alert for subterfuges, by which it imagines it can remove the blame of its own wickedness from itself to some other quarter' (*Institutes*, I. i. xv).

Philosophers of the school of Plotinus, on the other hand, might return an open verdict, since they see the alliance of soul with body as both 'good and necessary' *and* as 'a result of its impurity and of its vices.'[6] The philosophical problem of dualism is an ancient one, constantly being updated. For the earlier seventeenth century, this updating was provided by Descartes who takes a progressive scientific line in his *Discours de la Méthode* (1637),[7] where he separates mind and matter, allowing only for a possible point of intersection in the pineal gland. This new-style Cartesian dualism aroused as much hostility as interest among the old-style Platonic dualists like Henry More.[8] And if Descartes' theory helps to explain how Marvell's Soul and Body manage to perceive themselves as separate entities, it should be added that the poem criticises rather than endorses this perception.

Apart from its small niche in the history of ideas, *A Dialogue between the Soul and Body* has a more easily definable niche in the history of a genre. It is part of a revival of soul/body dialogues in the seventeenth century, which has antecedents in medieval debate.[9] The result of investigations into these generic connections is to prove once again that Marvell cuts something exceptional out of material with a common pattern. For example, he easily outstrips other emblematic writers in describing how it feels, figuratively, to be imprisoned in a body. The Soul begins with a sequence of remarkable anatomical images:

Soul

O who shall, from this Dungeon, raise
A Soul inslav'd so many wayes?
With bolts of Bones, that fetter'd stands
In Feet; and manacled in Hands.
Here blinded with an Eye; and there
Deaf with the drumming of an Ear.

> A Soul hung up, as 'twere, in Chains
> Of Nerves, and Arteries, and Veins.
> Tortur'd, besides each other part,
> In a vain Head, and double Heart.

(ll. 1–10)

Marvell reanimates a commonplace, partly by the etymological game that has been labelled 'unpunning'.[10] Yet, as Edmund Arwaker's translation of Hugo's original emblem proves, this device might be applied more mechanically, less strikingly.[11] What Marvell does is to electrify the images of immobilisation, like some Frankenstein, with a charge of nervous energy. Set beside this verbal description, the pictorial emblems of figures trapped within skeletons appear primitive.[12] Stylistically, he is verging on Clevelandism: the rhyme of the couplet, 'A Soul hung up, as 'twere, in Chains/Of Nerves, and Arteries, and Veins', echoes lines from Cleveland's *The Antiplatonick*

> The souldier, that man of Iron,
> Whom Ribs of *Horror* all inviron,
> That's strung with Wire, in stead of Veins,
> In whose imbraces you're in chains. . . .

(ll. 33–6)[13]

But where Cleveland's conceit dehumanises, turning the soldier into a grotesque robot, Marvell's conceit jolts the reader into awareness of common humanity beneath the skin. To the searching accuracy of an anatomical drawing,[14] he adds the appalling dimension of consciousness. Paradoxically, although the Soul argues that its capacity is dulled not heightened by the senses which cut it off from 'reality', the impression is that of hypersensitive awareness of the body itself, which is as exposed as if it were literally flayed alive. For a similar effect in poetry, Marvell's true peers are Donne or Pope. The direct parallel with *The Second Anniversary*—

> Thou shalt not peepe through lattices of eies,
> Nor heare through Laberinths of eares, nor learne
> By circuit, or collections to discerne.
> In Heaven thou straight know'st all—[15]

alerts us to the epistemological implications, for, like Donne, Marvell is making a point about the inadequacy of sensory perception. Pope also addresses himself to human limitations in the *Essay on Man*, though from a different philosophical angle. Where Marvell represents the normal human senses as instruments of torture, Pope evokes the torture of human senses abnormally heightened.[16] Dying of a rose in aromatic pain belongs to the same imaginative order of sensations as being deafened by the drumming of one's own ear. But the Soul ends by reminding us that the torture is not just physical. The phrases 'vain Head' and 'double Heart' superimpose a moral, even biblical, language on physiology.[17] Vanity and doubleness characterise fallen man:

> They speak vanity every one with his neighbour:
> with flattering lips and with a double heart do they speak.
>
> (Psalm 12: 2)

When the Body is given the right of reply, it adopts the same tactics as its antagonist. Instead of setting a literalist against a maker of metaphors, or one mode of discourse against another, Marvell gives Soul and Body a shared mode of imagery and wordplay:

> *Body*
> O who shall me deliver whole,
> From bonds of this Tyrannic Soul?
> Which, stretcht upright, impales me so,
> That mine own Precipice I go;
> And warms and moves this needless Frame:
> (A Fever could but do the same.)
> And, wanting where its spight to try,
> Has made me live to let me dye.
> A Body that could never rest,
> Since this ill Spirit it possest.
>
> (ll. 11-20)

The Body echoes the Soul's appeal for release, an appeal which underlines their mutual sense of impotence, of being unable to choose (although, significantly, the Body *does* impute the power of choice to the Soul). If the Soul is 'hung up', the Body is 'stretcht upright'. Critics often quote Marvell's inspired satirical attack on Samuel Parker in *The Rehearsal Transpros'd:*

> But after he was stretch'd to such an height in his own fancy, that he could not look down from top to toe but his Eyes dazled at the Precipice of his Stature; there fell out, or in, another natural chance which push'd him headlong.[18]

In both contexts the word 'Precipice' leaps out, creating an instant impression of teetering anxiety, comic to others, threatening to the self. Proud man has to contemplate the precariousness of his own dignity. But in the prose satire Marvell attacks an individual's absurd pride, putting a banana-skin under Parker. In the verse dialogue, the Body complains of the universal posture that makes it recognisably human. Left to itself, it would presumably revert to a comfortable all-fours or even recumbent position, finding its animal level (as indeed it does, temporarily, in *The Garden*, where the poet plays the banana-skin joke on himself). It is because man has a soul that he walks 'Godlike erect': it is a sign of his domination.[19] Here Marvell touches wittily on a classical and hexaemeral topic to raise the question of what is 'natural'. The Body believes that the Soul maliciously destroys its contentment, making it live to let it die. Instead of being 'needless'—needing nothing—it is now constantly restless. Yet death and rest are conspicuously *not* equated. Unlike Hugo's Latin poem or *Thyrsis and Dorinda, A Dialogue between the Soul and Body* never entertains the idea of suicide overtly. Nevertheless there is something disturbingly suicidal in the Body's image of itself,[20] and, later, in the Soul's death-wish. The Body speaks almost as though it were already dead, feeling itself to be possessed or haunted by its personal ghost in the machine which cannot be exorcised (the pun on 'ill Spirit' in line 20 is well taken).

Although the Body takes a clear and uncompromising dualistic line, the poet contradicts and satirises that dualism by making images cross and recross stanza boundaries. So the Soul reinforces the Body's superstitious allusion in its retort—

Soul

What Magick could me thus confine
Within anothers Grief to pine?

(ll. 21–2)

If the floating echo of *The Tempest*—the witch Sycorax confining Ariel, the 'spirit too delicate', within 'a cloven pine'—is not entirely fortuitous,[21] it might tempt the reader to reconstruct the dialogue as a contest between Ariel and Caliban, with Prospero conspicuous by his absence. It would be a pleasant conceit, but not one that the Soul would appreciate. He prefers philosophy to the black arts, posing the ancient conundrum of spiritual suffering—'I feel, that cannot feel, the pain' (l. 24). Plotinus had distinguished between knowledge of pain, which is unmoved, and the sensation itself:[22] but Marvell's Soul collapses the distinction into paradox. Theoretically it 'cannot feel', but it does. Contemplation does not remove pain; on the contrary, throughout the dialogue physical and mental suffering are expressed in terms of each other.

Pain triggers off the instinct for self-preservation: but which self?

And all my Care its self employes,
That to preserve, which me destroys:
Constrain'd not only to indure
Diseases, but, whats worse, the Cure:
And ready oft the Port to gain,
Am Shipwrackt into Health again.

(ll. 25–30)

Both Body and Soul share a survival instinct, but it tugs them in diametrically opposite directions. For the Soul, the only safe harbour is beyond this life, a familiar metaphor which, for instance, is employed by Spenser's Despair as a temptation to suicide:

> Sleepe after toyle, port after stormie seas,
> Ease after warre, death after life does greatly please.
> *(The Faerie Queene*, I. ix. 40)

Marvell's Soul is more metaphysical in its wit (the phrase 'Shipwrackt into Health' recalls a Crashaw epigram),[23] but not much less morally suspect in its self-pitying tone. Yet the real difference from Spenser is precisely that, for all the suicidal overtones, there is no question of voluntary suicide. The Soul wishes for the Body's death but cannot *will* it. It is 'constrain'd', not just by disease but more ironically by health, to accept ungraciously its bondage to flesh.

The Body in turn reminds the Soul that the physician cannot minister to a mind diseased:

Body

> But Physick yet could never reach
> The Maladies Thou me dost teach;
> Whom first the Cramp of Hope does Tear:
> And then the Palsie Shakes of Fear.
> The Pestilence of Love does heat:
> Or Hatred's hidden Ulcer eat.
> Joy's chearful Madness does perplex:
> Or Sorrow's other Madness vex.
> Which Knowledge forces me to know;
> And Memory will not foregoe.
>
> (ll. 31–40)

Here above all the interaction of mind and body, of language and experience, is indisputable. Today such disorders as 'Hatred's hidden Ulcer' would be termed psychosomatic, a word which in its very form denies the dissociation of mind and body. In the seventeenth century, the idea was also familiar: writers such as Robert Burton in *The Anatomy of Melancholy*[24] correlated states of mind and physical symptoms, backing up theory with case histories and noting cause and effect with keen interest. The Body, which cannot 'know' in one sense, is forced to 'know' in another.

Although the Body imputes spiteful motives to the Soul earlier (ll. 17–18), its list of mental faculties—passions, intellect, memory—omits direct mention of the will. Until this point in the dialogue, the language on both sides is predominantly determinist, a language of constraint and coercion. But in the extra quatrain allotted to the Body, which ends the dialogue in the Folio text, the question of choice is thrust suddenly into prominence:

> What but a Soul could have the wit
> To build me up for Sin so fit?
> So Architects do square and hew,
> Green Trees that in the Forest grew.

(ll. 41-4)

This quatrain is disturbing in more ways than one: it radically shifts the formal and argumentative balance of the dialogue; it introduces an explicitly theological concept of guilt ('Sin'),[25] and a powerful Marvellian image ('Green Trees'); and it challenges the reader to regard it as 'a conclusion in which nothing is concluded'. The conjecture that it is *not* the original conclusion, although it receives dubious support from the Bodleian manuscript, MS. Eng. poet. d. 49, has not deterred readers from bringing to these lines their own sense of an ending.[26]

In particular, the analogy 'So Architects do square and hew/Green Trees that in the Forest grew' unexpectedly throws open a window in the claustrophobic cell which the Soul and Body have so far occupied. However ambivalent emotionally or intellectually, the image marks a moment of imaginative release from previous constraint. And it gives readers a choice. Marvell is famous for ambiguous endings, and in this case the possible ambiguity stems from the traditional debate of art versus nature which permits various permutations.[27] Some would argue that here it is the Body, not Marvell, which insists on moral categories: that man's capacity to shape nature has both creative and destructive possibilities, finely balanced in this couplet.[28] Others would argue that the image is not in perfect equilibrium, but that it implies a judgment for or against the Body's innocent—or naïve—naturalism.[29] But the judgment is not an easy one to make, even on an intertextual basis. How much weight should be given to Marvell's distinctive phrasing, 'square and hew' set against 'Green Trees'?

Both the architect image and the symbolic greenness of nature occur in Marvell's writing in contexts which give them peculiar intensity. The former tends to represent the life of action, the latter contemplation, pleasure, beauty. It is hardly surprising, then, to find Marvell using architectural metaphors constructively when writing of historical and political processes,[30] as in *The First Anniversary*, lines 87-98, but negatively in a more contemplative setting like *Upon Appleton House*. He is fully conscious of architectural malpractice and violation of nature—'That unto Caves the Quarries drew,/And Forrests did to Pastures hew'—and associates them with pride.[31] In *A Dialogue between the Soul and Body*, the architect metaphor seems also to be an indictment of pride. Although in one sense 'the Soul is the *Architect* of her own dwelling-place',[32] it did not design that dwelling-place. But it can pervert that design, just as man can pervert his natural environment. Underlying the analogy is the concept of the divine Architect, who, as Cowley reminds us in his essay *The Garden* chose not to build a city for newly-created man, but to place him in a garden: the dubious honour of being the first city-planner belongs to Cain. Another of Cowley's verse and prose essays, *Of Solitude*, contains a stanza which has a strong imaginative affinity with Marvell's architects/green trees opposition:

> Here Nature does a House for me erect,
> Nature the wisest Architect,
> Who those fond Artists does despise
> That can the fair and living Trees neglect;
> Yet the Dead Timber prize.
>
> (stanza 3).[33]

Of course this is special pleading, like the Body's. But it is just because 'green' is such a special quality in Marvell's poetry that its potency should not be underestimated. It is the colour of Eden, of the unfallen world. Trees provide a much-needed emotional continuity with the beginning of time; Fairfax, lord of Nunappleton, shared something of this feeling with Marvell, to judge from his awkward enchanting translation from the French:

> O how myn eyes are pleas'd to see
> Oakes that such spreadinge branches beare
> W^ch from old Time's n[a]tivity
> And th'envy of so many yeares
> Are still greene beautiful & faire
> As att the world's first day they were.[34]

To read such emotions into Marvell's lines in *A Dialogue between the Soul and Body* is not necessarily to assert the Body's innocence, but it is to recognise an intuition of innocence denied to the sophisticated Soul.

Yet the Soul is not as much the master of its fate as the Body thinks it is. In another, political, context, Marvell was to argue eloquently on behalf of both body and mind:

> That the Body is in the power of the mind; so that corporal punishments do never reach the offender, but the innocent suffers for the guilty. That the Mind is in the hand of God, and cannot correct those perswasions which upon the best of its natural capacity it hath collected: So that it too, though erroneous, is so farr innocent.
>
> (*The Rehearsal Transpros'd*)[35]

The passage is a salutary reminder that in the world of action there are worse kinds of imprisonment and torture than those envisaged by the Soul and Body in their dialogue.[36] But it is also a reminder that their contemplation is misdirected in its self-centredness. If the proper sphere of the Soul is contemplation—'*whose act*, exercise, or office, *is the perpetuall contemplation of truth*'[37]—it should look to a truth beyond itself, acknowledging that it is indeed 'in the hand of God'. If the proper sphere of the Body is action, it should not seek to regress to vegetable passivity. Neither Soul nor Body can make sense of their suffering, because they have thrown away the key to their own prison.

(v) The Garden of Contemplation: The Nymph complaining for the death of her Faun

The Nymph complaining for the death of her Faun is another poem in which a naïve speaker tries to make sense of suffering in a sustained act of contemplation. Not for the first time in a Marvell poem, the reader's own powers of contemplation are put to the test, but in this case the poet withholds the formal protection of dialogue or emblem, and the authorial voice is silent. We are thrust into the middle of an emotional crisis, made recipients of the Nymph's confidences, with only the unusually extended title of the poem to guide us. The guidance is usually assumed to be generic: 'nymph' and 'faun'[1] locate the poem in pastoral, in a shadowy green medium between myth and human or animal existence. The mourning of a dead pet is a classical topos, treated in the Greek Anthology and Roman elegy.[2] Yet the form and subject, seemingly simple and precise, have generated more interpretative difficulties than almost any other poem in the Folio.[3] These difficulties centre on concepts such as 'allegory' and 'voice', but the most illuminating attempts to mark out a *templum* for observation start not from a concept but from the poem's own space and time, garden and narrative.

In contrast with *A Dialogue between the Soul and Body*, *The Nymph complaining* has leisure for fiction; but the relation between fiction and grief is even less easy to establish than is usual in pastoral elegy.[4] Such fictions tend towards self-contemplation, and some would say that the Nymph is as self-centred in her own way as the Soul and Body in theirs. Indeed her story, and her garden, can be read as an allegory of the soul[5] defending itself against intrusive pain as best it may. But without denying this insight, we might want to distinguish this form of self-contemplation from that practised by the Soul and Body. The choice of narrative form and extended pastoral metaphor enlarge the possibilities in a way only glimpsed in the 'Green Trees' of the preceding dialogue. Where that dialogue ends—on an image of nature violated by human initiative—*The Nymph complaining* begins.

With a difference however:

> The wanton Troopers riding by
> Have shot my Faun and it will dye.

> (ll. 1–2)

This act of violation is more acutely felt because it is 'wanton': it cannot be dignified even as a deliberated choice, although in a sense it arises from a prior commitment to the active life. Soldiers, like architects, behave according to professional type. In this instance, men conditioned to destroy show none of the respect for living nature which is a principle of the contemplative life. And, unlike the architects, they have no particular purpose in view.[6] If the use of the term 'Troopers' makes a specific political point, it is probably secondary.[7] If they do represent Cromwellian militarism, they simply link what is happening in a contemporary England at war with a centuries' old fear of the damage done by marauding soldiers. Their opportunism is not essentially different from that of Ascanius in the Virgilian episode which has been connected with Marvell's poem.[8] What is difficult is not the nature of the action, but the response to it. The Nymph, the voice of pastoral, is called upon to test the assumptions not only of pastoral but of the contemplative life itself when its values are outraged.[9]

She begins by expressing an uncomprehending emotional gap between her world and theirs:

> Ungentle men! They cannot thrive
> To kill thee. Thou neer didst alive
> Them any harm: alas nor cou'd
> Thy death yet do them any good.
> I'me sure I never wisht them ill;
> Nor do I for all this; nor will:
> But, if my simple Pray'rs may yet
> Prevail with Heaven to forget
> Thy murder, I will Joyn my Tears
> Rather then fail.
>
> (ll. 3–12)

Like other contemplatives, she turns to the language of religion, a language familiar yet distinctively hers in its ingenuous vocabulary and its awkward syntax. Although these lines, at least, are not beyond the scope of a pious child, there is much at issue here. Her intuitive response can scarcely measure up to the problem—metaphysical, not just psychological—that confronts her: why evil? why innocent suffering? if God is just.[10] A little later she hints, consciously or not, at Christ's supreme sacrifice. Here she seems almost to essay an *imitatio Christi* on her own account, praying heaven 'to forget/Thy murder'. But she gets it a little wrong, by substituting 'forget' for the more exemplary Christian 'forgive'—'Father, forgive them; for they know not what they do'[11]—and indeed she cannot bring herself to believe that God is capable of forgetting even the least of His creatures,[12] that heavenly justice is not part of the scheme of things:

> It cannot dye so. Heavens King
> Keeps register of every thing:
> And nothing may we use in vain.
> Ev'n Beasts must be with justice slain;
> Else Men are made their *Deodands*.
>
> (ll. 13–17)

In claiming animal rights as analogous to human rights, she borrows an unexpectedly esoteric term from legal usage: a *deo dandum*, thing to be given to God, is usually non-human, a personal possession which is forfeit because it has caused the death of a rational being. In this context, 'Marvell reverses the natural order',[13] bringing the customary categories of rational and non-rational into question, a little like Swift in Book IV of *Gulliver's Travels*. But the Nymph's crisis goes too deep for this kind of ironic logic, which is not natural to her. The idea of expiation leads her beyond law, to a direct emotional apprehension of religious sacrifice which does not depend on making logical connections.

> Though they should wash their guilty hands
> In this warm life-blood, which doth part
> From thine, and wound me to the Heart,
> Yet could they not be clean: their Stain
> Is dy'd in such a Purple Grain.
> There is not such another in
> The World, to offer for their Sin.

(ll. 18–24)

The point of the oblique reminder of the Passion can only be one of essential contrast.[14] It is simply unavailable to the Nymph in her world, as, in a different sense, it is claimed to be unavailable to the troopers in theirs. Although from the Nymph's viewpoint, the fawn is unique in its innocence and perfection, its sacrifice is unlike Christ's precisely because it cannot be efficacious. Nature's innocence cannot redeem human guilt. The image of washing in blood is as close to primitive ritual as to its biblical counterpart, hovering between superstition and spirituality. And the Nymph's two propositions do not fit together logically (if the first is true, the second is redundant). Logic is not, however, her strongest point.[15]

What she can do is to feel, and it is through her gift for feeling that she mediates the pain of the universe through a single innocent death. Yet she has been criticised for this as well. Her reaction to the fawn's death is often regarded as disproportionate, and either explained in terms of her own limitations, or else redefined in terms of the 'real' object of her grief.[16] Alternatively, the responsibility can be placed on the reader. Frank Kermode observes, 'the figure [of the archetypal sacrifice] is excessive, unless we revise it in obscure and complicated ways, so that our complexity finally joins her simplicity.'[17] All too many readings of the poem do 'revise it in obscure and complicated ways,' without the complexity finally joining her simplicity. But it is just her simplicity that goes to the root of the matter. If she does not analyse, 'does not attempt to consider *why* such acts take place',[18] it is because her spiritual energy is concentrated on dealing with consequences rather than causes. She is one of the walking wounded of the contemplative life; and a basic test of that life is whether it enables one to accept and transform grief. The Nymph's first attempt to reconcile her experience of pointless evil and suffering to a simple theological scheme may fail, but we should hesitate to conclude that Marvell attributes the failure to naïve egotism or a restricted imagination. The quality of her moral vision eclipses her faulty logic in its very directness. Like certain other ironists, Marvell honours, perhaps even envies, pure and simple spiritual intuitiveness. The dewdrop soul, the Bermudan Puritans, the Nymph: all have been denigrated as escapists, but all possess a kind of integrity which heightens their capacity for contemplation, and for feeling pleasure and pain.

The Nymph herself has known both pleasure and pain before this all-consuming grief came upon her. The pastoral world also has its losses and choices, as the story she tells illustrates:

> Unconstant *Sylvio*, when yet
> I had not found him counterfeit,
> One morning (I remember well)
> Ty'd in this silver Chain and Bell,
> Gave it to me: nay and I know
> What he said then; I'me sure I do.
> Said He, look how your Huntsman here
> Hath taught a Faun to hunt his *Dear*.
> But *Sylvio* soon had me beguil'd.
> This waxed tame, while he grew wild,
> And quite regardless of my Smart,
> Left me his Faun, but took his Heart.
>
> (ll. 25-36)

Her sad mimicry of Sylvio's double language seems as foreign to her as the sophisticated term 'deodand'. She has painstakingly memorised it, caught the linguistic trick of erotic male poetry: but this does not mean that she has been corrupted by it. If instead of conducting an inquisition into the Nymph's chastity we compare this episode with Marvell's treatment of pastoral love generally, it does not seem at all exceptional in itself. Distrust of sexuality is pervasive in Marvell's poems. Here Sylvio[19] represents erotic desire, which often figures as the destroyer of innocence and, therefore, of a paradisal relationship with the natural world.[20] What does make *The Nymph complaining* exceptional is that the pattern is reversed. Just as the troopers invade the contemplative world as intruders from the world of action, so Sylvio earlier invaded the Nymph's peace of mind with the specious promise of love and pleasure. But the consequences are strikingly different. One outcome is life and nature, the other death and art. Although her contact with the *vita voluptuosa* in its erotic form has hurt and disillusioned the Nymph, yet from her first experience of loss springs a new life of innocent pleasure and contemplation combined. Love of nature displaces unsatisfactory passion, and the garden displaces the huntsman's domain.

In order to bring this about, the Nymph has to make a choice, which she herself recognises as a choice of life:

> Thenceforth I set my self to play
> My solitary time away,
> With this: and very well content,

> Could so mine idle Life have spent.
>
> (ll. 37–40)

Her description fits the classical ideal of *otium*, fruitful idleness, which is celebrated by pastoral poets and praised by philosophers. The choice itself may be right or wrong, according to circumstances. Although pastime has a valued place in pastoral, for certain readers the words 'play' and 'idle' denote criticism of the Nymph's solitary life.[21] But it is not only pastime that the fawn offers her. More important still, it is an object of love, spiritual purpose and responsibility:[22]

> it seem'd to bless
> Its self in me. How could I less
> Than love it? O I cannot be
> Unkind, t'a Beast that loveth me.
>
> (ll. 43–6)

If the fawn has to symbolise anything, it surely symbolises nature itself, as Marvell conceives it in an ideal environment: playful, loving, touched by grace. The tentative expression 'it seem'd to bless/Its self in me' takes on fresh meaning if the relationship between the Nymph and her fawn reflects that between humanity and the natural creation. The Nymph's mythic role does not exclude the human. Indeed, she has been assimilated not only into the more obvious Ovidian myth, but also into the Platonic myth of the human soul.[23] And as a human soul, she may be both nature's superior and its inferior in certain attributes. She herself will tell us that she is inferior to the fawn in whiteness, softness, and swiftness. Yet the contemplative soul, in partaking of the divine, transcends the natural creation and helps to raise it to another level. If the fawn 'blesses itself'[24] in the Nymph, it is because she can perceive and articulate the beauty and meaning of its existence. She is, so to speak, the fawn's High Priestess, in the sense of George Herbert's beautiful lines, 'Man is the worlds high Priest: he doth present/The sacrifice for all'.[25] The Nymph's sacrifice is both grief and praise.

It is true that a passing doubt shadows her faith retrospectively:

> Had it liv'd long, I do not know
> Whether it too might have done so
> As *Sylvio* did: his Gifts might be
> Perhaps as false or more than he.
>
> (ll. 47–50)

Nature too might eventually betray the heart that loves her, being mortal nature and corruptible. After all, the fawn was tamed and trained by Sylvio, as nature in general is tamed by the arts of man. Nevertheless, the Nymph's brief experience makes her conclude

> But I am sure, for ought that I

> Could in so short a time espie,
> Thy Love was far more better then
> The love of false and cruel men.
>
> (ll. 51–54)

Although the notion that loving (or being loved by) a fawn is better than the love of men may be as tongue-in-cheek as the similar notion in *The Garden* that one is better off loving trees than women, there is in both instances a more serious underlying point. The contemplative life is all too easily disrupted by sexual passion, most dominating and dangerous of pleasures. The love of nature offers an innocent delight, which presents no obstacle to the 'contemplative imagination', and which can be interpreted Platonically as a preliminary stage in a spiritual ascent to the divine beauty.[26] Describing her nurturing of the fawn, the Nymph also observes that it surpasses woman in beauty as it surpasses man in love:

> It had so sweet a Breath! And oft
> I blusht to see its foot more soft,
> And white, (shall I say then my hand?)
> NAY any Ladies of the Land.
>
> (ll. 59–62)

And it easily outruns her in 'the Race', a phrase which again has multiple significance so that allegory hovers in the air. The race is associated with mortality, divinity, love and loss—and metamorphosis. Once more *The Garden* suggests a parellel:

> The *Gods*, that mortal Beauty chase,
> Still in a Tree did end their race.
>
> (ll. 27–8)

The outcome of the fawn's race is suspended by its teasing behaviour, which is both very much in the nature of fawns and appropriate to a legendary creature treading 'as on the four Winds' (l. 70).[27] But the race will have an end: first in flowers, then in blood, finally in the stillness of alabaster. A sequence of metamorphoses, all enacted in a garden.

The Nymph's description of this garden, embroidered like a tapestry, has been painstakingly unpicked thread by thread in scholarly exegesis. It deserves, however, to be contemplated first as a whole:

> I have a Garden of my own,
> But so with Roses over grown,
> And Lillies, that you would it guess
> To be a little Wilderness.
> And all the Spring time of the year
> It onely loved to be there.
> Among the beds of Lillyes, I

> Have sought it oft, where it should lye;
> Yet could not, till it self would rise,
> Find it, although before mine Eyes.
> For, in the flaxen Lillies shade,
> It like a bank of Lillies laid.
> Upon the Roses it would feed,
> Until its Lips ev'n seem'd to bleed:
> And then to me 'twould boldly trip,
> And print those Roses on my Lip.
> But all its chief delight was still
> On Roses thus its self to fill:
> And its pure virgin Limbs to fold
> In whitest sheets of Lillies cold.
> Had it liv'd long, it would have been
> Lillies without, Roses within.
>
> (ll. 71–92)

The intensely lyrical, and inescapable, echoes of the Song of Solomon—'My beloved is mine, and I am his: he feedeth among the lilies'[28]—set the Nymph's garden apart as a special domain. And it is *her* domain. The idea that this is a *hortus conclusus*, a garden enclosed, or a *hortus mentis*, a garden of the mind, although open to challenge, has the virtue of being compatible with seventeenth-century symbolic modes, and with the unique influence of the Song of Songs on these modes.[29] A *hortus mentis* may not be all it is; and it lacks any mention of an enclosing wall, a traditional feature of the *hortus conclusus*. But it is a place created for contemplation and pleasure. And, like the mind it reflects, it is not totally ordered and open: it has its secret places, its confusions and apparent wildness, its intimations of death as well as growth. It is idyllic, but not perfect.

The roses and lilies that overrun this garden are also heavy with symbolism. Since these are the commonest of emblematic flowers, what they 'mean' in this setting is inseparable from a sense of what is going on in the poem as a whole.[30] The reader has to 'guess' what the garden signifies, and what the roses and lilies signify. If the point is to contrast them, then the red of passion and blood offsets the white of purity and virginity. If, on the contrary, the colours combine in a single code (roses-and-lilies, red-and-white), then together they are the flowers of love and beauty; but whether sacred or profane is again a matter for the reader. Or they may be a traditional reminder of transience and mortality: specifically, the red roses make the fawn's lips seem to bleed, the lilies enfold it like a shroud. The emphasis on illusion, on an unrealised metamorphosis—'Lilies without, Roses within' (l. 92)—makes it clear that the garden's meaning is not fixed and immutable. Yet that is all the more reason to see it as a source of pleasure (even those antagonistic to the retreat mentality usually admit its beauty), and as a challenge to the contemplative imagination.

How does the Nymph herself see it? She is less in control than some readers assume,[31] for she is both inside and outside the garden of contemplation. Not only is it, in the poem's present, a lost domain; but even at the height of the idyll she is in some sense separated from, an observer of, the natural unity of fawn and garden. The *hortus mentis* idea is not all-inclusive.[32] Although the fawn and garden are both hers to contemplate and take pleasure in, she is gently mocked by their otherness, the way they merge into one another. The race turns into a quest for a beauty which can only be found through its self-revelation:

> Among the beds of Lillyes, I
> Have sought it oft, where it should lye;
> Yet could not, till it self would rise,
> Find it, although before mine Eyes.

(ll. 77–80)

The capacity to *see*, to distinguish, is central to Marvell's contemplative poems. In *The Nymph complaining*, limits are set on seeing and knowing for both Nymph and reader. Just as the reader is dependent on a text which both conceals and reveals its meanings, so the Nymph is dependent on a natural creation which offers itself in a living relationship. Like the fruits of *The Garden* (stanza v), the fawn 'boldly' makes its innocent advances, imprinting its rose-kisses on her lips. In this version of the contemplative life, the pleasure of the senses does not conflict with spiritual contemplation, and nature is both reality and symbol. So, although it has been customary to regard the garden idyll as a flight *from* experience, it is also a flight *to* experience, a way of transforming reality.

For there is no reason why this imaginary garden should not also be a 'real' garden. When the Nymph uses the phrase 'a little Wilderness' (l. 74), it is a reminder of seventeenth-century gardening habits as well as seventeenth-century habits of Bible-reading. A 'wilderness' was part of a larger garden, set aside and planted with an eye to an informal natural effect.[33] Francis Bacon does not use the actual term, but his essay *Of Gardens* describes an area 'framed, as much as may be, to a natural wildness' where thickets of sweetbriar and a profusion of flowers—including red roses and *lilium convallium*—should grow.[34] Usually the wilderness and the *hortus conclusus* are opposites, literally in garden design and figuratively,[35] but the Nymph's garden combines suggestions of both (she does not say that it *is* a wilderness). The fawn is a wild creature, tamed, certainly, yet still elusive. Even its diet of rose-petals, it seems, is not pure invention for the sake of a conceit.[36] And spring is the appropriate season not only for symbolic gardens but also, within limits, for real ones, where English gardeners may by cunning planting 'have *ver perpetuum*, as the place affords.'[37]

Both gardeners and poets deal in illusion, and so does Marvell's Nymph. The idea of metamorphosis, incomplete in this passage, takes on its traditional function of displacing grief[38] when the Nymph returns to the present contemplation of her stricken beloved:

> O help! O help! I see it faint:

> And dye as calmely as a Saint.
> See how it weeps. The Tears do come
> Sad, slowly dropping like a Gumme.
> So weeps the wounded Balsome: so
> The holy Frankincense doth flow.
> The brotherless *Heliades*
> Melt in such Amber Tears as these.
>   I in a golden Vial will
> Keep these two crystal Tears; and fill
> It till it do o'reflow with mine;
> Then place it in *Diana's* Shrine.
>
> (ll. 93–104)

The fawn's tears are metamorphosed into something rich and rare: indeed, the most evocative comparison, in a beautifully cadenced couplet, recalls the ancient sorrow of the Heliades, sisters of Phaeton, 'who with such funerall lamentation bewayled the death of their brother, that the gods in commiseration of their sorrow, turned them into trees.'[39] The cult of tears is part of contemplation (as in *Eyes and Tears*). It is not surprising that religious imagery—'And dye as calmely as a Saint'—recurs and mingles with the classical allusions. Nor is it surprising that a literary connoisseur can detect a likeness to Crashaw's *The Weeper*.[40] These tears are not the product of raw pain, but healing, embalming, precious, like balsam and frankincense. Preserving them in 'a golden Vial' and offering them to the goddess of chastity and the hunt is an appropriate, if in some ways ironic, gesture: tear-bottles had their place both in devotional literature and in the rituals of bereavement.[41] The Nymph is, as it were, putting her affairs in order prior to her final resolution.

Her contemplation of the afterlife is slight, and briefly expressed:

> Now my Sweet Faun is vanish'd to
> Whether the Swans and Turtles go:
> In fair *Elizium* to endure,
> With milk-white Lambs, and Ermins pure.
> O do not run too fast: for I
> Will but bespeak thy Grave, and dye.
>
> (ll. 105–110)

Even compared with the pastoral Elysium of *Thyrsis and Dorinda*,[42] this description scarcely engages the imagination, confined as it is to the token emblems of faithful love, innocence, and purity. Her true choice of eternity takes a different direction, not an Elysium but an eternity of stone:

> First my unhappy Statue shall
> Be cut in Marble; and withal,
> Let it be weeping too: but there
> Th'Engraver sure his Art may spare;
> For I so truly thee bemoane,
> That I shall weep though I be. Stone:
> Until my Tears, still dropping, wear
> My breast, themselves engraving there.

> There at my feet shalt thou be laid,
> Of purest Alabaster made:
>   For I would have thine Image be
> White as I can, though not as Thee.

(ll. 111–122)

For choosing death instead of life, replacing nature with art, the Nymph has been found guilty of ultimate spiritual failure.[43] The charge of escapism, as well as narcissism, can always be levelled at the contemplative spirit, and the deathwish in particular seems to arouse hostility—perhaps because it is the one human wish which is sure of gratification sooner or later. Although the absence of the poet's own voice from *The Nymph complaining* is a critical commonplace, it has not prevented the assumption that he implicitly judges the choice she makes and exposes its inadequacy. Yet this attitude is almost too easy. The Nymph's renunciation of life is not a renunciation of feeling: on the contrary, her grief will be perpetuated till it wears away even marble—'I shall weep though I be Stone' (l. 116). And she herself believes that the sculptor's art falls short of nature, that it can only strive for perfection without attaining it (ll. 121–2). Nevertheless, it is through art—the poem, the imagined statue—that remembrance is possible, that contemplation extends beyond the individual existence. Judged as a work of art, the statue like the poem fulfils its purpose. Its beauty gives aesthetic pleasure (the materials, marble and translucent alabaster, and the pose suggest the kind of Italian or Greek sculpture that Marvell might have seen abroad). Its subject awakens memories of myth, especially the myth of Niobe,[44] bereft of her children and metamorphosed into weeping stone. Niobe is the epitome of memorial art: William Browne, for example, wrote of the Countess of Pembroke

> Marble piles let no man raise
> To her name: for after days
> Some kind woman born as she,
> Reading this, like Niobe
> Shall turn marble, and become
> Both her mourner and her tomb.[45]

At the end of Marvell's poem, as throughout, one kind of grief, for one loss, stands for all kinds: the mythic griefs of the Heliades and Niobe, human grief for a lost paradise, perhaps even divine grief for lost humanity. Art is not offered as recompense, but rather as register. Possibly the reader is meant to reflect ironically that marble statues, no less than living creatures, may be at the mercy of the barbarians and of time itself. 'How with this rage shall beauty hold a plea?' And yet it does, and continues to do so.

The Nymph complaining for the death of her Faun has long been a touchstone in Marvell criticism. It also occupies an unusually important place in the Folio, at a point of transition between poems that have religious or philosophical overtones, and those that are concerned, directly or indirectly, with sexual love. If the centre of the Nymph's poem is the garden of contemplation, it is a place under threat from the erotic life on one hand and the active life on the other. The garden experience uniting contemplation and innocent pleasure, and secure enough to absorb or withstand these threats, will not be recreated until *The Garden* itself. Meanwhile the poems that follow *The Nymph complaining* examine and develop more fully what is involved in the erotic life represented in Sylvio's role.

Part II

The Life of Love and Pleasure

> ... in respect of pleasure, love and desire
> flourish together and together perish.
> (Leone Ebreo. *Dialoghi d'Amore*)

In the myth of the Judgment of Paris, as the Renaissance interprets it, the *vita voluptuosa* is in the gift of Venus and made flesh in Helen, most beautiful of mortal women. Her sexuality both signifies and sums up the life of pleasure. But, as Paris was to discover, the gifts of Venus are ambiguous. In theory, the relation between beauty, love, and pleasure should unfold as harmoniously as the pose of the three Graces which is supposed to be its manifestation.[1] According to the Neoplatonists, whose ultimate authority is Plato's *Symposium*, 'Amor ... in voluptatem a pulchritudine desinit', 'Love begins in Beauty and ends in Pleasure.'[2] However, even the most inveterate Neoplatonic idealists distinguish between the perfect round of the divine triad and the broken arcs of human life. Not all that passes for love in the sublunary world begins to meet their criteria.

It is Ficino who refines upon the connection between love and the choice of life in his *Commentary* on the *Symposium*.[3] He classifies love into two extremes, the good 'daemon', or love of the divine beauty, and its opposite 'daemon', the physical urge to procreate. Between these extremes, he divides love into three kinds, corresponding to the three kinds of life:

> ... we are born or reared with an inclination to the contemplative, the practical, or the voluptuous life. If to the contemplative, we are lifted immediately from the sight of bodily form to the contemplation of the spiritual and divine. If to the voluptuous, we descend immediately from the sight to the desire to touch. If to the practical and moral, we remain in the pleasures only of seeing and the social relations.

These three loves are valued accordingly: 'love of the contemplative man is called divine; that of the practical man human; and that of the voluptuous man, animal'.[4] Clearly this implies a judgment which many love poets would—and did—resist. And there are alternatives, Leone Ebreo's *Dialoghi d'Amore*, for instance, acceptably modifies Neoplatonic theory by recognising physical union as integral to the highest form of love between the sexes. Yet Leone too warns that bodily pleasures, including sex, 'are such that, once enjoyed, not only is desire of them stilled, but in most cases love also, which often changes to disgust and loathing . . . so that, in respect of pleasure, love and desire flourish together and together perish.'[5] It seems from the love treatises that the definition of love in any sexual context may become dangerously unstable, easily confused with mere physical desire.

Whatever its origin and nature, earthly love is by no means guaranteed to end in pleasure as ordinarily understood. In Renaissance literary tradition it is just as likely to end in tears, the Petrarchan 'pleasure of grieving'. Nor do many Renaissance poets writing of love concur with the view 'It was my choyse, yt was no chaunce'—not even Wyatt, who wrote the line.[6] Paris at least had a choice, and moreover was granted his desire, although Helen came with a price tag, paid for in the blood of Greeks and Trojans and the flames of Troy. In Renaissance poetry, the lover often has no choice, and the blood and flames are his own: 'And all he saies, a Lover drest/In his own Blood does relish best.'[7] Yet even the lover's life offers alternatives, if only the alternative of ending it. Certain conditions are predetermined: just as the division between body and soul plays a crucial part in the *vita contemplativa*, so the division of the sexes plays a crucial part in the *vita voluptuosa*. Choice begins with the individual lover deciding what psychological stance to take, how to pursue his desire for union with the beloved or how to endure separation. Certain traditional options are open to him. Obviously he can aim at pleasure by attempting to persuade her to consummate their love—so forcing her to choose in her turn. Or, despairing of that pleasure, he may settle for a love that not only begins in beauty but also ends in beauty, transforming pain and cruelty into art. Or he may redefine the perfect love itself as intellectual beauty, accepting permanent physical separation as the condition of spiritual union. Or he may displace his hopeless passion into revenge and self-destruction. Marvell makes poetry out of all these possibilities, and in doing so exercises his own literary choice among conventional forms: persuasion, blazon, definition, pastoral complaint.

Not every poet writing of love conforms to a single ideology. Attitudes to the relation between the sexes are as varied and conflicting as attitudes to the relation of soul and body, and for much the same reasons. And those who write most passionately, like Shakespeare or Donne, of the expense of spirit in a waste of shame can write even more eloquently of the ecstasy that 'defects of lonelinesse controules'.[8] Marvell, however, in spite of the variety of stances his lovers adopt, seems consistently to take an exceptionally wary attitude to sexual love, distrusting it as a means to pleasure. Marvell's lovers are almost all trapped, by time, by fate, by each other and themselves, and by the violent fictions that they enact. Their world is recognisably that of the classical love poets and the love theorists, but with the emphasis on the principle of opposition. They dedicate their lives to armed Eros rather than to Pleasure and the Graces—*Voluptati et Gratiis*. Even the most innocuous of pastoral love songs, *Ametas and Thestylis making Hay-Ropes*, works through an emblem of opposition, the hay-rope itself. In this instance, the lovers end by simply abandoning their witty entanglement, and their task, and settle for a tumble in the (loose) hay. But they are the exception among Marvell's lovers in being able to opt so light-heartedly for pleasure, cutting the Gordian knot of sexual opposition rather than unravelling it. At the other extreme is *The Definition of Love*, which perfects a theory of opposition, and in the process intellectualises physical pleasure out of existence altogether.

Most of Marvell's poems about love involve pleasure only in a special sense. It is a pleasure that owes as much to intelligence as to passion—if not more—and derives from an exacting aesthetic standard. His lovers tend to be connoisseurs of their own pain. When writing love verses, the poet himself seems metaphorically to be gathering roses in the rain, exposing lyricism to the chill of irony:

> Gentler times for Love are ment.
> Who for parting pleasure strain
> Gather Roses in the rain,
> Wet themselves and spoil their Sent.
>
> (*Daphnis and Chloe*, ll. 85–8)

Marvell's times are not 'gentle', nor are his lovers. They damage themselves, each other, and the world; but the scent of their roses is not spoilt but heightened by such misguided behaviour. The Unfortunate Lover 'dying leaves a Perfume here'. If the pleasures of these poems have to be snatched 'with rough strife,' in the phrase from *To his Coy Mistress*, it is the rough strife of artistic creation. The reader who experiences the poems cumulatively, not just in isolation, may come to suspect that Marvell values beauty far beyond either love or sexual pleasure. The *vita voluptuosa* based on sexual activity is a delusion: it scarcely represents a valid choice of life in a universe that loads the dice against pleasure if only through ensuring that it cannot last. Beauty too will not last; but the poet's 'ecchoing Song', although unable to penetrate the tomb, still leaves 'Musick within every Ear'.[9]

In spite of this measure of consistency, the arrangement of the love poems in the Folio is less assured than that of the contemplative poems. Yet they do link up with each other, and indeed the sequence contains Marvell's most cohesive single group of lyrics, the Mower poems. Appropriately, the arrangement begins with two poems which take the form of persuasions to love, *Young Love* and *To his Coy Mistress*, both classical in theme, with the former concentrating on unripeness, the latter on ripeness threatened with rottenness. Following this pair are a cluster of poems beginning with *The Unfortunate Lover*. Whatever its subtext,[10] overtly *The Unfortunate Lover* is linked to the persuasions through the topos of love and time, and to the following poems—*The Gallery, The Fair Singer, Mourning*, and *Daphnis and Chloe*—through its ironic stylisation of sexual behaviour. All this group, directly or obliquely, treat love as an art with its own forms and laws. But these elegant and pleasurable performances (pleasurable for the spectator at least) are displaced in turn by the most contemplative of Marvell's love poems, which deliberately has nothing to do with the *vita voluptuosa*: *The Definition of Love*.

The Definition of Love would be a hard act to follow in any case, since it *is* so extraordinarily definitive. Perhaps significantly, the loose thematic continuity of the Folio does begin to break down at this point, the next three poems being *The Picture of little T.C. in a Prospect of Flowers*, *Tom May's Death*, and *The Match*. If we discount *Tom May's Death* as an obvious aberration, that still leaves two poems with nature and love in common but little else. It seems to me that there is a case for placing *The Match* immediately after *The Definition of Love*, both on formal grounds and because, unequal as they are, each is concerned with the metaphysics of love. As for *The Picture of little T.C. in a Prospect of Flowers*, it is so characteristic of Marvell's lyrical genius that it would scarcely seem out of place anywhere among the lyrics, and has links with many of them. Hardly a love poem as such, its place here may be accounted for by the fact that it shares certain motifs with love poetry: anticipation of future triumph and disaster, witty alarm at female power, the significance of plucking flowers and the analogy with a girl's fresh beauty. The choice of a girl child as the subject also relates *Little T.C.* to the very different *Young Love*, to the Maria episodes in *Upon Appleton House*, and with some qualification, to *The Nymph complaining*.

What does set *Little T.C.* apart from the preceding love poems is not so much the fact that the subject is still a child—there are many seventeenth-century lyrics where the point of the poem is the girl's immaturity[11]—but the centrality of the natural world. The child's present relationship with nature is at least as important as her future power over men's hearts, if not more so. Nature figures in all Marvell's love poems, but usually either as an abstraction or as a tantalising glimpse of landscape or seascape. With The Picture of *Little T.C. in a Prospect of Flowers*, despite the title, it becomes more than a setting: it is a source of beauty, power, and pleasure in its own right. Consequently, human beings have to learn respect for the natural world and not destroy it wantonly.

The note of warning—and the overtones of the Fall—sound again in the Mower poems, where man's two relationships, with nature and with woman, collapse in 'one common Ruine'. In this beautifully crafted quartet, Marvell ironically observes the excesses of erotic feeling as he does elsewhere, but he gives particular priority to the landscape. Through pastoral he can suggest other satisfactions, other kinds of love and pleasure offered by the natural world. For the speakers of *To his Coy Mistress* and *The Definition of Love* there are no such alternatives, and their arguments intentionally demolish hypothetical pleasures. For Damon the Mower, if only he were capable of regaining it, there is another choice of life which is a true *vita voluptuosa*. But it is a life prior to erotic experience. The only fortunate lovers are those who accept their condition, take it 'as [they] may': Ametas and Thestylis, for whom pleasure is as real and graspable as their hay-rope. Their brief lively dialogue succeeds Damon's melancholy monologues, and ends the sequence of love poems on the simplest choice of all

Then let's both lay by our Rope,
And go kiss within the Hay.
(Ametas and Thestylis making Hay-Ropes, ll. 15-16)

The comparative rarity of true *love* poems in the Marvell canon, the habit of scepticism, the coolness in the face of erotic artillery, all give the impression of a poet for whom woman is a source of less pleasure than the art which purports to celebrate her and the nature which she allegedly rivals. Marvell's *vita voluptuosa* lies elsewhere, and is ultimately at one with the *vita contemplativa*. But in spite of (or perhaps because of) this, his best love poems are uniquely satisfying in their ironic beauty, their despair of perfection, and their imaginative energy summoned up against hopeless odds.

(i) Persuasions to Love: Young Love, To his Coy Mistress

Young Love

Young Love claims to be precisely that, a persuasion to *love*. Unlike many persuasion poems, where the speaker's intention is to seduce the girl into bed, its promise of pleasure is delicately adjusted to its subject; for the poem's strategy is to select a girl who is still so young that she is free to return love in all innocence, unhindered by the consciousness of adult sexuality. It requires considerable literary skill to write on such a topic from an angle of erotic awareness without misjudging the tone. Classical poets had achieved it in a different cultural climate: some seventeenth-century poets met the challenge with varying success. As always, Marvell adapts a literary precedent to his own purposes, expressing his continuing concern with innocence and experience, choice and necessity, time and fate, through this apparently slight motif.

The motif itself has been shown to derive from epigrams in the Greek Anthology and two of Horace's odes.[1] One of the latter, ode II: 5, describes a girl-child not yet ready for sexual experience, her grapes unripened: only wait, Horace advises the would-be lover, and the grapes will turn purple, the girl turn pursuer. In the other ode, I: 23, the lover in person addresses a girl trembling on the brink of sexual initiation:

> atqui non ego te tigris ut aspera
> Gaetulusve leo frangere persequor:
> tandem desine matrem
> tempestiva sequi viro.

> Am I a fierce Gaetulian
> Lion or some tiger with a plan
> To seize and maul you? Come, now, leave your
> Mother: you're ready to know a man.[2]

Marvell's speaker matches this experienced, indulgently mature tone, but the situation is less straightforward. Suspicion slides into the opening stanza, even as it is being dismissed:

I

> Come little Infant, Love me now,
> While thine unsuspected years
> Clear thine aged Fathers brow
> From cold Jealousie and Fears.

(ll. 1–4)

In the equivalent Greek and Latin poems, the girl is not referred to as an

infant, nor does she possess a jealous father (a figure who seems to have
strayed in from a different, more Ovidian, scenario). 'Infant' is playful, yet its
literal meaning alludes to the most radical innocence of all, the state prior to
speech as well as sexuality. In this respect, little T.C. and Maria Fairfax
contrast with *Young Love*, since each of them can and does use language to
considerable purpose.[3] The purpose of language in *Young Love* is
manipulative, not least where the reader is concerned.

What an initially unsuspecting reader may not realise is that the speaker is
also being playful with us, misdirecting our expectations. The second stanza
invites us to view the picture from a different, symbolic, perspective:

II

Pretty surely 'twere to see
By young Love old Time beguil'd:
While our Sportings are as free
As the Nurses with the Child.

(ll. 5–8)

As elsewhere in Marvell's poetry, the jealous antagonist whom love has to
outwit turns out to be not a person but a personification. In *The Definition of
Love*, it is Fate who watches 'with jealous Eye' (l. 13); here the aged father is
revealed as Old Father Time, beguiled by the infant Love as in some
allegorical painting, an acceptably 'pretty' picture that erases the disconcerting
first impression.[4] The oddly Blakean image—'While our Sportings are as
free/As the Nurses with the Child'—suggests the harmless pleasures of a
relationship between adult and child. Yet how disinterested is the speaker in
drawing such an analogy? For readers who question tone and motivation,[5] he
may seem altogether too smooth, too ready to distract our attention as well as
Time's. But questions about motive may be beside the point. For Marvell,
what seems to matter most is the argument of the poem, the attempt to give
love a sporting chance against time by working out new rules for the game,
which require an 'infant' player.

His first rule concerns timing:

III

Common Beauties stay fifteen;
Such as yours should swifter move;
Whose fair Blossoms are too green
Yet for Lust, but not for Love.

(ll. 9–12)

The compliment implied in 'Common Beauties' is a conventional one:[6] 'stay'
means 'wait for',[7] and reflects a social assumption about the proper season for
entertaining thoughts of love. In urging this rare beauty to disregard

convention, her would-be lover makes a provocative point. He dissociates love and lust not on Platonic or moral grounds but simply in relation to the passage of time. Ripeness is all. And the phrase 'fair Blossoms... green' hints that the senses are not inactive, even if restrained. There is pleasure in physical beauty, unlike On a Drop of Dew where the 'blossoms green' of the body are shunned. Green is the colour of love, of hope and youth and spring: the blossoms that promise fruition have their own perfection. Momentarily we catch a glimpse of a *jeune fille en fleur*.

The shock is all the greater when, in the next stanza, she becomes a sacrificial animal victim:

IV

Love as much the snowy Lamb
Or the wanton Kid does prize,
As the lusty Bull or Ram,
For his morning Sacrifice.

(ll. 13–16)

In this context, Love seems more like a euphemism for Lust.[8] A psychoanalytic reading might conclude that the speaker has let his mask slip, revealing that he is a 'tiger with a plan' after all. On a more abstract level, the inconsistency might well be intentional: the difference between love and lust is entirely opportunistic, the divide between 'Infant Love' and the all-powerful undiscriminating deity simply bridged by puberty. And full-grown Love—it is disquieting to deduce from the imagery—may even cross back over that bridge.

Once the idea of sacrifice has been introduced, it splits the poem in two. If the child does not become a sacrific to Love, she may well become a premature sacrifice to Time. It is not much of a choice, but the speaker presents it to her as a winning strategy, in a stanza which is almost a reprise of his opening gambit:

V

Now then love me: time may take
Thee before thy time away:
Of this Need wee'l Virtue make,
And learn Love before we may.

(ll. 17–20)

The warning of her possible fate is the same as in *The Picture of little T.C.*, but the accompanying injunction is very different. He urges her to 'learn Love', not in the sense of sexual arousal 'before we may', but rather as an awakening to the existence of a new range of feeling and also, simultaneously, to its possible loss. 'Of this Need wee'l Virtue make' is a favourite idea of

Marvell's,[9] but here he gives it a sophistical twist. The syntax locks together necessity and choice as if by logic, but it is the lover's imagination that creates the 'necessity': after all, Time and Fate only *may* deprive them of future fulfilment. Indeed the agile mind inventing the argument sees the possible objection, and swiftly counters it in the next stanza which covers alternative contingencies:

VI

So we win of doubtful Fate;
   And, if good she to us meant,
We that Good shall antedate,
   Or, if ill, that Ill prevent.

(ll. 21-4)

'Win' fits the notion of love as a game, but it also touches on a serious philosophical conundrum. How can one 'win' from Fate? Is it conceivable to 'antedate' a future which is in any sense predestined? As for 'prevent', although the old meaning of 'anticipate' may be proposed,[10] it also raises the teasing possibility of preventing ill in the sense of averting it. The whole point of *Young Love* is present happiness. Why meet trouble halfway? The reading of 'prevent' as 'anticipate in action', given that the object of the verb is 'ill', undercuts the persuasion; an ironic double meaning is more plausible. It could be argued that to prevent Fate in the sense of averting it is a contradiction in terms, yet there is at least one precedent in Shakespeare's *Hamlet*, when Horatio says to the Ghost

If thou art privy to thy country's fate,
Which, happily, foreknowing may avoid,
O speak..

(I. i. 136-8)

(Interestingly, the First Quarto has 'prevent' instead of 'avoid'.)[11]

As it happens, it is the 'country's fate' that Marvell uses as the final analogy to clinch this persuasion to love:

VII

Thus as Kingdomes, frustrating
   Other Titles to their Crown,
In the craddle crown their King,
   So all Forraign Claims to drown,

VIII

So, to make all Rivals vain,
   Now I crown thee with my Love:

> Crown me with thy Love again,
> And we both shall Monarchs prove.

(ll. 25–32)

The conceit is beautifully attuned to the double awareness of innocence and experience running through the lyric. On one level, this is a gentle game of make-believe, played with crowns of paper or flowers; on another level, it recalls the literary symbolism of adult love. The lyric scale ranges from nursery rhyme—'Lavender's blue'?—to Donne's *The Anniversarie*[12] Yet this love ritual is not altogether reassuring: it does not cancel out the earlier sacrifical imagery. If the formal symmetry of *Young Love* is taken into account, it becomes clear that the first half ends with ritual sacrifice, the second with ritual crowning. Although the latter is less obviously disturbing than the former, they are suggestive parallels. Also, as history proves, the crowning of a king in the cradle did not necessarily ensure stability or frustrate other claims. 'Woe to thee, O land, when thy king is a child' (Ecclesiastes 10: 16). The book of Ecclesiastes, incidentally, has a great deal to say on the life of pleasure, and on the idea that 'To every thing there is a season' (3: 1). If the ethos of Ecclesiastes were allowed to challenge the ethos of Horace, it would put the argument of Marvell's poem in a very different light.

Of course that ethos, insisting that all is vanity, is not allowed to intrude on the 'happy' ending of *Young Love*. It is a condition of that ending that 'all Forraign Claims' have to be drowned. But for all its genuine charm and skill, Young Love barbs the persuasion to pleasure with a half-concealed threat. Time, which was a friend to contemplation (at worst, it could only hasten the liberation of the soul), is a deadly adversary to pleasure. But, ironically, pleasure itself threatens innocence: the blossoms wait to be plucked, the snowy lamb is prized as a sacrifice. The persuader creates an illusion of choice, since real choice would subvert his argument from 'necessity'. The illusion is all the more fragile because the poem is ostensibly addressed to a 'little Infant': for a much more powerful argument for the *vita voluptuosa* we have to turn to the next poem in the Folio, *To his Coy Mistress*, which applies the same logic to an adult sexual relationship.

To his Coy Mistress

Beginning with its title, *To his Coy Mistress* seems to promise a persuasion poem in the classic tradition. Many readers have accepted it as such, notably T.S. Eliot who located 'a whole civilisation' at its centre and defined that civilised quality in half a dozen names: Lucretius, Horace, Catullus, Propertius, Ovid, Jonson.[13] Yet, magisterial as this claim is, the reader of Marvell learns to be wary of easy categorisation. Even the title may not be simply what it seems. Does 'his' deliberately signal an unreliable persona, or is it merely an instance of the common sixteenth/seventeenth century practice of attaching a third person descriptive title to a first person lyric?[14] The point is a relatively minor one, but it may affect the degree and kind of irony which we expect in the poem itself.

However the epithet 'coy' certainly merits attention. Its root meaning, deriving from *quietus*, at rest, still, quiet, implies passivity: like the 'little Infant', the coy mistress has no voice of her own. The English meanings 'modest', 'shy', 'disdainful' acquire at an early stage an aura of affectation, and can be applied to behaviour which is a variety of sexual display.[15] The English coy mistress could therefore be the equivalent of the Roman *castae puellae*, who are not necessarily chaste but who 'withhold their favours' for whatever motive.[16] She does not have to be stereotyped as the frigid Petrarchan mistress,[17] who by the seventeenth century had given chastity a bad name among the more avant-garde love poets. For the libertine, the display of coyness may be a challenge; but it can also turn sour. Thomas Randolph, in *A Complaint against Cupid that he never made him in Love*, welcomes a certain amount of resistance:

> Give me a Mistresse in whose looks to joy,
> And such a Mistresse (*Love*) as will be coy,
> Not easily wonne, though to be wonne in time;
> That from her nicenesse I may store my rhime...[18]

At a later date, Rochester's curse on *his* coy mistress contrasts brutally with Randolph's attitude:

> Then if to make your ruin more,
>   You'll peevishly be coy,
> *Dye* with the scandal of a *Whore*,
>   And never know the joy.
>   (*Phillis, be gentler*, ll. 13–16)[19]

Marvell's version of the coy mistress is more subtle than either, allowing us to play with the idea of her motives. Within the poem her lover slyly imagines her hunting for rubies, a pastime more perhaps in the line of the Roman *meretrix*[20] than the Petrarchan lady; and we discover that her physical disposition is governed by moist and warm humours, giving the lie to frigidity.[21] But although touches like these add flesh and blood to the description 'Coy Mistress', they are marginal nevertheless. All that is really essential to the argument is that she has to be both beddable and coy. And it is the precise nature and tone of the argument, not the personality of the mistress or the lover, on which critics are most divided. Is *To his Coy Mistress* a persuasion to love, a critique of persuasions to love, or a treatment of another system of ideas altogether, for which *carpe diem* serves as a metaphor?[22]

The tripartite structure is designed to attract admiring attention: this is a poem elegant in its bones. But once the syllogistic form has been recognised—'Had we... But... Now therefore'—the difficulties are only beginning.[23] It undoubtedly mimics logic, and with considerable panache; but *is* it logic? The critics who address themselves to this question have demonstrated the technical fallacy involved, without necessarily agreeing on the effects of that fallacy. This is especially true in relation to the intended audience. One of the simplest and yet most challenging methods of testing the argument is to construct an imaginary answer from the coy mistress herself.[24] For the fallacy is not just a technicality. The speaker structures a view of reality to be accepted or rejected, a view centred on the reality of bodies, copulating or corrupting. Persuasion presupposes choice: the coy mistress can say yes, or go on saying no. But the syllogism makes it seem as though there is only one logical choice for her to make, if she accepts the premises and does not detect the flaw. In a poem, however, as in life, there are other considerations besides logic. Ultimately the strength of *To his Coy Mistress* as a persuasion poem resides in its magnificent predatory assault on the imagination, disguised as an assault on the reason. Like the Pyramids, in Johnson's eloquent image, it bears witness to 'that hunger of imagination which preys incessantly upon life'.[25]

Indeed the speaker begins, like a number of Marvell's lovers, by creating a fiction. He takes, as it were, a deep breath of airy imagination, and puffs up time and space virtually to their utmost historical and geographical limits, before eventually collapsing them to the real shrunken dimensions of a human grave.

> Had we but World enough, and Time,
> This coyness Lady were no crime.
> We would sit down, and think which way
> To walk, and pass our long Loves Day.
> Thou by the *Indian Ganges* side
> Should'st Rubies find: I by the Tide
> Of *Humber* would complain. I would
> Love you ten years before the Flood:
> And you should if you please refuse
> Till the Conversion of the *Jews*.
>
> (ll. 1–10)

The first line might be uttered by an Antony in love with a Cleopatra; but the second, with its suave alliteration and significant rhyme,[26] is too calculated and ironic quite to sustain the illusion of a grand passion. He, of course, intends to prove to her that coyness *is* a crime, and he begins by indulging a fantasy, making world enough and time for her idea of pleasure, which is to be left free and yet courted to infinity. In effect, it parodies the life of contemplation. The daydream is familiar, even banal ('If you were the only girl in the world'...) but Marvell's wit makes it extraordinary. In such circumstances his lovers are almost comically at a loss, spoiled for choice as the idiom has it. After consideration, they come up with occupations which reflect unsatisfactory sexual stereotypes: he complains poetically, while she is preoccupied with her rubies (the price of a virtuous woman, it may be recalled from Proverbs 31: 10, is far *above* rubies);[27] and instead of being together, they are half a world apart.

The time-scale, measured according to sacre dhistory, might be felt to cast a long shadow across the frivolous pair. The references to the Flood and the conversion of the Jews (which, it was believed, would precede the millennium) are a reminder not only that time is finite, however extended, but also that its events are effectively beyond human control. More serious than conventional literary *adunata* (impossibilities),[28] these points of reference are at the same time sharper and wittier. Marvell may indeed have chosen his dates for reasons of topicality as well as unconventionality.[29]

As for the landscape, that too is unconventional, in startling contrast to the sensuous beauty of most love idylls. The divide between the glamorous Ganges and the homely Humber (Marvell's local river) relies simply on name association (the only epithet the poet himself uses is a strictly geographical one). Nor does the lover evoke the transient beauty of the flesh by means of flowers, the staple of *carpe florem*.[30] In this respect he is even more self-denying than the speaker of *Young Love*. Instead of the rose, he resorts to the notorious 'vegetable' to define not beauty but love:

> My vegetable Love should grow
> Vaster then Empires, and more slow.
>
> (ll. 11-12)

The exact connotations of 'vegetable Love' have provoked an astonishing, often entertaining, controversy among scholars.[31] 'Vegetable' can be taken as a philosophical term, alluding to the Aristotelian division of the soul into three, the vegetable, the sensible, and the rational. This Aristotelian theory, usefully summarised for the seventeenth century in Robert Burton's *The Anatomy of Melancholy*,[32] holds that the vegetable or 'vegetal' faculty of the soul is the one which is responsible for nutrition, growth, and generation: it is the distinguishing and sole faculty in plants, but in man it is inferior, subordinated to the higher faculties. Such a scheme has a certain affinity with other tripartite divisions like Ficino's classification of love (see above, part II, 'The Life of Love and Pleasure'), and attempts have been made to relate it to the tripartite structure of the poem. But there is no critical consensus on exactly how this might work. If Marvell does intend a philosphical gloss, then at most it might ironically imply the real inferiority of the love on offer, as well as intensifying the hyperbolic growth which is the point of the couplet. As an additional bonus, the reader is free to imagine 'some monstrous and expanding cabbage,' or the more dignified bulk of a great tree, or even a marrow with an expanding love-inscription[33]—depending on his or her learning or inclination.

Imagining the mistress's physical attributes is the chief purpose of this life of delayed pleasure and extended contemplation:

> An hundred years should go to praise
> Thine Eyes, and on thy Forehead Gaze.
> Two hundred to adore each Breast:

> But thirty thousand to the rest.
> An Age at least to every part,
> And the last Age should show your Heart.
> For Lady you deserve this State;
> Nor would I love at lower rate.
>
> (ll. 13–20)

The lover's proposed *blason* turns out to be as hypothetical as the time it requires, for he does not actually describe her at all. Instead he compliments her beauty indirectly through the arithmetical conceit. This type of conceit (originally Catullan), coupled with the later phrase 'vast Eternity' (l. 24), leads to comparison with Cowley's poem, *My Dyet*:[34]

> O'n a *Sigh* of Pity I a year can live,
>   One *Tear* will keep me twenty at least,
>   Fifty a gentle *Look* will give;
> An Hundred years on one *kind word* I'll feast:
>   An thousand more will added be,
>   If you an *Inclination* have for me;
>   And all beyond is vast *Eternity*.
>
> (stanza 3)

But Cowley is not attempting a *blason*, a catalogue of the mistress's beauties: his is a catalogue of hoped-for responses. Marvell's lover expects no response. Because this courtship is supposed to be on her terms, he is not allowed to touch, only to look, devoting centuries and millennia to the idolatry of a body dissected into its constituent parts.

The naming of parts serves two functions. It is an erotic tease, tantalising the voyeur because of the lack of specific detail, which incidentally contrasts with the kind of eroticism found in persuasion poems such as Carew's *A Rapture*;[35] and it also tests the lady's wits, since like any catalogue that is not completely random it betrays the maker's priorities. There is some reason to believe that Marvell reworked this passage to alter its balance. The rather garbled Haward manuscript text, discovered by W. Hilton Kelliher,[36] allots thirty thousand years to her 'Thighes' (which have disappeared from the Folio version), and omits the delicately weighed century assigned to 'each Breast'. However it maintains a roughly similar sequence, moving from the more intellectual 'Platonic' parts of the body to the more sexually suggestive. 'How much they stray that set out at the face' declares Donne in *Loves Progress*;[37] but Marvell's lover knows what he is doing. The point is that although the higher faculties are placed first they are in fact given less time. Any reader familiar with Donne's elegies or Cavalier libertine poetry would think with pleasure of what the decorous phrases 'the rest' and 'every part' comprise, and recognise from the time-scale the speaker's scale of values. Yet the final twist still keeps us guessing—'And the last Age should show your Heart' (l. 18)—for the last age heralds the Day of Judgment, and the heart of a mistress is so often a hard or dubious or unknown quantity. Exposure might be a threat, not a promise. She would be unwise to take his praise at face value, or to be reassured by the ambiguous conclusion, however sonorous. 'For Lady you deserve this State/Nor would I love at lower rate' begs the question of what she has indeed deserved, and uses a phrase which tacitly admits that love *can* be had at cutprice rates.[38]

If she has been entranced by his perfectly blown bubble of illusion, it and her world are about to burst:

> But at my back I alwaies hear
> Times winged Charriot hurrying near:
> And yonder all before us lye
> Desarts of vast Eternity.
> Thy Beauty shall no more be found;
> Nor, in thy marble Vault, shall sound
> My ecchoing Song: then Worms shall try
> That long preserv'd Virginity:
> And your quaint Honour turn to dust;
> And into ashes all my Lust.
> The Grave's a fine and private place,
> But none I think do there embrace.
>
> (ll. 21–32)

'Times winged Charriot' is a splendidly classical conception, with, apparently, no single classical source.[39] As in a nightmare, it bears down terrifyingly on the vulnerable human being dwarfed by the 'Desarts of vast Eternity', out of which Time came and to which everything must return. The idea of oblivion is as appalling as the idea of Time the destroyer. Brilliantly, Marvell translates this fear into images of space, conjuring up two opposite but related phobias: terror of wide open spaces, heightened by the fear of pursuit, and terror of confined spaces. The 'fine and private place' becomes a hideous travesty of the *locus amoenus* of the life of pleasure, just as the 'Desarts of vast Eternity' suggest a peculiarly bleak version of the contemplative solitude. In both environments, human action and pleasure cease—and they can be contemplated only from this side of the grave. Not even the conventional solace remains, the immortality of the poet's art defying physical dissolution. And he describes that dissolution in terms that play upon the woman's most intimate horror of physical violation. There is no need to dwell on the sexual *double entendre* to take the point.[40] The much praised flesh—eyes, breasts, private parts—must yield involuntarily to the rapacious worms. The argument for sexual enjoyment *because* flesh is mortal is, of course, at the heart of *carpe diem*, and classically educated readers do hear echoes in the vault: echoes of Catullus (Carmen V) and of an epigram by Asclepiades in the Greek Anthology:

You would keep your virginity? What will it profit you? You will find no lover in Hades, girl. It is among the living that we taste the joys of Kypris. In Acheron, child, we shall be only bones and dust.

(tr. Forrest Reid)[41]

But the same readers are conscious of difference as well as likeness. The echoes are not transmitted as pure imitation, but are mutated into a new and distinctive sound.[42]

And there are more recent precedents. The imagery of dissolution runs like a black current through much seventeenth-century literature, from Jacobean tragedy, where it gleams satirically, to sermons, where it broadens into meditation on the Four Last Things. Under certain kinds of imaginative pressure, the link between sex and physical corruption becomes inescapable and is reinforced by contemporary medicine and ethics. For a poet writing on love and time, this imagery offers one means of avoiding bland commonplaces; yet too strong a fascination with such a link could subvert a persuasion to love.[43] Sir Walter Ralegh, author of a lyric modelled on Catullus beginning 'Now Serena bee not coy' nevertheless reserves is most sombre and powerful imagery of dissolution for a more impersonal lyric on love and time:

> The Light, the Belly, lipps and breath,
>   He dimms, discolours, and destroyes,
> With those he feedes, but fills not death,
>   Which sometimes were the foode of Joyes;
> Yea Time doth dull each liuely witt,
> And dryes all wantonnes with it.
>   (*A Poem of Sir Walter Rawleighs*, ll. 25–30)[44]

Marvell, in contrast, combines this kind of writing with the 'coy mistress' address. Whereas *A Poem of Sir Walter Rawleighs* is entirely fatalistic in outlook, *To his Coy Mistress* uses fatalism as a means to an end which appears to involve choice.

But what kind of choice is it? It has been argued that the *ars moriendi*, the art of dying well, is more crucial for an understanding of Marvell's poem than the *carpe diem* tradition as such, in that Marvell both parodies the features of *ars moriendi* and inverts its purpose, which is to terrify and disgust men and women into sexual abstention by reminding them of the end of all flesh. If that is so, then the lover's case can be reformulated as follows:

> the choice presented to the mistress specifically precludes any issue of honor or virginity; in any event, the mistress must relinquish her virginity. The only question is when and how ... He presents the mistress with a choice—not between pleasure and pain, youth and age, death and life (for if she chooses correctly, she must only hasten death)—a choice of the time, place, and manner of her death.
> (Stanley Stewart, 'Marvell and the *Ars Moriendi*')[45]

The narrowing down of choice to when and how to 'die' (with the usual sexual quibble) ingeniously obscures the choice of life which is intentionally *not* offered. Certainly she has no choice about dying in the primary sense; but the lover disguises the fact that she does have a choice about the way to live by assuming that 'living' means only one thing—the gratification of the senses. According to this philosophy, it is pleasure, above all the pleasure of sex, that assures us that we are alive. The persuasion poem is caught in a pradox of choice without choice: in that the lover's aim is to manoeuvre the girl into going to bed with him, it assumes that she is free to choose; but his method is to argue as if she had no choice but to do so, no acceptable alternative. As for the choice of eternity, that too is precluded. The coy mistress is not allowed to think about eternity under any aspect other than 'Desarts', or of death as anything other than annihilation. Though the earlier allusions to biblical history might have alerted her to other ideas, these are swept aside by the onrush of Time's chariot.[46]

Yet the imagery of graves and worms might have the opposite effect, that of forcing the hearer to confront the choice of eternity in the starkest possible terms. For example, that is the intended function of the Cardinal's warning to the lecherous Duke in Middleton's *Women Beware Women*:

> Is she a thing
> Whom sickness dare not visit, or age look on,
> Or death resist? Does the worm shun her grave?
> If not, as your soul knows it, why should lust
> Bring man to lasting pain, for rotten dust?
>
> (IV. i. 247–51)[47]

The question 'Is it worth it?' can be asked concerning either coyness or lust; but the answers depend on different views of man's eternal destiny, views which nevertheless coincide in emphasising the death of the body. For Marvell's speaker, not only is the body mortal, but love as well. He deliberately cuts out one traditional consolation, the idea lovers cling to, that an embrace may be possible even in the grave.[48] Not for him the wishful thinking of Davenant's Dying Lover:

> Yet we hereafter may be found,
>   By Destinies right placing,
> Making, like Flowers, Love under Ground,
>   Whose Rootes are still embracing.
>
> (ll. 53–6)[49]

A more ghoulish version of the embrace with a corpse is the amorous grinding of bone on bone described by Propertius.[50] In place of such imaginings Marvell supplies a sceptic's irony which, out of context, can sound almost wistful:

> The Grave's a fine and private place,
> But none I think do there embrace.
>
> (ll. 31–2)

The lover is therefore justified in turning to living embraces. After what seems like the ultimate negation, the erotic energies of the poem at last tear through the iron gates of its logic.

It is not until the final stage of *To his Coy Mistress* that sex becomes a tangible reality; and it is not eyes, nor breasts for that matter, which have most allure, but young, moist, gleaming skin, which promises the pleasures of physical contact. The effect, after the deliberate holding back of sensuality, is electrifying:

> Now therefore, while the youthful glew[51]
> Sits on thy skin like morning dew,
> And while thy willing Soul transpires
> At every pore with instant Fires,
> Now let us sport us while we may...

(ll. 33-7)

Yet the exact words producing this effect are controversial, for the first couplet contains the best-known textual crux in Marvell's poetry. In the Folio, the rhyme is 'hew'/'glew'; in Bodleian MS. Eng. poet. d. 49, it is 'glew'/'dew'; in the Haward manuscript it is 'Glue'/'Dew'. The recurrence of the apparently unlikely glew/glue is striking, and it obviously fits the first line better than the second, where the simile 'like morning dew' (originating with Cooke's emendation) has found general editorial acceptance.[52] In an attempt to explain 'glew', some scholars adopt the suggestion that it is a northern dialectal form of 'glow'.[53] Yet this anxiety to avoid the obvious meaning is unnecessarily fastidious. The image of skin sticky with its own youthful glue, or sweat, (the Haward manuscript reading 'Stickes' in place of 'Sits' insists on the sensation) may embarrass editors who prefer to believe that ladies only glow. Renaissance poets knew better. Spenser and Donne both describe sweat as erotic (and the hands of the lovers in *The Exstasie* are 'cimented'—glued together—by 'fast balme').[54] Not only is the strong physicality of the glue image completely appropriate to Marvell's poem,[55] but the glue/dew reading has an interesting, and surely intentional, consequence. It makes the description entirely tactile, without the intrusion of the visual 'hew'. In the first part of the poem, the mistress's beauty is the cynosure of the worshipping lover's eyes, but here he is fascinated by the texture of skin, which can only be fully appreciated through the sense of touch. And touch is traditionally the lowest sense in the hierarchy, and most closely associated with sex.[56] The comparison of sweat to dew also fits, since dew was considered to be the 'sweat of the earth's bodily organism'.[57] Unlike the dewdrop-soul, the mistress's affinities are clearly with earth, not heaven. She exudes her 'willing Soul' through 'every pore'. If Marvell is adapting the words of Crashaw's hymn, *To The Name Above Every Name, The Name of Iesus*—

> What did Their weapons but with wider pores
> Inlarge thy flaming-brested Louers
>   More freely to transpire
>   That impatient Fire
> The Heart that hides Thee hardly couers—[58]

it sharpens the distinction between sacred and profane rather than obliterating it.

However, other distinctions become more difficult to make as the poem gathers momentum towards its climax. The symbolism crushes elementary distinctions such as that of sex into a single mass:

> Now let us sport us while we may;
> And now, like am'rous birds of prey,
> Rather at once our Time devour,
> Than languish in his slow-chapt pow'r.
> Let us roll all our Strength, and all
> Our sweetness, up into one Ball:
> And tear our Pleasures with rough strife,
> Thorough the Iron gates of Life.
> Thus, though we cannot make our Sun
> Stand still, yet we will make him run.
>
>   (ll. 37–46)

Much critical heat and energy have been generated over the sources and significance of the extraordinarily potent images,[59] but nothing to match the heat and energy of the images themselves. Is energy, in this instance, eternal delight? It does not lack purpose: the speaker emphatically contradicts Marvell's own world-weary observation in The Rehearsal Transpros'd that 'the world will not go the faster for our driving' (I. 135).[60] When he wrote that, it was out of much experience of the life of action and its constraints. Apparently without this awareness, the lover of To his Coy Mistress proposes to remake the life of pleasure in the image of the active life, not the contemplative life which he has already rejected. In the process, the very idea of pleasure becomes deeply compromised, difficult to distinguish from what we would normally regard as pain. For Marvell's lover, to act is to devour, to roll up (compress), to tear: disturbing verbs, even if their object is not the human body itself. Whether we flinch or feel exhilarated, it is impossible to ignore the ruthlessness which, although ostensibly directed against the enemy, Time, inevitably colours their sexual relationship with each other. 'Am'rous birds of prey' are destined for a wild mating. 'Slow-chapt pow'r' alludes to the devouring jaws of Time, tempus edax rerum.[61] In such a sophisticated literary context, the level of retaliation is curiously primitive. It is not surprising to find critics arguing that what is presented here is animal, not rational, love.[62] For the price the coy mistress is asked to pay for pleasure is not just her virginity, but in some sense her humanity.

The 'one Ball' comprising their male and female attributes is essentially an abstraction, a concentration of qualities kneaded, compressed, moulded from the more awkward and subtle components of individual personality. Whatever the ball represents—and conjectures include the emblematic sphere of perfection, the phoenix' egg, the globular hermaphrodite of Plato's Symposium, another sun, 'the great globe itself', not to mention a cannon-ball, a pomander, or a sweetmeat[63]—its properties are singular, in more senses than one. By an interesting coincidence, the phrase 'one Ball' also occurs in Lovelace's poem *Paris's Second Judgement*, in which Paris regrets that there is only one apple to offer three equally glorious deities—'*What pity the whole World is but one Ball*'.[64] Marvell's lover is too single-minded for regret or a divided soul: his judgment is cast entirely for pleasure, a pleasure for which the world is well lost, and which is powerful enough to smash through life's intractable opposition.

'The Iron gates of Life' present an equally intractable puzzle to the critic. Again a textual crux complicates the line, since the Bodleian MS. Eng. poet. d. 49 has the reading 'grates' for 'gates', which reinforces the impression of life as a prison, but diminishes the grandeur of 'Iron gates'.[65] Explanations of the latter phrase range from the philosophical to the physiological, and literary analogues (none of which exactly reproduce all three components of the phrase) range from Lucretius[66] to Spenser and beyond. Although Marvell specifies that these are the gates of life, it is unclear whether they are marked 'entrance' or 'exit'. (In Spenser's Garden of Adonis, there are double gates in walls of gold and iron, and the usual inference is that the iron gate readmits souls returning from earthly existence.[67]) But whether we envisage a two-way or a one-way system, what is striking here is the speaker's insistence that the lovers can *choose* to break through the gates. Naturally he is advocating physical sex, not a double suicide, as a means to this end. The metaphor of tearing through gates, we are told, 'certainly refers to the act of defloration.'[68] This is not necessarily the same as saying that 'Iron gates' must allude directly to the female *labia*,[69] a suggestion that would make the 'Pleasures' exceptionally painful: even a misogynistic poet, let alone a would-be seducer, might hesitate over the image. But it does imply that the sexual act is an act of strife. Marlowe had so described it in *Hero and Leander*:

> She trembling strove; this strife of hers (like that
> Which made the world) another world begat
> Of unknown joy.
>
> (Sest. II. ll. 291–3)[70]

Like that which made the world: the idea recalls the Lucretian cosmos, and Epicurean philosophy, which seems more relevant to this section of the poem than Neoplatonism.[71] The contemplative mode of the Neoplatonics was ironically rehearsed in the first section; here it is replaced by the philosophy of pleasure. This holds, even if the lover bases his case on a distortion of original Epicurean teaching. From one point of view, Marvell's lovers are at odds with the universe, challenging and upsetting its fundamental rhythms; but from another point of view, their 'rough strife' enacts one of the most fundamental rhythms of all. Pleasure is achieved only against formidable resistance, a resistance that is built into the nature of things; but without resistance, there is perhaps no pleasure (an argument that the coy mistress herself might have used to justify her original stance).

The final arrogant couplet—'Thus, though we cannot make our Sun/Stand still, yet we will make him run'—makes a claim for the life of pleasure which is in direct competition with the power of the spirit.[72] Joshua, the man of God, had commanded the sun to stand still to further the Israelite's active cause; and it had obeyed him (Joshua 10: 12-14).[73] His contemporary parallel, in Marvell's eyes, is Cromwell, also a man of prayer and action.[74] But as for lovers, however much they may want to delay the sun and abolish time's swift passing, they are powerless to do so. All that pleasure achieves is to intensify and, paradoxically, accelerate subjective experience. Nothing changes outside themselves (the Folio reading 'our Sun' against the Haward manuscript's 'the Sun' underlines the point). It has been argued that 'in the "Coy Mistress" mere epicureanism is *rejected* for a more rigorous coming to terms with reality.'[75] But the true rejection does not happen *in* the poem: if it happens, it is within the reader's mind; and what is rejected is not 'mere epicureanism'. The voluptuous life is embraced in the poem not just as an alternative to the 'reality' of the grave, but as the only alternative. In other words, the version of reality offered in *To his Coy Mistress* is a heavily edited one. Only if there is no choice of eternity can this particular choice of life seem valid. The lovers are checkmated not just by the nature of time but by the nature of sexuality itself. They are playing a losing game: the division of sexes is as much of a metaphysical trap as the division of soul and body, and even their ideas of pleasure are incompatible. Despite appearances, the persuasion to love does not liberate, but restricts choice. The voluptuous life is self-limiting.

(ii) *Ars amatoria: The Unfortunate Lover, The Gallery, The Fair Singer, Mourning, Daphnis and Chloe*

The Unfortunate Lover

In recent times, *The Unfortunate Lover* has been brought, as it were, out of the closet; the code has been cracked. At least, so it is claimed. But the decoding experts do not necessarily agree on the right key to use, even in literary terms: epic, allegory, sonnet, emblem, masque, all have been tried, and each has unlocked part of the enigma. One result has been to deconstruct the poem's genre, and to shift the centre of interest from the erotic life to philosophy, religion, or politics.[1] Although the political interpretation in particular has opened up an important new line of investigation, it seems unlikely that any one reading will, or should, gain an exclusive purchase on the poem's meaning. Even if we accept that Marvell did choose to conceal a political message or a religious or philosophical meditation in a lyric ostensibly concerned with the sufferings of an Unfortunate Lover, the ostensible subject remains. It could perhaps be reclassified as a poem of the contemplative or the active life, but the first compiler of the *Miscellaneous Poems* evidently decided that it belongs among the poems of love. There is good reason for following his example, while keeping other options open.

Certainly *The Unfortunate Lover* departs from the persuasion format, but the attitude to love has something in common with *Young Love* and *To his Coy Mistress*. Just as *Young Love* boasted a ritual sacrifice, and *To his Coy Mistress* its 'am'rous birds of prey', so *The Unfortunate Lover* has its cormorants and 'a spectacle of Blood' (stanzas V and VI).

> Love is not full of pity (as men say)
> But deaf and cruel where he means to prey.
> *(Hero and Leander*, Sest. II. 287–8)[2]

Marlowe's *sententia* applies in some measure to all three Marvell poems, but most cogently to *The Unfortunate Lover*. And another preoccupation of the persuasion poems that carries over into this different mode is the idea of time and fortune as the lover's principal antagonists. Indeed the title spotlights the key epithet 'Unfortunate', which is even more central than 'Young' or 'Coy', and equally generic. The lover is unfortunate simply by virtue of being a lover.[3] He has no other role but is, one might say, a born lover in an unusually ironic sense of the phrase. He is 'my poor Lover' (l. 11), not a first-person persona as in the persuasions, but a being pointedly set apart from the narrator who claims a proprietorial interest in him.[4] The precise tone of the narrative voice is a matter of dispute: patronising, amused, flippant, compassionate, outraged, or any permutation of these. Certainly it imposes itself from the outset with the plangent 'Alas...' that sets the mood of the poem in ironic juxtaposition with 'pleasant'.

The first stanza might be a Spenserian stanza in miniature, a Garden of Adonis or Temple of Venus:

I

Alas, how pleasant are their dayes
With whom the Infant Love yet playes!
Sorted by pairs, they still are seen
By Fountains cool, and Shadows green.
But soon these Flames do lose their light,
Like Meteors of a Summers night:
Nor can they to that Region climb,
To make impression upon Time.

(ll. 1–8)

The Infant Love here has not yet grown to his full menacing stature as armed Eros, but is more like one of the *putti* in an Italian painting, sportive in an idyllic scene. The scene itself is the familiar *locus amoenus*[5] with its most precious attributes, water and shade, the traditional setting for the life of love and pleasure. Spenser's Temple of Venus is surrounded by a similar environment:

Fresh shadowes, fit to shroud from sunny ray;
  Faire lawnds, to take the sunne in season dew;
  Sweet springs, in which a thousand Nymphs did play;
        . . .
  And therein thousand payres of louers walkt,
  Praysing their god, and yeelding him great thankes...
        . . .
All these together by themselues did sport
  Their spotlesse pleasures, and sweet loues content.
(*The Faerie Qveene*, IV. x. 24–6)

As for Marvell's 'Shadows green', 'Green indeed is the colour of lovers' according to Armado in *Love's Labour's Lost* (I. ii. 82). But, as at the end of Shakespeare's comedy, the darker shadow of time and mortality falls across Marvell's garden of love. It is worth noting that, although Spenser's Garden of Adonis is likewise afflicted by Time, in the Temple of Venus the poet separates ordinary happy lovers from those Platonic lovers whose love is immune to decay.[6] Marvell's pairs clearly belong to the former category, deserving compassion rather than envy or condescension.[7] Their love, in a common metaphor made brilliant by the precise technical terms 'Meteors' and 'impression',[8] is destined to burn out rapidly; their summer's night of love passes all too soon. Jonson uses the same phrasing in his version of Catullus V:

> But if once we lose this light,
> 'Tis with us perpetual night.
>
> (*Song. To Celia*, ll. 7–8)[9]

If happy love is regarded as not only transient but illusory, the image can be still more finely tuned. Donne does this in *Loves Alchymie*–

> So, lovers dreame a rich and long delight,
> But get a winter-seeming summers night.
>
> (ll. 11–12)[10]

In this comparable Renaissance framework, Marvell's single stanza holds its own as a definitive image of the triumph of Time over love and pleasure, its irony subdued to an elegiac regret.

When the poem switches abruptly to its main narrative and isolates its hero, the allegorical colouring persists. Storm, shipwreck and war are fundamental and ubiquitous spiritual metaphors, so much so that source-hunting seems scarcely necessary. Yet the choice of sources can make a radical difference to our reading of *The Unfortunate Lover:* the sea of life, the sea of passion, the sea of political troubles all have their storms, but each represents human experience under a different, more or less generalised aspect. To begin with, what Marvell emphasises is the primary association of storm and shipwreck with violent and traumatic birth:

II

> 'Twas in a Shipwrack, when the Seas
> Rul'd, and the Winds did what they please,
> That my poor Lover floting lay,
> And, e're brought forth, was cast away:
> Till at the last the master-Wave
> Upon the Rock his Mother drave;
> And there she split against the Stone,
> In a *Cesarian Section.*
>
> (ll. 9–16)

This association too is an ancient one (though Marvell redeems it from the commonplace by the '*Cesarian Section*' conceit[11]). It is found, for example, in Lucretius, *De rerum natura*, V. 222–5,[12] and in the allegorical commentary of Fulgentius on Virgil's *Aeneid:* 'Birth and the dangers attending birth are symbolized by the great storm'... Aeneas, at first a 'new-born infant', becomes 'youth', and 'leaps into the life of passion personified by Queen Dido'.[13] Although the Unfortunate Lover has no Dido to humanise his passion, he reenacts this heroic paradigm.

Closer to Marvell's own time, Sidney[14] and Shakespeare transmute the storms and shipwrecks of romance into something rich and strange. If the lovers of stanza I are reminiscent of those in early Shakespearian comedy, the main lyric narrative is more strongly reminiscent of the symbolism of the late plays:

> Did you not name a tempest,
> A birth and death?
>
> (*Pericles*, V. iii. 33–4)

A common link would be the influence of masque;[15] and there is also the sense of arcane meaning, the deep interfusion of political and private life working through sexual love as both metaphor and reality. Marvell's Unfortunate Lover is precipitated by the circumstance of birth, not volition, into a world of hostile and inexplicable passion. In terms of his sexual nature, 'the confluence of lusts make a great Tempest, which in this sea disturbes the sea-faring soule, that reason cannot governe it'.[16] To be deprived of reason is to be deprived of choice, if, as Milton asserts, 'reason is but choosing'.[17] And indeed in the next stanza he undergoes a sea change, becoming a human emblem of the irrational elements:

III

> The Sea him lent these bitter Tears
> Which at his Eyes he alwaies bears.
> And from the Winds the Sighs he bore,
> Which through his surging Breast do roar.
>
> (ll. 17–20)

Yet it is not just the seas and wind but Petrarch and his followers who lend the Unfortunate Lover his tears and sighs. Marvell's 'unfortunate and abject Heir' (l. 30) inherits a literary legacy from Petrarchism which is pushed to its extravagant limits.[18] Unlike the Petrarchan lover, however, his emotions have no focus. In this respect, he is closer to the art of the emblem books like Otto van Veen's *Amorvm Emblemata* (Antwerp, 1608), to which Marvell's images have been compared.[19] These emblems stylise emotional states to the point where love becomes entirely a spectator sport: the pictures freeze Petrarchan metaphors into impersonal visual clichés, usually represented by plump childish figures. Often the emblems overdo their message, as in the standard *amor vincit omnia* illustration, crammed with creatures and spiky with love's arrows.[20] Although *The Unfortunate Lover* shares the language of emblem, its excesses are more complicated and disturbing, if only because we are left to imagine the pictures for ourselves. Marvell's ironic scrutiny forces a reappraisal of the emblem tradition itself, its adequacy and its appeal.

The same is true of masque, which contributes striking special effects in the style of Inigo Jones:[21]

> No Day he saw but that which breaks,
> Through frighted Clouds in forked streaks.
> While round the ratling Thunder hurl'd,
> As at the Fun'ral of the World.

> IV

> While Nature to his Birth presents
> This masque of quarrelling Elements ...

(ll. 21–6)

Whether or not the use of masque is a central *political* statement,[22] it again draws attention to art as a source of contemplation and pleasure, a means of controlling powerful and not always conscious emotions. Both emblem and masque require cooperation on the part of reader or audience, and they ensure that cooperation through producing pleasure. But at the same time they restrict and manipulate their subject-matter, providing (in the case of masque) a substitute for reality in which only one outcome is possible. The Unfortunate Lover himself is brought up on illusions, fed and starved by his guardian cormorants:

> V

> They fed him up with Hopes and Air,
> Which soon digested to Despair.
> And as one Corm'rant fed him, still
> Another on his Heart did bill.
> Thus while they famish him, and feast,
> He both consumed, and increast:
> And languished with doubtful Breath,
> Th'*Amphibium* of Life and Death.

(ll. 33–40)

At this stage of development, the lover is passive; instead of dominating like a predator, he is the victim. He cannot choose either life or death, but hangs suspended in a limbo between.[23]

However, he is soon forced into action of a peculiarly ritualistic kind against Fortune and 'Tyrant Love'—ritualistic, but in deadly earnest, for this is no mock battle: the weapons are 'at sharp'. Once again the erotic life parodies the active life in a wincingly accurate blow-by-blow account:

> VI

> And now, when angry Heaven wou'd

> Behold a spectacle of Blood,
> Fortune and He are call'd to play
> At sharp before it all the day:
> And Tyrant Love his brest does ply
> With all his wing'd Artillery.
> Whilst he, betwixt the Flames and Waves,
> Like *Ajax*, the mad Tempest braves.
>
> (ll. 41-8)

The lesser Ajax had provoked the wrath of the gods on account of his
blasphemy; his punishment, transfixed on a rock in fire and tempest,
obviously parallels the Unfortunate Lover's plight. In one version, his original
offence was sexual and sacrilegious, the violation of Cassandra in Athene's
temple. Although Marvell might intend to suppress that part of Ajax Oileus's
story,[24] for any reader who did make the connection it would tend to confirm
a sex/violence/heroism/blasphemy equation. But whereas Ajax brought his
fate on himself, the Unfortunate Lover is 'call'd' arbitrarily by an 'angry
Heaven' for its entertainment. As in *To his Coy Mistress* and *The Definition of
Love*, the universe is antagonistic to lovers as a matter of course, but *The
Unfortunate Lover* has even less room for manoeuvre. The protagonist has no
choice offered to him, no prospect of change or release except by death, no
conjunction of the mind to offset the stars' opposition.[25] It might be argued
that he has a choice of stance, if nothing else, and that his heroism consists in
choosing the line of most resistance. Yet even his heroic resistance is
stagemanaged by 'angry Heaven'—and, it must be remembered, the poet—to
provide it, and the reader, with 'a spectacle of Blood' fit for a Roman mob.
The life that is thrust upon the Unfortunate Lover is the opposite of
pleasurable: the pleasure is ours, not his. Or is it?

The next stanza is perhaps the most ambiguous in the poem. It is here, not
at the poem's beginning, that the characteristic Marvellian 'See how' intrudes,
asking us to contemplate this strangely triumphant icon:

VII

> See how he nak'd and fierce does stand,
> Cuffing the Thunder with one hand;
> While with the other he does lock,
> And grapple, with the stubborn Rock:
> From which he with each Wave rebounds,
> Torn into Flames, and ragg'd with Wounds.
> And all he saies, a Lover drest
> In his own Blood does relish best.
>
> (ll. 49-56)

In this context, 'See how' invites the spectator's complicity with the artist,
and is a reminder that if heaven inflicts pain it is human beings who turn it into
art for all kinds of reasons, not always laudable. The Unfortunate Lover can

be interpreted as a proto-Romantic figure of rebellion, or even as a Promethean type of the artist himself,[26] but such readings may overestimate his tragic stature, and the degree of responsibility he takes for himself. On the other hand, the element of self-conscious performance, the hint almost of bathos as he cuffs the thunder, and rebounds, or bounces back, with each wave, may make the reader underestimate his quasi-mythical status. The stanza concludes with a much-debated couplet which writes the question of the precise response (whose?) into the text itself:

> And all he saies, a Lover drest
> In his own Blood does relish best.

> (ll. 55–6)

'Saies' may be a form of the verb 'assay', to test, as some commentators believe, and it could also mean 'says', giving the lover an unexpected speaking part.[27] Whatever the meaning, it stands for that to which 'a Lover'—this lover, or any lover?—responds. And that response is clearly positive. Disquietingly so: the culinary metaphor implicit in 'drest' and 'relish' conveys a pleasure heightened for the élite who can, so to speak, taste blood. The Unfortunate Lover is a sacrifice to that pleasure as much as to love itself.

His sacrificial role is fulfilled in the final stanza:

VIII

> This is the only *Banneret*
> That ever Love created yet:
> Who though, by the Malignant Starrs,
> Forced to live in Storms and Warrs;
> Yet dying leaves a Perfume here,
> And Musick within every Ear:
> And he in Story only rules,
> In a Field *Sable* a Lover *Gules*.

> (ll. 57–64)

Images of action, pleasure and contemplation combine in multiple association. The word *'Banneret'*, for instance, derives in the first place from the world of arms, where it denotes a man knighted on the battlefield for valour, but it almost certainly reached Marvell through a literary borrowing from Lovelace—'Love neere his Standard when his Hoste he sets/Creates alone fresh-bleeding *Bannerets.'*[28] Heraldry, an even more rigid and specialised code than emblems, is art in the service of the active life, but in the form of the *impresa* it can have a private, often erotic, meaning.[29] Perfume and music are associated with religious contemplation as well as the pleasure of the senses;[30] there is also a biblical association with the righteous king, Josias, which leads back to the political sphere.[31] Another beautiful variation on the figure occurs in Crashaw's *A Hymne of the Nativity, sung by the Shepheards*, which imagines perfumes displacing the grim wounds of war:

> Winter chid the world, and sent
> The angry North to wage his warres:
> The North forgot his fierce intent,
> And left perfumes, in stead of scarres...

(ll. 23–6)[32]

However, if perfume and music compensate for storms and wars, it is at best a doubtful compensation in Marvell's *Unfortunate Lover*. 'Though... yet' balances a life governed by 'malignant' forces against a kind of eternity, but it is not the dying lover himself who will enjoy his immortality. 'He in Story *only* rules' (l. 63, my italics). The line's double meaning poises the epitaph finely between a sense of waste and a sense of vindication.[33] But the final symbol, 'In a Field *Sable* a Lover *Gules*', is also the most dehumanising, a near-abstract design of a blood-red figure on a black background contrasting sharply with the living green of the opening stanza. (The parallel image of half-cooked lobsters, discovered in a political satire by Cleveland,[34] is even more reductive, though pleasingly absurd, when transferred to an anguished martyr-lover.)

Whatever else *The Unfortunate Lover* may be about, it relates love and the art inspired by love in a peculiarly disturbing way.[35] By depriving his lover of choice, Marvell paradoxically forces choice on the reader: the choice of how to respond to his 'Story'. It is impossible to condemn an unfortunate, of whom, in the last analysis, we know so little, and whose enemies are perceived to be the immortals; yet sympathy cannot preclude irony, and the more we collaborate with the text, the more that irony seems to be directed against us. The Unfortunate Lover's pain is our privileged pleasure. If we enjoy his *agon*, we perpetuate its cruelty; but if we do not, we nullify the only eternity he has.

The Gallery

It is likely that *The Unfortunate Lover* and *The Gallery* are close to each other in date of composition,[36] as well as being placed next to each other in the Folio. There are also similarities of structure: they share the same stanza form, and are arranged as a sequence of iconographic images. Although the structural principle of *The Unfortunate Lover* is evidently temporal and that of *The Gallery* spatial,[37] *The Unfortunate Lover* freezes into stasis at the end and, conversely, a suppressed narrative in *The Gallery* finally breaks through in the lover's appeal to the past. What links them perhaps most closely is the interdependence of love and art, love as an art in itself—the *ars amatoria*—and love as a subject for art, existing to give pleasure to the uncommitted even if its tenor is the pain of commitment.

In the case of *The Gallery*, the roles of spectators and participants theoretically overlap, as Marvell returns to the guise of lover and directs his 'See how' formula—here 'come view'—to a named mistress:

I

Clora come view my Soul, and tell
Whether I have contriv'd it well.
Now all its several lodgings lye
Compos'd into one Gallery;
And the great Arras-hangings, made
Of various Faces, by are laid;
That, for all furniture, you'l find
Only your Picture in my Mind.

(ll. 1–8)

Marvell often represents the mind by a metaphor of place, as an ocean, or a summer meadow, or a garden, or a building. Here it is a picture gallery, a logical extension of the common notion that the lover's heart contains the image of his beloved.[38] Obviously the expanded conceit gives the poet-lover more scope for invention, and permits a semi-mythological treatment of the relationship, such as we might find in allegory. Just as the garden in The Unfortunate Lover resembles a scaled-down Spenserian garden, so this gallery would not be out of place in one of Spenser's great houses in The Faerie Queene. The House of Malecasta, for example, is hung with arras depicting Venus and Adonis.[39] Marvell's lover, however, in a spring-cleaning of his imagination, puts away the outdated arras recording previous loves (he is clearly no novice).[40] He is, in effect, refurbishing his memory.

This points to one practical function of the mind-as-gallery in Renaissance psychology: pictorial images as mnemonic. Ever since classical antiquity the psychology of memory has been linked in a variety of ways with the visual arts, and the Greek poet, Simonides, is credited with the discovery that the key to the art of memory is systematic visualisation.[41] It is therefore possible to see The Gallery as 'perhaps . . . a memory-poem, more likely a parodied memory-poem, in which his lady's moods are forever recorded.'[42] But the only strong retrospective slant is right at the end of the lyric, and in any case the images suggest that the lover is fantasising rather than remembering. Indeed, Spenserian allegory again provides a parallel, the chamber inhabited by Phantastes in the House of Alma, which is 'dispainted all within,/With sundry colours, in the which were writ/Infinite shapes'—including hags, lovers, and dames.[43] The obvious difference between this and Marvell's gallery is that Spenser's allegory is appropriately generalised, but Marvell's paintings are all of a single subject.

Simonides is also credited with the famous analogy between poetry and painting, which, in its Horatian form—ut pictura poesis—was taken over into Renaissance aesthetic theory. The 'sister arts'[44] shared an extensive area of subject-matter: classical mythology, in particular, was a vital common source. The logical next step is to write poems about paintings and sculpture as Giambattista Marino does in La Galeria (Venice, 1620), a work which may have supplied Marvell with his title. Marino, an Italian poet of the baroque, had access to a range of superb masterpieces, and was himself a collector.[45]

Marvell's scale is tiny in comparison, but it reflects the interest in art which had become part of the life of civilised pleasure in Charles I's England. He mentions Charles's exceptionally fine collection, supplemented by the Mantuan acquisition, in *The Gallery* (ll. 47-8), a collection which had been dispersed early in the Interregnum.[46] Foreign travel, combined with the fashion set by royalty, also educated the English eye. Since Marvell himself had visited the centres of European culture, it is not improbable that *The Gallery* is a memory-poem in another sense, drawing on recollections of paintings and details of paintings to create composite images.[47]

Marino devotes the first section of *La Galeria* to mythological works, including two beautifully tinted Auroras and a rosy Venus in her shell.[48] Marvell depicts comparable figures, but, unlike Marino, he deliberately arranges his pictures in symmetrical contrast to discriminate between different kinds of female image. The alternating device, with the moment of choice at the end, is familiar from the dialogue poems. It effectively illustrates Clora's dual nature; or, perhaps more accurately, the dualism inherent in sexual love, of pain and pleasure, attraction and repulsion. The stanzas divide accordingly between two ideas of woman, woman as the active agent of man's destruction, practising the black arts, and woman as passive object of man's pleasure, radiating a calm luminosity:

II

Here Thou art painted in the Dress
Of an Inhumane Murtheress;
Examining upon our Hearts
Thy fertile Shop of cruel Arts:
Engines more keen than ever yet
Adorned Tyrants Cabinet;
Of which the most tormenting are
Black Eyes, red Lips, and curled Hair.

III

But, on the other side, th'art drawn
Like to *Aurora* in the Dawn;
When in the East she slumb'ring lyes,
And stretches out her milky Thighs;
While all the morning Quire does sing,
And *Manna* falls, and Roses spring;
And, at thy Feet, the wooing Doves
Sit perfecting their harmless Loves.

IV

Like an Enchantress here thou show'st,
Vexing thy restless Lover's Ghost;
And, by a Light obscure, dost rave

> Over his Entrails, in the Cave;
> Divining thence, with horrid Care,
> How long thou shalt continue fair;
> And (when inform'd) them throw'st away,
> To be the greedy Vultur's prey.
>
> V
>
> But, against that, thou sit'st a float
> Like *Venus* in her pearly Boat.
> The *Halcyons*, calming all that's nigh,
> Betwixt the Air and Water fly.
> Or, if some rowling Wave appears,
> A Mass of Ambergris it bears.
> Nor blows more Wind than what may well
> Convoy the Perfume to the Smell.

(ll. 9–40)

Within the broadly delineated contrasts, the iconographical details are invariably apt and witty. The *femme fatale* stanzas concentrate on her 'cruel Arts', the craftsmanship and self-display involved in the *ars amatoria* which is here equated with the gentle art of murder. But Clora's instruments of torture turn out to be cosmetic ones, such as the 'curled Hair' (l. 16) that marks her out as devious and possibly worse. Thomas Fuller in *The Profane State* is darkly suspicious of '*whorish attire*: As crisping and curling, (making her hair as winding and intricate as her heart)'.[49] Whereas Fuller views his Harlot and Witch with uncompromising moral censure, Marvell relishes his Murderess and Enchantress, making the flesh creep enjoyably with his horrors. Clora reading her lover's entrails like a Roman *haruspex* is simply a logical development from her earlier manifestation in stanza II. What links the two portraits is her sublime indifference to love, her preoccupation with her own beauty, and her practicality evinced in her 'horrid Care' and her convenient disposal of the remains '(when inform'd)'. 'The greedy Vultur'[50] parallels the cormorants of *The Unfortunate Lover*, another emblem of love's cruel and predatory nature. But within *The Gallery* it is offset by the doves and halcyons (ll. 23–4 and l. 35) which symbolise faithful love and tranquillity. This kind of matching detail is what we would expect in portraits designed as matching pairs. On the one hand, Marvell's Dark Lady represents the pains of love; on the other hand, in her guise as Aurora or Venus, she represents *voluptas*—naked, accessible, yet unpossessed. The natural settings indulge every sense, going well beyond a purely pictorial limit: the soft 'milky' or 'pearly' tones, the quality of light, blend with birdsong and airborne sweetness and perfume.

What remains intriguing, however, is the precise nature of the opposition between the images of Clora as murderess/enchantress and Clora as goddess of the dawn or love. For although the aspects are contrary, she is clearly the same woman, no more to be trusted when promising pleasure than when inflicting pain. In both sets of portraits, she is characterised by her emotional separateness, whether callous or serene (indeed as Aurora she is—unconventionally—still sleeping).[51] She is not painted in love: the source of pleasure in all these pictures is beauty, and they are aesthetically rather than morally differentiated. The art-lover can take pleasure in both styles, Renaissance and baroque.[52] Even Clora's lover may derive pleasure of a kind, if only a *frisson* of erotic excitement, from all her poses.

Image-making is a form of power, and both sexes want power over each other.[53] With whom in *The Gallery* does the ultimate power—or the ultimate responsibility—lie?

VI

> These Pictures and a thousand more,
> Of Thee, my Gallery do store;
> In all the Forms thou can'st invent
> Either to please me, or torment . . .

> (ll. 41–4)

Although the male lover has staked first claim in 'contriving' his gallery, which implies that he can select and vary her image at will, it is she who 'invents' the images that please or torture him. Yet, since these images pre-exist in some form in art and mythology and are culturally conditioned, neither poet-lover nor mistress can claim exclusive rights in them. The more powerful tribute is not to compare the beloved to myth, but to assert that the beloved turns myth into truth, makes 'fables histories'.[54] This too becomes a convention: Habington and Waller both profess to find Ovidian metamorphoses being enacted in contemporary love affairs:

> . . . they whose wisdome did discusse
> Of these as fictions: shall in us
> Finde, they were more then fabulous.
> (Habington, *To Castara*, ll. 31–33)

> To these old tales such Nymphs as you
> Give credit, and still make them new.
> The Am'rous now like wonders find
> In the swift changes of your mind.
> (Waller, *To the mutable faire*, ll. 55–8)[55]

Instead of criticising his Celia, Waller complies with her 'swift changes'. So too does Marvell's lover, although he runs more risk of being taken over as his mutable fair reverses the more usual process of sexual imperialism and colonises *him:*

> For thou alone to people me,
> Art grown a num'rous Colony;

> And a Collection choicer far
> Then or *White-hall's*, or *Mantua's* were.
>
> (ll. 45–8)

Yet the final choice is his: for, as the allusion to the royal collection reminds us, it is the patron, not the artist nor even the sitter, who pays the piper and calls the tune.

In stanza VII he chooses, both as lover and as connoisseur:

VII

> But, of these Pictures and the rest,
> That at the Entrance likes me best:
> Where the same Posture, and the Look
> Remains, with which I first was took.
> A tender Shepherdess, whose Hair
> Hangs loosely playing in the Air,
> Transplanting Flow'rs from the green Hill,
> To crown her Head, and Bosome fill.
>
> (ll. 49–56)

Had the lyric ended with stanza VI, it is unlikely that readers would have suspected their private view of the Clora exhibition to be incomplete. After all, the first six stanzas have a satisfactory self-contained structure with a beginning, a middle, and an 'end' inviting the spectator to step back and marvel at the extent of the entire collection. Four pictures have been singled out and balanced so that none can take precedence.[56] But the addition of the seventh stanza (the number of creation and of mutability) radically changes the structure of the poem,[57] turning it into a private view in another sense. By destroying the impression that all his imaginary paintings are in a way equal, Marvell asserts the reality of choice. The lover chooses a pastoral image which evokes the voluptuous life at its most innocent, when ordinary human sexuality is closest to the beauty and pleasure of nature. For once, love and pleasure, nature and art, are in visible harmony.

Of course, the pastoral pose is no less a product of art than the others: the inspiration for Clora-as-shepherdess may be Ovidian, or Spenserian, or derived from a diffuse heritage of pastoral poetry and painting.[58] Nor has the male-female relation necessarily changed: 'took' retains, however unobtrusively, the notion of the woman captivating the man with beauty's bait. Presumably, like Congreve's Restoration shepherdess, Clora is 'Affecting to seem unaffected.'[59] Yet the illusion, if it is one, remains exquisitely intact, with no nudge of complicity from the poet. What *has* changed is the quality of feeling. And what sustains that feeling is the natural landscape, which transcends the earlier, more sophisticated symbolism. It is simplified to the essentials—a movement of air, flowers, the *green* hill—which are inseparable from the only image of Clora that strikes the heart.[60] The shepherdess is 'tender' and her beauty natural. Indeed she may owe more than she realises to the power of purely natural beauty over her poet.[61] She borrows from nature, 'transplanting' flowers to her head and bosom; but transplants tend to be fragile. How fragile, we are reminded by *The Coronet* where the poet undoes his own pastoral—'Dismantling all the fragrant Towers/That once adorn'd my Shepherdesses head' (ll. 7-8). Yet values are relative, and within *The Gallery* the shepherdess clearly represents the highest form of pleasure, gentle and unalloyed, nostalgic and safe. The medium of love in these poems is art; but here at least its message is nature.

The Fair Singer

In *The Fair Singer*, the medium of love is again art, but the art of music instead of painting. Ovid had advised in his *Ars Amatoria* that women should learn to sing, on the grounds that the voice is a powerful aid to seduction (more efficacious, for many, than the face).[62] In the Renaissance, that power might be overrated or underrated in comparison with visual beauty; but it could scarcely be ignored. Music invades the emotions and produces a pleasure so intense that the association with the equally intense sexual emotions is unavoidable, though Renaissance writers differ over exactly how the association works, and how it relates to the theories of love based predominantly—sometimes exclusively—on sight.[63] Marvell is not among those who relegate hearing to a subordinate position. Clearly he was deeply attracted to both music and the visual arts, but on the evidence he grants equal, sometimes superior, power to the former. In *A Dialogue between the Resolved Soul and Created Pleasure* he places music at the height of created pleasures, and both there and in *The Fair Singer* it is the *mind* that is susceptible to harmony.[64] Music is dangerous because it appeals to, and tests the resolution of, the highest faculty—'None can chain a mind/Whom this sweet Chordage cannot bind'.

The speaker of *The Fair Singer* is assaulted on two fronts simultaneously, and proves himself no Resolved Soul in his fatalism:

I

> To make a final conquest of all me,
> Love did compose so sweet an Enemy,
> In whom both Beauties to my death agree,
> Joyning themselves in fatal Harmony;
> That while she with her Eyes my Heart does bind,
> She with her Voice might captivate my Mind.

(ll. 1-6)

Normally in Renaissance literature, 'harmony' is a word strongly charged with positive and creative force. The epithet 'fatal' subverts this usage. Lovelace too describes a harmony which is metaphorically fatal in *Gratiana dauncing and singing*, a lyric sometimes compared with *The Fair Singer*; but in the Lovelace poem, the lady's performance imitates the harmonies of the universe, transcending the destructive aspect which is kept finely impersonal— 'The floore lay pav'd with broken hearts' (1.18).[65] Whereas the controlling metaphor of *Gratiana dauncing and singing* is cosmic harmony, that of *The Fair Singer* is conflict, love as war. Highly traditional of course; but Marvell never uses it inertly where sexual relations are concerned. Here it edges the pleasure with resistance, however vain.

In *The Gallery*, the lover was merely colonised by Clora, but here the unnamed singer conquers and enslaves him:

II

> I could have fled from One but singly fair:
> My dis-intangled Soul it self might save,
> Breaking the curled trammels of her hair.
> But how should I avoid to be her Slave,
> Whose subtile Art invisibly can wreath
> My Fetters of the very Air I breath?[66]

(ll. 7–12)

Marvell's apparent obsession with entanglement, and his recurrent imagery of fetters,[67] relates closely to his view of the soul's involvement in the material world and the difficulty (if not the impossibility) of choosing freedom. The sensation of being fettered is ambiguous, half-pleasurable, half-painful, depending on what the fetters are—tears, flowers, briars, a woman's hair—and the degree of submission. The verb 'wreath' recalls *The Coronet*: nature is almost too pliable in an artist's hands. The singer is a fellow-artist, whose performance conjures beauty literally out of thin air. As a description of the insidious power of vocal music (pointed by the pun on 'air') the verse is as subtle as its subject. A number of Cavalier lyrics on similar topics may be compared to *The Fair Singer*, but none surpasses Marvell's skill.[68] Perhaps it is necessary to look to the old maestro, Ben Jonson himself, for a consummate example of this kind of conceit in a different context. In *My Picture Left in Scotland*,[69] Jonson makes witty play on the rival perceptions of eye and ear: the girl's sight of the heavy, fleshy contours of his portrait blocks her response to the airy music of verses meant to enchant her. In this lyric, eye and ear work against each other, to the poet's downfall: in Marvell's lyric, eye and ear are in collusion—also to the poet's downfall.

Logically, the poem which opened with the prospect of 'a final conquest of all me' (1.1) ends on a surrender without a struggle:

III

> It had been easie fighting in some plain,
> Where Victory might hang in equal choice,
> But all resistance against her is vain,

Who has th'advantage both of Eyes and Voice,
And all my Forces needs must be undone,
She having gained both the Wind and Sun.

(ll. 13–18)

The experience that enthralls mind and heart also paralyses the will. Although the lover has not descended to the lowest level of the besotted senses, neither has he been raised to the heights of divine contemplation. He inhabits a kind of limbo where the soul is, as it were, recalled and suspended like the winds and rivers of *A Dialogue between the Resolved Soul and Created Pleasure*. The second and third stanzas of *The Fair Singer* entertain the notion of escape or resistance purely as hypotheses: 'I could have fled ... But how should I avoid to be her Slave ...?'; 'It had been easie fighting ... But all resistance against her is vain'. Elsewhere in his poetry, for example in *Upon Appleton House* (stanza LXXVI), Marvell does devise tactics of evasion and resistance to beauty which appear to work. But here the situation permits the lover not even the 'equal choice' that might exist in the real life of action, where battles are tactically decided. All he can do is gracefully submit, 'She having gained both the Wind and Sun' (l.18).

However, the lover's lack of choice is taken relatively lightly, if only because the pleasure is so obviously rewarding.[70] In spite of the continuing metaphor of conflict, the power of music dissolves emotional tensions in its own harmony. His capitulation to the inevitable does not entail any kind of psychic damage—rather the reverse. His fetters are the strongest but also the lightest imaginable, and when the musical performance ends in silence, as end it must, they too will vanish.

Mourning

Mourning is not on the face of it an activity analogous with singing or sitting for one's portrait: yet this Chlora seems to have brought the shedding of tears to a fine art, perfecting her practice of what might be termed *ars dolendi*, the art of grieving. 'Seems': for the point of the poem is that Chlora's tears can be variously interpreted, that the art itself may be nature. The poem begins with an ironic appeal to one group of professional interpreters, seventeenth-century equivalents of psychoanalysts (and sometimes regarded just as ambivalently), the astrologers:

I

You, that decipher out the Fate
Of humane Off-springs from the Skies,
What mean these Infants which of late
Spring from the Starrs of *Chlora's* Eyes?

(ll. 1–4)

With his interest in Fate, Marvell might be expected to be intrigued by the claims of astrology, but his references to astrologers register amusement or scepticism ('Th'*Astrologers* own Eyes are set...').[71] His Latin verse-letter addressed 'To a Gentleman that only upon the sight of the Author's writing, had given a Character of his Person and Judgment of his Fortune' treats this graphologist with exaggerated solemnity, calling him 'Astrologus *certior* Astronomo' (l.26), 'an astrologer more certain than an astronomer.'[72] Coincidentally, in the same epistle he uses the phrase '*stellarum... divina propago*' (l.41), 'the divine offspring of the stars', which recalls the imagery of the first stanza of *Mourning*. Both epistle and lyric, unlike in almost every other way, reflect Marvell's preoccupation with 'Judgment' and the validity of evidence.

The other Marvell poem inevitably brought to mind by the description of Chlora's eyes and tears in stanzas II and III is, of course, *Eyes and Tears*. Both poems owe a clear debt to the 'lachrymose' convention.[73] Yet the two lyrics differ sharply in orientation, and possibly this is why they are separated in the Folio. The wit of *Eyes and Tears* is contemplative, homiletic, universalised; *Mourning* is specific, sexual, secular. The latter advertises its irony much more openly. When *Mourning* records physical phenomena, it uses language— 'confus'd', 'doubled ore', 'molding'—which encodes mental processes involving duplicity and manipulation:[74]

II

Her Eyes confus'd, and doubled ore,
With Tears suspended ere they flow;
Seem bending upwards, to restore
To Heaven, whence it came, their Woe.

III

When, molding of the watry Sphears,
Slow drops unty themselves away;
As if she, with those precious Tears,
Would strow the ground where *Strephon* lay.

(ll. 5–12)

Chlora's tears might be motivated by true grief, not just decorum (in which case, she could retort with Hamlet, 'I know not "seems" ').[75] If she does weep in piety and remembrance, then these tears find a parallel in *On a Drop of Dew* on the one hand, and in *The Nymph complaining* on the other.[76] But the presumptive doubt is strong, and repeated.

The cynics offer worldly expertise instead of astrology:

IV

Yet some affirm, pretending Art,

Her Eyes have so her Bosome drown'd,
Only to soften near her Heart
A place to fix another Wound.

V

And, while vain Pomp does her restrain
Within her solitary Bowr,
She courts her self in am'rous Rain;
Her self both *Danae* and the Showr.

(ll. 13-20)

The phrase 'pretending Art' (l. 13) is ambiguously poised, like so much else in this poem.[77] This alternative explanation in fact deepens the enigma of Chlora's behaviour: is she acting from choice, or under the constraint of social pressures which she then exploits as best she may? She mourns ostentatiously, as 'vain Pomp' requires, yet in privacy. The 'solitary Bowr', which should be a place of devout contemplation, becomes a closet of secret involuted pleasure. On this showing, Chlora outdoes her near-namesake of *The Gallery* by enacting an entire hermaphroditic love-myth, which makes her independent of the male and incidentally solves the problem of waiting for love's new 'Wound'. 'Her self both *Danae* and the Showr':[78] the story of Zeus gaining access to the incarcerated Danae in a shower of golden rain is perfect for Marvell's purposes—slyly suggestive, with a strong element of calculation, yet irrationally magical. What comes across powerfully is the voluptuousness of Chlora's alleged self-courtship, without any breach of decorum.

However her pleasure may arise from antedating the consummation of a new love:

VI

Nay others, bolder, hence esteem
Joy now so much her Master grown,
That whatsoever does but seem
Like Grief, is from her Windows thrown.

VII

Nor that she payes, while she survives,
To her dead Love this Tribute due;
But casts abroad these Donatives,
At the installing of a new.

(ll. 21-28)

Chlora is far from being the first woman to be suspected of such ulterior motives (indeed here she dwindles from Danae into more of a stereotype).[79] She *is* a survivor: life goes on, and with it the possibility of choosing. Contemplation (true mourning) and pleasure (a new lover) are the woman's options, but there is the merest hint of a political option as well. A dead ruler in the public world may be replaced as easily as a dead lover in the private one.[80] Although the coarse domestic comparison of tears to slops thrown into the street (l. 24) appears to clash with the ceremonious 'Donatives' (l. 27), which refers to largesse distributed at the installation of a new ruler, they are linked by the image of casting something abroad. Tears are as disposable as their object.

And yet: the artist refuses to see Chlora's tears as worthless, whatever the motives that prompt them. The cynics delude themselves with shallow speculation:

VIII

How wide they dream! The *Indian* Slaves
That sink for Pearl through Seas profound,
Would find her Tears yet deeper Waves
And not of one the bottom sound.

(ll. 29–32)

The alternative reading 'dive' for 'sink' (l.30, Bodleian MS. Eng. poet. ld. 49) is less mysterious and apt. In this subaqueous world everything should move in dream-like slow motion, like the tears untying themselves away. From the viewpoint of human values, Chlora's tears may be meretricious; but from the poet's viewpoint, their beauty makes them genuinely precious, deeper than the seas of the world and traditionally symbolised by sought-after pearls.[81] Yet irony is not absent. The play on 'sound' (l. 32) as verb and adjective richly confuses the sense:[82] this ocean of tears may be too deep to test or understand, or it may lack any firm basis in feeling.

As in *The Gallery*, the pleasure given by art is, paradoxically, most acute when mediated through an image that turns art back upon nature. Unlike *The Gallery*, however, *Mourning* does not conclude on its most memorable image. In another of his deceptive endings, Marvell swings the poem from lyricism to sub-satire, reserving rather than giving judgment:

IX

I yet my silent Judgment keep,
Disputing not what they believe:
But sure as oft as Women weep,
It is to be suppos'd they grieve.

(ll. 33–6)

The ironic double meaning in the last two lines leaves both the speaker and his audience with their options open. We can either connive at 'a polite pretence',[83] a social observance, or else accept that weeping is indeed the effect of grief and nothing else. We have our choice: there is no way of knowing what Chlora's true choice has been, whether heavenly contemplation, or a life of renewed sexual pleasure, or even a life of inverted pleasure disguised as devoutness, like that of the nuns of *Upon Appleton House* (who find tears a useful cosmetic aid).[84] The first possibility seems the least likely, but to endorse the others is to join the school for scandal. The ironic gallantry of the last stanza arises from sexual and social complicity; and this encroaches upon another form of complicity characteristic of this group of poems, the complicity of artist, subject, and spectator. In *The Fair Singer*, music brings about a total, if temporary, capitulation to pleasure, and the poet involves himself most closely in his fiction. In the other lyrics, lovers and mistresses sustain fictions of themselves, and the poet invites the reader to see through the fiction with him, and to count the cost of maintaining it in real or imaginary pain. At the same time, he invites us to share his pleasure in what art can make of sexual conduct and display.

Daphnis and Chloe

Daphnis and Chloe develops the study of the art of love to an ultimate sophistication. Its plot hinges on the separation of lovers,[85] allowing Marvell to play off determinism against free will, and the laws of nature against the laws of an artificial society. From this material he could easily have produced yet another variant on Love versus Time or Fate; but as the situation evolves, it becomes clear that this is a problem not of Time but of timing (and, it is tempting to add, of two-timing)—a very different thing.[86]

The first stanza leads, or rather misleads, the reader into believing that the lovers' imminent separation is from necessity:

I

> *Daphnis* must from *Chloe* part:
> Now is come the dismal Hour
> That must all his Hopes devour,
> All his Labour, all his Art.

(ll. 1–4)

Even so, the choice of how to behave is theirs, and it turns out to be a choice beset by more than one kind of pressure and misconception. They want to play by the rules, although the status of the rules is dubious, and their skill in applying them clearly variable. In the opening phase it looks as if Daphnis's male 'Art' is being set against Chloe's female 'Nature'. But neither is privileged at this point:

II

> Nature, her own Sexes foe,
> Long had taught her to be coy:
> But she neither knew t'enjoy,
> Nor yet let her Lover go.

(ll. 5–8)

Women beware women! Chloe is confronted with a dilemma in which her earlier instinctive knowledge fails her. She resolves it, not by abandoning Nature but by copying Nature's own female inconsistency on which the world's continuance depends[87] (stanzas III and IV). To begin with, Chloe was 'natural' but not natural *enough*: equally, Daphnis was artful, but not artful enough. If she did not know 't'enjoy', he lacked the crucial bit of information to ensure enjoyment:

V

He, well read in all the wayes
By which men their Siege maintain,
Knew not that the Fort to gain
Better 'twas the Siege to raise.

(ll. 17–20)

The element of apparent naïveté has already been prepared for by Marvell's ironic choice of title following the Greek romance by Longus, and its exploitation by a sophisticated narrator has a closer antecedent in Marlowe's *Hero and Leander*.[88] Marvell's lovers, like Marlowe's, are at cross-purposes. Chloe and Hero share conflicting instincts of coyness and come-hither; Daphnis and Leander have read all the books. But Daphnis is far more devious than Leander, and his priorities are different.

When Chloe drops her defences at the news of her lover's departure, Daphnis himself is so preoccupied by the set pattern of behaviour that art prescribes for the parting lover that he cannot—will not—adjust to the changed situation. If we are to believe the narrator, he is so self-absorbed that he does not perceive it:

VI

But he came so full possest
With the Grief of Parting thence,
That he had not so much Sence
As to see he might be blest.

(ll. 21–4)

Chloe's yielding has thrown out Daphnis's calculations (only at the end of the poem do we realise by how much), threatening to deprive him of his role.[89] Finding himself 'Between Joy and Sorrow rent' (l. 32), he becomes the outraged purist, eloquently justifying his rejection of a pleasure once desired but now, so he claims, emotionally contaminated.

Eloquently, and at length: his case takes up stanzas XII to XXIV, yet rests on a single sophistry. He argues through analogies spun from the parting=death equation,[90] all tending to the same point—'Joy will not with Sorrow weave' (l. 91). But art, as well as psychology, contradicts him. He asks rhetorically 'Why should I enrich my Fate?' (l. 65), yet that is precisely what he is doing, assembling his metaphoric jewels to enhance his (self-chosen) fate. He relishes his powers of fantasy, deliberately offsetting the macabre and sensational—execution, cannibalism, necrophilia, sorcery—with another of the heightened natural images which transform these *ars amatoria* poems:

XXII

> Gentler times for Love are ment.
> Who for parting pleasure strain
> Gather Roses in the rain,
> Wet themselves and spoil their Sent.

(ll. 85–88)

The source of this image is a speech from Suckling's *Aglaura* (1638),[91] in which Aglaura strives to dissuade Thersames, who is in mortal danger, from his 'strong preservative of happinesse', the consummation of their love:

> Gather not roses in a wet and frowning houre;
> They'll lose their sweets then, trust mee they will Sir.
> What pleasure can Love take to play his game out,
> When death must keepe the Stakes—

(III. i. 62–5)

Marvell's adaptation decentres human tragedy ('who' has not even an antecedent) and erases, momentarily, Daphnis's egotism. Rain-soaked roses with their ruined scent still evoke the freshness of their pristine state as ungathered roses signifying true pleasure.[92]

True pleasure is what Daphnis shows no sign of recognising. He prefers the perverse pleasures of the unnatural or the supernatural: the magical fernseed gathered at midsummer midnight (stanza XXI) is more potent for his purpose than roses gathered in the rain. And so the imagery of seed, fruit, and flowers is twisted from its innocent connotations of fertility; the life of pleasure with its sensual satisfactions—eating, drinking, adorning oneself, making love—is similarly twisted (see stanzas XIV and XVII to XIX). Corruption even creeps into the text itself in the case of stanza XX. The Folio reads

XX

> And I parting should appear
> Like the Gourmand *Hebrew* dead,
> While he Quailes and *Manna* fed,
> And does through the Desert err.

(ll. 77–80)

Not surprisingly, editors from Cooke onwards emend lines 79 and 80 to 'While with Quailes and *Manna* fed,/He does through the Desert err.'[93] Yet the obviously garbled original does throw up a real and bizarre confusion between feeding and being fed on, which seems central to Marvell's treatment of erotic love in certain poems. The lover in *To his Coy Mistress* offers a choice between devouring and being devoured; *The Unfortunate Lover* has the hero experiencing both simultaneously; Daphnis begins by having his hopes devoured (ll. 3–4) and later declares that he will starve defiantly rather 'Than be fatted up express/For the *Canibal* to dine' (stanza XVIII). He assumes the 'manly' right to choose, regardless of Chloe's feelings.[94] In fact, he concludes by asserting a choice which lets him have it both ways:

XXIV

Fate I come, as dark, as sad,
As thy Malice could desire;
Yet bring with me all the Fire
That Love in his Torches had.

(ll. 93–6)

He wants to retain the 'Fire' of passion which fuels his performance, but to renounce passion itself. As a self-conscious poseur, he does 'pollute' imaginary grief with the pleasure of fantasy, and the discrimination on which his argument is supposed to be based breaks down. As an unfortunate lover, he is a fraud.

It only remains for us to discover that he is a fraud because he is *too* fortunate with women:

XXVI

But hence Virgins all beware.
Last night he with *Phlogis* slept;
This night for *Dorinda* kept;
And but rid to take the Air.

(ll. 101–4)

Not Fate but personal whim governs Daphnis. His behaviour is caught and placed by the beautifully irresponsible reason for his departure, as much as by his appointments with ladies of easy virtue.[95] The ironically named Daphnis ends up as a cultivated creature who sallies out to 'take the Air', not a native inhabitant of a pastoral world. The tone foreshadows the decline of pastoral into fashionable affectation, and anticipates the skilled light verse of the Restoration and eighteenth century. Compare Swift's *vers de société*, 'Apollo Outwitted':

OVID had warn'd her to beware,
    Of Stroling God's, whose usual Trade is,
Under pretence of Taking Air,
    To pick up Sublunary Ladies.

(ll. 21–4)[96]

Ovid, not Longus, is the true patron of Daphnis.

And, true to type, Daphnis has the last word. He evades responsibility for his insolent freedom of choice by appealing through the narrator to 'the Lawes':

XXVII

> Yet he does himself excuse;
> Nor indeed without a Cause.
> For, according to the Lawes,
> Why did *Chloe* once refuse?

(ll. 105–8)

What laws are these? Hardly Nature's, for all her inconsistency: more likely the laws of the *ars amatoria*, as formulated by a libertine élite (a possible allusion to the 1647 tract, *A Parliament of Ladies: with their Lawes newly enacted*, has been proposed).[97] It looks as if the 'Cause' is deliberately left open to male and female judgments. But, at least for some readers,[98] the flippant ending does not obliterate the lingering taste of pleasure spoilt and sexuality frustrated or squandered—not through accident, but through human perversity. *Daphnis and Chloe* interprets love as possession and freedom as licence. In the next poem in the Folio, *The Definition of Love*, these assumptions are radically challenged, and the separation of lovers gives birth to a completely different philosophy. The poet exchanges the equivocal laws of *ars amatoria* for the sounder laws of geometry.

(iii) Definitions of Love:
"The Definition of Love", "The Match"

The Definition of Love

Not the least of the difficulties involved in this deliberately difficult poem is
its title: so much so, that one critic asks tentatively if it might have been
'attached to the poem by mistake'.[1] But the pun on definition, which conflates
the modern usage with the older Latinate sense of 'restriction',[2] seems very
Marvellian, and makes the possibility of mistake unlikely. Nevertheless, the
title does raise expectations of a definitive statement that will bring all these
'love' poems into clearer focus, giving us a recognisable landmark from which
to take our bearings in the shifting half-concealed landscape of erotic
experience. Instead the reader finds that like the titles of certain abstract
paintings—and, in its way, *The Definition of Love* is like abstract art, based on
geometric rather than human figures—the title begs more questions than it
answers.

For a start, how is a definition defined? The criterion of universal validity
scarcely applies to this poem, beginning as it does with an assertion of the
special, not to say unique, status of its subject—'My Love is of a birth as
rare...' (1. 1).[3] Yet the proposition, 'A definition is universally valid',
depends on a kind of circular thinking, since to say that definitions are *by
definition* universally valid has to be self-validating. Technical formulae, as in
seventeenth-century handbooks of logic and rhetoric, are more rigorous.
Marvell himself uses such a formula when he writes that a definition 'alwaies
consists, as being a dialectick animal, of a body, which is the genus, and a
difference, which is the soul of the thing defined'.[4] Even more germane to *The
Definition of Love* is the use of the term in geometry.[5] Hobbes writes

> ... in Geometry, (which is the onely Science that it hath pleased God hitherto to
> bestow on mankind,) men begin at settling the significations of their words; which
> settling of significations, they call *Definitions*; and place them in the beginning of
> their reckoning.
>
> (*Leviathan*, I. iv)

Germane, because in structure and imagery Marvell's poem draws upon the
shape of a Euclid theorem: given, love itself; required, its definition;
construction, the images of space and line; proof, the argument from those
images which culminates in the q.e.d. of the last stanza.

Few if any definition poems recall such exact disciplines. Cut loose from its
more specialised contexts, a definition is simply the attempt to answer the
question 'What is is?'. Earlier lyrics in the definition-of-love genre incorporate
question and answer, for example, Peele's *What thing is love?*, or *Now what is
love*, attributed to Ralegh.[6] In mood these lyrics are a world apart from

Marvell's *Definition*, not just because they define more directly and superficially, but because the love defined is so emotionally different (a difference accentuated by metre). 'It is a pretty pretty thing', warbles Peele, an enchanting and bawdy game that, as the Ralegh lyric points out, may end in tears. The question might be rephrased as 'What is being in love like?' and the answers rely on emotional paradoxes which are a feature of the genre, and can also be traced in French examples like this *Chanson* from *Thronus Cupidinis*:[7]

> C'est un plaisir tout rempli de tristesse,
> C'est un tourment tout confit de liesse,
> Vn desespoir ou tousjours on espere,
> Vn esperer ou l'on se desespere.
>
> (11. 5–8)

Marvell's paradoxes are both more private and more philosophical, and the question which his definition answers is less easy to formulate. However, the philosophical concerns of his poem are familiar from Renaissance debate. For the Renaissance intelligentsia, defining love is a serious intellectual occupation as well as a social pastime: the origins and end of love, the relative importance allotted to body and mind, conjunction and separation, all these issues recur in the love treatises and are reflected in the literature.[8] Marvell's *The Definition of Love* might almost be written as a direct refutation of certain ideas worked out in the prose of Leone Ebreo and the poetry of Donne.

The opening stanza of *The Definition of Love* immediately issues a challenge:

I

> My Love is of a birth as rare
> As 'tis for object strange and high:
> It was begotten by despair
> Upon Impossibility.
>
> (11. 1–4)

The vocabulary expands from austere monosyllables, 'rare', 'strange', 'high', into the magnificent polysyllabic 'Impossibility', which, keyed into 'despair', sets the code of the poem. It is a code both subjective and objective. This love has come into existence not despite impossibility but because of it. Yet, according to Leone, this is a contradiction in terms. Philo and Sophia, the participants in his dialogue, debate precisely this problem,[9] and Philo contends that it is not in human nature to sustain desire for the self-evidently impossible:

> you will observe that a man has no desire to reach heaven on foot, or to fly with wings, or to be a star or to take one in his hands, and such like; for although these things are excellent enough in themselves, and although man is both deficient in them and conscious of their value, yet he does not desire them, for they are clearly impossible, and where there is no hope of achievement neither is there desire. For

> the hope of acquiring something pleasurable which we know and lack, gives rise to love and desire to possess it: where the hope is small the love is never intense nor the desire hot, and where all hope fails because the possession is impossible the love and desire of the knower also fail.
>
> (p. 329)

His analogies strike a modern reader as dubious support, and indeed fail to account for the Renaissance phenomenon of the 'aspiring mind', a Leonardo or a Faustus; but Sophia's only exception to Philo's rule is the human desire to escape death, which Philo reinterprets as a not impossible desire for immortality. 'Possibility' is therefore accepted as a necessary condition of both heavenly and earthly love, the choice of life or eternity.

The argument that the object of Marvell's 'Definition of Love' is divine not human has its attractions, but it does not by itself solve the conundrum of an impossible love.[10] On the contrary, perfect union with God in a future state, of the kind desired by the soul in *On a Drop of Dew*, is more conceivable than perfect union with another human being in this life. Ironically, the very heart of Leone's love theory relating to the sexes is in a sense an 'Impossibility':

> the proper definition of the perfect love of a man for a woman is: the conversion of the lover into the beloved together with a desire for the conversion of the beloved into the lover. And when such love is equal on both sides, it is defined as the conversion of each lover into the other.
>
> (p. 55)

Sir Thomas Browne points out the flaw, writing of those who love that they 'desire each to be truely the other, which being impossible, their desires are infinite, and must proceed without a possibility of satisfaction'—a passage which has been used to throw light on Marvell's poem.[11] It is obviously true that in a sexual relationship individuals cannot merge completely into one being, except metaphorically, and that the frenzy of lovemaking can be presented as a constantly renewed failure to achieve the impossible (Lucretius so presents it in *De Rerum Natura*).[12] But if Marvell's lovers want to imagine an ideal unity beyond intercourse, there are symbols available to express that unity (for instance, the traditional circle or sphere or androgyne, or the much-debated seventeeth-century concept of 'penetration'). It should be noted, however, that the poet does not avail himself overtly of these, although implicit allusions have been deduced.[13] Instead he chooses to refer 'Impossibility' to the ancient antagonists of humanity, Fate and the stars, which oppose the union of 'two perfect Loves' (stanzas III, IV, and VIII). Two *perfect* loves: that is the point. The inevitable separateness of human beings may be regarded as the penalty of the Fall, or as a fact of physics, according to taste. But the condition applies to all lovers indiscriminately, and one matter on which *The Definition of Love* is explicit is that its subject is the special, the unique case.

Despite this claim to uniqueness, however, other writers besides Marvell were intrigued by the idea of a love springing not from the hope of pleasure but from the contemplation of impossibility. Among the sources and analogues proposed for *The Definition of Love* is a passage from Sidney's *Arcadia* (1590),[14] which sounds very like a variation on Leone:

> ... unpossible desires are punished in the desire it selfe. O then, ô tenne times unhappie that I am, since where in all other hope kindleth love; in me despaire should be the bellowes of my affection: and of all despaires the most miserable, which is drawn from impossibilitie.... The most ambitious wight vexeth not his wittes to clime into heaven; Why? because it is impossible.
>
> (*Arcadia*, II. iv)[15]

But Philoclea's despair is both motivated and removable. She believes Pyrocles, with whom she is in love, to be a woman, a situation which romantic convention creates and also resolves. Unlike *The Definition of Love*, there is a supporting narrative which ensures that the reader knows that the impossibility is not absolute.

A closer analogy to Marvell's poem is Cowley's lyric titled *Impossibilities*,[16] with its metaphysical conceit upon 'Conjunction' and its association of impossibility with hostile Fortune. But Cowley recommends resistance:

> As *stars* (not powerful else) when they *conjoin*,
> Change, as they please, the Worlds estate:
> So thy *Heart* in *Conjunction* with mine,
> Shall our own fortunes regulate;
> And to our *Stars themselves* prescribe a *Fate*.
>
> (ll. 11–15)

Another Cowley poem, *The vain Love*,[17] includes lines which might have stayed in Marvell's mind, or at any rate in his ear:

> Now my desires are worse, and fly
> At an *Impossibility*.
>
> (ll. 41–42)

Whatever the degree of specific influence, these lyrics may at least have stimulated Marvell into re-examining the clash between love and impossibility, and into coming up with a different attitude to the so often deplored gap between what is desirable and what is possible. Cowley in *Impossibilities* professes to believe not only that lovers have a choice, but that their choice can 'regulate' their circumstances. His answer is to bridge the gap by will-power and the force of human, not astrological, conjunction. Marvell, more subtly, concludes that conjunction *depends* on there being a gap of some sort.

Similarly he reassesses the role of hope and despair in love, so familiar as attributes of a lover's state of mind that they are often an integral part of the definition. Usually hope precedes despair, like prologue and epilogue, in an unhappy love affair (hence Nashe's summary description of Sidney's *Astrophil and Stella*).[18] This is the sequence in *The Unfortunate Lover* (ll. 33–4). But in

The Definition of Love, despair takes precedence and hope flutters feebly in limbo, a butterfly broken upon fate's wheel:

II

> Magnanimous Despair alone
> Could show me so divine a thing,
> Where feeble Hope could ne'r have flown
> But vainly flapt its Tinsel Wing.

(ll. 5–8)

Hope and the life of pleasure are alike denigrated: the supreme value here is contemplation. What Despair—significantly defined as great and generous of soul—has to offer is a spiritual revelation, seen but untouchable.

What contemplation cannot achieve is to complete the trajectory of desire, reintegrating the lover with his own soul which is 'fixt' in the beloved:

III

> And yet I quickly might arrive
> Where my extended Soul is fixt,
> But Fate does Iron wedges drive,
> And alwaies crouds it self betwixt.

(ll. 9–12)

Whether or not there is a witty play on the new Cartesian notion of extension considered as a property not of spirit but of matter,[19] the image of the extended soul makes it clear that there is no deficiency of will or commitment on the lover's part. He is prevented from following up contemplation with action, not because he so chooses but because Fate intervenes. The *locus classicus* of the 'Iron wedges' is Horatian:[20]

> te semper anteit serva Necessitas,
> clavos trabalis et cuneos manu
>   gestans aena, nec severus
>   uncus abest liquidumque plumbum.

> Before thee stalks Necessity, thy servant,
> Who in her brazen hand grips the strong wedges
>   And nails, and with them brings
>   Her molten lead, her unrelenting clamp.

(*Odes* I.xxxv. 17–20, tr. J. Michie)

In Cesare Ripa's *Iconologia* (1593), Necessitá is represented as 'a young Woman, holding in her right Hand a Hammer, and in her left a Handful of Nails' (fig. 224).[21] Although wedges and nails have opposite practical functions, both symbolise Fate's power of irresistible coercion. In a famous parallel image from the second part of *The Rehearsal Transpros'd*, Marvell writes of the kind of Necessity that dominated even the deities 'and drove the great Iron nail thorough the Axle-tree of Nature', but emphasises that this is only one concept among 'several Families of the Necessities'.[22] Earlier in the first part he had quoted Juvenal on Fortune (both contexts are of course satiric)—

> —sed te
> *Nos facimus Fortuna Deam Coeloque locamus.*
>
> *But we make thee Fortune a Goddess, and place thee*
> *in Heaven.*[23]

This is also pertinent, because the Fate of *The Definition of Love* should not be placed in heaven either: she operates in the material world, and is necesary to its continuance. When 'two perfect Loves' collide with this universal principle, the result is, paradoxically, both a loss and a confirmation of freedom. Their love is raised to the level of a universal principle itself. The conflict becomes a metaphysical deadlock. Although Fate has the power to separate the lovers permanently, she cannot destroy their will to love; she exercises that power *because* perfect love can hypothetically annihilate her and the material universe she governs. In the world of action and pleasure she has the power of veto, but the contemplative 'Conjunction of the Mind' (l. 31) cannot be undone.

Stanzas IV to VI define the deadlock through their own grammatical conjunctions 'For... And therefore... Unless':[24]

IV

For Fate with jealous Eye does see
Two perfect Loves; nor lets them close:
Their union would her ruine be,
And her Tyrannick pow'r depose.

V

And therefore her Decrees of Steel
Us as the distant Poles have plac'd,
(Though Loves whole World on us doth wheel)
Not by themselves to be embrac'd.

VI

Unless the giddy Heaven fall,
And Earth some new Convulsion tear;
And, us to joyn, the World should all
Be cramp'd into a *Planisphere.*

(ll. 13–24)

The imagery of these stanzas has provoked much learned discussion of cartography, astronomy and astrology, which extends to the parallel and oblique lines—lines of latitude and longitude?—of stanza VII.[25] There is disagreement over whether 'the distant Poles' (l. 18) are the terrestrial or celestial poles, and about the implications of either interpretation. A planisphere is a flat map showing the projection of a sphere or part of a sphere; the quotation used to gloss the term comes from Thomas Blundeville's *Exercises* (1594):[26]

> Astrolabe . . . is called of some a Planispheare, because it is both flat and round, representing the Globe or Spheare, having both his Poles clapt flat together.

Although the exact technical significance of the imagery may elude the reader, the literary affinities are more likely to register. This is the kind of writing expected from a metaphysical poet: almost inevitably, and with good reason, readers are reminded of Donne. Not only the Donne of the love poetry (especially the valedictions), but also the Donne of the divine poetry and prose:[27] Donne's fascination with maps, stars, the cosmos, the meeting of East and West, is well known. From the sermons, it is possible to pick out forerunners of Marvell's planisphere.[28] In one instance, he turns a flat map back into a globe—

> In a flat Map, there goes no more, to make West East, though they be distant in an extremity, but to paste that flat Map upon a round body, and then West and East are all one.
>
> (Sermon LV)

The reverse process happens in another instance:

> If you looke upon this world in a Map, you find two Hemisphears, two half worlds. If you crush heaven into a Map, you may find two Hemisphears too, two half heavens . . .
>
> (Sermon LXVI)

Turning a globe into a planisphere (not *vice versa*) involves a measure of force, so that it is not surprising to find a correspondence between Blundeville's 'clapt flat', Donne's 'crush', and Marvell's 'cramp'd'.

Indeed Marvell's imagery in stanzas IV to VI is conspicuously violent. As in other poems, the thought of a physical embrace attracts into its orbit words connoting physical damage: 'giddy . . . fall'; 'Convulsion tear'; 'cramp'd'. Nor is the world's destruction an alien idea in Marvell's poetry—on the contrary.[29] His imagination of destruction encompasses the small-scale and the vast, from the fall of the grass to the fall of the heavens (or, as Pope would put it, the bursting of a bubble or of a world). Since human history is bounded by the Fall and the Day of Judgment, 'some new Convulsion' (l. 22) looks back and forward. What is highly unusual is that it is the *union* of lovers, not their separating or ceasing to love, that brings chaos.[30] Marvell, it has been argued, is deliberately and starkly differentiating his position from that of Donne, while borrowing Donne's style.[31] Too starkly for some critics: an attempt has been made in the past to reclaim *The Definition of Love* for more recognisable human emotions by inventing a shadowy relationship with an unattainable woman.[32] But the poem itself makes no concessions in this direction. The reader's sympathy slides off the surface, for there is nothing to get a purchase on emotionally.

But if the emotions are starved or rarefied, according to viewpoint, there is intellectual compensation. The laws of geometry, like the laws of poetry, have a satisfying formal beauty perceived by the mind:

VII

As Lines so Loves *oblique* may well
Themselves in every Angle greet:
But ours so truly *Paralel*,
Though infinite can never meet.

(ll. 25–8)

In this, his seventh stanza, Marvell rewrites the mathematical language of the cosmos as a language of love. And it is not purely mechanical: 'Themselves in every Angle greet' nails wittily and precisely the kind of love that haunts dark corners.[33] Against this lustful pleasure is set a love at once infinite (an often loosely used word made strikingly exact in this context) and never to be consummated. Ironically, the acceptance of separation in space seems to annihilate the threat of time, as though Fate has to surrender her alternative weapon. Some achieve Platonic love, others have it thrust upon them.[34] Whatever is the case with Marvell's lover, he has learnt to see his contemplative love as superior to the pleasure to be had in the act of love. In a sense he might be said to choose eternity instead of life.

The final stanza clinches the definition and the proof:

VIII

Therefore the Love which us doth bind,
But Fate so enviously debarrs,
Is the Conjunction of the Mind,
And Opposition of the Stars.

(ll. 29–32)

If this is Marvell's true definition of an ideal love, then it cuts away much of what human beings value. A literal or hostile reading might put it down to sour grapes, or making the best of a failed relationship. Yet it holds to a crucial perception. Love not only can survive without hope of sexual consummation, but its continuing perfection is actually conditional upon the deprivation of pleasure. Love and pleasure almost always have an ambiguous or strained relation in Marvell's poetry. In *The Definition of Love* their divorce is, so to speak, made final by a decree absolute. It is a contemplative poem which has love for its subject. The extreme discrepancy between the personal subject and the impersonal mode reflects the tension of forces within the poem itself, as 'a dialectick animal'. Within a sequence of poems in which sexual love is usually imperfect, either in its nature or as an answer to time and fate, *The Definition of Love* stands for a joyless but powerful equilibrium.[35] Choice meets necessity on its own ground, and is not defeated.

The Match

Although *The Match* does not immediately follow *The Definition of Love* in the Folio, it is in its way a definition of love, which ends by apparently reversing the argument of the more highly rated poem.[36] Marvell invents an aetiological myth, involving personified Nature and Love and their strategy for defeating the ravages of time: but the love affair between the speaker and Celia that this 'explains' is disappointingly conventional despite its claim to uniqueness. What differentiates this love from 'the Conjunction of the Mind' is not just the impotence of mind against the consuming demands of sexuality ('all that burns the Mind', l. 24). It is also the fact that the conceits balance on the idea of union, not separation, and that the conclusion equates love with selfish pleasure.

The title *The Match* puns on sexual union and on the means of causing an explosion.[37] Again the dominant metaphor is one of violence beyond personal control. As far as the lover and Celia are concerned, their situation is brought about by laws analogous to the laws of chemistry: proximity accomplishes everything. Unlike the lovers who challenge inexorable law, the lover of *The Match* cooperates blandly with it, for it is in his interest to do so. Nature and Love are not outmanoeuvred by human choice but undone by their own precautions.[38]

The first section of the poem reworks a very familiar, not to say tired, compliment on Nature's handiwork,[39] with the added twist that the creation of her masterpiece, Celia, happens when Nature's back is turned:

I

> Nature had long a Treasure made
> Of all her choisest store;
> Fearing, when She should be decay'd,
> To beg in vain for more.

II

> Her *Orientest* Colours there,
> And Essences most pure,
> With sweetest Perfumes hoarded were,
> All as she thought secure.

III

She seldom them unlock'd, or us'd,
But with the nicest care;
For, with one grain of them diffus'd,
She could the World repair.

IV

But likeness soon together drew
What she did separate lay;
Of which one perfect Beauty grew,
And that was *Celia*.

(ll. 1–16)

In other versions of this hyperbole, Nature is very much the active agent, for example in this song from William Browne's *Britannia's Pastorals*:

> *Nym.* But what is it, wherein Dame *Nature* wrought
> The best of workes, the onely forme of Heauen;
> And hauing long to finde a present sought,
> Wherein the worlds whole beautie might be giuen;
> Shee did resolue in it all Arts to summon,
> To ioyne with natures framing?
> *God.* Tis this woman.[40]

'Nor was dame *Nature* onely busied in this Work, but all the Graces did consult and cooperat with her' writes James Howell, flattering the Marchioness of Winchester in similar vein.[41] So standard is the compliment that it enters the repertoire of all those aspirants to social and literary success for whom such works as *The English Parnassus* (1657) were compiled. Under the headings 'Beautie' and 'Beautifull', Poole's *Parnassus* displays the convention in all its varying plumage. Even the notion of Nature's undoing is a variation going back, at least, to Marlowe's *Hero and Leander*.[42] Marvell, then, could have appropriated the basic idea from almost anywhere. But it is typical of Marvell that the 'one perfect Beauty' should be simply a by-product of natural creation, rather than its aim and end. Repairing the fallen world is of more consequence to Nature than adorning Celia. And she is right to be worried, according to the belief in her senescence so widely diffused in the early seventeenth century.[43] Great creating Nature is a more vividly realised and sympathetic figure than the utterly passive Celia, whose beauty is less convincing than that of her unnamed counterpart offered and rejected in *A Dialogue between the Resolved Soul and Created Pleasure* (ll. 51–4).

Similarly, in the second section of this 'matched' piece,[44] personified Love is a more interesting and less conventional figure than the combustible Petrarchan lover himself. The process, metaphorically described, is more original than what it produces:

V

Love wisely had of long fore-seen
   That he must once grow old;
And therefore stor'd a Magazine,
   To save him from the cold.

VI

He kept the several Cells repleat
   With Nitre thrice refin'd;
The Naphta's and the Sulphurs heat,
   And all that burns the Mind.

VII

He fortifi'd the double Gate,
   And rarely thither came;
For, with one Spark of these, he streight
   All Nature could inflame.

VIII

Till, by vicinity so long,
   A nearer Way they sought;
And, grown magnetically strong,
   Into each other wrought.

IX

Thus all his fewel did unite
   To make one fire high:
None ever burn'd so hot, so bright;
   And *Celia* that am I.

(ll. 17–36)

If *The Definition of Love* models itself on the formal beauty of a Euclid theorem, *The Match* injects a banal affair with the excitement of an experiment performed with unstable materials. Specifically, it employs language connected with the technology of explosives and their military use. Even if this lyric is an early piece, for seventeenth-century Englishmen such connotations are hardly innocuous. This Eros is armed with more up-to-date weaponry than the traditional arrows. Yet the speaker seems to make light of the destructive potential of explosives inadvertently ignited, and his conclusion smugly accepts personal pleasure as all-sufficient and self-justifying:

X

So we alone the happy rest,
   Whilst all the World is poor,

> And have within our Selves possest
> All Love's and Nature's store.

(ll. 37–40)

The love defined in *The Match* is indeed a love that separates, but it separates the lovers from the world and not from each other. By the standard of *The Definition of Love*, it is a 'love oblique' which, morally speaking, cuts corners. What is missing from the final assertion is any counting of the cost of pleasure. Although the speaker defines love in terms which evoke the world's creation and destruction, he does so irresponsibly, and unlike the speaker of *The Definition of Love* he is prepared to consign the universe to perdition in the cause of happiness. With 'All Love's and Nature's store', he has the illusion of security: the poem ironically transfers the fear of decay and age from individual human lovers to Nature and Love themselves. Yet the reminder of destruction pervades *The Match*, even in the last stanza with its glib contrast between happy lovers and impoverished world.

If the poem is read as calculated irony,[45] a critique of the attitude it professes and the conventions it uses, it certainly appears more characteristic of Marvell. Even so, the irony lacks its customary verbal edge. Less memorably phrased than most of his poems, it is also weaker in conception.[46] It might have been written by Cowley on an average day (and it is not in fact unlike certain poems in *The Mistress*).[47] Marvell's full powers are not engaged. Although the essential elements are present—nature, love, time—the imaginative spark fails to ignite, in defiance of the chosen image.[48] We expect Love and Nature to be set in more revealing relationship, and pleasure and beauty to come alive to the senses. But the poem has no landscape, internal or external, in which to take root. Emotionally or otherwise, it is perhaps the most rootless of Marvell's lyrics.

(iv) Love in a Garden:
The Picture of little T.C. in a Prospect of Flowers

The Picture of little T.C. in a Prospect of Flowers returns the reader to
Marvell's roots in more senses than one, and to his most contemplative mode
of writing. The title clears a space not only for immediate observation but for
augury. 'Prospect' is a characteristic bit of Marvellian wordplay: in
seventeenth-century usage, a prospect is a landscape, a view to be looked at;
but it also carries the meaning of looking forward in time, so that little T.C.'s
prospect of flowers both frames the child in the present and draws the
spectator's imagination into her possible future.[1]

As so often, the poet starts with the directive 'See'—

I

See with what simplicity
This Nimph begins her golden daies!

(ll. 1–2)

Little T.C. shares that simplicity with other Marvellian figures, from the
dewdrop-soul to the sister-nymph who complains for the death of her fawn.
They appear as transparent as water, yet they hold, for the onlooker, teasing
reflections and depths. Little T.C. however is closer to human individuality
than the protagonists of those purely contemplative poems, and exercises a
rather different claim to our attention. In fact, the poem written about her
turns into a kind of love poem, although a very special kind. She is more nearly
'nature's self' than any of Marvell's profane mistresses, but she is neither a
mistress nor a goddess—yet. Instead she is a flesh-and-blood child, whose
closest counterpart in Marvell's poetry is his girl pupil, Mary Fairfax.[2]
Modern readers are indebted to Marvell's editor for identifying little T.C. as
Theophila Cornewall, whose mother came from the Skinner family, well
known to Marvell, and for also bringing to light the poignant fact that the
child had been called after a sister, another Theophila, who had died as an
infant.[3] This fact enhances the elegiac note struck in the concluding stanza,
and illumines the phrase 'Darling of the Gods' (l. 10) which is an English
equivalent of the Greek name.[4] Presumably Marvell is encoding personal
information, as well as drawing upon a deep reserve of emotional forebodings
and on literary recollections of a genre of poems written for the deaths of
children. Like the innocents lyrically mourned by Herrick, Theophila is 'a
pretty bud' which may be prematurely plucked by death.[5] The tone of such
poems is finely judged, often distinguished by a ceremonious delicacy which
was later to find musical expression in Ravel's *Pavane pour une Infante
Défunte*. But while adopting something of this tone, Marvell is not writing
about a dead child but a living one, caught and held in the sunlight and shadow

of possible choices. Like a character from Henry James, 'she[seems] to stand with little nipping scissors in a garden of alternatives.'[6]

For the present, her choice of life is spontaneous and self-fulfilling, bounded by the golden age of childhood and the miniature green horizon:

> In the green Grass she loves to lie,
> And there with her fair Aspect tames
> The Wilder flow'rs, and gives them names:
> But only with the Roses playes;
> And them does tell
> What Colour best becomes them, and what Smell.
>
> (ll. 3–8)

How far Marvell associates little T.C.'s 'golden daies' with the golden age of humanity is debatable.[7] Her activity is likely to impress upon the reader an idea of Eden rather than a classical version of the golden age. Although harmony between human beings and the natural world characterises all types of earthly paradise, it can take different forms; and here, appropriately, the child engages in a blissful game of education which is more serious than she knows.[8] The flowers of Eden are woman's special responsibility.[9] To read the poem with *Paradise Lost* in mind is to remember Eve's beautiful lament over her flowers which she 'bred up with tender hand/From the first opening bud, and gave... names' (XI. 276–7). According to Francis Bacon, to name truly will be to regain our lost command of the creatures.[10] But in a fallen world, 'naming destroys the unnamed innocence of the thing itself' (John Carey).[11] Or the untamed innocence: in Milton's Eden the 'taming' of flowers is permissible, but Milton presents it as real gardening activity, whereas little T.C. is doing something both more magical and more dangerous to the flowers of her world and ours. Dangerous, for the moment, in a purely metaphysical sense, for like the fauns and fairies of Damon's meadows her influence is more a matter of presence—'her fair Aspect'—than of skill.[12] At the same time, she is a human creature learning about power and about discrimination. The phrase 'Wilder flow'rs' introduces a standard of comparison foreign to Eden. In this environment there is scope for choice,[13] and little T.C. gives her preference to the roses of pleasure. Yet she is not content with nature as it is. Instead of surrendering to natural beauty in a spirit of contemplation beyond her years, she lectures even the roses in a spirit of improvement. In her childlike behaviour, the contemplative spectator sees the seeds of the human desire to dominate that leads inexorably to action. It is her very power to choose that sets her apart from nature,[14] ensuring that, like Mary Fairfax, she only '*Seems* with the Flow'rs a Flow'r to be' (*Upon Appleton House*, (l. 302; my italics). She believes that the world exists for her pleasure, innocent as that pleasure is, and so she dictates her terms.

But little T.C. does not have a monopoly of power in the poem: the gods are also watching. In dealing with human beings, Marvell constantly acknowledges destiny as well as choice:

II

Who can foretel for what high cause
This Darling of the Gods was born!

(ll. 9–10)

This is the challenging rhetoric of the active life, fitted for kings and heroes (in fact, Carew uses the 'Darling of the Gods' phrase in a royal or aristocratic context).[15] In suddenly applying it to the little girl whom we have been watching at play, Marvell insinuates a gentle parody, while reminding his readers that this human life, like any individual life, is not only precious to heaven but chosen out for a purpose. Risking hubris, the poet is prepared to prophesy:

Yet this is She whose chaster Laws
The wanton Love shall one day fear,
And, under her command severe,
See his Bow broke and Ensigns torn.
Happy, who can
Appease this virtuous Enemy of Man!

(ll. 11–16)

According to this description of her future career, T.C. is indeed destined for action in the wars of love, in which she will challenge and overcome the power of Eros. But is her destiny her choice? What is the true nature of this triumph of Chastity,[16] and how does it fit into the poem?

Much depends on the emphasis and placing of individual words as well as the arrangement of stanzas. 'Happy', for instance, is ironically isolated at the beginning of its brief Latinate line, 'Happy, who can...', and it balances 'virtuous' as 'chaster' balances 'wanton'. But the latter is not a perfect balance, since 'chaster' takes the comparative form. The reason for this (scansion apart) might be to complement 'Wilder' in the previous stanza (l.5).[17] The effect of both comparatives is to make distinctions, which are not absolutes but a matter of degree. Throughout the poem little T.C. is being urged to distinguish degrees of wildness, of ripeness, and even of chastity and innocence. As she learns about adult love, her severity will initially be directed against the god who stands for its wanton and arbitrary force: hostility to man is secondary, the corollary of a war in which male lovers are merely the poor bloody infantry. But is this chastity ideal or excessive? Does it exact too high a price? Does the prophecy allow or exclude marriage? These questions have sharply divided readers of the poem, who recognise only the gulf between innocence and experience.[18] The child may follow her instincts (at least up to the point starkly defined in the final stanza) but the nubile girl has to choose between virtue and pleasure. Of course marriage might provide an escape clause, as it does in the case of Mary Fairfax who also knows how to resist the onslaught of wanton love.[19] Little T.C.'s triumph need not preclude a Spenserian solution to the dilemma. The overthrow of wanton Eros does not have to mean that 'there will no more marriages.'[20] Indeed, in the original ending of Book III of *The Faerie Queene*, such a triumph of Chastity is the precondition of happy marriage. And in *The Picture of little T.C.* Marvell wryly permits at least the possibility of pleasure reconciled to virtue—'Happy, who can/Appease this virtuous Enemy of Man!'[21]

If Marvell is being ironic at the expense of his own sex, he immediately diverts the irony to himself in particular. In the next stanza he declares himself anxious to adopt the role of appeaser, though he negotiates more perhaps from his privileged position as poet than as potential lover. The device is his favourite one of 'antedating':

III

> O then let me in time compound,
> And parly with those conquering Eyes;
> Ere they have try'd their force to wound,
> Ere, with their glancing wheels, they drive
> In Triumph over Hearts that strive,
> And them that yield but more despise.

(ll. 17–22)

The motif here, summed up in the phrase 'Young beauty's power foretold',[22] has an ancient history going back to the Greek Anthology, and is still popular. It is easily trivialised—even the beautiful phrasing of Waller's version, 'Why came I so untimely forth',[23] cannot conceal a slight vapidity—but not by Marvell. For all his exaggerated alarm, he hints at a power to inflict pain which is not to be taken lightly. Whatever the reactions of T.C.'s lovers, whether they strive or acquiesce, they are all victims beneath the 'glancing wheels' of her eyes (a wincingly apt conceit). Once the heart is committed, neither an active nor passive role will protect it in the conflict between passion and chastity.

The secret is to avoid the lover's commitment, and the poet has his own resources for doing so. He can diplomatically make his peace with beauty while she is still the artist's subject, not the lover's; and he can withdraw strategically from the unequal contest between virtue and pleasure. He ends this stanza by choosing the philosophic pleasure of contemplation before the pains of enlistment in the wars of Eros:

> Let me be laid,
> Where I may see thy Glories from some shade.

(ll. 23–4)

The reading of 'laid ... shade' as an allusion to the grave has been proposed, defended, and attacked by various critics.[24] Certainly the traditional verbal associations are very strong, especially in conjunction with 'Glories'—'*I have seen the Glories of the world*' murmured Isaac Barrow on his death-bed,[25] making an exemplary seventeenth-century end. But although Marvell clearly has mortality on his mind in this poem, it is not obvious that he should, as it were, keep a watching brief on T.C.'s conquests from the grave itself. Perhaps he quietly mocks the persona of the superannuated lover-poet, gone to his eternal rest but still haunted by earthly beauty. Renaissance poetry is hardly lacking in graveyard perspectives on love. However, *this* poet may simply consider a contemplative retreat to be appropriate and graceful in the circumstances, surrendering himself to the 'shade', as in *Upon Appleton House* or *The Garden*, the more securely to contemplate the world's glories.

'Mean time' little T.C. is to practise on nature her powers of enchantment:

IV

Mean time, whilst every verdant thing
It self does at thy Beauty charm,
Reform the errours of the Spring;
Make that the Tulips may have share
Of sweetness, seeing they are fair;
And Roses of their thorns disarm:
But most procure
That Violets may a longer Age endure.

(ll. 25–32)

Just as the Nymph's fawn 'seem'd to bless/Its self in [her]' (*The Nymph complaining*, ll. 43–4), so all green things charm themselves—realise their own beauty—in and at little T.C.'s.[26] Nevertheless this beauty is imperfect, as the child herself, for all her innocence, is morally imperfect by reason of original sin. She is asked to assume an impossible responsibility for reforming a fallen earth.[27] For Maria in *Upon Appleton House* such grace is effortlessly exercised, as she turns her world into a paradise just by passing through it.[28] For little T.C. it is not so simple. In the first stanza, the child's instruction of the flowers was touched by pastoral make-believe, and her powers of organisation and selection were not unduly taxed. Undoing the effects of the Fall, reforming 'the errours of the Spring', is categorically different. It is possible for human beings to alter plant species by acting upon nature, as the Mower bitterly observes in *The Mower against Gardens*, but not to change the fundamental reality of a world that always falls short of the ideal.[29] In any case, little T.C.'s creative powers are less operative in action than in the transforming imagination. She is taught to imagine perfection; and again she learns her lesson in awareness through the flowers. To begin with, she was concerned only with degrees of pleasure, but now she is made to confront the knowledge that the life of beauty and pleasure is irrevocably flawed. Tulips deceive, roses draw blood, violets die. Emblematically, these flowers are chosen to correspond to different kinds of 'errour': the rose offers pleasure inseparable from pain, the tulip a meretricious beauty appealing to the eye but 'good for nothing', and the violet 'Beauty that must die'.[30] Because of their emblematic significance, the poet's naming of flowers has encouraged other allegorical readings of the stanza.[31] Since it is only in the inner garden that such errors can even begin to be reformed, little T.C.'s prospect of flowers may be both without and within. The traditional identification of the rose with woman's sexuality, opening itself to love but also 'fenc'd with prickles of a sharp denyall',[32] has led some readers to regard T.C. herself as the rose which needs to be disarmed. But this reading, relevant as it is to the sense of sexual threat in stanzas II and III, requires caution if it is not to unbalance the poem (and it applies less obviously to the rest of stanza IV). Marvell's concern is with the fallen condition as such, and with the shadow of transience that lies across the garden.

The final stanza is a reminder that little T.C. herself lives in that shadow. That is precisely why her choices, her actions, matter so much:

V

> But O young beauty of the Woods,
> Whom Nature courts with fruits and flow'rs,
> Gather the Flow'rs, but spare the Buds;
> Lest *Flora* angry at thy crime,
> To kill her Infants, in their prime,
> Do quickly make th'Example Yours;
>   And, ere we see,
> Nip in the blossome all our hopes and Thee.

(ll. 33–40)

The ultimate lesson for little T.C. is that her freedom even in her golden age is conditional. Like the Resolved Soul, she is courted by fruits and flowers, but while she is encouraged to respond innocently to Created Pleasure she is required to respect the divinity within nature as well as above nature. Marvell makes the point by adding a rider to the traditional *carpe florem* injunction: 'Gather the Flow'rs, but spare the Buds'.[33] Gathering flowers is a conventional image for both the life of pleasure and the life of action, but what is unconventional is the demand for restraint. Even within this charmed circle, this golden age, not everything is permitted. The buds and the child herself, with all that they represent of hope within the natural scheme of things, need to be under special protection. However, protection and destruction complement each other as aspects of power, whether human or divine. Here Marvell mediates the idea of divine power through the classical guise of Flora, who can also spare or destroy at will. From a human viewpoint, the infanticide analogy must be disturbing. As flowers to wanton girls are we to the gods...? Though the goddess Flora is said to kill in judicious anger, not for sport, that is scarcely reassuring. Tender-hearted readers may feel the need to rationalise their shock at such a clear-sighted—though far from pitiless—view of the child's mortality:[34] not because it is unrealistic, certainly not in terms of seventeenth-century statistics let alone the family history;[35] but because Marvell interprets little T.C.'s possible fate in the language of crime and punishment, at odds with the myth of childhood innocence which the lyric can be read as reinforcing. Yet it is this latter assumption that is at fault. In spite of the classical trappings, the poem's ending has a Puritan cast, particularly in the warning against plucking what is forbidden, and Puritans tend not to subscribe to the myth of childhood innocence.[36] The warning is as uncompromising as some of Bunyan's. For all his sense of its 'simplicity', Marvell does not sentimentalise childhood, in that he treats a child as a morally responsible being, capable of 'crime'. On the other hand, he does not overemphasise original sin, nor does he evince (here at least) an absolute distrust of natural instinct. He has already urged upon little T.C. a relationship with nature that is morally discriminating and at the same time deeply and instinctively pleasurable. Now he reminds her that sinful humanity has to relearn its lesson from Eden, that privilege means also responsibility and that responsibility means choice. The poem is held together by this principle.

The threefold life of contemplation, action, and pleasure is within the child's grasp in the garden if she chooses wisely; and she is watched over by the love of all those whose hopes centre on her and on what she symbolises. But, ironically, the same virtue that protects her childhood will alienate her from certain kinds of relationship in adulthood. Not all kinds of love and pleasure can enter a garden and flourish there. As the Mower poems demonstrate, Eros can have the power to destroy Flora through human agency.

(v) Love in a Landscape: The Mower Poems, Ametas and Thestylis making Hay-Ropes

The Mower poems, like the Folio itself, seem to be arranged in sequence. Indeed the sequence of movements resembles a musical form such as a sonata, with a prominent leitmotif and contrasts of mood and tempo within a single structure. (*Ametas and Thestylis making Hay-Ropes* could take the place of a coda.) Each of the four poems is metrically distinct: the Jonsonian elegiac distichs of *The Mower against Gardens*; the familiar eight-line stanza of *Damon the Mower*; the alternately rhymed quatrains of *The Mower to the Glo-worms*; and finally *The Mower's Song* with its unique scything refrain. Thematically the group is united by the dramatic irony which ensures that the Mower, who passes judgment on 'Luxurious Man' and fallen nature, himself falls and attempts to involve nature in 'one common Ruine'. Without each lyric in its place, Damon's drama would be incomplete.[1]

The Mower against Gardens

The first poem, *The Mower against Gardens*, states the theme from Damon's point of view. At this stage the speaker is as much against sex as he is against gardens, confusing the lascivious practice of both activities. His version of the *vita voluptuosa* immediately challenges seventeenth-century susceptibilities: although mowers might exemplify the traditional enemy of gardens, Time,[2] for this Mower to denounce gardening as a kind of refined brothel-keeping violates something sacred. True, the symbolic status of the garden varies, depending on what is being held sacred. If it is love of country, the garden is England; if it is woman, the garden is her face or body; if it is art, the garden is a poem; if it is the life of the spirit, the garden is the mind or soul.[3] But of course a garden may be sacred on its own account, simply because God created it so. Sir William Temple, writing in the 1680s, sums up a widely-held conviction as a self-evident truth:

> If we believe the Scripture, we must allow that God Almighty esteemed the life of a man in a garden the happiest He could give him, or else He would not have placed Adam in that of Eden; that it was a state of innocence and pleasure; and that the life of husbandry and cities came in after the Fall, with guilt and with labour.
>
> (*Upon the Gardens of Epicurus*)[4]

Powerful as this argument is in a theological age, its application in a fallen world could be controversial. On the one hand, the chorus of horticulturists who endorse it extend the state of innocence to the labour of husbandry, since Adam was placed in the garden to dress it and keep it (Genesis 2: 15). Writers such as Adolphus Speed, Abraham Cowley, and John Evelyn claim that gardening was God's choice of life for man, and direct their exhortations to *Adam out of Eden*.[5] On the other hand, the Catholic writer, Walter Montague, points out that after all God fenced off Eden after the Fall, and deduces 'That God did not expulse Man out of *Paradise*, to allow him the making another Paradise for himself out of the Earth'. This view, expressed in *Miscellanea Spiritualia* (1648), is supported by Thomas Vaughan in *Magia Adamica* (1650):[6]

> For if God had excluded him from *Eden*, and Continued the *Earth* in her *Primitive Glories*, he had but turned him out of *one Paradise* into *Another*, wherefore he fits the *Dungeon* to the *Slave*, and sends a *Corruptible Man* into *a Corruptible World*.

For many seventeenth-century enthusiasts, however, making another paradise out of the earth remains the highest justification of gardening, and it is this position that Marvell's Mower challenges.

In the first place, he cuts the ground from under the theological defence by giving a highly idiosyncratic slant to the myth of nature's fall (in effect, he says, it didn't fall, it was pushed):

> Luxurious Man, to bring his Vice in use,
>   Did after him the World seduce:
> And from the fields the Flow'rs and Plants allure,
>   Where Nature was most plain and pure.
>
> (ll. 1–4)

In the second place, by destroying the presumed innocence of gardening, he contaminates the pleasure of the garden itself:

> He first enclos'd within the Gardens square
>   A dead and standing pool of Air:
> And a more luscious Earth for them did knead,
>   Which stupifi'd them while it fed.
>
> (ll. 5–8)

The villains are the improvers and planners, often represented in Marvell's poetry by the figure of the architect (the pejorative phrase, 'standing pool of Air', has been traced to Sir Henry Wotton's *The Elements of Architecture*, first published in 1624).[7] Yet although the air is dead, the plants continue to exist in a drugged half-life, ripe for exploitation:

> The Pink grew then as double as his Mind;
>   The nutriment did change the kind.
> With strange perfumes he did the Roses taint.
>   And Flow'rs themselves were taught to paint.
> The Tulip, white, did for complexion seek;
>   And learn'd to interline its cheek:

Its Onion root they then so high did hold,
That one was for a Meadow sold.

(ll. 9–16)

Marvell does not choose the flowers at random. The tulip and rose appear together as fallen flowers in *Little T.C.*; and the wildly fashionable and expensive tulip in particular is a target for contemporary disapproval, because of the Dutch tulipomania of the 1630s.[8] It becomes an emblem of worthless beauty, 'Neither for *Physick* good, nor *Smell*, nor *Tast*' (Cowley), at the bottom of Jeremy Taylor's list of flowers—he 'had rather see Time and Roses, Marjoram and Julyflowers, that are fair and sweet and medicinal, then the prettiest Tulips, that are good for nothing'.[9] The disappointed lover of James Shirley's *The Garden* associates tulips with the artificial garden he rejects, bitterly describing them as behaving like flirtatious women—

> This Garden does not take my eyes,
> Though here you shew how art of men
> Can purchase Nature at a price
> Would stock old Paradise agen.
>
> ...
>
> Those Tulips that such wealth display,
> To court my eye, shall lose their name,
> Though now they listen, as if they
> Expected I should praise their flame.

(ll. 1–4 and 13–16)[10]

It is a short step to typecasting the tulip as the painted harlot of the garden, and this puts a figuratively different complexion on their appeal. More generally, the overvaluing of tulips stands for the wrong approach to garden pleasures. When Sir Thomas Browne warns that 'In Garden Delights 'tis not easie to hold a Mediocrity; that insinuating pleasure is seldome without some extremity' and gives illustrations of those who love gardens not wisely but too well, he notes '*Cato* seemed to dote upon Cabbadge; While the Ingenuous delight of Tulipists stands saluted with hard language, even by their own Professors'.[11]

Other writers besides Browne feel it necessary to distinguish between garden lovers and garden fanatics, between self-improvement and self-indulgence. Justus Lipsius makes his mentor, Langius, castigate plant collectors 'who take the death of one of these *New Flowers* more to heart, then of one of their *Old friends*'; he also discriminates between sensual sloth and spiritual recreation, despising those idle persons who 'onely *sit, walke, gape*, and *sleep*' in their gardens.[12] Nor has Evelyn any time for the lazy pleasure-seeker, briskly dismissing the notion that the garden life should be valued because of the 'ease and opportunity which ministers to *volupty*': on the contrary, 'there is not amongst *Men* a more laborious life then is that of a good *Gard'ners;* but a labour ... such as (if any) contributes to *Piety* and

Contemplation...'.[13] The pleasures of the garden life can more easily be defended when they are subsumed into either the contemplative life or the active life. And like Renaissance apologists for poetry, apologists for gardens rest their case on the distinction between use and abuse.

Marvell's Mower admits no such distinction. He is an absolutist, rejecting all gardens as a travesty of nature marked out by sexual malfunction. Man might grudgingly be allowed his 'Rarities' such as the Marvel of Peru (so named by Parkinson in 1629),[14] since he had been originally invested with the overlordship of the natural creation (ll. 17–20), but arbitrary interference with the sex life of plants goes beyond the biblical limits:[15]

> Had he not dealt between the Bark and Tree,
>   Forbidden mixtures there to see.
> No Plant now knew the Stock from which it came;
>   He grafts upon the Wild the Tame:
> That the uncertain and adult'rate fruit
>   Might put the Palate in dispute.
> His green *Seraglio* has its Eunuchs too;
>   Lest any Tyrant him out-doe.
> And in the Cherry he does Nature vex,
>   To procreate without a Sex.

(ll. 21–30)

Other writers use grafting as a sexual metaphor;[16] Marvell, while retaining its full metaphoric force, makes it literal. Although disquiet over sophisticated grafting processes was no new phenomenon, ancient authorities on horticulture were also fascinated by the multiple possibilities of the new garden technology. As well as Pliny, Columella and Palladius go into the subject in considerable detail, and in the seventeenth century Gervase Markham describes the method of propagation apparently alluded to by Marvell.[17] The allusion is highly specialised, but the implications go further than turning flowers into prostitutes and cherry-trees into eunuchs. The basic human drives towards pleasure and power are held responsible for destroying self-respect and respect for all other living things. In condemning grafting, the Mower is not merely condemning man's projection of his own voluptuousness on to the garden, but exposing the perversion of that voluptuousness with regard to his own species. The gardener's activities are those of a pander,[18] his pleasures those of a sultan: the 'green *Seraglio*' parodies a mechanical dehumanising form of eroticism, sex as experiment or exploitation, not as an expression of love.

The image of man the gardener dealing between the bark and tree will be ironically re-enacted by Damon the Mower, cutting between earth and root. But the speaker of *The Mower against Gardens* does not recognise the irony lying in wait. In fact, he does not identify himself within the poem. Were it not for the title, the only clue to his precise occupation would be his choice of life in the neglected 'sweet Fields' and meadows. Here, he believes, is an unspoilt innocence to set against the perverted pleasures of the garden:

'Tis all enforc'd; the Fountain and the Grot;
While the sweet Fields do lye forgot:
Where willing Nature does to all dispence
A wild and fragrant Innocence:
And *Fauns* and *Faryes* do the Meadows till,
More by their presence then their skill.

(ll. 31–6)

Willing nature as opposed to enforced nature: the epithets are both sexual and political,[19] invoking the myth of a paradise or golden age when everything is freely given and received. The problem of cultivation or control, the need for labour,[20] is gracefully evaded in the fauns and fairies who bring pleasure and beauty simply by being—or by being believed in. The fairies in particular, who reappear in *Damon the Mower* (ll. 61–4), are readily politicised in mid-seventeenth century England just because of their association with a vanished age of innocence. 'There never was a merry World since the *Fairies* left Dancing', said John Selden, and he was not alone in his sentiment.[21] Farewell rewards and fairies: but Marvell's Mower claims that they are still to be found, if sought in the right place. The reader who patronises him for his superstition runs the risk of underestimating the powerful feeling he evokes.

Native nostalgia is reinforced by a version of the classical commonplace, that the gods themselves make their choice of life a pastoral one:[22]

Their Statues polish'd by some ancient hand,
May to adorn the Gardens stand:
But howso'ere the Figures do excel,
The *Gods* themselves with us do dwell.

(ll. 37–40)

Like 'the Fountain and the Grot', statues of pagan deities were a feature of European gardens in the Italianate style, and an easy target for the Mower's polemical distinction between art and nature.[23] While conceding that art may 'excel' in its own context, he refutes the Lipsian idea that the garden is 'the *only* seat of *Venus*, and the *Graces*'.[24] His own claim, however, is dangerously hubristic, and in the following Mower poems the advent of a deity unforeseen and all-powerful will bring him to disaster. And yet: although his choice may be deeply biased, fallible, and about to be compromised, the life he chooses does have enduring value as a source of pleasure, if only as a literary fiction. This becomes all the more apparent when his meadow paradise turns into a paradise lost.

Damon the Mower

In *Damon the Mower*, as the title reveals, the occupation which was excluded or suppressed in *The Mower against Gardens* is brought into the foreground, and the reasons for Marvell's unusual choice of pastoral protagonist become clearer.[25] Damon, named for the first time, is much preoccupied with his own identity. As is common in pastoral, though for shepherds rather than mowers, his experience of unhappy love connects on the one hand with the nature of his work and on the other with the landscape itself:

I

> Heark how the Mower *Damon* Sung,
> With love of *Juliana* stung!
> While ev'ry thing did seem to paint
> The Scene more fit for his complaint.
> Like her fair Eyes the day was fair;
> But scorching like his am'rous Care.
> Sharp like his Sythe his Sorrow was,
> And wither'd like his Hopes the Grass.

(ll. 1–8)

But where the narrator uses simile, Damon will collapse the comparisons into metaphor. His emblematic scythe joins his labour to his pain (l. 68), as well as marking him out as an avatar of Time and Death. *A Mower*, observes Wye Saltonstall,[26]

> Is one that barbes the overgrowne fields, and cuts off the greene lockes of the meddowes. Hee walkes like the Embleme of Tyme, with a Sith upon his backe, and when he cuts the grasse, hee shewes the brevity of mans life, which commeth forth like a flower, and is cut downe.

Like Marvell, Saltonstall merges the figurative and the functional and his mower too is active enough to sweat from his exertions, 'He stands in a bending posture, and so fetching a compasse stroake, sweepes downe the grasse before him, while the sweat seemes to spring in his forehead.' But the conclusion effaces the character with the season, in a final reminder of mutability: 'Lastly, he comes in with the two months of Iune, and Iuly, and when they are done. He is never thought on till next yeare'.

Not surprisingly, poets tend to find mowing a melancholy spectacle:

> Ay me, ay me! I sigh to see the scythe a-field;
> 　Down goeth the grass, soon wrought to withered hay:
> Ay me, alas! ay me, alas! that beauty needs must yield,
> 　And princes pass, as grass doth fade away.

(Thomas Proctor?)[27]

All the more so when they write as lovers: in Aurelian Townshend's beautiful *A Dialogue betwixt Time and a Pilgrime* the lover dreads that the aged mower may chance to cut down his love's lily before his own stalk 'in some Thistle or some spyre of grasse'.[28] When, as in Marvell's pastoral, the lover *is* a mower, then all he can do is to cut down himself.

But that is to anticipate. Damon's occupation is initially important because he (like the gardener) is man acting upon nature and in relationship with it, a relationship which is prior to his relationship with woman and which shapes the meaning of his existence. He begins his complaint by concentrating on the present state of nature on which he projects his disordered emotions:

II

> Oh what unusual Heats are here,
> Which thus our Sun-burn'd Meadows sear!
> The Grass-hopper its pipe gives ore;
> And hamstring'd Frogs can dance no more.
> But in the brook the green Frog wades;
> And Grass-hoppers seek out the shades.
> Only the Snake, that kept within,
> Now glitters in its second skin.

(ll. 9–16)

There is precedent for this intolerable heat in Virgil's Second Eclogue, where Corydon's psychic state finds a parallel in the normal temperature of a Mediterranean summer which drives all creatures to the shade except the heat-loving cicadas.[29] But in the English lyric the abnormal heat wave catches the meadow creatures literally on the hop. They too have their literary identity, the grasshopper as the singer celebrating ephemeral joys—'Epicuræan Animal!'—and even the humble frog, which the Greek poet also associates with the life of pastoral pleasure.[30] Their retreat from the meadows is a comic anomaly, for this is the season when pleasure should be at its height: instead of nymphs and shepherds, it is frogs who dance no more.[31] Damon, himself a singer and dancer, should take warning. But nature's creatures, unlike him, can find natural succour in water and shade. Ominously, the only being that actually flourishes in the sun's full glare is the snake, turning Damon's world into an ironic 'True Paradise' like Donne's *Twicknam Garden*.[32] The innuendo locates the source of the trouble—woman.

III

> This heat the Sun could never raise,
> Nor Dog-star so inflame's the dayes.
> It from an higher Beauty grow'th,
> Which burns the Fields and Mower both:
> Which mads[33] the Dog, and makes the Sun
> Hotter then his own *Phaeton.*
> Not *July* causeth these Extremes,
> But *Juliana's* scorching beams.

(ll. 17–24)

The convention that Marvell is adapting here is sometimes called pastoral hyperbole, and is rooted in a myth of power: the beloved's presence brings the spring season, his or her absence brings winter.[34] But this power can be abused, particularly if the relation between human and natural beauty is seen as essentially competitive. In Cavalier poetry, the mistress's presence darkens the sun, banishes inferior flowers, charms not the birds but the leaves off the trees, so substituting autumn for an expected spring.[35] In such beauty contests, Nature invariably loses. Marvell makes the compliment to Juliana's powers, refracted as it is through Damon's distorting consciousness, an even more back-handed one. Instead of resuscitating crippled plants and gracefully withdrawing when her beauty threatens to become too much for them (like Cleveland's Phillis), Juliana exercises an influence which is almost entirely baleful. Her regime is not merely unnatural but anti-nature. Her effects are madness and loss of control. The mesmerised Mower can see no retreat:

IV

Tell me where I may pass the Fires
Of the hot day, or hot desires.
To what cool Cave shall I descend,
Or to what gelid Fountain bend?
Alas! I look for Ease in vain,
When Remedies themselves complain.
No moisture but my Tears do rest,
Nor Cold but in her Icy Breast.

(ll. 25–32)

His helpless rhetorical question recalls *Clorinda and Damon*, where cave and fountain are images of pleasure sternly challenged by his namesake.[36] But the very fact that the question is rhetorical suggests that this Damon has abandoned any idea of choosing. He does not perceive his pastoral landscape as offering either the satisfaction of desire or a contemplative refuge from desire; he can only transmute it into the weary conceits of the courtly lover. For the Mower the natural world is no longer an all-sufficient choice of life.

Yet, as the following stanzas show, it might have been. In V and VI, Damon develops a distinctively pastoral persona as giver and receiver of gifts. As giver, he inherits a tradition first established by Theocritus' Cyclops and Virgil's Corydon, and transmitted through Marlowe's Passionate Shepherd and a host of others.[37] Damon tries their method of seducing the recalcitrant beloved with pastoral gifts, and is conspicuously unsuccessful:

V

How long wilt Thou, fair Shepheardess,
Esteem me, and my Presents less?
To Thee the harmless Snake I bring,
Disarmed of its teeth and sting.
To Thee *Chameleons* changing-hue,
And Oak leaves tipt with hony due.
Yet Thou ungrateful hast not sought

Nor what they are, nor who them brought.

(ll. 33–40)

Admittedly, his chosen catalogue makes Juliana's ingratitude more understandable.[38] Although the oak leaves distilling honey are straight out of Ovid's Golden Age, the disarmed snake and the inconstant chameleon hardly typify prelapsarian sexual bliss. If these are emblems of the life of pleasure, they are ambiguous rather than innocent. It is only in the next stanza, when Damon solemnly offers his credentials, that he evokes the meadow life glimpsed in *The Mower against Gardens*, with its 'wild and fragrant Innocence'.

VI

I am the Mower *Damon*, known
Through all the Meadows I have mown.
On me the Morn her dew distills
Before her darling Daffadils.
And, if at Noon my toil me heat,
The Sun himself licks off my Sweat.
While, going home, the Ev'ning sweet
In cowslip-water bathes my feet.

(ll. 41–8)

Here Damon is not the giver, but the receiver of nature's gifts. Partly because of the presence of the Cyclops and Corydon in the literary middle distance, some readers find the Mower's pretensions throughout the poem absurdly narcissistic, even grotesque. But it depends on perspective, and Marvell's perspectives are notoriously adjustable. Is Damon hopelessly naïve, or is his folly a kind of natural wisdom? Is his description of his privileged relationship with a willing and gracious nature responsive to his every need pure wish-fulfilment, a compensation for sexual failure? Or does it reflect a true pleasure far superior to '*Juliana's* scorching beams'? We do not have to exclude either possibility. On the one hand, Damon exaggerates in taking such attentions as his personal due. It is already clear from *The Mower against Gardens* that he is guilty of spiritual pride, the sin by which the angels fell; to that is added inordinate sexual passion, the sin by which Adam fell. Marvell colours these lyrics with the imagination of the Fall,[39] but Damon is spiritually colour-blind and does not recognise or accept his own fallen nature. Yet, on the other hand, there is a remnant of unfallen innocence in his very belief in natural beneficence. If he is not exempt from the consequences of the Fall, at least he can take comfort from the notion that the sweat of his brow, the sign of the curse, is licked off by 'the Sun himself'. Besides, the solace of morning dew and cowslip-water is real and tangible, nature's own beauty aids, however incongruous their application may seem.[40] Damon thinks he knows how to value such pleasures; but there is an irony in his use of the historic present tense. The natural paradise to which he feels himself entitled is already lost to him, its dews dried up by the drought of passion. Significantly, the flowers that he names are the flowers of the past spring.[41] Yet, whatever happens to the Mower himself, the pastoral life of pleasure endures, with its daily and seasonal beauties and compensations.

Although Damon has attempted to arrogate nature's benefits to impress his mistress, he does reluctantly acknowledge the existence of his rival the shepherd, if only to belittle his claims:

VII

What, though the piping Shepherd stock
The plains with an unnum'red Flock,
This Sithe of mine discovers wide
More ground then all his Sheep do hide.
With this the golden fleece I shear
Of all these Closes ev'ry Year.
And though in Wooll more poor then they,
Yet am I richer far in Hay.

(ll. 49–56)

It is understandable that the Mower, comparing his own calling to that of the shepherd, should present mowing as a constructive activity, as another more magical kind of shearing. He imagines himself not as a rustic clown but as a hero like Jason of the Golden Fleece (though the story of Jason, with his disastrous marriage and possible suicide, is hardly a hopeful portent). With this image, he claims a role in the world of action. But the discourse of the active life is usually at variance with pastoral discourse, and in trying to compete with the shepherd as a producer of wealth Damon seems to have an imperfect grasp of the unworldly pastoral ideal which he was defending in *The Mower against Gardens*. Mowing is neither as harmless nor as heroic as his analogy asserts. Later in the poem the analogy breaks down, and the language recalls the active life in its grimmest aspect: he no longer shears but slaughters.

Meanwhile, however, stanza VIII completes a triptych of the Mower's self-portraits, as he contemplates his own reflection:

VIII

Nor am I so deform'd to sight,
If in my Sithe I looked right;
In which I see my Picture done,
As in a crescent Moon the Sun.

(ll. 57–60)

At this point the Virgilian echo—*informis*/'deform'd'—is heard most clearly.[42] The visual image is, characteristically, a mirror-image, an enchanted glass that distorts what it reflects. Damon cannot look 'right' in a crooked scythe: the crescent moon reflects only a sliver of the sun. And since Damon's scythe symbolises and puns upon his self-absorbed sorrow,[43] it follows that unhappy love destroys the true image of the self. Yet Damon may be deluded about his own worth and still possess the artist's vision:

> The deathless Fairyes take me oft
> To lead them in their Danses soft;
> And, when I tune my self to sing,
> About me they contract their Ring.
>
> (ll. 61–4)

The numinous description acts as a reminder that the pastoral world remains a perfect setting for Pleasure and the Graces.[44] To see only the Mower's self-aggrandisement and superstition is to underrate his moments of lyrical insight which make his dreams a kind of truth. He fails to sustain the pastoral ideal he creates for himself, not because the ideal of communion with nature is a total illusion, but because it cannot survive the emotional obsession which fatally, and in the end literally, unbalances him.

Damon turns everything around him into an emblem of his pain, but the change is in himself:

> IX
>
> How happy might I still have mow'd,
> Had not Love here his Thistles sow'd!
> But now I all the day complain,
> Joyning my Labour to my Pain;
> And with my Sythe cut down the Grass,
> Yet still my Grief is where it was:
> But, when the Iron blunter grows,
> Sighing I whet my Sythe and Woes.
>
> (ll. 65–72)

'Thistles' again hints at the contrast between paradise and a fallen earth (Genesis 3: 18), and the iron metaphorically enters the Mower's soul (*The Book of Common Prayer*, Psalm 105: 18)[45] as it will literally enter his ankle:

> X
>
> While thus he threw his Elbow round,
> Depopulating all the Ground,
> And, with his whistling Sythe, does cut
> Each stroke between the Earth and Root,
> The edged Stele by careless chance
> Did into his own Ankle glance;
> And there among the Grass fell down,
> By his own Sythe, the Mower mown.
>
> (ll. 73–80)

The switch to the narrator's voice permits a slightly callous humour, and also sharpens the sense of what has *happened* to Damon. Unlike the love-smitten shepherd of pastoral convention, he does not neglect his occupation:[46] on the contrary, he pursues it more energetically if more carelessly. But his relationship with nature, or how he perceives that relationship, has fundamentally altered. The crucial word 'Depopulating' turns him into its tyrant and destroyer. The activity does not change, but its meaning does (the fact that the meaning was always latent increases the irony). The ultimate, cruelly comic, irony is that he is part of nature and that in cutting between earth and root he cuts down himself. The Mower mown, like the mocker mocked, is a brilliant much-praised image of reversal and alienation.[47] And the appropriate instrument is the scythe, representing the pain and potency of love, which brings about his mock 'fall'. It is love that exposes Damon to Fate, 'careless chance' not choice. Yet like Marvell's other lovers confronting the power of Fate he has still a choice of attitude, which he articulates in the last stanza.

Et in Arcadia ego, I also am in Arcadia, says Death;[48] and Damon ends by saluting his fellow-Mower:

XI

Alas! said He, these hurts are slight
To those that dye by Loves despight.
With Shepherds-purse, and Clowns-all-heal,
The Blood I stanch, and Wound I seal.
Only for him no Cure is found,
Whom *Julianas* Eyes do wound.
'Tis death alone that this must do:
For Death thou art a Mower too.

(ll. 81–8)

He can be stoical about natural misadventure, for which natural remedies exist (the efficacy of the plants he names is on record in Gerard's *Herball*).[49] Even in this extremity, nature offers a support system, comforting and healing, ameliorating the physical ills humanity is heir to since the Fall. But nature, at least in Damon's view, has no remedy for the effects of love which divides the self and alienates man from the universe. Damon's unrequited passion has separated him from the harmonious rhythms of his natural existence. Whereas in Virgil's Second Eclogue the shepherd's complaint is reintegrated with pastoral harmony as evening falls, there is not the same poetic closure in *Damon the Mower*.[50] But there is a recognition. Unlike Corydon, the Mower has no choice of life remaining—pleasure, contemplation and action have all failed him—but he does have a choice of death which he duly makes. Death, not nature, is finally acknowledged as his ally and refuge.

The Mower to the Glo-Worms

The Mower to the Glo-Worms continues the argument that nature cannot minister to a mind displaced, but with a variation that refreshes the subject, like the transition from the glare of noon to a summer night. This brief nocturne which separates the two complaint poems modulates their tone into a gentler, more self-effacing grief: the structure delays despair, and the skilled lyric phrasing soothes the ear. In contrast with the feverish human activity thrust on the reader's attention in the other Mower poems, here the natural creation is 'shining, or singing'[51] in serene contemplation:

I

Ye living Lamps, by whose dear light
The Nightingale does sit so late,
And studying all the Summer-night,
Her matchless Songs does meditate...

(ll. 1–4)

In *The Mower against Gardens* and *Damon the Mower* it was the human being who was the artist, for better or worse. Here nature supplies a supreme artist of her own, traditionally the nightingale. In a perfect image of the contemplative life, the nightingale becomes the wandering scholar of the woods, burning the glow-worms' midnight oil as she meditates her songs.

The glow-worms themselves are, according to Pliny, surrogate stars.[52] Not only do they serve a practical purpose as a sign of the seasons; but they also serve a contemplative purpose, arousing wonder at the mystery of the heavens. Sir Thomas Browne loses himself in this particular mystery:

> Now whether the light of animals, which do not occasionally shine from contingent causes, be of Kin unto the light of Heaven; whether the invisible flame of life received in a convenient matter, may not become visible, and the diffused ætherial light make little Stars by conglobation in idoneous parts of the *compositum;* whether also it may not have some original in the seed and spirit analogous unto the Element of Stars, whereof some glympse is observable in the little refulgent humor, at the first attempts of formation; Philosophy may yet enquire.[53]

The wonder that Browne spins out into the web of a complicated prose sentence Marvell wraps up in the cocoon of a phrase, 'Country Comets':

II

Ye Country Comets, that portend
No War, nor Princes funeral,
Shining unto no higher end
Then to presage the Grasses fall...

(ll. 5–8)

The belief in comets as portents of great and disastrous events in history is familiar: 'When beggars die, there are no comets seen;/The heavens themselves blaze forth the death of princes' (*Julius Caesar*, II. ii. 30–1).[54] Marvell is using the rhetorical trick, a favourite of Milton's, of associating ideas by explicitly dissociating them. By excluding heroic death from the pastoral world, he recalls to us that all flesh is grass.[55] Although 'Country Comets' may register a comfortingly small scale of significance on a first reading, on further reflection it becomes one of Marvell's especially resonant phrases. These omens are innocent, the hay harvests recur yearly; but human experience encompasses a world where omens are not innocent, and finality has to be accepted.

Nevertheless, nature offers 'long wandered man'[56] beauty, service, and protection:

III

> Ye Glo-worms, whose officious Flame
> To wandring Mowers shows the way,
> That in the Night have lost their aim,
> And after foolish Fires do stray...

(ll. 9–12)

The 'foolish Fires', *ignes fatui* or will-o'-the-wisp, are described by John Smith, the Cambridge Platonist:

> those foolish fires that fetch their birth from terrene exudations, that doe but hop up & down, and flit to and fro upon the surface of this earth. serve not so much to enlighten, as to delude us; nor to direct the wandring traveller into his way, but to lead him farther out of it.[57]

In contrasting these with the officiously helpful glow-worms that guide the mowers back to the true path, Marvell creates a country parable. Other seventeenth-century lyric poets might use glow-worm imagery in a context of love and pleasure: Herrick's *The Night-piece, to Julia*, for instance, begins 'Her Eyes the Glow-worme lend thee', and places his mistress, not errant mowers, under the magical protection of the night-creatures ('No *Will-o'th'-Wispe* mis-light thee').[58] Herrick anticipates a lovers' meeting at the end of the journey: not so Marvell.

The Mower to the Glo-Worms ends with irredeemable loss and exile, touched with a deeper spiritual meaning:

IV

> Your courteous Lights in vain you wast,
> Since *Juliana* here is come,
> For She my Mind hath so displac'd
> That I shall never find my home.

(ll. 13–16)

Damon is so disorientated by passion that 'home'—natural or spiritual—is lost to him for ever. There can be no paradise within when man has lost his integrity of mind, and after the transition from innocence to experience there is no return to a natural paradise either. In *Damon the Mower* Juliana brought unnatural heat; here she is the false light that distracts the Mower from what Jeremy Taylor calls 'the little images of beauty and pleasure'. As her devotee, Damon might wish to emulate Taylor's worshipper who easily forsakes the object of his devotion:

> so long as the light shines bright, and the fires of devotion, and desires flame out, so long the mind of a man stands close to the altar ... but as the fires die and desires decay, so the mind steals away and walks abroad to see the little images of beauty and pleasure, which it beholds in the falling stars and little glow-wormes of the world.[59]

Damon cannot escape from or renounce his desires so easily. Instead, his feeling for natural beauty, still intense, is poisoned at its source. Having fallen himself, he becomes obsessed with 'the Grasses fall' to the point where he turns it into a ritual sacrifice.

The Mower's Song

The Mower's Song completes the cycle. It enacts the pastoral equivalent of sophisticated man's corruption of nature in *The Mower against Gardens*; it is also the last act in the drama of *Damon the Mower*, and the fulfilment of the omens in *The Mower to the Glo-Worms*. When Damon resumes his complaint at the beginning of *The Mower's Song* he is not simply repeating himself, for he has recast his drama as a revenge tragedy (a point made in one of the most perceptive criticisms of the poem).[60] Nature, the discarded lover, becomes the betrayer. Moreover, his retrospect on their lost relationship, continuing the emphasis on 'Mind' at the end of *The Mower to the Glo-Worms*, is in a more contemplative vein than before:

I

> My Mind was once the true survey
> Of all these Medows fresh and gay;
> And in the greenness of the Grass
> Did see its Hopes as in a Glass;
> When *Juliana* came, and She
> What I do to the Grass, does to my Thoughts and Me.

(ll. 1–6)

Behind this account lies a concept of the ideal relation of the mind to external reality which is similarly expressed in *The Garden*. For the true contemplative, this relation is reflective in every sense: 'the truth of being and the truth of knowing are one'.[61] In Damon's case, the truth of eeling might be substituted for the truth of knowing, since what the meadows reflect are his 'Hopes' (appropriately, for green in the emblem-books is the colour of Hope).[62] Hopes of love? Hopes of Salvation? Hopes of the millennium? Or simply the state of undifferentiated youthful hope, a state of unconscious and anticipatory joy aptly imaged in a spring meadow? Whatever its object, some readers will equate hope with delusion and argue that Damon's 'true survey' was never true in any verifiable sense.[63] All along he sees in the meadows what he chooses to see, distorting them in the enchanted glass of his mind, which only he believes is a clear mirror. And yet: even if Damon's claim to an original correspondence between himself and nature is egotistic and exaggerated, it still aspires to a contemplative ideal. It is the business of the contemplative mind to discover correspondences, to recreate the world in language and metaphor. When the reflection is blurred and broken by emotional disorder, then the correspondence breaks down, and the human being is divided both from nature and from the self ('my Thoughts and Me').

Damon recognises that a divorce has taken place, but blames it on the innocent party:

II

But these, while I with Sorrow pine,
Grew more luxuriant still and fine;
That not one Blade of Grass you spy'd,
But had a Flower on either side;
When *Juliana* came, and She
What I do to the Grass, does to my Thoughts and Me.

III

Unthankful Medows, could you so
A fellowship so true forego,
And in your gawdy May-games meet,
While I lay trodden under feet?
When *Juliana* came, and She
What I do to the Grass, does to my Thoughts and Me.

(ll. 7–18)

In his view, the meadows flaunt their luxuriance and fineness—the choice of words brings his accusation ironically close to his indictment of gardens, which also had sexual overtones.[64] As for 'gawdy May-games' in the next stanza, 'gaudy' with its Latin connotations of festive rejoicing[65] underscores his awareness that the pastoral life of pleasure is going on without him. It is conventional in lyric poetry for a lover to lament the discrepancy between his mood of dark despair and the uncaring springtime world:[66] the Mower is unusual in having the means of doing something about it. He resorts to action to restore the metaphoric correspondence between himself and the grass.[67]

The reiterated deadening sweep of the refrain[68] insists on the further correspondence between what man does to nature and what woman does to man. The change in the last two stanzas of the poem from 'When *Juliana* came' to 'For *Juliana* comes' marks a subtle shift from narrative past tense to present justification.

Damon decides, in effect, 'to bring his Vice in use', to involve the whole world—his world—in his fall:[69]

IV

But what you in Compassion ought,
Shall now by my Revenge be wrought:
And Flow'rs, and Grass, and I and all,
Will in one common Ruine fall.
For *Juliana* comes, and She
What I do to the Grass, does to my Thoughts and Me.

(ll. 19–24)

However the relationship between man and nature defines itself, through pleasure, contemplation, or action, in Damon's eyes it should be fundamentally indissoluble. From the beginning until the end of time, man's mortal being is locked into the natural creation. And so the Mower envisages their common destiny, paralleling past and future, fall and apocalypse:[70]

V

And thus, ye Meadows, which have been
Companions of my thoughts more green,
Shall now the Heraldry become
With which I shall adorn my Tomb;
For *Juliana* comes, and She
What I do to the Grass, does to my Thoughts and Me.

(ll. 25–30)

The 'solution' of turning violent love or grief into a permanent art form is Marvell's familiar mode of poetic closure, but here more than ever it seems to represent a kind of failure. In forcing the meadows to conform to the lover's state, Damon deprives them of all their essential qualities of life and growth and greenness. Withered grass is a singularly futile heraldic device, merging as it does into the surrounding landscape. In the end, Damon chooses neither life nor eternity, but oblivion. As Wye Saltonstall puts it, once the meadows are mown and July over, the Mower 'is never thought on till next yeare.'[71] For Damon, there will be no next year.

He began the cycle by deriding those garden-lovers who mistake the source of true pleasure, but he ends by being false to his own imaginative integrity, wantonly destroying his recognised source of pleasure and contemplation. And he has gained nothing in return, not even an idea of love and beauty powerful enough to explain his obsession. Although Juliana is conventionally taken to symbolise such an idea, the emotional pressure of the poetry is against her. Instead of the mistress being at the centre, Damon's relationship with nature occupies the true centre of interest. Like Adam, to whom he is so frequently compared, Damon loses his paradise through a woman; or, more precisely, through choosing to set a woman in place of his original deity. He sees himself as victim, yet he is not an unwitting victim, since he recognises the value of what he has lost. What that is we find more fully unfolded in Marvell's poem of restored harmony between man and nature in the absence of woman, *The Garden*. Meanwhile, the Mower group contains possibly his finest ironic commentary on the incompatibility between love of nature and love of woman.

Ametas and Thestylis making Hay-Ropes

In the next lyric in the Folio, however, the attitudes of the Mower poems are in turn delightfully mocked: love and nature are not incompatible. Ametas and Thestylis, whose dialogue this is, find a better use for hay than as an adornment for a tomb. Yet it is evident from the outset that the course of their pastoral love has not run smooth:

I

Ametas

Think'st Thou that this Love can stand,
Whilst Thou still dost say me nay?
Love unpaid does soon disband:
Love binds Love as Hay binds Hay.

(ll. 1–4)

As in the Mower poems, the rustic occupation—in this case making ropes of hay—becomes an emblem for love, but a debatable emblem. Ametas argues for reciprocal pleasure on the grounds that 'Love binds Love as Hay binds Hay'; Thestylis mischievously maintains that just as strands of a rope must be twisted in opposite directions if it is to hold, so the spirit of opposition is the essence of love (a creed advanced elsewhere in Marvell's love poetry):[72]

II

Thestylis

Think'st Thou that this Rope would twine
If we both should turn one way?
Where both parties so combine,
Neither Love will twist nor Hay.

(ll. 5–8)

If Damon had been allowed a dialogue with Juliana in place of his gloomy monologues, she might have made much the same point. But Damon and Juliana are not on the same social or occupational level, unlike Ametas and Thestylis, and Ametas is shrewder in the ways of women than Damon. He retorts that Thestylis is delaying pleasure for no good reason, since in any case love is a looser constraint on a woman's mind than a hay-rope (ll. 9–12).

Thestylis immediately takes advantage of this sexist—or sexually liberated—assumption, tossing the choice back to her partner:

IV

Thestylis

What you cannot constant hope
Must be taken as you may.

(ll. 13–14)

In a breath she blows lightly away all emotional constraints, the hopes that turn into despair for other Marvellian lovers, the oppressive awareness of the future that conditions their choice or deprives them of choice altogether. And Ametas completes the quatrain:

V

Ametas

Then let's both lay by our Rope,
And go kiss within the Hay.

(ll. 15–16)

This sharing of the last quatrain between the two speakers neatly signifies their concord, as does the pun on 'Hay' which is also the name of a country dance ending in the exchange of kisses.[73]

So the poem ends happily, with the emblematic hay-rope discarded, and the pastoral lovers about to take their pleasure in a manner more Shakespearean than Marvellian (their dialogue is as light-hearted as Autolycus's bird-songs, those 'summer songs for me and my aunts,/ While we lie tumbling in the hay').[74] This little lyric celebrates a rare, perhaps a unique, moment of unshadowed sexual pleasure in Marvell's poetry. Its sunlit frivolity allows a pause for relaxation, rounding off the Folio sequence not just of the Mower poems but of all the poems concerned with love. These began with persuasion and end with invitation. In *Ametas and Thestylis making Hay-Ropes* Marvell bids farewell to his tormented lovers: he leaves these two to their own pastoral devices, a life of pleasure undisturbed by guilt or overmuch reflection.

Part III

The Threefold Harmony

There is, therefore, this triple beauty:
of the soul, of the body, and of sound.
(Ficino, *Commentary on The Symposium*)

Musicks Empire, *The Garden* and *Hortus* occupy the central ground of Marvell's *Miscellaneous Poems*, if we reckon from the total number of poems included in the Folio rather than their relative length. They also mark the climax of the major lyric sequences: from this peak the Folio arrangement tumbles into a more uneven miscellany of occasional poems, translations, satire, political poems—everything from the small polished outcrops of epitaph and epigram to the broad vistas (some would say, meanders) of *Upon Appleton House*. It is as if these lyrics form a natural vantage point from which to survey the landscape of Marvell's poetry.

Such a claim seems orthodox in the case of *The Garden* which early became an anthology piece, attracting admiration and attention whenever Marvell's lyric poetry found readers and critics. But *Musicks Empire* is a different matter. Against a long list of entries for *The Garden* in *Andrew Marvell: The Critical Heritage*, *Musicks Empire* can boast only one, although the editor declares that it was, with certain others, 'beginning to come into [its] own' during the nineteenth century.[1] In fact, twentieth-century criticism has done something to promote this poem, as well as putting *The Garden* at risk of over-exposure. However, possibly the most surprising assessment of its merit comes from an eighteenth-century source: Giles Jacob's remark that *Musicks Empire* is 'one of the best of Mr *Marvel's*' (*Historical Account of the Lives and Writings of Our Most Considerable English Poets*, 1720).[2] Just as surprisingly perhaps, Jacob fails to mention *The Garden*, although both lyrics had been printed among a small selection of Marvell's poems in Tonson's *Miscellany*, 1716. But the two poems are seldom bracketed together for discussion in spite of their juxtaposition in the Folio, and not merely because modern critical judgments usually contradict Jacob's. Genre also comes into it. *The Garden* is self-evidently related to Marvell's other garden poetry and to seventeenth-century garden poetry in general, whereas *Musicks Empire* is classified with poems which have or include music as a topos. Beyond this classification, problems arise, since *Musicks Empire* may be read as either a predominantly religious or a predominantly political poem, and in each case it slots into a different group in the Marvell canon. However, it is safe to say that it and *The Garden* are normally regarded as poems of different genres, which can claim much closer relations than each other in the extended family of seventeenth-century lyric as well as in Marvell's own work. So why—unless by accident—place them next to each other?

If we look for links other than generic, one possibility lies in the Fairfax/Nunappleton connection. *Musicks Empire* can be taken as a Fairfax poem, *The Garden* as a Nunappleton poem, though there is no indisputable evidence for either association (the evidence for the former will be reviewed in due course). On the other hand, there is nothing to disprove the belief that the two poems are chronologically close, products of the same period of composition. Both are free from explicit personal or local reference. What they have in common is a concern with the phenomena of the created world, and with certain concepts such as time and eternity, that are central to Marvell's lyric writing. One main contention of this study has been that *Miscellaneous Poems* has at least the semblance of thematic organisation, and it follows from that contention that *Musicks Empire* and *the Garden* complement each other more than has been recognised. Through two of the primary pleasures known to humanity—music and gardens—Marvell interprets the potential fullness and ultimate aim of earthly life as his culture conceived it.

Yet the connection is not a simple one. Music and gardens are not only pleasures, but also two of the most powerful symbols available to Renaissance artists: if on one level they are recreation, on another they are bound up with the myth of creation itself. Traditionally, their function in human life is to contribute to its completeness. Through the making and enjoying of music and gardens, human beings can participate actively in a divine creative process, rediscover their origins, and contemplate their eternal destiny. If a poet wants to create an image of the threefold life, with contemplation and pleasure paramount but also with scope for constructive action, then the worlds of music and the garden offer complementary models. The former is to time as the latter is to space: a harmony perceived by the mind and engaging the senses. From this it appears that *Musicks Empire* and *The Garden* do present related themes, and that their juxtaposition need not be accidental. The likenesses and differences between these poems are therefore especially interesting.

One likeness arises from the nature of the experience described. For the individual, it is threefold: physical, intellectual, spiritual. It also includes different kinds of experience, in that political and erotic metaphors become the means of remaking a fallen world in an ideal and comprehensive image. Both *Musicks Empire* and *The Garden* confront the idea of imperial power: *Musicks Empire* deals with it by accepting and transforming it—this is a myth of an imperialism at once irresistible and bloodless—whereas *The Garden* metamorphoses the imperial garland into innocent greenery. Clearly the idea is much more dominant and developed in *Musicks Empire*, as the title suggests, but it is a reminder of the *vita activa* present in both poems. Conversely, the erotic idea is more prominent in the witty sublimations of

The Garden and *Hortus*, where gods have love affairs with trees, but it is also present in the conceits of *Musicks Empire*, where 'Virgin Trebles wed the manly Base' and procreate harmony. Music and the garden are their own societies, with their own systems of order, more harmonious than human society and setting it an example of conquest without violence, guiltless passion, and striving satisfied. Both poems comment on the relation of human civilisation, 'the world, as it is mans', to the divine creation, 'the world, as it is Gods'[3]; both have their versions of history. Yet it is precisely in this area that they are most strikingly differentiated. In *The Garden* there is a haunting almost self-mocking consciousness of the Fall; but in *Musicks Empire*, in spite of its historical structure, the Fall is conspicuous by its absence.[4] Partly because of this, *The Garden* is more complicated in mood, more Marvellian in a sense, than *Musicks Empire*. But behind both poems is a pressure of tradition which is both resisted and assimilated, and which the interpreter too must resist and assimilate.

(i) Music and triplex vita: Musicks Empire

The musico-literary tradition, like that relating to gardens, speaks in many voices, some of which contradict each other. And as with the garden, it is the association between music and pleasure that forces many apologists to discriminate between the use and abuse of such a powerful psychological and physiological influence. The distinction between the ends of contemplation and pleasure goes back to Plato:

> music ... in so far as it uses audible sound, was bestowed for the sake of harmony. And harmony, which has motions akin to the revolutions of the Soul within us, was given by the Muses to him who makes intelligent use of the Muses, not as an aid to irrational pleasure, as is now supposed, but as an auxiliary to the inner revolution of the Soul, when it has lost its harmony, to assist in restoring it to order and concord with itself.[1]

Behind the claim that music is an adjunct of the contemplative life lies the idea that not only the soul but the universe is a harmony. The complex and beautiful Pythagorean system of world harmony, including the music of the spheres and the image of the soul as a sleeping musician, was transmitted to the Christian Middle Ages and Renaissance through Cicero's *Somnium Scipionis* and Macrobius's commentary, and given new resonance by the Neoplatonists.[2] It is Ficino who synthesises the theories of the power of music over the hearer, bringing together the idea of world harmony and the Greek theory of *ethos* which explained the psychological function of the different musical modes.[3]

Like Ficino's concept of the threefold life, musical theory may also reveal a tripartite pattern: for example, Sir John Davies's *Hymne in Prayse of Musicke*— 'Prayse, Pleasure, Profit, is that three-fold band'.[4] Although the ancient musical modes number more than three, it is possible to summarise their effects in three broad categories:

> In general, music was thought to affect the mind in three ways: it could stimulate to action; it could strengthen (and conversely undermine) the will; or ... it could excite the listener to the point where he rose above and beyond himself, to a state of ecstasy ...[5]

These in turn have a bearing on the different modes of life. The Dorian and Phrygian musical modes, the only ones that Plato permits in his ideal state, promote a balanced life with the emphasis on virtuous action. The seventeenth-century musicologist, Charles Butler, describes the Phrygian as 'a manly and coorragious kinde of Musik, which, with his stately, or loud and violent tones, rouseth the spirit, and inciteth to arms and activiti'. On the other hand, the Ionian and certain Lydian modes (excluded from Plato's

Republic)[6] are associated with pleasure. But Butler makes a further distinction, effectively linking the Lydian mode with contemplation and the Ionian with the *vita voluptuosa*: the former he describes as 'heavenly harmoni' which raises the mind 'from the regarde of earthly things, unto the desire of celestiall joyz'; the latter is 'an effeminate and delicate kinde of Musik, set unto pleasant songs and sonnets of loov'.[7]

The differences, however, may be more in the ear of the listener than in the music itself. If he is Sir Thomas Browne, 'even that vulgar and Taverne Musicke' will strike in him 'a deepe fit of devotion, and a profound contemplation of the first Composer'.[8] But this very power of music caused more cautious heads to distrust it. The seventeenth-century controversy over the use of instrumental music in religious worship has deep roots in the history of ideas, and sharpens the practical and theoretical distinctions between sacred and profane. According to Humphrey Sydenham, a supporter of Church music, in his sermon *The Wel-Tvned Cymbal*—

> there is nothing more betraying us to sensuality, than some kind of Musicke; than other, none more advancing unto God. And therefore there must be a discreet caution had, that it be grave and sober, and not over-wanton'd with curiositie or descant . . .

> The over-carving and mincing of the ayre either by ostentation or curiositie of Art, lulls too much the outward sense, and leaves the spirituall faculties untouch'd, whereas a sober mediocritie and grave mixture of *Tune* with *Ditty*, rocks the very soule, carries it into extasies, and for a time seemes to cleave and sunder it from the body, elevating the heart inexpressably, and resembling in some proportion those *Halleluiahs* above, the Quire and unitie which is in Heaven.[9]

This is an interesting gloss on one kind of music that Marvell distinguishes in *Musicks Empire*.

Music occupies a central, if controversial, place in seventeenth-century culture and ideology, and for that reason alone it is a natural subject for Marvell as for Milton. Elsewhere in his poetry Marvell links music with contemplation (*Bermudas*), with pleasure (*The Fair Singer*), and with action (*The First Anniversary*). He pays tribute to its power by having the Resolved Soul reject it outright in the first poem of the Folio. But just as Created Pleasure will be rehabilitated in *The Garden*, so music's 'sweet Chordage' is rehabilitated in *Musicks Empire*.[10] And only in *Musicks Empire* does music become the planet that attracts everything else into its orbit. Modern readings of the poem have tended to polarise it as either political (pertaining to the active life) or religious (pertaining to the contemplative life).[11] But its structure appears deliberately inclusive of different modes, as are its metaphors of space and time.

With one highly significant exception: as already observed, the idea of the Fall is conspicuous by its absence. Just how conspicuous that absence is becomes apparent from a comparison with other versions of the world harmony theme in seventeenth-century literature. Donne and Milton, two famous exponents of the idea, both distinguish three states, unfallen, fallen, and redeemed. Donne speaks musically of Fall and Redemption in a Lent sermon:

> God made this whole world in such a uniformity, such a correspondency, such a concinnity of parts, as that it was an Instrument, perfectly in tune: we may say, the trebles, the highest strings were disordered first; the best understandings, Angels and Men, put this instrument out of tune. God rectified all again, by putting in a new string, *semen mulieris*, the seed of the woman, the *Messias*: And onely by sounding that string in your ears, become we *musicum carmen*, true musick, true harmony, true peace to you.[12]

In *At a Solemn Music*, Milton is equally eloquent in his desire that 'we on earth' should once again harmonise with the divine music—

> As once we did, till disproportioned sin
> Jarred against nature's chime, and with harsh din
> Broke the fair music that all creatures made
> To their great Lord, whose love their motion swayed
> In perfect diapason, whilst they stood
> In first obedience, and their state of good.
>
> (ll. 19–24)[13]

The first stanza of *Musicks Empire* also represents the pristine state of the world as a condition of music:

I

> First was the World as one great Cymbal made,
> Where Jarring Windes to infant Nature plaid.
> All Musick was a solitary sound,
> To hollow Rocks and murm'ring Fountains bound.
>
> (ll. 1–4)

But Marvell's primeval music is in a very different mode from Milton's. Indeed the superficial similarities in their descriptive language only emphasise a deeper divergence. 'Jarring' echoes 'jarred', 'chime' and 'cymbal' are cognate: yet the context modifies them significantly. In *At a Solemn Music* the phrase 'Jarred against nature's chime' carries heavy moral weight; in *Musicks Empire* the 'Jarring Windes' are a natural rather than a moral phenomenon, part of the ordained *discordia concors* of the natural world which is essentially harmonious.[14] Even so, the landscape of this and the following stanza is unusually bleak, isolated and constricted ('solitary', 'bound', 'sullen Cell'), a far cry from the exuberant hymning creation imagined by most writers on world harmony.

As for Marvell's 'one great Cymbal', it too is unusual enough to invite explanations, for although the world-as-instrument is a standard emblem, it is normally either an organ or a stringed instrument like a lute.[15] Much has been made of the singularity of the cymbal, perhaps unnecessarily.[16] Sydenham's 'well-tuned cymbal', for example, is a perfectly straightforward and positive allusion to sacred music. The cymbal, like Milton's 'nature's chime', might derive symbolically (the pun is often noted) from the Latin *in cymbalis bene sonantibus*, interpreted as 'the musical harmony of the universe.[17] At least the Old Testament precedents for its being an instrument of general rejoicing appear stronger than the New Testament comparison of empty eloquence with a tinkling cymbal, since the latter refers specifically to a *human* lack of charity. And what is missing from Marvell's landscape is precisely any human presence—which also accounts for the absence of the Fall. The function of the cymbal is to rouse 'infant Nature'; but the music itself is nature, solitary, self-engendered and self-contemplating. If this is joy, it is of a particularly austere kind. Infant nature cannot remain at this self-contemplative stage, but must emerge into society and action. What sets this poem apart from the majority of Marvell's lyrics is the lack of regret that this process should take place.

The agent of the process is Jubal, 'the father of all such as handle the harp and organ' (Genesis 4: 21):

> *Jubal* first made the wilder Notes agree;
> And *Jubal* tuned Musicks *Jubilee:*
> He call'd the *Ecchoes* from their sullen Cell,
> And built the Organs City where they dwell.
>
> (ll. 5–8)

Jubal's lineage should make him an ambivalent figure, since he is descended from Cain and half-brother of Tubalcain (both have parallels in pagan mythology).[18] He takes after his ancestor in being a founder of cities ('God the first Garden made, and the first City, *Cain*')[19]; but his city is one of harmony. Although in orthodox terms Jubal's musical invention is a product of the Fall, his role in *Musicks Empire* appears to be entirely constructive and liberating. The word-play on *'Jubilee'* introduces an allusion to rejoicing, to the Jewish year of emancipation and restoration,[20] and Jubal's tuning paradoxically frees music from its natural prison, its 'sullen Cell'. And although making 'the wilder Notes agree' might remind the reader of little T.C. taming 'the Wilder flow'rs', the phrase in this instance does not seem to carry any encoded warning against the exercise of creative powers. Read in the light of *Paradise Lost*, the stanza acquires different overtones; but it was not written in that light.[21] With its glorious sonority and capacity, the organ is an obvious choice of instrument to represent the city of music as it represents cosmic harmony, and the seventeenth-century cathedral organ might, it was speculated, have its origin in Jubal's own invention. 'But whether it had or not', adds Sydenham, 'doubtlesse in many it doth sublimate devotion, sets their contemplation a soaring ...'. Yet concealed in this jubilation is the old snare of pleasure, the captivation by music, and neglect of meaning, against which Augustine warned. 'Sacred sensualitie' is Sydenham's phrase; he regards music as a divine strategy designed to catch human nature through its propensity 'to the wayes of pleasure'.[22] Marvell—deliberately?—avoids the controversy over sacred music, leaving it uncertain whether 'the Organs City' is a *civitas dei* or not.[23] He circumvents the problem of sensual pleasure by displacing it. Apart from the archetypal figure of Jubal, he simply removes the human element: music is self-delighting, as nature was self-contemplating.

The next two stanzas therefore concentrate on the volition of the notes themselves, as if they were independent of any performer.[24] Whereas Milton describes Jubal's music in metaphors of flight and pursuit (*Paradise Lost* XI. 561–3), Marvell describes it in terms of seeking and finding, allowing more imagined freedom to music personified than to most of his human subjects. In effect, these stanzas are an allegory of choice:

III

Each sought a consort in that lovely place;
And Virgin Trebles wed the manly Base.
From whence the Progeny of numbers new
Into harmonious Colonies withdrew.

IV

Some to the Lute, some to the Viol went,
And others chose the Cornet eloquent.
These practising the Wind, and those the Wire,
To sing Mens Triumphs, or in Heavens quire.

(ll. 9–16)

The initial choice embraces pleasure and beauty, appropriately imaged in the metaphor of an ideal union of the sexes in a *locus amoenus*—'that lovely place'. But it immediately passes into a politicising metaphor (ll. 11–12), and in the following stanza the choice of instruments expands to serve the alternative ends of the active and the contemplative life—'To sing Mens Triumphs, or in Heavens quire.' This two-stanza central unit of the poem forms a paradigm of the threefold life in hierarchical order: pleasure, action, and contemplation.

In keeping with the design of universal harmony, these values are complementary, not competing. Pleasure, for instance, is not merely sensual and erotic: when it is sanctified, so to speak, by a marriage metaphor—and 'consort' plays on the double meaning of musical harmony and marriage partner—it ceases to be libertine. Instead sexual fulfilment is the beginning of communal responsibility. From the individual to the family; from the family to the state: such is music's progress. The colonising image is of course appropriate to the basic concept of *Musicks Empire*, but it is important that it is *harmonious* colonising, in all senses.[25] These colonies come into existence voluntarily, as a consequence of happy procreation. The precise distinction between string and wind instruments in stanza IV is traditional, but not in this instance invidious.[26] Wind instruments such as the eloquent cornet have military uses on the parade-ground and battlefield; Marvell selects the least ominous ceremonial function, 'to sing Mens Triumphs'. Stringed instruments, on the other hand, often accompany the singing voice, and are therefore associated with a more contemplative music, including hymns of praise—'in Heavens quire.' The fine balance struck here should act as a corrective to readings of the poem which are exclusively political or exclusively religious.

Indeed the penultimate stanza insists on inclusiveness:

V

Then Musick, the Mosaique of the Air,
Did of all these a solemn noise prepare:
With which She gain'd the Empire of the Ear,
Including all between the Earth and Sphear.

(ll. 17–20)

The most striking word in that stanza, 'Mosaique', itself enfolds multiple meanings. Because the phrase 'Mosaique of the Air' can be compared with 'light *Mosaick*' in *Upon Appleton House* (stanza LXXIII), it has been argued that there is a parallel allusion to Moses, prophet and law-giver, and to the combined wisdom of the three civilisations, '*Rome, Greece, Palestine*'. One commentator, while making the application cautiously, remarks that 'certainly the word, with its three-fold connections, is appropriate to a fantasy with three threads, in the same way as "Mosaick", in *Appleton House*, answers to the three-fold wisdom of "Rome, Greece, Palestine".'[27]

A connection with *Upon Appleton House* receives support from another direction, with the illuminating discovery that Marvell echoes lines from *Gondibert* in stanza III of *Musicks Empire*. Since he also borrows from Davenant in *Upon Appleton House* (stanza LVII), this is a useful chronological pointer, another reason for associating *Musicks Empire* with Fairfax.[28] But it is more than that. It significantly recalls the Temple of Astragon sequence in *Gondibert*, in particular the House of Praise, which is one of three fanes dedicated to Praise, Penitence, and Prayer (II. vi. 4).[29] Davenant compresses a history of music into two stanzas, connecting, as Marvell does, sacred and secular music, and differentiating three musical modes that correspond to contemplation, pleasure, and action:

In Statue o're the Gate, God's Fav'rite-King
    The author of Celestial praise) did stand;
His Quire (that did his sonnets set and Sing)
    In *Niches* rang'd, attended either Hand.

From these, old *Greeks* sweet Musick did improve;
    The Solemn *Dorian* did in Temples charm,
The softer *Lydian* sooth'd to Bridal Love,
    And warlick *Phrygian* did to Battail warm!

(II. vi. 48, 49)

Davenant's 'Praise' encompasses both human achievement and divine worship. The congregation in the House of Praise, bridal in their appearance (stanzas 77–8), do their utmost to express 'Heav'n's renown' in their singing 'Though Tongues ne'r reach, what minds so nobly ment':

> Yet Musick here shew'd all her Art's high worth;
>   Whilst Virgin-Trebbles, seem'd, with bashfull grace,
> To call the bolder marry'd Tenor forth;
>   Whose Manly voice challeng'd the Giant Base.
>
> To these the swift soft Instruments reply;
>   Whisp'ring for help to those whom winds inspire;
> Whose louder Notes, to Neighb'ring Forrests flie,
>   And summon Nature's Voluntarie Quire.
>
> (II. vi. 80, 81)

Apart from his verbal indebtedness to Davenant, Marvell appears to be influenced by the combination of motifs in the House of Praise: the antiquity and diversity of music are similarly represented in both contexts. Not only that, but Davenant too has a hero who, like Marvell's 'gentler Conqueror', joins in offering 'Heav'ns praise':

> Hither, with borrow'd strength, Duke *Gondibert*
>   Was brought, which now his rip'ning wounds allow;
> And high Heav'ns praise in musick of the heart,
>   He inward sings, to pay a Victor's vow.
>
> (II. vi. 83)

Although Davenant does not provide an exact model for Marvell's paradox, he does construct a politically loaded antithesis between the harmony of praise and the discord of sectarian prayer:

> *Praise,* is devotion fit for mighty Minds!
>   The diff'ring World's agreeing Sacrifice;
> Where Heav'n divided Faiths united finds;
>   But Pray'r in various discord upward flies.
>
> (II. vi. 84)

Even praise, however, is a dangerous and unstable quantity when targeted on a fallible human being—

> Its utmost force, like Powder's, is unknown!
>   And though weak Kings excess of Praise may fear,
> Yet when 'tis here, like Powder, dang'rous grown,
>   Heav'ns Vault receives, what would the Palace tear.
>
> (II. vi. 87)

In the final stanza of *Musicks Empire*, it looks as if Marvell is acting on a hint from *Gondibert* in insisting that it is wisdom, not weakness, to fly from the music of one's own praise.

It is this sixth stanza that decisively shifts the balance of the poem, and offers a perplexing key to its meaning:

VI

Victorious sounds! yet here your Homage do
Unto a gentler Conqueror then you;
Who though He flies the Musick of his praise,
Would with you Heavens Hallelujahs raise.

(ll. 21–4)

Who is the 'gentler Conqueror'? The answer can only emerge from a reading of the poem as a whole, although any external evidence should not be ignored. Those who claim that *Musicks Empire* is a typological poem, and support their case with numerology, conclude that it culminates in the sixth age with the coming of Christ.[30] But there seems to be no very convincing answer to the question of why Christ should need to fly the music of his praise, whereas a very similar phrase is used of Fairfax in *Upon the Hill and Grove at Bill-borow*—'That Courage its own Praises flies' (l. 76).[31]

Moreover, Fairfax rather than Cromwell (the other contender for the role of 'gentler Conqueror')[32] might seem to deserve the description. His self-effacing modesty is consistently remarked upon by those who knew him: Marvell himself, Joshua Sprigge, his chaplain, Thomas May, Parliamentary historiographer.[33] The tone of his *Short Memorials ... Written by Himself* bears out this general impression.[34] And his epitaph, written by his son-in-law, the Duke of Buckingham, records his combination of valour and gentleness—

Both Sexes Vertues were in him combin'd,
He had the fierceness of the Manliest mind,
And all the meekness too of Woman-kind.[35]

Although Amphion/Cromwell is credited with a 'gentle hand' in *The First Anniversary* (l. 50), the role designates his qualities as a statesman rather than a military leader. It is not altogether easy to see Cromwell as a gentle *conqueror*, though the musical topos is comparable.

A final reason for specifically identifying this figure with Fairfax is on thematic grounds: the last stanza of *Musicks Empire*, like its central stanzas, enacts a choice. The poet commands the 'victorious sounds' to acknowledge an even greater victory over self and ambition, a turning from one kind of glory to another. Milton interprets Fairfax's decision to retire in just these terms:

You have defeated, not only the enemy, but ambition as well, and the thirst for glory which conquers all the most eminent men, and you are reaping the reward of your virtues and noble deeds amid that most delightful and glorious retirement which is the end of all labors and human action, even the greatest.[36]

Compare Marvell's reference to 'securer Glory' in *Upon the Hill and Grove at Bill-borow* (l. 16), and stanza XLV of *Upon Appleton House*. It is true that Fairfax, understandably in the political circumstances, was condemned as well as praised; his withdrawal from public life, however principled, could be presented as a strategic retreat from responsibility. Arguably, both Milton and Marvell betray a certain ambivalence even in their panegyric.[37] Yet both of them, Marvell in particular, are qualified to enter imaginatively into such a choice. For Marvell it becomes even more than a choice of the life of contemplation and pleasure over the life of action. It is, rather, a choice of eternity.

At least this is the dominant impression left by *Musicks Empire*. The first five stanzas embody an allegory of civilised life, as a threefold harmony attainable through, and symbolised by, music. Religion is one strand of that harmony. But in the final stanza, music pays homage to the man who has conquered himself and transcended earth's glories, who now looks only to eternity and 'Heavens Hallelujahs'. The Resolved Soul has won its victory again in *Musicks Empire*, yet not at the expense of Created Pleasure. The end is harmony, as both are made God's music.

(ii) The Poet in the Garden: vitae melioris anhelus: The Garden

The Garden invites readers to recreation—re-creation—both of themselves and of the text. We recreate ourselves through vicarious enjoyment of its green shade; we re-create the text through our attempts to understand its green thought. But, in the case of the text, to recreate is often to deconstruct or, to use a Marvellian word, to annihilate what the poet has made. So architects do square and hew...

The process begins with the subjective presence in the poem whom earlier readers in their innocence were allowed to call Marvell but who now has to submit to a circumlocution such as 'the speaker'. What is his stance, given the internal evidence that he is male and a poet like his creator? Are his attitudes endorsed or criticised? Are they indeed ascertainable? Such problems are commonplace in Marvell's lyrics, but that does not make them any less acute, especially in this, the quintessential Marvell lyric. Although the text itself is stable, with only the slightest of textual variations, it presents other kinds of difficulty and challenge: its generic and formal properties are disputed; its thesis, assuming it has one, is dismembered and refracted through the history of ideas; the simplicity of its language is held to be deceptive. As Huck Finn says of Pilgrim's Progress, its statements are interesting, but tough. Perhaps too tough for many modern readers to swallow: it is easier to argue that The Garden subtly discredits its own claim to establish an integrated 'better' life by excluding politics, sex and society, than to accept that claim. Those critics who appear most anxious to separate the writer ideologically from his poem, who describe its argument as outrageous (usually with the implication that they are too scholarly actually to be outraged), show how much the ostensible meaning goes against the grain.[1] Marvell must be joking: mustn't he? But he may be joking to protect his seriousness. All readings of The Garden, including the following one, fall into the poet's traps, but we can only trust to a soft fall like his own.

There are many ways into The Garden, and one of the most enticing is through its Latin shadow, Hortus. If Hortus represents a simpler version of The Garden, possibly an earlier experiment,[2] it offers a rare opportunity to watch Marvell in the act of making literary and linguistic choices. The Latin poem is more explicit, spilling out its beautiful polysyllables and spelling out the Ovidian mythology that braces its structure: this is a much more populous place than The Garden itself, and the sense of solitude is correspondingly less intense. Naturally the omission of lines directly parallel to the English stanzas V–VII changes the balance of the poem, though something numinous is implicit in the phrases used to describe the silence and secrecy of the Penetralia veris, 'the sanctuaries of spring'.[3] If Hortus confines itself decorously to classical limits, it also clarifies the central issue as, precisely, a choice of life. The poet refers to himself as 'panting for a better life' (mihi... vitae melioris anhelo, ll. 12-13); and, more than *The Garden*, *Hortus* emphasises crucial comparatives as in l. 40: Arbore *nunc melius potiuntur quisque cupita*, 'Each [god] achieves his desires better now in a *tree*'.

The quality of this better life is more simply defined in the Latin poem, but even so it goes beyond the familiar divide between action and contemplation.[4] Although the poet ostentatiously rejects the active life, Roman-style (temples, palaces, circus, forum), he remakes the socio-political world in the image of the garden kingdom:[5]

> *Municipem servate novum, votoque potitum,*
> *Frondosae Cives optate in florea Regna.*
>
> Preserve your new citizen, and me, having attained my wish,
> Leafy citizens, accept in the flowery kingdom.
>
> (ll. 14-15)

And he crucially transforms the life of pleasure. Like Paris, the speaker is set up as judge in a beauty contest—*me judice*, l.22—and he gives his verdict in favour of trees not girls. He drives the point home with a double comparison outdoing *The Garden*: a girl's beauty surpasses the whitest snow or the deepest red, but is itself surpassed by nature's green. The description that follows plays with the notion of the living tree in true Ovidian style. In fact, over half the poem is devoted to developing the idea that the true beauty, the true pleasure, is to be found in making love to trees: Cupid, as in a Spenserian allegory, lays aside his wings and weapons, inverts his torches or falls asleep, and the gods are infatuated with oak, ash, or myrtle.[6] Because this wit of choosing is so central to *Hortus*, it is more difficult to brush aside its counterpart in *The Garden* as merely peripheral or perverse. Both poems move between negative and positive poles in a sustained act of discrimination which ends in an image of the better life constructed in herbs and flowers.

The similarities between *Hortus* and *The Garden*, particularly evident in their emblematic openings and closure, do not however extend to their central structure. In *The Garden*, Marvell not only prunes back the verbal luxuriance of *Hortus* but also substitutes nine regular stanzas, V–VII containing new material, for the Latin verse paragraphs. Theoretically, this should make the structure and internal relations of *The Garden* easier to analyse; in practice, a reader may opt for different patterns, with different explanations ranging from numerology to classical rhetoric.[7] Given nine units, it might seem obvious to look first for a threefold principle, which would correspond to universal triplicity: 'every Element is *threefold*, this *Triplicity* being the exprèsse Image of their *Author*, and a Seal he hath laid upon his *Creature*' including the human organism.[8] *The Garden* seems to acknowledge this in the three stanzas missing from *Hortus*, which narrate the activities of body, mind, and soul. Nevertheless, these raise further questions. Are they to be considered as a unit, or separately? Why, if they are the centre of the argument, are they not the central three stanzas—IV, V, and VI, instead of V, VI, and VII? (Numerology has an answer to this conundrum). Other ways of dividing *The Garden* reflect different concepts: for example, two equal units of four stanzas, with a separate summarising stanza in conclusion; or two unequal units of five and four stanzas, with a decisive break after stanza V; or three opening stanzas (I–III) balanced against one closing stanza (IX).[9] Symmetries have been noted between stanzas IV and VIII, and between stanzas I and IX ('How vainly'/'How well'). Seventeenth-century writers were themselves prepared to accommodate alternative models of this kind without compromising a sense of unity. If every element is threefold, every element is also binary,[10] and beyond all there is the One. Whatever structure is proposed for *The Garden* does not close down other possibilities, and only confirms its inclusiveness. The obvious binary oppositions—action/contemplation, society/solitude, man/woman, self/outside world—are not rigid but subject to realignment, splitting open or merging. Even the dominant prepositions function to merge and include: in, among, upon, into. Yet there can be no inside without an outside, and the world of *The Garden* like that of *Bermudas* is defined against knowledge of what is exterior to it and the text.

In the opening stanza, what is 'outside' is the active life, ironically symbolised by nature's own greenery:

I

How vainly men themselves amaze
To win the Palm, the Oke, or Bayes;
And their uncessant Labours see
Crown'd from some single Herb or Tree.
Whose short and narrow verged Shade
Does prudently their Toyles upbraid;
While all Flow'rs and all Trees do close
To weave the Garlands of repose.

(ll. 1–8)

Unusually for Marvell, the lyric begins with a judgment presupposing a choice already made. In fact, it expresses an adverse judgment on the choice of those who pursue the rewards of worldly success.[11] The rewards are made entertainingly literal, to 'prove' their inadequacy. The fresh eye turned on status symbols is a Utopian eye which sees only semicircles of green leaves severed from their natural habitat, of no practical use for shade or repose.[12] Further, the active life of 'uncessant Labours' is itself subdivided into three categories, symbolised by the palm (military honour), the oak (civic honour), and the writer's laurels. While the first two are self-evidently linked with public life and the exercise of power, the third implies a further choice between alternatives directly involving the poet. What is being rejected is a style and a vocation, writing as a political act, not just a way of life. Of course there is a case to be made on the other side; of course this opening invites the reader, including the academically successful reader, to turn the judgment back on the so-called naïve speaker who so casually dismisses the pressures and achievements of success. But the reader is also pleasurably drawn in by an interwoven language[13] that paradoxically asserts its own integrity. The generous offer of 'all Flow'rs and all Trees' is an offer of wholeness, of reintegration (in *Hortus*, l.6, the epithet for the wood is *integra*).

> If Life should a well-order'd Poem be
> 　(In which he only hits the white
> 　Who joyns true Profit with the best Delight)
> The more Heroique strain let others take

—so writes Cowley, choosing the Pindaric way, in life as in literature.[14] The poet of *The Garden* chooses the lyric mode, replanting his laurels among the flowers. By the end of the poem, both the symbolic plants and human labour will be restored to their pristine environment. Nothing, including time, is lost or wasted.

The second stanza begins the restorative process:

II

> Fair quiet, have I found thee here,
> And Innocence thy Sister dear!
> Mistaken long, I sought you then
> In busie Companies of Men.
> Your sacred Plants, if here below,
> Only among the Plants will grow.
> Society is all but rude,
> To this delicious Solitude.

(ll. 9–16)

Again his form of expression is supposed to cast the speaker in the role of *naïf*, or *faux-naïf*, according to taste.[15] Who else would search for quiet and innocence 'in busie Companies of Men'? But it is difficult to take this line without sounding altogether too dismissive. This stanza is both a confession and a conversion, and as such it brings out the enthusiast in the speaker, the sceptic in the hearer. Yet if scepticism is suspended, the effect of the poetry is that of joyous revelation, a weary quest consummated. Quiet and Innocence, so long elusive, manifest themselves as the sister graces of the garden like something out of Spenser (the former is not only beautiful but gracious, *Alma Quies* in the Latin version).[16] Nor is it incidental that their presence also admits female attributes and relationship,[17] although only in allegory: 'such company decks such solitarines.'[18] Their origin is heavenly, like Milton's haemony[19]—'Your sacred Plants, if here below'—but they can be naturalised in the contemplative garden environment. No wonder the stanza ends with a happy and absurd paradox, to be enjoyed rather than taken as evidence of maladjustment. The real power of the poet, the power of naming, comes into play, so that society can be called 'all but rude' and solitude delicious.

This readiness to rewrite the labels, as well as a readiness to fall in love, links up with stanza III, which appropriately introduces the third choice of life, the lover's:

III

> No white nor red was ever seen
> So am'rous as this lovely green.
> Fond Lovers, cruel as their Flame,
> Cut in these Trees their Mistress name.
> Little, Alas, they know, or heed,
> How far these Beauties Hers exceed!
> Fair Trees! where s'eer your barkes I wound,
> No Name shall but your own be found.

(ll. 17–24)

This choice is treated in its own right, not simply as an adjunct of the active life,[20] and with good reason. For whereas the men of action tend to ignore nature, making only a token use of its plants, the lover traditionally invades and takes over the natural world as the theatre of his passion. Whether the location is the libertine garden of pleasure or the melancholy love solitude, it derives meaning exclusively from his sexual obsession. Marvell reverses this attitude, giving the prize for beauty to 'this lovely green' instead of woman's white or red, and sowing the seeds of discord as surely as Paris. The critical quarrel over the precise sense of 'am'rous' is a case in point.[21] Occurring so soon after 'delicious' (l. 16) with its Latinate overtones,[22] 'am'rous' in its root meaning carries more emotional force than its English equivalent 'lovely'. Whether active or passive, the green offers a real challenge to the red and white. Usually in seventeenth-century verse, when woman and nature are in competition as rival beauties, nature comes off badly: swans moult, glow-worms shrivel, trees go bald from envy or excessive devotion.[23] This is the extreme self-reversing form of the more familiar pastoral hyperbole in which the mistress enhances nature by her presence. If nature does show itself 'am'rous', it is towards her, in homage to her supremacy. In *The Garden*, for once, nature is avenged. But, cry Marvell's readers, he cannot be serious. Possibly not, but it is not enough to react to the proposition that trees are preferable to women purely on the assumption that it is self-evidently wrong (or right, for that matter). The stanza needs to be considered in context, and in more detail.

Marvell's predilection for green is often remarked upon, and linked with Renaissance colour coding in general.[24] But even apart from its symbolism, green might be preferred to red and white for practical reasons, reinforced by theological underpinning. God chose green as the colour of grass and herbs, because it was most soothing to the human eye. Henry More argues in *An Antidote against Atheism* (1653) that 'it was not at all necessary that grasse and herbs should have that *colour* which they have, for they might have been red or white, or some such colour which would have been very offensive and hurtfull to our sight'; Sir Thomas Browne concurs in this view—'and therefore providence hath arched and paved the great house of the world, with colours of mediocrity, that is, blew and green, above and below the sight, moderately terminating the *acies* of the eye' (*The Garden of Cyrus*, 1658).[25] In *The Garden*, Marvell conjures with literal and metaphoric colours to confuse the usual criteria on which judgments are made.

Similarly, human behaviour towards trees becomes a test of judgment.[26] Carving the loved one's name on a tree is a universal symptom of the lover's malaise, wherever trees are available, and it is a favourite cliché in Renaissance literature. Cruelty to trees, according to Marvell, results from what might now be termed a displacement activity—'Fond Lovers, cruel as their Flame...'. But Cowley (himself a genuine tree-lover) in his poem *The Tree* describes it as accidental, a choice that goes wrong:

> I Chose the flouri'shingst *Tree* in all the Park,
>   With freshest Boughs, and fairest head;
> I cut my Love into his gentle Bark,
>   And in three days, behold, 'tis *dead*;
> My very *written flames* so vi'olent be
>   They'have burnt and wither'd up the Tree...

This lover goes on to ask the tree's forgiveness, and to reflect, with slightly risible pathos, 'I thought her *name* would thee have happy made'.[27] Ineptitude of this order might well appeal to Marvell as a comic fiction of the damage man in love inflicts on everything, himself included. Yet The *Garden* speaker's own credentials as a tree-lover can be called in question, since he does not propose necessarily to refrain from assaulting trees (it is intriguing that the hypothetical '*si... unquam*', 'if ever', of *Hortus*, 1.28, becomes the less hypothetical 'where s'eer' in the English poem). He intends to make reparation by carving their own names on the trees instead. It is impossible not to smile; at the same time, the implications cut deep, and expose disturbing connections between language and sex as *acts*, arbitrary ways of appropriating something, or someone. By claiming to restore the 'proper' relation between sign and signified, the tree-namer makes the reader think about relationship in general.

The logical extension of writing names on beloved trees is making love to those same trees; and the *locus classicus* for such an imagined pleasure must be Ovid's myths of metamorphoses:

IV

> When we have run our Passions heat,
> Love hither makes his best retreat.
> The *Gods*, that mortal Beauty chase,

> Still in a Tree did end their race.
> *Apollo* hunted *Daphne* so,
> Only that She might Laurel grow.
> And *Pan* did after *Syrinx* speed,
> Not as a Nymph, but for a Reed.

(ll. 25–32)

The narrative implication of the opening couplet should not be overlooked in any estimate of the choice of life represented by *The Garden*. It parallels the retrospect of the second stanza, by suggesting that other choices have already been tried and exhausted. Passion, like action, can no longer satisfy. For those who are inclined to attribute this attitude to sour grapes, it is worth pointing out that the wordplay on 'heat' and 'retreat' could equally convey welcome relief, a sense of earned respite.[28] Also, this is a strategic withdrawal from passion but not from Love—that Love which is present in *Hortus*, disarmed of his active accoutrements. The superlative 'best' expresses a judgment from experience.

The gods too are credited with discriminating judgment when it comes to the pursuit of pleasure. In the original stories[29] Apollo and Pan gained their experience reluctantly, but Marvell puts it down to their own volition. Of course he is not the only seventeenth-century poet to rewrite Ovidian myths for an ulterior motive (Carew did so dazzlingly in *A Rapture* in support of the libertine ethos).[30] But what is the ulterior motive here? Some would have it that the speaker's argument is self-serving and self-undermining: no confidence can be placed in a case which rests on such blatant tampering with the evidence.[31] If, however, something worth attending to *is* being said about the right end of passion, its consummation and quietus, then the familiar myths take on a different kind of imaginative potency.

But potency is part of the problem. The suggested pun on 'race'[32] pinpoints one obvious objection to making love to trees not women, namely the failure to propagate. For some reason, almost everyone seems to assume that Marvell must be in favour of human fertility and against celibacy, at least in his capacity as a poet. Yet this can hardly be taken for granted: in fact, in one witty epigram, *Upon an Eunuch: a Poet*, which may not be altogether tongue-in-cheek, he turns the slur of sterility into an idiosyncratic triumph—*Tibi Fama perennè/Praegnabit*, 'Fame will be continually pregnant by you'.[33] In a similar connection, another way of interpreting lines 29–32 of *The Garden* is to turn laurel and reed into symbols of poetry and music. But although this reading has sound analogues, it comes up against the difficulty that the symbolic bays have already been rejected.[34] It is more logical to conclude that as in the first stanza the true plants replace the symbols. Laurel and reed are valued for precisely what they are, growing plants ('Only that She might Laurel *grow*'—my italics). Even in the Ovidian source, the tree itself becomes an erotic object, quivering to Apollo's embrace.[35] Presumably this sensation is inferior to the real thing; but the notion that trees (like angels) might have a superior sex life to humans had its own eccentric attraction for seventeenth-century writers. Probably the most famous expression of wishful thinking is Sir Thomas Browne's: 'I could be content that we might procreate like trees, without conjunction, or that there were any way to perpetuate the world without this triviall and vulgar way of coition...[36]. The desire to escape 'this triviall and vulgar way of coition 'by behaving like plants is self-parodying. John Evelyn, for once advocating *Publick Employment and Active Life*, adds his own heavy irony: 'Indeed if all the world inhabited the *Desarts*, and could propagate like *Plants* without a fair Companion...we might all be contented, and all by happy.'[37] According to Pliny, the Esseni come closest to this mode of life: 'Women they see none: carnall lust they know not...they lead their life by themselves, and keepe companie only with Date trees.'[38] What all these have in common is an image of life made simple. Whether or not it is a life of pleasure is a matter of taste: hugging a tree is not everyone's idea of fulfilment.

In the next stanza of *The Garden*, however, the pleasures on offer are both sensuous and accessible:

V

What wond'rous Life in this I lead!
Ripe Apples drop about my head;
The Luscious Clusters of the Vine
Upon my Mouth do crush their Wine;
The Nectaren, and curious Peach,
Into my hands themselves do reach;
Stumbling on Melons, as I pass,
Insnar'd with Flow'rs, I fall on Grass.

(ll. 33–40)

The first line is sometimes emended to 'What wond'rous Life is this I lead!' following the Thompson edition of 1776,[39] but, slight as it is, the change is reductive, turning the exclamation into more of a cliché—'This is the life!' Like the other prepositions in the poem, 'in' is important because it draws attention to the enabling environment that makes the wondrous life possible. Also the line initiates both the middle stanza of *The Garden* and the sequence of three stanzas corresponding to the threefold nature of man: body, mind, and soul. The garden accommodates itself to the needs of each, filling the senses, stimulating the innate creativity of the mind, and—temporarily— liberating the soul. These functions are interdependent and simultaneous. Their formal separation simply reflects different kinds of need, physical, intellectual, and spiritual: it should not be taken as an adverse sign of self-division in the usual sense of sinful man being self-divided and at war with himself.[40] In *The Garden* love of nature heals and integrates man without denying the fact of his composite being. This ''wond'rous Life', for all the reservations that have been expressed about it by neo-Puritans and others, offers an image of completeness and joy. And it also offers one way of envisaging the threefold life. Pleasure, contemplation, and action no longer compete with each other, although they are not given the same priority. As might be expected, pleasure and action are remade, as it were, in the image of contemplation: the pleasures of the body and the active energies of the mind are given their own scope, with only oblique reminders that in other times and places that scope could bring disaster ('Insnar'd', 'fall', 'Annihilating' are all words that have to be purged of guilt). Under these conditions, 'What wond'rous Life in this I lead!' applies to all three stanzas, and might stand as epigraph to the whole lyric.[41]

It follows from this reading that stanza V both celebrates and transforms the *vita voluptuosa*. It is not the simple life: the fruits that delightfully thrust themselves upon the poet are virtually all luxuries, cultivated for a big house, esoteric because they grow in an English garden rather than because of any strained symbolism attached to them.[42] There is an almost identical list in a poem by Sir Aston Cokayne, praising his mother's garden at Ashbourne in Derbyshire:

> What gallant Apricocks, and Peaches brave,
> And what delicious Nectorins you have?
> What Mellons that grow ripe without those Glasses
> That are laid over them in other Places?
> What Grapes you have there growing? and what wine
> (Pleasant to tast) you made last vintage time?[43]

(Presumably Marvell's melons are also free range.) Another more famous garden which compares with Marvell's is that described by Jonson in *To Penshurst*: the descriptions share the classical topos of nature spontaneously offering itself to be enjoyed.[44] In the case of *The Garden*, some readers feel threatened by the onslaught of the vegetable creation, and assume that the poet feels the same—a reaction particularly marked in certain male critics, who believe that nature is behaving like an aggressive female wooer, and that the poet's masculinity insufficiently asserts itself.[45] Of course the aggressive female wooer and the reluctant male are stereotypes of Ovidian narrative, but there seems no reason to transplant a similar relationship into this poem, or to suppose that the poet could, or should, be anything other than blissfully cooperative. The point is surely the one frequently made, that *this* fall is happy, harmless, and mutually loving.[46] In the garden, among the fruits, the body which complained so eloquently in *A Dialogue between the Soul and Body* of being forced to walk upright—'mine own Precipice I go'—is allowed to find its natural level.[47] Here it rolls like a plucked fruit itself, wholly absorbed in its own life of pleasure. The question of the sexuality of the plants and the suggested Hermetic explanation have proved unnecessarily troublesome (anyway it is unclear why bisexual plants should bother to make love to a monosexual poet).[48] What matters is that although sexual passion has been excluded from this garden neither love nor the satisfaction of the senses have been given up. As Ficino knew, it is dangerous to deny the claims of the goddess of pleasure altogether. And the purpose, as the next stanzas show, is not sheer hedonism but a necessary condition of mental and spiritual liberty.

Stanza VI begins by defining two kinds of relation with what precedes it, a temporal relation and a comparative relation:

VI

Mean while the Mind, from pleasure less,
Withdraws into its happiness:
The Mind, that Ocean where each kind
Does streight its own resemblance find;
Yet it creates, transcending these,
Far other Worlds, and other Seas;
Annihilating all that's made
To a green Thought in a green Shade.

(ll. 41–8)

'Mean while' underlines the totality of the experience which simultaneously involves body and mind; 'pleasure less' and its rhyme word 'happiness' distinguish between the levels of experience accessible to body and mind. To debate over possible ambiguity in the phrase 'pleasure less' might increase the critic's pleasure, but tends to lessen the reader's.[49] It is sufficient to point out that 'less' may simply state the traditional assumption that the pleasures of the senses are to be ranked below those of the mind—an assumption which need not carry overtones of moral condemnation. Or, to put it another way, the *vita contemplativa* takes precedence over the *vita voluptuosa*. Hence a further significance can be read into the distinction between 'pleasure' ('pleasures' in the Bodleian manuscript text) and 'happiness', since according to Aristotle happiness is contemplation, 'a virtuous activity of the mind and spirit'.[50]

Here, more than anywhere in his poetry, Marvell confronts the difficulty of describing what contemplation actually *is*, the central mystery of consciousness addressed by the philosophers. Like many seventeenth-century writers, he does so through analogy; and contemplation turns out indeed to be a kind of activity, a seeking out and matching up of ideas and forms. Just as the garden comes to meet the body, so the universe does not passively await discovery but comes to meet the mind—'The Mind, that Ocean where each kind/Does streight its own resemblance find' (ll. 43-4). The notion that every land creature has a parallel in the sea has been well documented from Sylvester's du Bartas, Sir Thomas Browne, and Cleveland,[51] and is obviously a conceit to appeal to a witty poet, since 'a true piece of *Wit*', in Cowley's definition, is comparable to the original all-inclusive creation—

... the *Primitive Forms* of all

> (If we compare great things with small)
> Which without *Discord* or *Confusion* lie,
> In that strange *Mirror* of the *Deitie*.[52]

Whether Marvell subscribed to the literal belief or not, it serves his purpose, like the Platonic or Neoplatonic epistemology which many find in this stanza.[53] But the importance of philosophical sources for the professional scholar—and scholastic or Cartesian theories of knowledge have also been cited—may distort the lyrical effect. Marvell is describing how the mind functions, in what are essentially a poet's terms. And a poet contemplates in order to create, for *his* happiness is in creating: he cannot be satisfied with a simple two-way transaction of the Baconian kind, in which, ideally, 'the truth of being and the truth of knowing are one, differing no more than the direct beam and the beam reflected.'[54] For the poet, 'the mind of man...is rather like an enchanted glass': in Marvell's lines

> Yet it creates, transcending these,
> Far other Worlds, and other Seas;
> Annihilating all that's made
> To a green Thought in a green Shade.

(ll. 45–8)

To quote Bacon again, poetry 'was ever thought to have some participation of divineness, because it doth raise and erect the mind, by submitting the shews of things to the desires of the mind; whereas reason doth buckle and bow the mind unto the nature of things.' Marvell's important conjunction 'yet' implies that the reflective relation between things and the mind is not enough. It needs to go beyond known reality to the otherness of its own creation. 'Transcending' turns into 'annihilating', a transition that readers often find obscurely disturbing, or at least requiring explanation.[55] Both verbs are transitive, and in naming their objects—'these', 'all that's made'—the speaker perforce affirms the existence of the created world which is the starting point for contemplation. Neither the transcendence nor the annihilation are absolute. What happens is not the cutting loose of the mind to float into some ecstatic nirvana, but its anchorage in nature, the wonderful interpenetration of God's creation and man's in which each shares the epithet 'green'. Green links the body's life of pleasure with the mind's life of contemplation. And its significance is as various as the light rippling through the soul's plumage in stanza VII: it is the colour of hope, love, innocence, renewal, meditation, sanctity, but above all it is nature's own colour, 'the dearest freshness deep down things'.[56] A green thought in a green shade glimpses a perfection in which the imagination transcends nature *through* nature, becoming one with the natural world yet retaining the power of thought that makes it distinctive in the creation, Pascal's 'thinking reed'. Choosing between outer and inner states, between sensation and thought, between pleasure and contemplation, is not impossible: it is simply not necessary.

In the crucial seventh stanza the contemplative soul takes wing, but not very far:

VII

> Here at the Fountains sliding foot,
> Or at some Fruit-trees mossy root,
> Casting the Bodies Vest aside,
> My Soul into the boughs does glide:
> There like a Bird it sits, and sings,
> Then whets, and combs its silver Wings;
> And, till prepar'd for longer flight,
> Waves in its Plumes the various Light.

(ll. 49–56)

Attempts to pin down Marvell's meaning too often end by clipping his poetic wings. Here the symbolism—fountain, tree, bird, light—is so traditional and fundamental that it is inevitably surrounded by its own bright nimbus of associations. The fountain, like the green shade of the previous stanza, is part of classical pastoral, and the Latinate 'sliding foot'[57] reinforces the oneness of the human body with nature; also, as in *Clorinda and Damon*, it may be a symbol of spiritual regeneration. Similarly the fruit-tree, like those growing in Ralph Austen's orchard, may be of spiritual use, bearing 'the figure, and resemblance of many high and great Mysteries in the Word of God'.[58] But it is also a tree belonging to the natural garden, offering rest and shade at its 'mossy root', where the body can relax while the soul goes about its own affairs. Yet, although the soul in this stanza is out of the body, it is not itself out of the garden. Like the body earlier in stanza V it finds its proper level, but in the green branches not the blue empyrean, so that it is still very much within nature. The key preposition is not 'from'—despite 'Casting the Bodies Vest aside'—but '*into* the boughs' (l. 52, my emphasis), a phrase which creates a fleeting impression of yet another metamorphosis.[59] In that sense, the ecstasis is not complete. But the effect is one of joyful freedom, intensified in the second half of the stanza.

The comparison of the soul to a bird is again deeply traditional. Many beautiful instances of this trope have been quoted, originating with Plato;[60] perhaps the closest seventeenth-century parallel is Francis Quarles's emblem—[61]

> My Soule is like a Bird, my Flesh, the Cage...

> From Sense she climbes to Faith; where, for a season,
> She sits and sings; then, down againe to Reason...

Quarles, however, is preoccupied with confinement rather than escape, and envies the 'happier birds' who

> can spread their nimble wing
> From Shrubs to Cedars, and there chirp and sing,
> In choice of raptures, the harmonious story
> Of mans Redemption, and his Maker's Glory...

It is these 'happier birds' that Marvell's bird-soul most resembles emblematically. But it has been criticised, if not envied, for the form its happiness takes, as though the absence of Quarles's explicit piety is somehow a flaw. Sitting and singing may be all very well, but the whetting and combing of silver wings has come under particular suspicion as betraying an unworthy degree of vain self-contemplation. It is difficult to argue over what must be ultimately a question of tone and nuance. What to one reader might seem like a spiritual shortcoming, to another might seem like a legitimate expression of joy in God-given spiritual powers. The former is inclined to interpret the spontaneity and lightness of the soul's movements, its evident lack of effort, as frivolous irresponsibility; the latter may or may not describe the experience as mystical, but will recognise a quality of vision that has something in common with mysticism.[62] Even if it is qualified, the second reading is preferable. To locate the source of the soul's joy in self-regard, instead of the contemplation of beauty which includes itself and also the entire 'various Light'[63] of the divine creation which it reflects and mediates, is to lose too much of what The Garden has to offer. In effect, it is to run the risk of being like Milton's Satan, first of critics, who in Eden 'Saw undelighted all delight'.[64]

The soul's delight is poured out in song, and the imagery of the stanza is appropriate to poetic inspiration, since the bird with its plumes figures the poet and his plume, or pen. In his epic inductions, Milton makes powerful use of flight metaphors, and Marvell compliments him with the same allusion in On Mr Milton's Paradise lost.[65] Again this links pleasure and contemplation with creative action. They also serve who only sit and sing. But Marvell does go on to make a crucial distinction in The Garden between the soul's present flight and the 'longer flight' (l. 55) which it is not yet ready to undertake. Like almost everything else in the poem, the phrase 'longer flight' can bear more than one construction, and once more a comparative invokes a standard of comparison. In terms of poetic choices, 'longer flight' could refer to epic, the height of literary endeavour, in contradistinction to the shorter flights of pastoral and lyric. But a more fundamental distinction, especially in view of Marvell's treatment of time,[66] is that between earthly life and eternity. The soul's choice must ultimately be a choice of eternity, though the bird-soul of The Garden unlike the dewdrop-soul of On a Drop of Dew does not shun 'the various Light' in order to regain union with 'th'Almighty Sun.' Instead its garden life foreshadows that final transcendence. It comes as close as possible in this world to the paradise of God in which redeemed souls sing forever in praise of the ineffable and uncreated Light.

Analogically it also comes as close as possible to that first paradise in which God placed Adam. But the comparison takes an unexpected turn:

VIII

Such was that happy Garden-state,
While Man there walk'd without a Mate:
After a Place so pure, and sweet,
What other Help could yet be meet!
But 'twas beyond a Mortal's share
To wander solitary there:
Two Paradises 'twere in one
To live in Paradise alone.

(ll. 57–64)

If critics usually feel that the preceding stanzas need to be explained, some feel even more strongly that stanza VIII needs to be explained away. Modern readers are likely to be uncomfortable with the apparent misogyny of Marvell's option for the celibate life. One popular way out of the embarrassment is to laugh at the proposition that Adam would have been happier without Eve, and the real wit of the argument invites such a response. Even so, a few are not amused.[67] In any case, a refusal to take the argument seriously has to reckon with the existence of powerful and widespread precedents for seeing woman as the source of all mankind's woe. 'How witty's ruine!' Donne exclaims, elaborating the conceit

For that first mariage was our funerall:
One woman at one blow, then kill'd us all,
And singly, one by one, they kill us now.[68]

Of course the difference between Donne's point here and stanza VIII of *The Garden* is that of context: Donne recognises that a good purpose—'Gods purpose'—in the creation of woman has been frustrated. Marvell simply omits that part of the Genesis story, while mischievously signalling his awareness of the original text by his play on 'Help...meet' (God says in Genesis 2: 18 'It is not good that the man should be alone; I will make him an help meet for him'). And readers continue to rise to the bait, accusing Marvell's speaker, with more or less amused tolerance, of blasphemy[69] as well as male chauvinism. The accusations are levelled against the persona rather than against Marvell himself, since poets are not supposed to think like this. At least one scholar stoutly maintains in the face of 'all the misogynist literature of the ancient and medieval and Renaissance worlds' that 'such a belief was never central nor widely held by poets.'[70] But this proves nothing either way in an individual case: it only underlines the sense that there is a case to be met. Others shift the emphasis from misogyny to the argument that solitude is better than society, or explain that what is being rejected is marriage.[71] But this is scarcely a defence against those readers of the poem who find the central flaw in its argument to be precisely the evasion of human responsibilities and a 'full' life, who regard the garden as an inferior substitute for sex and society, not vice versa. If no man is an island,[72] no man should be a garden either.

What all this goes to prove is that stanza VIII touches an exceptionally sensitive nerve, and that it is both more integral and more challenging than is sometimes acknowledged. Its relevance to contemporary controversies helps to bring this out. More than one seventeenth-century writer is prepared to take the argument for solitude back to the Fall itself. Sir George Mackenzie, for example, grasps the nettle in *A Moral Essay, preferring Solitude to Publick Employment:*

> It was I confess GODS own verdict of man, that it was not good for him to be alone, but this was when because of his congenial innocence, he needed not fear the contamination of society; but to demonstrat what the hazard of being in company is: even *Adam* could not live one day in it, and live innocent, for the first news we hear of him, after that *Eve* was associat to him, is, that he had forefeited that native purity.[73]

And Cowley versifies the same *post hoc ergo propter hoc* argument:

> Oh Solitude, first state of Human-kind!
> Which blest remain'd till man did find
> Even his own helpers Company.
> As soon as two (alas!) together joyn'd,
> The Serpent made up Three.[74]

It is not a difficult argument to refute, and Evelyn answers Mackenzie by pointing out that it was Eve's solitary straying 'from the company and presence of her *Husband*' that created the Serpent's opportunity.[75]

If however it is Eve's sex rather than her solitude that is the crucial factor in the Fall, then what is to be deplored is the division of sexes. According to the Hermetic writings, this division did not exist in the original perfect creation, which was '*Hermaphroditicall*':[76] the sexual split is a result rather than a cause of man's fall into imperfection. The legend of the androgynous Adam has been used to explain Marvell's 'two Paradises . . . in one' (l. 64).[77] But it seems an unnecessary gloss, since the poem itself defines the double paradise as the condition of being not only in the garden but being there alone. When a seventeenth-century poet does choose to exploit the notion of an androgynous Adam, it is characteristically to endorse marriage not celibacy:

> *Adam*, till his Rib was lost,
> Had the Sexes thus ingrost.
> When Providence our Sire did cleave,
> And out of *Adam* carved *Eve*,
> Then did Man 'bout Wedlock treat
> To make his Body up compleat.
> Thus Matrimony speaks but thee
> In a Grave Solemnity:
> For Man and Wife make but one right
> Canonical Hermaphrodite.
>
> (*Vpon a Hermaphrodite*)[78]

And naturally the praisers of women, like Randolph, consider Adam fortunate at least in Eve's creation—although the tone is tongue-in-cheek:

> Who had he not your blest creation seen,
> An Anchori[t]e in Paradice had been.
> *(In praise of Woemen in Generall)*[79]

What Marvell acknowledges is the impossibility of sustaining the anchorite Adam's state, whether desirable or undesirable. By foreshortening the Fall narrative in more ways than one, the poet reminds us of mortality—'But 'twas beyond a Mortal's share/To wander solitary there' (ll. 61–2).[80] However far back we go, mortality and loss are potentially within the human condition, and the two paradises continually retreat. But not beyond the reach of imagination: it can surmise a state of ultimate happiness and wholeness which is repossessed in the garden.

Stanza VIII, then, continues to argue that pleasure is contingent upon one kind of life, the garden-life. What has changed is that the ideal is no longer presented as a possible *choice* of life. In the earlier stanza IV, which it parallels, the gods might deliberately choose trees instead of women; Adam is not given the choice of solitude rather than Eve. Indeed this is perhaps the most remarkable aspect of the obvious contrast between Milton's approach to the Genesis story and Marvell's: if Marvell takes startling liberties with Genesis, Milton too departs from the strict letter of the text in making Adam discover loneliness for himself, and not only choose to have a companion but actively debate the issue and pester God into giving him one.[81] Long before *Paradise Lost* itself, it is clear from the divorce tracts how passionately Milton felt about the statement that it is not good for man to be alone, and the idea that Eve was created for 'mutual help, comfort, and solace'.[82] Marvell, on the contrary, implies that man had no choice by virtue of being 'Mortal'. Ironically in *The Garden* it is fallen man who *can* choose to be solitary within the limits of space and time; but he cannot altogether regain the paradise which could not even be assured to innocent Adam. Whether or not Marvell 'accepts with good grace' the necessity of woman's creation—and the tenor of *The Garden* suggests that humorous reluctance is closer to the mark—he does recognise that necessity.[83] But what he does about it is finally to affirm more powerfully than ever the completeness of the garden-life that is available to mortals, and how it can order time and space into its own kind of perfection, including and transforming more than it excludes.

From thoughts of Genesis it is a natural transition to a reminder of Adam's first occupation, gardening:

IX

> How well the skilful Gardner drew
> Of flow'rs and herbes this Dial new;
> Where from above the milder Sun
> Does through a fragrant Zodiack run;

And, as it works, th'industrious Bee
Computes its time as well as we.
How could such sweet and wholsome Hours
Be reckon'd but with herbs and flow'rs!

(ll. 65–72)

The varying shades of seventeenth-century opinion on the subject of gardening have already been reviewed in connection with *The Mower against Gardens*.[84] Here the emphasis is entirely on the gardener's constructive skills. 'Like *Adam*, hee is put into some Gentlemans Garden, to dresse the Trees, and to make it if he can, a Paradise of pleasure . . . He can make diverse curious Mazes, and knots, but'—also like Adam—'hee thinkes the worst knot he ever made was the knot of Marriage.'[85] Wye Saltonstall's character is the earthy, and earthly, embodiment of *A Gardiner*. His toil is the paradisal equivalent of the active life, and by introducing a similar figure in the concluding stanza of his poem Marvell compensates for the apparent total rejection of the active life in the counterbalancing first stanza. Instead of vainly seeking inadequate garlands, the gardener makes a 'Dial new' which is functional as well as symbolic.[86] It is often claimed that stanza IX represents a return to reality, however that is understood, and the gardener in his very ordinariness, his comforting sense of routine, helps to create this impression.

Yet by no means all readers find this gardener or his activity ordinary. Obviously other possibilities present themselves to those who read *The Garden* as an allegory or emblem of the *hortus conclusus*. Marvell himself identifies Fairfax as a spiritual gardener, weeding ambition but tilling conscience, in *Upon Appleton House* (stanza XLV). And beyond the human level the idea of the Divine Gardener is sanctioned by both Old and New Testaments. In Eden, as Sylvester's translation of du Bartas describes it, 'God himself (as Gardner) treads the allies . . . He plants, he proins, he pares, he trimmeth round/Th'ever green beauties of a fruitfull ground';[87] and at the Resurrection, as Lancelot Andrewes expounds in a sermon, Christ appeared to Mary Magdalen as 'no other, then *He* was: A *Gardiner He* was, not in shew alone, but *opere & veritate*'.[88] There is therefore some justification for seeing Marvell's Gardener as a figure of the Creator and Redeemer of mankind—if, that is, *The Garden* is an essentially religious poem.[89] A symbolic reading can also extend to 'this Dial new'; but another approach, investigating the available evidence about floral horologes in the seventeenth-century gardener's world,[90] directs attention back to the practical skills of the active life. The gardener is an artist in his own right, a maker like the poet himself. Making poems is partly inspiration, the soul sitting and singing in the green boughs, but it is also the craft of setting words, as the gardener sets plants, in a satisfying design.[91] Since *The Garden* is a self-referential poem, it is likely that 'this Dial new' is also self-referential.

If gardener and poet are fellow-workers, so too is 'th'industrious Bee':

And, as it works, th'industrious Bee

> Computes its time as well as we.
>
> (ll. 69–70)

The pun on time/thyme (confirmed by *Hortus*)[92] collapses the abstract into the natural in another 'green Thought'. Outside the garden, the active life is a race against time; the contemplative life aspires to timelessness; the life of pleasure is constantly threatened by time. But inside the garden, in this version of the threefold life, time is distilled into honey, 'sweet and wholsome Hours'. Certainly the herbs and flowers flourish briefly and fade,[93] but as certainly they spring again. The bee guarantees their survival. As for the bee itself, it is a traditional emblem not only of the active life as such, but of the political life.[94] Its presence in the garden hints at an assimilation of a political and communal ideal into an environment already perfectly adapted to the individual's experience of pleasure and contemplation. And the honey-bee is poetical as well as political. So many bees buzz pleasantly through classical and post-classical poetry, that Marvell's is only one of a veritable swarm: but the most appropriate source which has been proposed is in one of the Odes of Horace. Horace compares himself to a small bee gathering thyme and painstakingly constructing poems like honeycombs, in contradistinction to those poets who earn their laurels by praising Caesar.[95] If this is indeed the direct ancestor of Marvell's bee, then *The Garden* has come full circle in its final judgment of life and literature.

The final couplet of the poem is a formal closure, yet grammatically it may be read as a question as well as an exclamation:

> How could such sweet and wholsome Hours
> Be reckon'd but with herbs and flow'rs!
>
> (ll. 71–2)

Either this is an assertion with the full weight of the poem behind it, or it is open-ended, equivocal, querying its own premisse, drawing attention to its own limitations. Or both. Many modern readers take it for granted that *The Garden* is an interlude poem, signifying a temporary and self-consciously fantasising withdrawal on the poet's part. At the end, it is assumed, the poet tacitly acknowledges the necessity of returning to the 'real world'. It is an assumption reinforced by hindsight in the case of critics who find it difficult to erase their knowledge of Marvell's own life, and the fact that he did in the longer term choose a public career. But this knowledge is strictly irrelevant to the (undated) text of *The Garden*, and there is nothing in the last stanza that makes such an implication inescapable. On the contrary, the poem stands by the choices made.

It is true that *The Garden* deliberately excludes a great deal of what humanity lives for in this world: material and career advancement, sexual fulfilment and reproduction. But it is not simply a retreat *from* experience; it is a retreat *to* experience. It enfolds the possibility of a 'wond'rous Life' which allows pleasure, action, and contemplation, body, mind, and spirit, their due.

Marvell protects his creation of this 'wond'rous Life' by making it comic, setting intellectual booby-traps. Yet the poem remains surprisingly secure in its essential happiness. The choice of eternity is seen not to be in conflict with the choice of life but a natural extension of it, a 'longer flight'. In quite a different sense from *A Dialogue between the Resolved Soul and Created Pleasure* it might be said of *The Garden*–'The World has not one Pleasure more'.

Abbreviations and Short Titles

Principal editions

Misc. Poems, 1681	*Andrew Marvell: Miscellaneous Poems 1681*, Scolar Press Facsimile, Scolar Press, Menston, 1969.
Margoliouth/ Legouis	*The Poems and Letters of Andrew Marvell*, ed. H.M. Margoliouth, 2 vols., 3rd edn., rev. by Pierre Legouis with the collaboration of E.E. Duncan-Jones, Oxford, 1971.
RT and *RT II*	*Andrew Marvell: The Rehearsal Transpros'd and The Rehearsal Transpros'd The Second Part*, ed. D.I.B. Smith, Oxford, 1971.

Other editions (in order of publication)

Grosart ed. *Prose Works*	*The Complete Works of Andrew Marvell*, III and IV, ed. A.B. Grosart, Fuller Worthies Library, London, 1872–5.
Macdonald ed. *Poems*	*The Poems of Andrew Marvell*, ed. Hugh Macdonald, The Muses' Library, London, 1952.
Winny ed. *Some Poems*	*Andrew Marvell: Some Poems*, ed. James Winny, Hutchinson English Texts, London, 1962.
McQueen/ Rockwell	*The Latin Poetry of Andrew Marvell*, ed. and tr. William A. McQueen and Kiffin A. Rockwell, Univ. of North Carolina Press, Chapel Hill, 1964.
Kermode ed. *Selected Poetry*	*Andrew Marvell: Selected Poetry*, ed. Frank Kermode, Signet Classics, NY and London, 1967.
Lord ed. *Complete Poetry*	*Andrew Marvell: Complete Poetry*, ed. George deF. Lord (1st edn. 1968), Everyman's Library, London, 1984.
Donno ed. *Complete Poems*	*Andrew Marvell: The Complete Poems*, ed. Elizabeth Story Donno, Penguin English Poets, Harmondsworth, 1972.

Marvell criticism and biography

Berthoff (1970)	Ann E. Berthoff, *The Resolved Soul: A Study of Marvell's Major Poems*, Princeton U.P., Princeton, N.J., 1970.

Bradbrook and Lloyd Thomas (1940)	M.C. Bradbrook and M.G. Lloyd Thomas, *Andrew Marvell*, Cambridge, 1940.
Brett ed. *Essays* (1979)	*Andrew Marvell: Essays on the tercentenary of his death*, ed. R.L. Brett, Oxford for the University of Hull, 1979.
Carey ed. *Critical Anthology* (1969)	*Andrew Marvell: A critical anthology*, ed. John Carey, Penguin critical anthologies, Harmondsworth, 1969.
Chernaik (1983)	Warren L. Chernaik, *The Poet's Time: Politics and Religion in the Work of Andrew Marvell*, Cambridge, 1983.
Colie (1970)	Rosalie L. Colie, '*My Ecchoing Song*': *Andrew Marvell's Poetry of Criticism*, Princeton U.P., Princeton, N.J., 1970.
Craze (1979)	Michael Craze, *The Life and Lyrics of Andrew Marvell*, London, 1979.
Davison (1964)	Dennis Davison, *The Poetry of Andrew Marvell*, Studies in English Literature no. 18, London, 1964.
Donno ed. *Critical Heritage* (1978)	*Andrew Marvell: The Critical Heritage*, ed. Elizabeth Story Donno, The Critical Heritage Series, London, 1978.
Friedenreich ed. *Tercentenary Essays* (1977)	*Tercentenary Essays in Honor of Andrew Marvell*, ed. Kenneth Friedenreich, Archon Books, Hamden, Conn., 1977.
Friedman (1970)	Donald M. Friedman, *Marvell's Pastoral Art*, London, 1970.
Hodge (1978)	R.I.V. Hodge, *Foreshortened Time: Andrew Marvell and Seventeenth Century Revolutions*, D.S. Brewer, Cambridge, 1978.
Hunt (1978)	John Dixon Hunt, *Andrew Marvell: His Life and Writings*, London, 1978.
Hyman (1964)	Lawrence Hyman, *Andrew Marvell*, Twayne's English Authors Series, NY, 1964.
King (1977)	Bruce King, *Marvell's Allegorical Poetry*, The Oleander Press, Cambridge and NY, 1977.
Kelliher (1978)	Hilton Kelliher, *Andrew Marvell: Poet & Politician 1621-78*, British Library exhibition catalogue, BM Publications, London, 1978.
Klause (1983)	John Klause, *The Unfortunate Fall: Theodicy and the Moral Imagination of Andrew Marvell*, Archon Books, Hamden, Conn., 1983.
Legouis (1968)	Pierre Legouis, *Andrew Marvell: Poet, Puritan, Patriot*, 2nd edn., Oxford, 1968.
Leishman (1966)	J.B. Leishman, *The Art of Marvell's Poetry*, London, 1966.

Long (1984)	Michael Long, *Marvell, Nabokov: Childhood and Arcadia*, Oxford, 1984.
Lord ed. *Critical Essays* (1968)	*Andrew Marvell: A Collection of Critical Essays*, ed. George deF. Lord, Twentieth Century Views series, Englewood Cliffs, N.J., 1968.
Patrides ed. *Approaches* (1978)	*Approaches to Marvell: The York Tercentenary Lectures*, ed. C.A. Patrides, London, 1978.
Patterson (1978)	Annabel M. Patterson, *Marvell and the Civic Crown*, Princeton U.P., Princeton, N.J., 1978.
Pollard ed.	*Casebook* (1980) *Andrew Marvell: Poems. A Casebook*, ed. Arthur Pollard, Casebook Series, London, 1980.
Stocker (1986)	Margarita Stocker, *Apocalyptic Marvell: The Second Coming in Seventeenth Century Poetry*, The Harvester Press, Brighton, Sussex, 1986.
Toliver (1965)	Harold E. Toliver, *Marvell's Ironic Vision*, Yale U.P., New Haven and London, 1965.
Wallace (1968)	John M. Wallace, *Destiny His Choice: The Loyalism of Andrew Marvell*, Cambridge, 1968.
Wilcher (1985)	Robert Wilcher, *Andrew Marvell*, Cambridge, 1985.
Wilding ed. *Modern Judgements* (1969)	*Marvell: Modern Judgements*, ed. Michael Wilding, Modern Judgements Series, London, 1969.

First references to all other sources in the notes are cited in full, and thereafter by author's name and a short title (books) or author's name, abbreviated title and date of periodical (articles).

Abbreviations of periodical titles

AJP	*American Journal of Philology*
BuR	*Bucknell Review*
CentR	*Centennial Review*
CL	*Comparative Literature*
CQ	*Critical Quarterly*
CS	*Critical Survey*
ELN	*English Language Notes*
ELH	*A Journal of English Literary History*
ELR	*English Literary Renaissance*
Eng. Misc.	*English Miscellany*

ES	*English Studies*
EiC	*Essays in Criticism*
EA	*Études Anglaises*
FMLS	*Forum for Modern Language Studies*
HR	*Hudson Review*
HLQ	*Huntington Library Quarterly*
JRLB	*John Rylands Library Bulletin*
JEGP	*Journal of English & Germanic Philology*
JHI	*Journal of the History of Ideas*
MLN	*Modern Language Notes*
MLQ	*Modern Language Quarterly*
MLR	*Modern Language Review*
MP	*Modern Philology*
NLH	*New Literary History*
NDQ	*North Dakota Quarterly*
N&Q	*Notes and Queries*
OUR	*Ohio University Review*
PLL	*Papers in Language and Literature*
PQ	*Philological Quarterly*
PMLA	*Publications of the Modern Language Association*
RN	*Renaissance News*
RQ	*Renaissance Quarterly*
RES	*Review of English Studies*
SeR	*Sewanee Review*
SoR	*Southern Review*
SEL	*Studies in English Literature*
SP	*Studies in Philology*
TSLL	*Texas Studies in Literature and Language*
TLS	*Times Literary Supplement*
UTQ	*University of Toronto Quarterly*
YES	*The Yearbook of English Studies*

Other abbreviations

CPW	*The Complete Prose Works of John Milton*, Yale U.P., New Haven and London, I–VIII, 1953–82.
FQ	Edmund Spenser, *The Faerie Queene*
OED	*Oxford English Dictionary*
PL	John Milton, *Paradise Lost*
PR	John Milton, *Paradise Regained*
UAH	Andrew Marvell, *Upon Appleton House*

Notes

Introduction

1. i.e. the first half reckoning by number of titles, not actual length.
2. v. bibliographical summary prefacing *Misc. Poems*, 1681; Margoliouth/Legouis I. 224–237; Macdonald ed. *Poems*, xvii–xx; Lord ed. *Complete Poetry*, xxx–xxxiv; Donno ed. *Complete Poems*, 9–12.
3. v. C.E. Ward, 'Andrew Marvell's Widow', *TLS*, 14 May, 1938, p. 336, and F.S. Tupper, 'Mary Palmer, Alias Mrs Andrew Marvell', *PMLA*, 1938, pp. 367–392. William Empson rebuts the case against the marriage in *Using Biography*, London, 1984 (pp. 43–95, The Marriage of Marvell').
4. T.S. Eliot, 'Andrew Marvell', *Selected Essays*, 3rd enlarged edn., London, 1951, p. 303.
5. A. Alvarez confers 'the title of poet of judgment' on Marvell in precisely this sense (*The School of Donne*, London, 1970, p. 107).
6. v. Bradbrook and Lloyd Thomas (1940), chapter III; George deF. Lord, 'From Contemplation to Action: Marvell's Poetical Career' (1967, repr. Lord ed. *Critical Essays*, 1968, pp. 55–73); Don Parry Norford, 'Marvell and the Arts of Contemplation and Action', *ELH*, 41, 1974, 50–73.
7. v. Marsilio Ficino, *Opera*, Basle, 1576, I. Epistolarum. Lib. x, 919–920: Seneca also discusses the threefold life in *De Otio*, (*Epistulae Morales*, VIII). For seventeenth-century examples v. Christine Rees, 'Some Seventeenth-Century versions of the Judgment of Paris', *N&Q*, 24, 1977, 197–200.
8. v. Milton, *CPW*, IV. 1650–1655, Part I, ed. Don M. Wolfe, 1966, p. 624 and note 322.
9. A number of critics discuss this theme e.g. John Creaser, 'Marvell's Effortless Superiority', *EiC*, 20, 1970, 403–423; Chernaik (1983), passim; Klause (1983), passim.
10. v. Donno ed. *Critical Heritage* (1978), pp. 8, 142, 150, 158–9, 222, 286.
11. v. *RT II* (p. 169) for comments on his lifelong addiction to 'modest retiredness' —not necessarily ironic—and on the proper function of the clergy 'consisting in the sweetness of a contemplative life' and 'freedom from the Mechanical drudgery of raking together a fortune' (pp. 237–8).
12. v. *RT* (p. 135): 'Whether it were a War of Religion, or of Liberty, is not worth the labour to enquire.'

Part I

1. *On a Drop of Dew*, l.1; *The Picture of Little T.C. in a Prospect of Flowers*, l.1; *Upon the Hill and Grove at Billborow*, l.1; *UAH*, l.657; *Damon the Mower*, l.1. All quotations from Marvell's poetry are from Margoliouth/Legouis vol. I, unless otherwise identified.
2. Francis Bacon, *Works*, edd. J. Spedding, R.L. Ellis, and D.D. Heath, 14 vols., London, 1857–74, III. 266 and 267. v. also Sir Walter Ralegh, *The History of the World*, ed. C.A. Patrides, London, 1971, I. ii. 5.

3. v. *RT II*, pp. 203-4; Legouis (1968), chapter I, 'Early Life'; Klause (1983), pp. 127-8 and p. 183 n.9.

4. v. Louis L. Martz, *The Poetry of Meditation*, Yale U.P., New Haven, 1954, rev. edn., 1962; W.H. Halewood, *The Poetry of Grace*, Yale U.P., New Haven. 1970; Barbara K. Lewalski, *Protestant Poetics and the Seventeenth-Century Religious Lyric*, Princeton U.P., Princeton, N.J., 1979.

5. *The Saints' Everlasting Rest*, London, 1650, IV. vi. 7, pp. 694-5.

6. *Saints' Everlasting Rest*, IV. xi. 4, pp. 762-3.

7. For Marvell and Cambridge Platonism v. Toliver (1965), chapter I; Friedman (1970), pp. 23-32; Muriel Bradbrook argues against the connection, chiefly on chronological grounds (*RQ*, 24, 1971, 584-5).

8. *The Cambridge Platonists*, ed. C.A. Patrides, Stratford-upon-Avon Library 5, London, 1969: John Smith, 'The True Way or Method of Attaining to Divine Knowledge' (p. 134); Benjamin Whichcote, *Moral and Religious Aphorisms* (p. 334); Ralph Cudworth, 'A Sermon Preached before the House of Commons. March 31, 1647' (p. 98). Although these texts are all later than Marvell's Cambridge period, they represent relevant aspects of Cambridge Platonist thought.

9. Whichcote, *Aphorisms* (Patrides, p. 334); Smith, 'The True Way' (Patrides, p. 129).

10. John Calvin, *Institutes of the Christian Religion*, tr. Henry Beveridge, 2 vols., London, 1953, I. xv. 4 (I. 164).

11. *Macrobius' Commentary on the Dream of Scipio*, tr. W.H. Stahl, NY, 1952, II. i-iii (pp. 185-197). v. Henry More, *An Antidote against Atheism*, 1653 (Patrides, p. 223).

12. *Institutes*, I. xv. 6 (Beveridge, I. 166).

13. Beveridge, I. 169.

14. v. Plotinus, *Enneads* IV; for Augustine's position on Neo-platonism v. *Confessions and Enchiridion*, ed. and tr. A.C. Coulter, The Library of Christian Classics, VII, London, 1955, pp. 144-156.

15. Hermann Hugo: see below p. 207 n.4.

Part I, section i: *A Dialogue between the Resolved
Soul and Created Pleasure*

1. With some notable exceptions: e.g. Frank Kermode, 'The Banquet of Sense', *JRLB*, 44, 1961-2, pp. 68-9 (repr. *Shakespeare, Spenser, Donne: Renaissance Essays*, London, 1971, chapter 4); H.E. Toliver, 'The Strategy of Marvell's Resolve against Created Pleasure', *SEL*, 4, 1964, pp. 57-69.

2. Matt. 7: 13-14.

3. v. Bradbrook and Lloyd Thomas (1940), p. 70; Legouis (1968), p. 12.

4. *Christian Warfare*, 1604, chapter VII, pp. 38-9, cit. William Haller, *The Rise of Puritanism* (1st edn. 1938), NY, 1957, p. 156. For varying emphases on Marvell's use of the warfaring topos v. Friedman (1970), pp. 74-5; Joseph Pequigney, 'Marvell's "Soul" Poetry' (Friedenreich ed. *Tercentenary Essays*, 1977, pp. 77-8); Barbara K. Lewalski, 'Marvell as religious poet' (Patrides ed. *Approaches*, 1978, pp. 258-9).

5. Miltonic parallels are proposed by Leishman (1966), pp. 31–2; v. also Kermode (1971), pp. 84–5.

6. C.A. Patrides ed. *The English Poems of George Herbert*, Everyman's University Library, London, 1974, p. 107 and p. 132. All quotations from Herbert's poetry are from this edition.

7. e.g. Leishman (1966), p. 204; Friedman (1970), p. 76 and p. 81.

8. v. Margoliouth/Legouis I. 242 (Duncan-Jones); Spenser, *FQ* II. xii. 77; Marlowe, *The Passionate Shepherd to His Love*, l.9; Thomas Carew, *A Rapture*, ll. 35–44.

9. *Emblemes*, London, 1635, I. vii, p. 30.

10. Bradbrook and Lloyd Thomas (1940), p. 71.

11. Genesis 3: 5.

12. e.g. *The Mower's Song*, ll. 1–4; *UAH*, stanza LXXX; *The Garden*, stanza VI. For discussion of Marvell's mirror imagery v. Christopher Ricks, 'Its own resemblance' and John Carey, 'Reversals transposed' (Patrides ed. *Approaches*, 1978, especially pp. 109–110 and 149–50).

13. Gilbert Ryle, *The Concept of Mind*, London, 1949, p. 159.

14. *Bartas his Devine Weekes & Workes*, tr. Josuah Sylvester, London, 1605–6, 'The First Day of the First Week', p. 6.

15. *Hermes Mercurius Trismegistus, his Divine Pymander, in Seventeen Books*, tr. Dr Everard, London, 1657, p. 24.

16. Lucan, *De bello civili*, VI. 469–474. I am indebted to Dr Gareth Roberts for this reference.

17. For seventeenth-century attitudes to music v. John Hollander, *The Untuning of the Sky: Ideas of Music in English Poetry 1500–1700*, Princeton U.P., Princeton, N.J., 1961, chapter V; Gretchen Ludke Finney, *Musical Backgrounds for English Literature: 1580–1650*, Rutgers U.P., N. Brunswick, N.J., n.d., chapter III; and for the Puritan view, Lawrence A. Sasek, *The Literary Temper of the English Puritans*, Louisiana State U.P., Baton Rouge, 1961, pp. 115–7.

18. v. William G. Madsen, *From Shadowy Types to Truth: Studies in Milton's Symbolism*, Yale U.P., New Haven and London, 1968, chapter 5, 'The Eye and the Ear'; cf. the role of the senses in Milton's *Comus*.

19. Hollander, *Untuning of the Sky*, p. 42 and p. 48; William Empson classifies the pun in *Seven Types of Ambiguity*, (1st edn. 1930), 2nd rev. edn. London, 1947, chapter III. K.W. Gransden extends the wordplay in 'Time, Guilt and Pleasure: A Note on Marvell's Nostalgia', *Ariel*, I. ii. 1970, pp. 83–97 (88–90).

20. Kermode, *Renaissance Essays*, p. 87.

21. e.g. Joseph Hall, *The Arte of Divine Meditation*, London, 1607; Robert Bolton, *A Discourse about the State of True Happinesse*, 4th edn., 1698; Jeremiah Burroughs, *The Rare Iewel of Christian Contentment*, 1652.

22. *Works*, edd. Spedding et al., VI. 467. Kermode (*Selected Poetry*, p. 49) and Leishman (1966, pp. 203–4) both conjecture that the poem might have been intended for a musical setting.

23. v. Margoliouth/Legouis, I. 242.

24. *Renaissance Essays*, p. 86.

25. tr. C.B. Gulick, Loeb Classical Library, 1933, V. 294–5: Hallett Smith quotes this passage in *Elizabethan Poetry: A Study in Conventions, Meaning, and Expression* (1st edn., 1952), Harvard U.P., Cambridge, Mass., 1964, p. 294.

26. *Selected Poetry*, p. 51.

27. v. Margoliouth/Legouis, I. 242: Margoliouth quotes the 1647 text. My quotation is from *Abraham Cowley: Poems*, ed. A.R. Waller, Cambridge, 1905, p. 83.

28. *Poems*, ed. C.H. Wilkinson (1st edn., 1930), Oxford, 1953, p. 71.
29. *An Apologie for Paris*, London, 1649, p.69 c.f. George Peele, *The Araygnement of Paris*, IV. iv.
30. For Marvell's likely knowledge of Montemayor's *Diana* v. Leishman (1966), p. 106. For the Judgment of Paris debate v. J.M. Kennedy ed. *A Critical Edition of Yong's Translation of George of Montemayor's Diana*, Oxford, 1968, p. 81.
31. Friedman (1970, p. 81) mentions both the Faust legend and *Paradise Regained* in this connection.
32. *Georgics* II. 490: Margoliouth/Legouis I. 243.
33. *Works*, ed. L.C. Martin (1st edn., 1914), 2nd edn., Oxford, 1957, p. 349, *Life of Paulinus*, 11. 19-22.
34. Barbara K. Lewalski writes 'the combat is designed to exhibit and prove the soul's elect state' ('Marvell as religious poet', Patrides ed. *Approaches*, 1978, p. 257).
35. *CPW*, II, ed. Ernest Sirluck, 1959, pp. 514-5: warfaring/wayfaring is a textual crux (v. editor's footnote). The passage is cited in this connection by Joseph Pequigney, 'Marvell's "Soul" Poetry' and Warren L. Chernaik, 'Marvell's Satires' (Friedenreich ed. *Tercentenary Essays*, 1977, p. 79 and p. 273); also by Wilcher (1985), p. 58.

Part I, section ii: *On a Drop of Dew*

1. D.M. Friedman, 'Sight and insight' (Patrides ed. *Approaches*, 1978, pp. 313-20).
2. v. Ruth Wallerstein, *Studies in Seventeenth-Century Poetic*, Univ. of Wisconsin Press, 1950, pp. 162-4; J.E. Saveson, 'Marvell's "On a Drop of Dew"', *N&Q*, 203, 1958, pp. 289-90; Harry Berger Jr., 'Andrew Marvell: The Poem as Green World', *FMLS*, 3, 1967, pp. 290-309 (298-302); Louis L. Martz, *The Wit of Love*, Univ. of Notre Dame Press, Notre Dame, 1969, pp. 161-2; Friedman (1970), pp. 64-5; Donald R. Dickson, *The Fountain of Living Waters*, Univ. of Missouri Press, Columbia, 1987, pp. 2-8.
3. v. citation with translation in Henry Vaughan, 'Man in Darkness, or, A Discourse of Death', *The Mount of Olives*, 1652, (*Works*, ed. L.C. Martin, 2nd edn., Oxford, 1957, p. 173).
4. *Ros*, tr. McQueen/Rockwell, pp. 15-17.
5. cf. Donne's Latin epitaph in St. Paul's: 'aspicit eum/Cujus nomen est Oriens'.
6. *The Carelesse Merchant (THRENOIKOS The House of Mourning*, 1640), cit. Barbara K. Lewalski, *Donne's 'Anniversaries' and the Poetry of Praise*, Princeton U.P., Princeton N.J., 1973, p. 200; Lewalski also cites the following Donne quotation (p. 209).
7. *Sermons*, edd. Evelyn M. Simpson and George R. Potter, Univ. of California Press, Berkeley and LA, 1962, X. 187.
8. e.g. in the collection of commonplaces 'Sic Vita', 1.4 and 1.11 (attrib. Henry King: v. *The Poems of Henry King*, ed. Margaret Crum, Oxford, 1965, pp. 148-9 and Appendix III).
9. v. Bradbrook and Lloyd Thomas (1940), p. 58; Colie (1970), pp. 115-7; Lewalski (Patrides ed. *Approaches*, 1978), p. 262. Bradbrook and Lloyd Thomas compare,

Colie and Lewalski contrast.

10. *Poems*, ed. Waller, 1905, p. 321.

11. *Otia Sacra*, London, 1648, p. 13.

12. *Poems*, ed. L.C. Martin, Oxford, 1956 and 1965, p. 393.

13. *Poems*, ed. Ian Donaldson, Oxford, 1975, p. 266. In his note on l. 55 Donaldson cites the Senecan image of the soul as 'a god dwelling as a guest in a human body' (*Epist.* xxxi. 11).

14. v. *Enneads*, especially IV. viii. For discussion of the problems involved in Plotinus's view of the soul (which I have greatly simplified) v. Émile Bréhier, *The Philosophy of Plotinus*, tr. Joseph Thomas, Univ. of Chicago Press, Chicago and London, 1958, chapter V, and J.M. Rist, *Plotinus: The Road to Reality*, Cambridge, 1967, chapter 9.

15. v. Richard Crashaw, *Poems*, ed. L.C. Martin, Oxford, 1957, *The Teare*, p. 84. Crashaw parallels are noticed by Leishman (1966), p. 202; Friedman (1970), p. 62; Craze (1979), p. 279.

16. *Poems*, ed. Donaldson, p. 265.

17. e.g. Klause (1983), p. 54; Long (1984), pp. 114–6; Wilcher (1985), pp. 63–8.

18. v. Bréhier, *Philosophy of Plotinus*, p. 39; Augustine, *The City of God*, tr. John Healey, XX. xxi, cit. King (1977), p. 33.

19. v. Leishman (1966), p. 200, n. 3; King (1977), p. 31.

20. v. Saveson (*N&Q*, 1958), p. 289.

21. *Areopagitica*, *CPW*, II. 515.

22. Edmund Gosse, *The Life and Letters of John Donne, Dean of St. Paul's*, London, 1899, II. 9.

23. e.g. Berger (*FMLS*, 1967), pp. 299–302.

24. v. George M. Muldrow, 'The Forty Lines of Andrew Marvell's "On a Drop of Dew" ', *ELN*, 23, 1985–6 (1986), pp. 23–7.

25. v. Leishman for Vaughan/Crashaw comparisons (1966, pp. 196–202).

26. v. Ryle, *Concept of Mind*, pp. 15–16 and passim.

27. But cf. the opposite Hermetic view that water is the primary element of commerce between heaven and earth: v. Thomas Vaughan, *Euphrates*, 1655 (*Works*, ed. Alan Rudrum assisted by Jennifer Drake-Brockman, Oxford, 1984, pp. 538–41). Vaughan also theorises on the link between dew and manna (pp. 548–9).

The Coronet

28. e.g. Michael McKeon, 'Pastoralism, Pluralism, Imperialism, Scientism: Andrew Marvell and the Problem of Mediation', *YES*, 13, 1983, pp. 46–65 (49–50); Long (1984), pp. 129–32. For theological readings v. also Margaret Carpenter, 'From Herbert to Marvell: Poetics in "A Wreath" and "The Coronet" ', *JEGP*, 69, 1970, pp. 50–62; Bruce King, 'A Reading of Marvell's "The Coronet" ', *MLR*, 68, 1973, pp. 741–9; Annabel Patterson, '*Bermudas* and *The Coronet*: Marvell's Protestant Poetics', *ELH*, 44, 1977, pp. 478–99 (490–7).

29. v. Berthoff (1970), pp. 46–7; Carpenter (*JEGP*, 1970), pp. 52–3.

30. v. Izaak Walton, *The Life of John Donne* (*Lives*, London, 1670), pp. 36–7.

31. *Poems*, London, 1640, p. 160.

32. v. Colie (1970), p. 80.

33. v. Patterson (*ELH*, 1977), pp. 491–2.

34. v. Giorgio Vasari, *The Lives of the Artists*, a selection tr. by George Bull, Penguin Books, Harmondsworth, 1965, p. 377.
35. *Divina Commedia, Purgatorio* xxvii. 94–108. For commentary on the allegory v. W.W. Vernon, *Readings on the Purgatorio of Dante chiefly based on the commentary of Benvenuto da Imola*, 3rd rev. edn., London, 1907, II. 419–22. v. also Renato Poggioli, *The Oaten Flute: Essays on Pastoral Poetry and the Pastoral Ideal*, Harvard U.P., Cambridge, Mass., 1975, p. 141; A.J. Smith, *The Metaphysics of Love*, Cambridge, 1985, pp. 50–5.
36. Ps. 24; 7–10. The importance of the Psalms for seventeenth-century Protestant poetics is attested by Patterson (*ELH*, 1977) and Lewalski, *Protestant Poetics* (1979). Marvell strives not just to imitate but to outdo. Patterson points out that *The Coronet* 'deliberately abandons the solution of a poetry based on and validated by the Psalms of praise' (p. 490).
37. v. King (*MLR*, 1973), p. 745.
38. v. Herbert, *Jordan (II)*.
39. For Herbert/Marvell comparisons v. Martz, *Wit of Love*, pp. 154–6; Joseph H. Summers, *The Heirs of Donne and Jonson*, London, 1970, p. 132; Carpenter (*JEGP*, 1970); Laurence Lerner, *The Uses of Nostalgia*, London, 1972, pp. 181–2; Patterson (*ELH*, 1977) pp. 495–6.
40. v. Patterson (*ELH*, 1977), p. 491.
41. v. H.R. Swardson, *Poetry and the Fountain of Light*, London, 1962, pp. 86–7.
42. v. Leishman (1966), p. 195, n. 2.
43. *Modern Painters*, III. 222, cit. Vernon, *Readings on the Purgatorio*, II. 422.
44. tr. Beveridge, I. 253.
45. v. Leishman (1966), p. 196; Thomas Randolph, *Poems*, 2nd edn., Oxford, 1640, pp. 84–7 (86).
46. Among those who find a resolution in the ending are E.W. Tayler, *Nature and Art in Renaissance Literature*, Columbia U.P., NY and London, 1964, pp. 164–5; Lewalski (Patrides ed. *Approaches*, 1978), p. 257; Stocker (1986), pp. 113–21. v. also Klause (1983), pp. 119–20; McKeon (*YES* 1983), pp. 49–50.
47. 'this curious frame': George Chapman, *Ovids Banquet of Sence*, st. 117 (*Poems*, ed. Phyllis Brooks Bartlett, NY and London, 1941, p. 82); 'allegorie's curious frame': Sir Philip Sidney, *Astrophil and Stella*, xxviii.1 (*Poems*, ed. William A. Ringler Jr., Oxford, 1962, p. 178).
48. v. Patterson (*ELH*, 1977), p. 496; Long (1984), pp. 131–2.
49. The phrase is Martz's (*Wit of Love*, p. 156).
50. Carpenter (*JEGP*, 1970), p. 61 (following Toliver).
51. *Works*, ed. Martin (2nd edn., 1957), p. 539.
52. op. cit., p. 508. Swardson makes the general association between the Magdalen's repentance and *The Coronet* (*Poetry and the Fountain of Light*, pp. 87–8).
53. v. Stocker (1986), pp. 113–21: she stresses *renovatio* coming out of *desolatio*.
54. v. St Augustine, *Confessions*, VII. ix. 15. v. also Joshua Reynolds, *Mythomystes*, cit. Sasek, *Literary Temper of the English Puritans*, pp. 51–2.

Eyes and Tears

55. v. Margoliouth/Legouis I. 245. For comments on the poem's structure, v. Leishman (1966), pp. 38–9; Legouis (1968), p. 65; Wilcher (1985), p. 20.
56. v. Martz, *Poetry of Meditation* (rev. edn.), pp. 199–203.

57. e.g. Leishman (1966), pp. 38–42; Legouis (1968), p. 35; Lewalski (Patrides ed. *Approaches*, 1978), pp. 265–8; Craze (1979), pp. 91–3; Wilcher (1985), pp. 13–20.
58. Lewalski represents the dichotomy as that of nature and grace (Patrides ed. *Approaches*, 1978, pp. 266–7).
59. For Marvell's use of optics in *Eyes and Tears* v. Friedman (Patrides ed. *Approaches*, 1978), pp. 321–4.
60. Herschel Baker, *The Wars of Truth*, London and NY, 1952, p. 304.
61. The phrase is from Galileo's *Dialogues Concerning Two New Sciences*, tr. Henry Crew and Alfonso de Salvio, 1939: Baker quotes part of the dialogue (op. cit., p. 315).
62. ll. 20–24 (*Works*, ed. Martin, 2nd edn., 1957, p. 397).
63. v. Friedman (Patrides ed. *Approaches*, 1978), p. 323; Klause (1983), pp. 148–9.
64. *Works*, ed. Martin (2nd edn., 1957), p. 159.
65. For the Magdalen's tears as a subject for ingenuity v. Leishman (1966), p. 40.
66. Bacon, *The Advancement of Learning*: v. *Works*, edd. Spedding et al., 1857–74, III. 287 and 394–5.
67. v. Ps. 19: 1 and Ps. 8: 3–4.
68. cf. Lewalski (Patrides ed. *Approaches*, 1978), p. 266.
69. v. Herbert, *Grief* (*English Poems*, ed. Patrides, 1974, p. 170); Vaughan, *The Mount of Olives* (*Works*, ed. Martin, 2nd edn., 1957, p. 159); Jeremiah 9.1.
70. For differing estimates of the poem's conclusion v. Thomas Clayton, ' "It is Marvel…" ' (Friedenreich ed. *Tercentenary Essays*, 1977), pp. 65–6; Lewalski (Patrides ed. *Approaches*, 1978), p. 267; Wilcher (1985), pp. 19–20.

Part I, section iii: *Bermudas*

1. Readings of *Bermudas* differ radically: a cross-section includes R.L. Colie, 'Marvell's "Bermudas" and the Puritan Paradise', *RN*, 1957, pp. 75–9; R.M. Cummings, 'The Difficulty of Marvell's "Bermudas" ', *MP*, 67, 1969–70, pp. 331–40; Tay Fizdale, 'Irony in Marvell's "Bermudas" ', *ELH*, 42, 1975, pp. 203–13; Toshihiko Kawasaki, 'Marvell's "Bermudas"—A Little World, or a New World?', *ELH*, 43, 1976, pp. 38–52; Annabel Patterson, '*Bermudas* and *The Coronet*: Marvell's Protestant Poetics', *ELH*, 44, 1977, pp. 478–99 (486–90); Philip Brockbank, 'The politics of Paradise: "Bermudas" ' (Patrides ed. *Approaches*, 1978, pp. 174–93); Long (1984), pp. 116–8; Stocker (1986), pp. 186–201.
2. Silvester Jourdan, *A Discovery of the Barmvdas*, London, 1610, p. 8.
3. Lewis Hughes, *A Plaine and Trve Relation of the Goodnes of God towards the Sommer Ilands, written by way of exhortation, to stirre vp the people there to praise God*, London, 1621, sigs. A2^v, A3^r'.
4. This is suggested by Cummings (*MP*, 1969–70), pp. 335–6.
5. The Ninth Pastoral, ll. 79–81 (*Poems*, ed. James Kinsley, Oxford, 1958, II. 908–9).
6. First known use on the Company's Book of Laws, 1622: v. T. Tucker, *Bermuda: Today and Yesterday*, London, Bermuda, NY, 1975, pp. 66–7.
7. e.g. Kawasaki (*ELH*, 1976), pp. 47–8; glosses are proposed by Colie (*RN*, 1957), p. 79; Fizdale (*ELH*, 1975), pp. 210–11; C.B. Hardman 'Marvell's Rowers',

EiC, 27, 1977, pp. 93–9; J.H. Summers, 'Some Apocalyptic Strains in Marvell's Poetry' (Friedenreich ed. *Tercentenary Essays*, 1977, pp. 180–203), p. 200.

8. 'The politics of Paradise' (Patrides ed. *Approaches*, 1978), p. 176; v. also Stocker (1986), p. 189.

9. v. Bradbrook and Lloyd Thomas (1940), pp. 64–5; Patterson (*ELH*, 1977), pp. 486–8; Lewalski (Patrides ed. *Approaches*, 1978), pp. 273–4. v. also Fizdale's contrasting interpretation (*ELH*, 1975), pp. 206–10.

10. v. C.B. Hardman, 'Marvell's "Bermudas" and Sandys's *Psalms*', *RES*, 32, 1981, pp. 64–7.

11. v. Hughes, *A Plaine and Trve Relation*, sig. A3ᵛ.

12. Relevant historical sources include Jourdan (1610) and Hughes (1621) already cited; also Hughes, *A Letter sent into England from the svmmer Ilands*, London, 1615; Captain John Smith, *The Generall Historie of Virginia, New-England, and the Summer Isles*, London, 1624, Lib. V; William Strachey, *A true reportory of the wracke, and redemption of Sir Thomas Gates Knight; vpon, and from the Ilands of the Bermudas (Purchas His Pilgrimes. In Five Bookes*, London, 1625, The Fourth Part, IX. 6). A useful modern history is H.C. Wilkinson, *The Adventurers of Bermuda*, 2nd edn., Oxford University Press, London, 1958.

13. v. Hughes, *A Letter*, sig. B2ʳ; Jourdan, *A Discovery*, p. 9; Smith, *Generall Historie*, p. 170.

14. v. Wilkinson, *Adventurers*, chapter XIV; Cummings (*MP*, 1969–70), pp. 332–3; Fizdale (*ELH*, 1975), pp. 204–5.

15. Roger Wood, cit. Wilkinson, *Adventurers*, p. 225.

16. v. John Oxenbridge, *A Seasonable Proposition of Propagating the Gospel by Christian Colonies in the Continent of Guaiana*, [?] London, 1670.

17. Both husband and wife: v. Marvell's epitaph for Jane Oxenbridge (Margoliouth/ Legouis I. 139–40).

18. v. Genesis 1: 21; Ps. 74: 14; Ps. 104: 25–6; Isaiah 27: 1.

19. *The Battell of the Summer Islands, Poems*, etc., 1645, pp. 52–9. For Marvell/ Waller comparison and contrast v. Warren L. Chernaik, *The Poetry of Limitation: A Study of Edmund Waller*, Yale U.P., New Haven and London, 1968, pp. 179–80; Kawasaki (*ELH*, 1976), pp. 41–4; Patterson (*ELH*, 1977), pp. 488–9. For ironic reading v. Cummings (*MP*, 1969–70), p. 334.

20. Jourdan, *A Discovery*, p. 17.

21. Cummings (*MP*, 1969–70), p. 334.

22. v. Kawasaki (*ELH*, 1976), p. 47; Stocker (1986), pp. 191–2. Kawasaki sees them as possibly both 'apocalyptic' and 'mock-heroic'.

23. v. Wilkinson, *Adventurers*, p. 22.

24. *The Tempest*, ed. Frank Kermode, Arden Shakespeare, 6th edn., London, 1958, repr. 1961, p. 45: v. Kermode's note explicating l.53.

25. v. Wilkinson, *Adventurers*, pp. 296–308.

26. Hughes, *A Plaine and Trve Relation*, sigs. A4ᵛ – B1ᵛ.

27. Hughes, op. cit., sig. B1ʳ; Strachey, *A true reportory (Purchas His Pilgrimes*, 1625), p. 1757 (second-hand report).

28. Wilcher (1985), p. 144, notes the interplay of tenses.

29. *Demonorum Insula:* v. Wilkinson, *Adventurers*, p. 23, quoting Diego Ramirez. Hughes denies 'the Ilands of diuels' report (*A Letter*, sig. A3ᵛ).

30. e.g. Ariosto, *Orlando Furioso*, VI, Alcina's isle; Spenser, *FQ*, II. xii, Acrasia's Bower of Bliss; Camões, *Os Lusiadas*, IX, Venus's isle.

31. Cummings (*MP*, 1969–70), pp. 337–9.

32. Fizdale (*ELH*, 1975), p. 207: for refutation of Fizdale's case v. Hardman (*EiC*, 1977), p. 96.
33. v. Patterson (*ELH*, 1977), pp. 488–9.
34. *The Earthly Paradise and the Renaissance Epic*, Princeton U.P., Princeton N.J., 1966, p. 119: v. also p. 86.
35. v. *Divina Commedia, Purgatorio*, XXVIII.
36. Poggioli, *The Oaten Flute*, p. 151.
37. Giamatti, *The Earthly Paradise*, p. 101, n.3; p. 142, n.10.
38. *Generall Historie*, p. 170.
39. Letter from Lord Thanet to John Aubrey, cit. Anthony Powell, *John Aubrey and His Friends*, rev. edn., London, 1963, p. 158: v. also Waller, *The Battell of the Summer Islands*, I. 40–3 (*Poems*, p. 53).
40. Exodus 16:13. *Generall Historie*, p. 171. cf. Strachey, *A true reportory* (*Purchas His Pilgrimes*, 1625), pp. 1740–1.
41. *A Plaine and Trve Relation*, sigs. A4ᵛ and B1ʳ.
42. *Generall Historie*, p. 171. Smith records that 'they were neere all destroyed, till there was a strict inhibition for their preseruation'.
43. cf. Matt. 10: 29–31.
44. Geoffrey Bullough ed. *Luis de Camões. The Lusiads in Sir Richard Fanshawe's Translation*, London, 1963: introduction p. 25; text p. 288.
45. This and the following Cowley quotation are from *Essays, in Verse and Prose, The Garden*, stanza 9 (*Essays* etc., ed. Waller, 1906, p. 426). Waller in *The Battell of the Summer Islands*, I. 7–8, says that Bermudan oranges surpass the golden apples of the Hesperides (*Poems*, p. 52). v. also John Raymond's ecstatic description of 'the Hesperian Apple, or Orange Tree' (*An Itinerary Contayning A Voyage, Made through Italy, in the yeare 1646, and 1647*, London, 1648, sig. a4ʳ). For stylistic analysis of the effect of Marvell's couplet v. Archie Burnett, *Milton's Style*, London and NY, 1981, Appendix, pp. 172–3.
46. *An Antidote against Atheism* (1653), II.v (*The Cambridge Platonists*, ed. Patrides, 1969, p. 259).
47. ibid.
48. *Antidote against Atheism*, II.vii (p. 266).
49. For associations between melons in *Bermudas* and *The Garden* v. Friedman (1970), p. 160; King (1977), p. 43.
50. Michael Wilding argues on symbolic and practical grounds against the apple/pineapple identification (' "Apples" in Marvell's "Bermudas" ', *ELN*, 6, 1968–9, pp. 254–7).
51. Governor Roger Wood in a letter to Lady Dorset (quoted by Wilkinson, *Adventurers*, p. 221).
52. v. Wilding (*ELN*, 1968–9), pp. 254–7; J.B. Winterton, 'Some Notes on Marvell's "Bermudas" ', *N&Q*, 213, 1968, p. 102, n.1; King (1977), p. 44; Lewalski (Patrides ed. *Approaches*, 1978), p. 272; Stocker (1986), p. 196. They may be regarded as the fruit of the Tree of Knowledge (Wilding), of the Tree of Life (Lewalski), or both in conjunction with the Tree of the Cross (Stocker). Cummings identifies them with the apples of the Hesperides (*MP*, 1969–70), p. 336.
53. v. Brockbank (Patrides ed. *Approaches*, 1978), pp. 176, 184, 188.
54. v. Smith, *Generall Historie*, pp. 176–8; Fizdale (*ELH*, 1975), p. 209.
55. Waller, *The Battell of the Summer Islands*, I.9–10 (*Poems*, p. 52); Sir William Davenant, *Madagascar*, ll. 391–2 (*The Shorter Poems, and Songs from the Plays*

and Masques, ed. A.M. Gibbs, Oxford, 1972, p. 20).

56. Colie (*RN*, 1957), p. 78: Jourdan was responsible for the report of pearls (*A Discovery*, p. 16).

57. v. A.P. Newton, *The Colonising Activities of the English Puritans*, New Haven, London and Oxford, 1914, pp. 124–5.

58. v. Bacon, *New Atlantis* (*Works*, edd. Spedding et al., 1857–74, III.137–9).

59. St Ambrose, *De Officiis Clericorum, Hexaemeron* etc., ed. R.O. Gilbert, Lipsiae, 1839, p. 52: there is a nice Latin pun on 'incentive'. Leo Spitzer cites the passage in 'Classical and Christian Ideas of World Harmony', Part I, *Traditio* II, 1944, pp. 409–64 (v. 424–30). The translation is mine.

60. v. Winterton (*N&Q*, 1968), p. 102, n.3: 'a witty reference to the old and the new cosmology'.

61. Scepticism: v. Cummings (*MP*, 1969–70), p. 339. Proper humility/diffidence/ reluctance: v. Hardman (*EiC*, 1977), p. 97; Summers (Friedenreich ed. *Tercentenary Essays*, 1977), p. 201; Wilcher (1985), p. 144.

62. For reflections on the narrator's mixed feelings v. Klause (1983), p. 92; Long (1984), p. 117.

63. *The New Arcadia* I (*The Countess of Pembroke's Arcadia*, ed. Victor Skretkowicz, Oxford, 1987, p. 11).

64. v. Christopher Ricks, *Milton's Grand Style*, Oxford, 1963, pp. 142–3; Hardman (*EiC*, 1977), pp. 94–5.

65. But v. Barbara Everett's subtle reading of '*Bermudas*' for a different emphasis on the effect on the reader ('The Shooting of the Bears', Brett ed. *Essays*, 1979, pp. 99–102).

Clorinda and Damon and *Thyrsis and Dorinda*

66. An alternative solution is available to editors who attempt a chronological arrangement of the lyrics since, if Marvell's authorship of the original version is accepted, it must be 'his earliest datable poem in English': v. Donno ed. *Complete Poems*, p. 221. For evidence for and against attribution v. notes 82–4 below.

67. *On the Victory obtained by Blake* shares with *Thyrsis and Dorinda*, and *Tom May's Death*, the distinction of being omitted from Bodl. MS. Eng. poet. d. 49 (v. Lord ed. *Complete Poetry*, p. xxxii).

68. The phrases are from Cowley's 'Of Agriculture', *Essays, in Verse and Prose* (*Essays* etc., ed. Waller, 1906, p. 401).

69. Donno finds the dialogue 'curious' and the ending speculative ('The Unhoopable Marvell', Friedenreich ed. *Tercentenary Essays*, 1977, pp. 39–40); but v. Lewalski's positive reading (Patrides ed. *Approaches*, 1978, pp. 269–71).

70. *FQ* II. xii. 50, cit. Leishman (1966), p. 119.

71. *The Poetical Works of Edmund Spenser*, ed. J.C. Smith and E. de Selincourt, Oxford, 1912, repr. 1960, p. 430. v. note on *FQ* II. xii. 50–5 in *The Faerie Queene*, ed. Thomas P. Roche, Penguin English Poets, Harmondsworth, 1978, p. 1139.

72. The Prayer Book and Isaiah allusions are noted by Wilcher (1985), p. 53: the primary source for the former is Isaiah 53: 6.

73. v. Patrick Cullen, *Spenser, Marvell, and Renaissance Pastoral*, Harvard U.P., Cambridge, Mass., 1970, pp. 165–7; Angus Easson compares the *converted* Clorinda's response to Damon with that of unfallen Eve to Adam ('Andrew Marvell's "Clorinda and Damon": An Echo of "Huius Nympha Loci"?', (*N&Q*,

225, 1980, p. 335). Friedman (1970), p. 50 and Lerner, *Uses of Nostalgia*, p. 190 both comment on the role reversal in a pastoral context.

74. cf. Lewalski (Patrides ed. *Approaches*, 1978), p. 269. For *vade* v. Leishman (1966), p. 118, n. 1.

75. Horace, *Odes* III. xiii. 10. For *frigus* in Virgil's *Eclogues* (e.g. I.52 and II.8) v. Michael C.J. Putnam, *Virgil's Pastoral Art*, Princeton U.P., Princeton N.J., 1970, p. 47. For another suggested echo v. Easson (*N&Q*, 1980), pp. 335–6.

76. *Regeneration*, ll. 49–52 (*Works*, ed. Martin, p. 398): Lewalski also cites this, with Scriptural and emblematic references (Patrides ed. *Approaches*, 1978), p. 278, n. 24; cf. Geoffrey Walton, *Metaphysical to Augustan*, London, 1955, pp. 122–3.

77. Malcolm Lowry, *Under the Volcano*, chapters 1 and 3 (v. Chris Ackerley and Lawrence J. Clipper, *A Companion to 'Under the Volcano'*, University of British Columbia Press, Vancouver, 1984, index *Clorinda and Damon*); T.S. Eliot, *Selected Essays*, p. 300. v. also Robert Ellrodt, *L'Inspiration Personnelle et l'Esprit du Temps chez Les Poètes Métaphysiques Anglais*, Première Partie, Tome II, Paris, 1960, p. 138; Long (1984), p. 46.

78. Henry Vaughan, *Corruption*, ll. 23–4 (*Works*, ed. Martin, p. 440).

79. Spenser, *Poetical Works*, ed. Smith and de Selincourt, p. 439; Milton, *On the Morning of Christ's Nativity*, ll. 89–90, *Complete Shorter Poems*, ed. John Carey, Longman Annotated English Poets, London, 1971 (1st pubd. 1968), p. 105 and note. v. Friedman (1970), pp. 54–5; Long (1984), p. 224, n. 5, argues for ambiguity.

80. v. *The Cambridge Platonists*, ed. Patrides, p. 306.

81. v. Donno (Friedenreich ed. *Tercentenary Essays*, 1977), pp. 39–40: Klause (1983), p. 118; Wilcher (1985), p. 54.

82. Margoliouth/Legouis I. 247.

83. v. Margoliouth/Legouis I. 247–8; Kelliher (1978), pp. 48–9.

84. v. Lord ed. *Complete Poetry*, p. xxxii and p. 261, note; Kelliher (1978), pp. 48–9; Chernaik (1983), Appendix, pp. 206–8.

85. v. Klause (1983), p. 170, n. 25, and p. 185, n. 28.

86. The text of this version is supplied by Craze (1979), pp. 31–2, with the later version pp. 258–9. He compares them (p. 260) without questioning the attribution.

87. *Select Sermons* (1698), Part I (*Cambridge Platonists*, ed. Patrides, p. 4). The title given to the sermon is Patrides' own (p. 42).

88. Johnson, *Rasselas* I. i. 2.

89. For the terms *musica speculativa* and *musica instrumentalis* v. Hollander, *Untuning of the Sky*, passim; for music of the spheres also v. Hollander, passim, on Pythagoras, Plato, Cicero/Macrobius. 'Chast Soul': cf. Milton, *Apology for Smectymnuus* (*CPW* I, ed. Don M. Wolfe, 1953, pp. 892–3).

90. v. *OED*, Antedate, 4 and 6.

91. v. note 73 above. For *Thyrsis and Dorinda*, v. Kenneth Friedenreich, 'The Mower Mown' (Friedenreich ed. *Tercentenary Essays*, 1977), p. 163.

92. 'The Sheepheard Carillo his Song', *England's Helicon*, ed. H.E. Rollins, Harvard U.P., Cambridge, Mass., 1935, I. 87–9: noted by Leishman (1966), p. 106.

93. Colie (1970), p. 129. For varying interpretations v. also Swardson, *Poetry and the Fountain of Light*, p. 91; Lerner, *Uses of Nostalgia*, pp. 182–3; Donno, pp. 38–9, and Friedenreich, pp. 164–5 (Friedenreich ed. *Tercentenary Essays*, 1977). Muriel Bradbrook offers a politicised reading of the dialogue in 'Marvell and the Masque' (*Tercentenary Essays*), pp. 211–13.

94. *pace* Lord ed. *Complete Poetry*, p. 261, note. A. Alvarez surveys relevant

seventeenth-century attitudes to suicide in *The Savage God*, London, 1971, IV. 2. Klause (1983) speculates on a possible link with the publication of Donne's *Biathanatos* in 1647 (p. 185, n. 28).

95. From Fanny Burney's *Diary:* v. *Diary & Letters of Madame D'Arblay*, 6 vols., ed. Austin Dobson after Charlotte Barrett, London, 1904, I. 398.

Part I, section iv: *A Dialogue between the Soul and Body*

1. But Kitty Scoular Datta significantly equates the attitudes of Soul and Body with different 'ways of life': v. 'New Light on Marvell's "A Dialogue between the Soul and Body"', *RQ*, 22, 1969, pp. 242–55 (253–4).
2. For an explanation of this and other features with reference to academic disputation v. Joseph Pequigney, 'Marvell's "Soul" Poetry' (Friedenreich ed. *Tercentenary Essays*, 1977), pp. 90–1.
3. Leishman (1966), p. 214.
4. Marvell's indebtedness to Hugo was first established by Datta (*RQ*, 1969, p. 243 ff.)
5. St Augustine (v. note 14 on p. 197 above); Calvin, *Institutes* tr. Beveridge, I. 60. Rosalie Osmond discusses the confusion between body/soul and flesh/spirit using another Augustinian reference: v. 'Body and Soul Dialogues in the Seventeenth Century', *ELR*, 4, 1974, pp. 364–403 (368).
6. The phrases are from Bréhier, *Philosophy of Plotinus*, tr. Thomas, p. 55. Friedman (1970) cites Plotinus and John Smith in connection with ll. 18–20 (p. 70 and p. 91, n. 53).
7. For Marvell's probable knowledge of Descartes v. Roger Sharrock 'Marvell's Poetry of Evasion and Marvell's Times', *English*, 28, 1979, p. 25; v. also Ellrodt, *Les Poètes Métaphysiques Anglais*, I. ii. 139.
8. v. *Antidote against Atheism*, I. xi (*Cambridge Platonists*, ed. Patrides, pp. 240–5; v. also Patrides' introduction, pp. 29–31); for shift in More's attitude to Descartes, v. P.G. Stanwood, introduction to More's *Democritus Platonissans*, 1646, Augustan Reprint Society no. 130, Los Angeles, 1968, pp. i–xi.
9. v. Leishman (1966), pp. 212–14; Osmond (*ELR*, 1974), passim.
10. v. Colie (1970), pp. 93–4; v. also Carey, p. 142, and Ricks, pp. 113–5 (Patrides ed. *Approaches*, 1978).
11. *Pia Desideria* ... Written in *Latine* by *Herm. Hugo.* Englished by Edm. Arwaker, London, 1686, p. 231. Datta cites Arwaker's version (*RQ*, 1969), p. 244.
12. cf. F.W. Bateson and F.R. Leavis, ' "A Dialogue between the Soul and Body": a debate', 1953, (Wilding ed. *Modern Judgements*, 1969, pp. 165–81).
13. *Poems*, ed. Brian Morris and Eleanor Withington, Oxford, 1967, p. 55. Leishman (1966) notes an affinity with Cleveland but does not cite this example (pp. 214–15).
14. Sharrock compares William Harvey's *Exercitationes anatomicae*, 1628 (*English*, 1979, p. 25).
15. ll. 296–9 (*The Epithalamions Anniversaries and Epicedes*, ed. W. Milgate, Oxford, 1978, p. 49).
16. v. *An Essay on Man*, ed. Maynard Mack, Twickenham edn., III. i, London and

New Haven, 1950, I. vi, pp. 36–40.

17. cf. 'double...Mind' (*The Mower against Gardens*, l.9). v. Christopher Hill's gloss, *Puritanism and Revolution*, London, 1958, p. 342, n. 1; also v. John Smith, 'There is *a double head*, as well as *a double heart*' (*Select Discourses*, 1660, *Cambridge Platonists*, ed. Patrides, p. 132).

18. *RT*, p. 30.

19. Milton, *PL* IV. 289 and VII. 505–16. v. Alastair Fowler's note on latter, *Paradise Lost*, Longman Annotated English Poets, London, 1971 (1st pubd. 1968), pp. 387–8: also v. Davis P. Harding, *The Club of Hercules: Studies in the Classical Background of 'Paradise Lost'*, Univ. of Illinois Press, Urbana, 1962, pp. 111–12. Lerner reads the poem as 'a dialogue between Fallen Man and Natural Man' (*Uses of Nostalgia*, p. 196).

20. cf. Ricks (Patrides ed. *Approaches*, 1978), p. 115.

21. I. ii. 272–7. Craze (1979) notes the echo (p. 288).

22. v. *Enneads* IV. iv. 18–19 (tr. Stephen MacKenna, 4th edn. rev. B.S. Page, London, 1969, pp. 301–2).

23. *Joann. 5. Ad Bethesdae piscinam positus* (*Poems*, ed. L.C. Martin, 2nd edn., Oxford, 1957, p. 15). v. Margoliouth/Legouis I. 250.

24. v. especially I. 2. 5. 1: 'Continent, inward, antecedent, next Causes, and how the Body works on the Mind' (*Anatomy of Melancholy*, 1621, ed. Holbrook Jackson, Everyman's Library, London, 1932, repr. 1978, pp. 374–6).

25. v. Pequigney (Friedenreich ed. *Tercentenary Essays*, 1977), p. 92. Osmond is mistaken in asserting that 'there is no mention of sin at all' (*ELR*, 1974, pp. 387–8).

26. In Bodl. MS. Eng. poet. d. 49 the quatrain is scored out and the annotation *Desunt multa* ('many are lacking') added. For speculation on this apparent lack of closure v. Leishman (1966), p. 216; v. also Catherine Belsey, *Critical Practice*, London and NY, 1980, p. 98.

27. The debate is surveyed by Tayler, *Nature and Art in Renaissance Literature*.

28. e.g. Lerner, *Uses of Nostalgia*, p. 196. Frank J. Warnke, 'Play and Metamorphosis in Marvell's Poetry', *SEL*, 5, 1965, pp. 23–30 (29).

29. Friedman (1970) emphasises the case against the Body (p. 73), Craze (1979) the case for the Body (p. 292): Rosemond Tuve does not think 'that it is possible to know the extent of the irony in the concluding figure' (*Elizabethan and Metaphysical Imagery*, Univ. of Chicago Press, Chicago, Illinois, 1947, Phoenix Books, 1961, p. 208). v. also Sharrock (*English*, 1979), p. 24.

30. v. Berthoff (1970), pp. 74–5, n. 5; but also v. Stocker (1986), pp. 39–40.

31. *UAH*, st. I, ll. 3–4. v. Pequigney (Friedenreich ed. *Tercentenary Essays*, 1977), p. 88.

32. v. E.E. Duncan-Jones (Margoliouth/Legouis I. 250).

33. *Essays* etc., ed. Waller, 1906, p. 395.

34. Bodl. MS. Fairfax 40, p. 552 (Saint-Amant, *La Solitude*, *Oeuvres poétiques*, ed. L. Vérane, Paris, 1930, p. 3).

35. *RT*, pp. 111–12: both Chernaik (1983), p. 103 and Klause (1983), p. 76 and pp. 175–6, n. 102 link this passage with the dialogue.

36. Both Hill (*Puritanism and Revolution*, p. 346) and Stocker (1986), pp. 38–40 connect the dialogue directly with civil war.

37. cit. Sir Walter Ralegh, *The History of the World*, ed. C.A. Patrides, London, 1971, p. 122.

Part I, section v: *The Nymph complaining for the
death of her Faun*

1. The etymology of 'faun' and the connotations of 'nymph' are frequently
discussed (v. critics cited below): Jonathan Goldberg re-examines the problem of
the signifiers in 'Marvell's nymph and the echo of voice', *Voice Terminal Echo:
Postmodernism and English Renaissance texts*, NY and London, 1986, pp. 14–37.
2. v. Don Cameron Allen, *Image and Meaning: Metaphoric Traditions in Renaissance
Poetry*, The Johns Hopkins Press, Baltimore, Maryland, 1960, rev. edn., 1968,
pp. 165–86: his article, 'Marvell's "Nymph" ', appeared in *ELH*, 23, 1956,
pp. 93–111.
3. There is an extensive secondary bibliography, much of which is devoted to
refuting, modifying, or extending established critical positions. Examples of the
main approaches are given in the notes below.
4. The classic correlation between 'leisure for fiction' and 'little grief' is
Dr Johnson's on *Lycidas*: v. *Lives of the English Poets*, ed. George Birkbeck Hill,
in 3 vols., Oxford, 1905, I. 163. For the converse discrepancy between a 'slight'
fiction and intense feeling in Marvell's *Nymph* v. T.S. Eliot, *Selected Essays*, p. 300.
5. For variations on 'allegory of the soul' readings v. inter al. Allen (*ELH*, 1956),
pp. 105–6; Ruth Nevo, 'Marvell's "Songs of Innocence and Experience" ', *SEL*, 5,
1965, pp. 1–21 (5–15); Geoffrey Hartman, ' "The Nymph Complaining for the
Death of Her Fawn": A Brief Allegory', *EiC*, 18, 1968, pp. 113–35.
6. Or none beyond a spot of target practice: for their behaviour and her perception
of it v. Pierre Legouis, 'Réponse à E.H. Emerson', *EA*, 8, 1955, pp. 111–12 (112).
7. 'Troopers'; first applied to Covenanters *c*. 1640: v. E.S. Le Comte, 'Marvell's
"The Nymph Complaining for the Death of her Fawn" ', *MP*, 50, 1952, pp.
97–101 (100); later applied generally; v. Martz, *The Wit of Love*, p. 180 and
pp. 203–4, n. 14.
8. v. Kenneth Muir, 'A Virgilian Echo in Marvell', *N&Q*, 196, 1951, p. 115; Allen
(*ELH*, 1956), p. 95 ff. and *Image and Meaning*, p. 167 ff.; Earl Miner, *The
Metaphysical Mode from Donne to Cowley*, Princeton U.P., Princeton, N.J., 1969,
pp. 246–70. Friedman (1970), pp. 102–3, questions the relevance of Virgil's
episode, and Phoebe S. Spinrad contrasts it with Marvell's in 'Death, Loss, and
Marvell's Nymph', *PMLA*, 97, 1982, pp. 50–9 (50–1).
9. cf. Toliver (1965), p. 92 and pp. 129–37.
10. For varying views of the theological problem and the Nymph's own position—
pagan? Christian?—v. John S. Coolidge, 'The Religious Significance of Marvell's
"The Nymph Complaining for the Death of Her Faun" ', *PQ*, 59, 1980,
pp. 11–25; Klause (1983) especially pp. 88–9; Wilcher (1985), pp. 83–4.
11. Luke 23: 34. cf. Acts 7: 60.
12. Coolidge cites Matt. 10: 29 (*PQ*, 1980), p. 12.
13. E.E. Duncan-Jones (Margoliouth/Legouis I. 251).
14. Those who support, refute, or modify the case for religious allegory include (in
addition to those already cited) Bradbrook and Lloyd Thomas (1940), pp. 47–50;
Le Comte (*MP*, 1952), pp. 97–101; Karina Williamson, 'Marvell's "The Nymph
Complaining for the Death of her Fawn": A Reply', *MP*, 51, 1954, pp. 268–71;
Leo Spitzer, 'Marvell's "Nymph Complaining for the Death of Her Faun":
Sources versus Meaning', *MLQ*, 19, 1958, pp. 231–43; Nicholas Guild, 'Marvell's
"The Nymph Complaining for the Death of Her Faun" ', *MLQ*, 29, 1968,

pp. 385–94; Cullen, *Spenser, Marvell, and Renaissance Pastoral*, pp. 170–2; Legouis (Margoliouth/Legouis I. 250–1).

15. But v. Coolidge who argues that the logical connective should be 'for' not 'and' (*PQ*, 1980, p. 13).

16. Those who criticise her naïvety or excessive self-preoccupation include Berger (*FMLS*, 1967), pp. 290–7; Colie (1970), pp. 87–90; Carolyn Asp, 'Marvell's Nymph: Unravished Bride of Quietness', *PLL*, 14, 1978, pp. 394–405; T. Katharine Thomason, 'Marvell's Complaint against his Nymph', *SEL*, 18, 1978, pp. 95–105. Those who explain her grief by redefining its object, for instance as the loss of innocence or even the loss of a child, include Jack E. Reese, 'Marvell's "Nymph" in a New Light', *EA*, 18, 1965, pp. 398–401 (answered by Legouis, pp. 402–3); Evan Jones, *Explicator*, 26, 1967–8, no. 73; John J. Teunissen and Evelyn J. Hinz 'What is the Nymph Complaining For?' *ELH*, 45, 1978, pp. 410–28. v. also the allegorical interpretations already cited, and Earl Miner, 'The Death of Innocence in Marvell's "Nymph Complaining for the Death of Her Faun" ', *MP*, 65, 1967–8, pp. 9–16.

17. *Selected Poetry*, p. xxvi.

18. Colie (1970), p. 89. Colie's criticism extends to another *naïf*, Damon the Mower (p. 90); but cf. John Creaser, who also compares the Nymph and Damon, for a much more sympathetic reading ('Marvell's Effortless Superiority', *EiC*, 20, 1970, pp. 403–23 [413]).

19. v. Goldberg on 'Sylvio', *Voice Terminal Echo*, pp. 21–2 and pp. 164–5, n. 6.

20. cf. the Mower poems.

21. e.g. Asp (*PLL*, 1978), pp. 398–9.

22. For the fawn as surrogate lover and the love chase tradition v. Allen, *Image and Meaning*, pp. 176–8; Michael J.B. Allen, 'The Chase: The Development of a Renaissance Theme', *CL*, 20, 1968, pp. 301–12 (308–12). Some critics argue that this relationship is lacking in responsibility, that the fawn 'makes no psychic or physical demands on her' (Asp, *PLL*, 1978, p. 399; v. also Berger, *FMLS*, 1967, p. 293).

23. For Ovidian myth in *Nymph* v. Coolidge (*PQ*, 1980), pp. 18–19; for Platonic myth v. Nevo (*SEL*, 1965), pp. 10–13.

24. Bless: v. Spitzer (*MLQ*, 1958), pp. 235–5; Coolidge (*PQ*, 1980), p. 16.

25. *Providence*, ll. 13–14 (*English Poems*, ed. Patrides, 1974, p. 129).

26. v. Nevo (*SEL*, 1965), pp. 10–13.

27. Margoliouth/Leguois, I. 251 cites Pliny. v. Williamson (*MP*, 1954), p. 270, for biblical references; also Coolidge (*PQ*, 1980), p. 17 and p. 25, n. 18.

28. The Song of Solomon 2: 16. A number of commentators note the echoes; v. especially Williamson (*MP*, 1954), pp. 268–71.

29. For the *hortus conclusus* tradition in general v. Stanley Stewart, *The Enclosed Garden: The Tradition and the Image in Seventeenth-Century Poetry*, Univ. of Wisconsin Press, Madison, Milwaukee, and London, 1966, pp. 31–59. For *hortus mentis* in *Nymph* v. Allen, *Image and Meaning*, pp. 179–81: challenged by Berthoff (1970), pp. 38–40.

30. For a range of associations v. Allen, *Image and Meaning*, pp. 182–3; Spitzer (*MLQ*, 1958), p. 238; King (1977), pp. 56–9; Thomason (*SEL*, 1978), p. 101; Spinrad (*PMLA*, 1982), pp. 55–6.

31. e.g. Berger (*FMLS*, 1967), pp. 292–3; Asp (*PLL*, 1978), p. 399.

32. But Nevo (*SEL*, 1965), p. 12, argues that the unity of the soul with the beloved is perfected in the garden.

33. v. *OED*, Wilderness, 1.c.
34. *Works*, ed. Spedding et al., 1870, VI. 485–92 (490–1).
35. Hence Berthoff's objection (1970, p. 40): for background v. Stewart, *Enclosed Garden*, pp. 38–40; Roy Strong, *The Renaissance Garden in England*, London, 1979, chapter V, p. 135. John Dixon Hunt examines 'the gardenist background for Marvell's poetry' (' "Loose Nature" and the "Garden Square"...', Patrides ed. *Approaches*, 1978, pp. 331–51).
36. v. E.E. Duncan-Jones (Margoliouth/Legouis I. 251).
37. Bacon, *Of Gardens* (*Works*, VI. 487).
38. But cf. Coolidge (*PQ*, 1980), pp. 21–2, who observes that the grief itself is eternised.
39. Thomas Heywood, *Gunaikeion*, 325, cit. DeWitt T. Starnes and Ernest W. Talbert, *Classical Myth and Legend in Renaissance Dictionaries*, Univ. of N. Carolina Press, Chapel Hill, 1955, p. 224. v. also Allen, *Image and Meaning*, p. 185. Marvell's couplet is singled out by T.S. Eliot, *Selected Essays*, p. 300, and Empson, *Seven Types of Ambiguity*, pp. 167–8.
40. v. Leishman (1966), pp. 159–60.
41. v. Ps. 56: 8; George Herbert, *Praise (III)*, ll. 25–36 (*English Poems*, ed. Patrides, 1974, pp. 165–6).
42. For the parallel v. Friedman (1970), p. 112.
43. e.g. by Toliver (1965), p. 137; Asp (*PLL*, 1978), pp. 402–5; Thomason (*SEL*, 1978), pp. 101–2. v. also the comments of Allen, *Image and Meaning*, p. 186 (slightly altered from his article, *ELH*, 1956, p. 111); Klause (1983), p. 90.
44. Ovid, *Metamorphoses*, VI. 148–312; in connection with *Nymph*, v. Spitzer (*MLQ*, 1958), p. 242; Colie (1970), p. 131; Coolidge (*PQ*, 1980), p. 23; Klause (1983), pp. 88–9.
45. *Poems of William Browne of Tavistock*, ed. Gordon Goodwin, introd. A.H. Bullen, The Muses' Library, London, 2 vols., 1904, II. 294, *On the Countess Dowager of Pembroke*, ll. 7–12. However, the attribution is doubtful (v. II. 350): the lines are omitted from the text of *William Browne: The Whole Works*, ed. W. Carew Hazlitt, repr. Hildesheim and NY, 1970 (v. p. 373).

Part II

1. v. Edgar Wind, *Pagan Mysteries in the Renaissance*, rev. edn., Penguin Books in association with Faber & Faber, Harmondsworth, 1967, chapter III, 'The Medal of Pico della Mirandola', pp. 43–4.
2. *Marsilio Ficino's Commentary on Plato's 'Symposium'*, The Text and a Translation, with an Introduction by Sears Reynolds Jayne, The University of Missouri Studies, Vol. XIX, no. 1, Univ. of Missouri, Columbia, 1944, Oratio Secunda, Capitulum II, p. 43 and p. 134.
3. v. Ficino, *Commentary*, tr. Jayne: text, Oratio Sexta, Capitulum VIII, pp. 85–6; translation, pp. 192–3. v. also John C. Nelson, *Renaissance Theory of Love*, Columbia U.P., NY, 1958, pp. 77–8; Smith, *Metaphysics of Love*, pp. 96–7, gives Pico della Mirandola's version.
4. Ficino, *Commentary*, tr. Jayne, p. 193.
5. Leone Ebreo [Judah Abrabanel], *The Philosophy of Love (Dialoghi d'Amore)*,

tr. F. Friedeberg-Seeley and Jean H. Barnes, introd. by Cecil Roth, London, 1937, Dialogue I, 'On Love and Desire', p. 16. For the argument concerning physical union v. pp. 52–7. v. also A.J. Smith, 'The Metaphysic of Love', *RES*, n.s.9, 1958, pp. 362–75 (368–9).

6. v. *The Collected Poems of Sir Thomas Wyatt*, edd. Kenneth Muir and Patricia Thomson, Liverpool U.P., Liverpool, 1969, no. CXCII (pp. 201–2). Contrast no. CXCIII, 'So vnwarely was never no man cawght' (pp. 202–3), and no. CCLIII, 'Synce loue wyll nedes that I shall loue,/Of very force I must agree' (pp. 249–50).

7. *The Unfortunate Lover*, ll. 55–6.

8. Donne, '*The Exstasie*', l.44 (*The Elegies and the Songs and Sonnets*, ed. Helen Gardner, Oxford, 1965, p. 60). For discussion of 'seventeenth-century love poetry, and the failure of love' after Donne v. Smith, *The Metaphysics of Love*, pp. 221–53.

9. v. *To his Coy Mistress*, ll. 26–7; *The Unfortunate Lover*, l.62.

10. For a range of attempts at decoding the subtext v. n. 1 to *The Unfortunate Lover*.

11. For examples v. Leishman (1966), pp. 169–81.

Part II, section i: *Young Love*

1. v. Leishman (1966), p. 166 ff.; Colie (1970), p. 52.

2. *The Odes of Horace*, tr. and introd. by James Michie, Penguin Classics, Harmondsworth, 1967 (first pubd. 1964), pp. 60–1.

3. v. *The Picture of little T.C. in a Prospect of Flowers*, ll. 3–8; *UAH*, st. LXXXIX.

4. For varying views of the love/time allegorisation v. Toliver (1965), pp. 162–3; Berthoff (1970), pp. 122–3; Long (1984), p. 7 and p. 218 n. 4.

5. e.g. Davison (1964), pp. 25–6; Legouis (1968), p. 31; Colie (1970), pp. 52–3: for an alternative view of 'young love' as 'a positive ideal' in contrast to adult love v. Klause (1983), p. 171 n. 33.

6. The phrase itself is a favourite of Carew's: v. Margoliouth/Legouis I. 252; Craze (1979), p. 45.

7. v. Leishman (1966), p. 173 n. 1.

8. Colie (1970), p. 53, assumes that they are synonyms; Leishman (1966), p. 172, notes a distinction, and a discrepancy between stanzas III and IV.

9. cf. *UAH*, l. 744.

10. This meaning is assumed by Legouis ('anticipate in action', Margoliouth/Legouis I. 252); Leishman (1966), p. 173 n. 2; Craze (1979), p. 46.

11. v. *Hamlet*, ed. Harold Jenkins, Arden Shakespeare, London and NY, 1982, p. 22.

12. cf. Bradbrook and Lloyd Thomas (1940), p. 50, who mention 'Ring a ring o' Roses'; Leishman (1966), p. 174, compares *The Anniversarie*.

To his Coy Mistress

13. *Selected Essays*, pp. 295–7.

14. Bruce King argues for a satiric persona ('Irony in Marvell's "To his Coy Mistress" ', *SoR*, n. s. 5, 1969, pp. 689–703: p. 155): for further comments on the title's significance, or lack of it, v. Craze (1979), pp. 312–13; B.J. Sokol, 'Logic

and Illogic in Marvell's "To His Coy Mistress" ', forthcoming (*ES*, 1989).

15. v. *OED*, 'coy' *a.* 2, a and b; 3; 5. For coyness/modesty distinction v. Thomas
Fuller, *The Profane State*, Cambridge, 1648, V. i. 344; v. also Stocker (1986),
p. 208 and p. 344 n. 14.

16. v. Propertius I. i. 5 (phrase tr. by R. Musker, *The Poems of Propertius*, London,
1972, p. 45). Classical scholars disagree over 'castas odisse puellas': *casta* may be
as ambiguous in this context as 'coy' in English. v. Georg Luck, 'The Woman's
Role in Latin Love Poetry' (G. Karl Galinsky ed. *Perspectives of Roman Poetry*,
Univ. of Texas Press, Austin and London, 1974, pp. 15-31), pp. 20-22;
J.P. Sullivan dissents from Luck's reading (*Propertius: A Critical Introduction*,
Cambridge, 1976, pp. 102-6).

17. As, for instance, by J.J. Moldenhauer, 'The Voices of Seduction in "To His Coy
Mistress": A Rhetorical Analysis', *TSLL*, 10, 1968-9, pp. 189-206 (195);
v. also John Hackett, 'Logic and Rhetoric in Marvell's "Coy Mistress" '
(Friedenreich ed. *Tercentenary Essays*, 1977, pp. 140-52: p. 146).

18. ll. 149-52: *Poems*, Oxford, 1638 (repr. 1640), cit. L.N. Wall, 'Thomas Randolph
and Marvell's "Coy Mistress" ', *N&Q*, 213, 1968, p. 103.

19. *The Poems of John Wilmot, Earl of Rochester*, ed. Keith Walker, Oxford, 1988
(first pubd. 1984), p. 36.

20. For the Roman *meretrix* v. Luck (Galinsky ed. *Perspectives of Roman Poetry*),
pp. 15-31. Frank O. Copley defines the classic type of 'ancient love affair', and
claims Catullus as an exception, in 'Emotional conflict and its significance in the
Lesbia-poems of Catullus' (Kenneth Quinn ed. *Approaches to Catullus*,
Cambridge and NY, 1972, pp. 78-9).

21. cf. Shakespeare, *Othello*, III. iv. 33-40.

22. For a survey of different critical approaches v. French Fogle, 'Marvell's "Tough
Reasonableness" and the Coy Mistress' (Friedenreich ed. *Tercentenary Essays*,
1977, pp. 121-39). More recent examples include a complex and challenging case
for a *carpe diem* reading, finely put by Patricia Coughlan ('Classical Themes in
the Non-Satiric Poetry of Andrew Marvell', London Ph.D. thesis, 1980, chapter 3,
pp. 93-180); Stocker's apocalyptic reading (1986, pp. 202-34); and Catherine
Belsey's 'Love and Death in "To His Coy Mistress" ' (Richard Machin and
Christopher Norris edd. *Post-structuralist readings of English poetry*, Cambridge,
1987, pp. 105-21).

23. For discussion of the poem's syllogistic structure v. J.V. Cunningham, *MP*, 51,
1953, pp. 33-41, and Barbara Herrnstein Smith, *Poetic Closure*, 1968, pp. 133-5
(both repr. Carey ed. *Critical Anthology*, 1969, pp. 213-23); Bruce E. Miller,
'Logic in Marvell's "To His Coy Mistress" ', *NDQ*, 30, 1962, pp. 48-9;
Anthony Low and Paul J. Pival, 'Rhetorical Pattern in Marvell's "To His Coy
Mistress" ', *JEGP*, 68, 1969, pp. 414-21; J.C. Maxwell, 'Marvell and Logic',
N&Q, 215, 1970, p. 256; Hackett (Friedenreich ed. *Tercentenary Essays*, 1977,
pp. 140-52); Hodge (1978), pp. 22-6; Sokol (forthcoming article, *ES*, 1989).

24. cf. B. Herrnstein Smith (Carey ed. *Critical Anthology*), p. 222; Hackett
(Friedenreich ed. *Tercentenary Essays*, 1977), pp. 146-7 and 149-51. But contrast
Colie (1970), p. 60; Berthoff (1970), p. 111.

25. *Rasselas* II. 32 (edd. Tillotson and Jenkins, p. 85).

26. cf. time/crime in Spenser's version of Tasso's song, *FQ*. II. xii, and A.C.
Hamilton's note, *FQ* (1980), p. 295.

27. Stocker (1986, p. 210) also cites this text, but to support a much more specialised
and radical identification of the Coy Mistress with the Scarlet Whore of Babylon.

28. For *adunata* v. Leishman (1966), p. 79; Colie (1970), p. 55.
29. v. Roger Sharrock, *TLS*, 31 October, 1958, p. 625, and 16 January, 1959, p. 33; E.E. Duncan-Jones, *TLS*, 5 December, 1958, p. 705; Christopher Hill, 'Milton and Marvell' (Patrides ed. *Approaches*, 1978, pp. 1–30), p. 2 and p. 24 n. 4.
30. v. Colie (1970), p. 54.
31. Bradbrook and Lloyd Thomas allot it a modest footnote (1940), p. 43 n. 1. Carey makes a representative selection in *Critical Anthology* (1969): v. J.V. Cunningham, pp. 217–18; René Wellek and Austin Warren, p. 224; H.E. Toliver, pp. 224–5. v. also Rufus Putney, ' "Our Vegetable Love": Marvell and Burton' (D.C. Allen ed. *Studies in Honor of T.W. Baldwin*, Univ. of Illinois Press, Urbana, Illinois, 1958, pp. 220–8); Patrick G. Hogan Jr., 'Marvell's "Vegetable Love" ', *SP*, 60, 1963, pp. 1–11; Low and Pival (*JEGP*, 1969), pp. 416–17; K. Gransden, 'Time, Guilt and Pleasure: A Note on Marvell's Nostalgia', *Ariel*, I. ii, 1970, pp. 83–97 (93). Craze (1979, p. 315) compares *Clarindon's House-Warming*, ll. 53–6; Stocker (1986, p. 215) detects an image of sexual tumescence.
32 . *Anatomy of Melancholy*, Pt. I, Sec. i, Mem. 2, Subs. 5: v. Putney (*Studies in Honor of T.W. Baldwin*, pp. 220–8).
33. The quoted phrase is Cunningham's (Carey ed. *Critical Anthology*, 1969), p. 217; cf. Patrides, 'a sort of lecherous cabbage' (*Approaches*, 1978), p. 33. For the tree analogy v. Margoliouth/Legouis I. 253. Robert Cummings has suggested to me that 'vegetable love' might derive from Jacob Cats, *Silenus Alcibiadis*, Amsterdam, 1622, which shows inscriptions growing on and with the marrows.
34. v. Margoliouth/Legouis I. 252; Cowley, *Poems*, ed. Waller, 1905, p. 89.
35. *Poems*, London, 1640, pp. 83–9.
36. W. Hilton Kelliher, 'A New Text of Marvell's "To His Coy Mistress" ', *N&Q*, 215, 1970, pp. 254–6: Kelliher argues that this MS is 'not simply a bad text' of the Folio version but that it may represent 'an earlier stage of composition' (p. 255). Craze (1979, p. 315 ff.) discusses the textual variants.
37. *Loves Progress*, l.40 (*Elegies and Songs and Sonnets*, ed. Gardner, Oxford, 1965, pp. 16–19).
38. This reading concurs with Friedman (1970), p. 185, and Gransden (*Ariel*, 1970), p. 93: coincidentally I have used the same term—cutprice—as Gransden. For an alternative response to the tone of ll.19–20 v. Sokol (forthcoming article, *ES*, 1989).
39. v. Erwin Panofsky, *Studies in Iconology: Humanistic Themes In the Art of the Renaissance*, NY/Oxford, 1939, pp. 69–93, Plates XXI–XL; Samuel C. Chew, 'The Allegorical Chariot in English Literature of the Renaissance' (Millard Meiss ed. *Essays in Honor of Erwin Panofsky*, New York Univ. Press, 1961, first pubd. 1960, I. 37–54: Chariot of Time, p. 38 and pp. 42–3; also II. 13). v. also Karl Joseph Höltgen's review of Legouis (*Anglia*, 84, 1966, p. 243). Dennis Davison quotes Quarles, *Emblems*, III. xii ('Notes on Marvell's "To His Coy Mistress" ', *N&Q*, 203, 1958, p. 521). A.G. Lee proposes an Ovidian influence, *Amores* 3.1 ('Tenerorvm Lvsor Amorvm', J.P. Sulivan ed. *Critical Essays on Roman Literature: Elegy and Lyric*, London, 1962, p. 178 n. 6). Coughlan comprehensively surveys the classical analogues ('Classical Themes in the Non-Satiric Poetry of · Andrew Marvell', pp. 132–53).
40. v. Margoliouth/Legouis I. 253.
41. V. 85: *Poems from the Greek Anthology*, London, 1943, p. 23.
42. v. Leishman (1966), pp. 76–7.
43. v. Stanley Stewart, 'Marvell and the *Ars Moriendi*' (Earl Miner ed. *Seventeenth-*

Century Imagery, Univ. of California Press, Berkeley, LA and London, 1971, pp. 133–50). v. also Belsey, 'Love and death in "To His Coy Mistress" ' (Machin and Norris edd. *Post-structuralist readings of English poetry*, pp. 105–21).

44. *The Poems of Sir Walter Ralegh*, ed. Agnes M.C. Latham, The Muses' Library, London, 1951, pp. 21–2. cf. 'Now Serena bee not coy' (p. 20) and note its title 'To his Love *when hee had obtained Her*' (my italics).

45. Miner ed. *Seventeenth-Century Imagery*, p. 137.

46. For a completely opposite interpretation v. Stocker (1986), pp. 215–16.

47. *Women Beware Women*, ed. J.R. Mulryne, The Revels Plays, London, 1975, p. 132.

48. v. D.C. Allen, 'Love in a Grave', *MLN*, 74, 1959, pp. 485–6.

49. *Song. The Dying Lover, Shorter Poems*, ed. A.M. Gibbs, pp. 168–70 (170).

50. *Elegies* IV. vii. 93–4, quoted against Marvell by Allen (*MLN*, 1959), p. 486.

51. Here I do not follow the Margoliouth/Legouis reading 'hew'.

52. Kelliher makes these points (1978, p. 53). v. also Thomas Clayton, ' "Morning Glew" and Other Sweat Leaves in the Folio Text of Andrew Marvell's Major Pre-Restoration Poems', *ELR*, 2, 1972, pp. 356–75.

53. v. Margoliouth/Legouis I. 253. v. the Marvell editions listed on 192 above for a range of editorial views.

54. cf. Spenser, *FQ* II. xii. 78; Donne, *The Comparison*, ll. 1–6 (admittedly offset by its repellent contrary) and *The Exstasie*, ll. 5–6 (*Elegies and Songs and Sonnets*, ed. Gardner, p. 5 and p. 59).

55. Donno (*Complete Poems*, p. 235) argues for its appropriateness on more metaphysical grounds.

56. v. Leone Ebreo, *Philosophy of Love*, tr. Friedeberg-Seeley and Barnes, pp. 53–5.

57. At least by 'some imaginative writers': v. S.K. Heninger, *A Handbook of Renaissance Meteorology*, Duke U.P., Durham, N. Carolina, 1960, p. 67.

58. ll. 211–15 (*Poems*, ed. Martin, 2nd edn., 1957, p. 245). v. John J. Carroll, 'The Sun and the Lovers in "To His Coy Mistress" ', *MLN*, 74, 1959, pp. 4–7 (he also cites a Herrick parallel); Friedman (1970), p. 197 n. 95; Stocker (1986), p. 220 (she also cites Spenser, p. 346 n. 53).

59. The final image sequence poses formidable interpretative problems: for a sceptical approach to critics' efforts v. Legouis (1968), p. 70 n. 1; among many commentators on the ending v. esp. Balachandra Rajan, 'Andrew Marvell: the aesthetics of inconclusiveness' (Patrides ed. *Approaches*, 1978 pp. 155–73), pp. 162–3 and p. 171 n. 13.

60. Chernaik cites this *RT* passage in connection with *To his Coy Mistress*, but argues that 'man's limited control over his surroundings does not make all action futile' (1983, p. 17).

61. lit. Time, consumer of things: Ovid, *Metamorphoses*, XV. 234.

62. v. Low and Pival (*JEGP*, 1969), pp. 418–21; contrast Putney (*Studies in Honor of T.W. Baldwin*), pp. 226–8.

63. For a range of suggestions v. inter al., Margoliouth/Legouis I. 254; F.W. Bateson, *English Poetry: A Critical Introduction*, London, NY and Toronto, 1950, p. 9; Carroll (*MLN*, 1959), p. 6; Lawrence W. Hyman, 'Marvell's "Coy Mistress" and Desperate Lover', *MLN*, 75, 1960, pp. 8–10 (10); J.B. Broadbent, *Poetic Love*, London, 1964, pp. 252–3; King (*SoR*, 1969), p. 699; Berthoff (1970), pp. 113–4. Carey shortlists unattributed explanations (*Critical Anthology*, 1969, p. 63).

64. l. 18 (*Poems*, ed. Wilkinson, p. 179): noted by Friedman (1970), p. 197 n. 98, and commented on by Roger Sharrock, 'Marvell's Poetry of Evasion and Marvell's

Times', *English*, 28, 1979, p. 21.

65. Donno is unusual among Marvell editors in adopting 'grates': v. her note (*Complete Poems*, p. 235), which also discusses the Spenserian 'gates'.

66. v. Craze (1979, p. 325) for parallels from Lucretius and Lucan.

67. *FQ* III. vi. 31-2: v. A.C. Hamilton's note, *FQ* (1980), p. 360. v. also Hyman (*MLN*, 1960), p. 10; for an alternative interpretation v. Stocker (1986), pp. 224-5 and p. 347 n. 65-9.

68. Kermode ed. *Selected Poetry*, p. 77.

69. Davison (*N&Q*, 1958, p. 521) compares Lovelace's 'rosy gates' (*Lucasta taking the waters at Tunbridge*), a suggestion dryly rejected by Legouis (Margoliouth/Legouis I. 254).

70. *Poems*, ed. Millar Maclure, The Revels Plays, London, 1968, p. 39. Maclure's note mentions Empedocles and Aristotle, but not Lucretius.

71. For the influence of Lucretius on *To his Coy Mistress* v. Coughlan, 'Classical Themes in the Non-Satiric Poetry of Andrew Marvell', pp. 171-8. For Marvell's ironic use of Neoplatonism v. King (*SoR*, 1969), pp. 689-703: v. also Toliver (1965), pp. 153-61.

72. King formulates a more extreme version of this contention (1977), pp. 74-5. The question of how to respond to the lover's claim is also raised by Klause (1983), p. 61, and Wilcher (1985) pp. 44-5.

73. The Joshua allusion may be supplemented by other Old Testament allusions: v. Hill, *Puritanism and Revolution*, 1958, p. 347 n. 1. v. also Donno's note, *Complete Poems*, p. 236.

74. v. *A Poem upon the Death of O.C..*, ll. 191-2. The *difference* between Cromwell and the lovers seems more to the point than a resemblance. But v. Stocker (1986), pp. 229-30, in the context of a fundamentally different interpretation of the lovers' activism.

75. Hill, *Puritanism and Revolution*, p. 348.

Part II, section ii: *The Unfortunate Lover*

1. For a wide variety of interpretations v. Rosemary Syfret (Bradbrook and Lloyd Thomas, 1940, pp. 29-30 n. 2); Ann Berthoff, 'The Voice of Allegory: Marvell's "The Unfortunate Lover" ', *MLQ*, 27, 1966, pp. 41-50 (also Berthoff, 1970, pp. 75-88 and pp. 214-16); E.E. Duncan-Jones, 'A Reading of Marvell's *The Unfortunate Lover*' (Reuben Brower, Helen Vendler, John Hollander edd. *I.A. Richards: Essays in his Honor*, Oxford/NY, 1973, pp. 211-26); Paulina Palmer, 'Marvell, Petrarchism and "De gli eroici furori" ', *Eng. Misc.*, 24, 1973-4, pp. 19-57; Peter T. Schwenger, 'Marvell's "Unfortunate Lover" as Device', *MLQ*, 35, 1974, pp. 364-75; Maren-Sofie Røstvig, '*In ordine di ruota:* Circular Structure in *The Unfortunate Lover* and *Upon Appleton House*' (Friedenreich ed. *Tercentenary Essays*, 1977, pp. 245-67), pp. 245-55; King (1977), pp. 77-88; Patterson (1978), pp. 20-5; Craze (1979), pp. 106-113; Klause (1983), pp. 58-60; Long (1984), pp. 16-19; Stocker (1986), pp. 257-305; P.R.K. Davidson and A.K. Jones, 'New Light on Marvell's "The Unfortunate Lover" ', *N&Q*, 230, 1985, pp. 170-2.

2. *Poems*, ed. Maclure, pp. 38-9.

3. Palmer compares Giordano Bruno's 'infortunato amante' (*Eng. Misc.* 1973-4, p. 35); v. also Røstvig (Friedenreich ed. *Tercentenary Essays*, 1977), p. 251; Klause (1983), p. 59.

4. Berthoff proposes an analogy with the formula 'our hero' (1970, p. 80); Schwenger speculates on a possible homosexual love (*MLQ*, 1974, pp. 369-70); Klause entertains the possibility of a female speaker (1983, p. 171 n. 35).

5. For the *locus amoenus* (pleasant place) v. E.R. Curtius, *European Literature and the Latin Middle Ages*, tr. Willard R. Trask, Bollingen Series, XXXVI, NY, 1953, pp. 192-3 and pp. 195-202. Duncan-Jones qualifies the association (*I.A. Richards: Essays in His Honor*, p. 215).

6. v. *FQ* III. vi. 39-41 and IV. x. 26-7.

7. Schwenger insists, perhaps too emphatically, on the inferiority of these lovers (*MLQ*, 1974, pp. 370, 374).

8. cf. Heninger, *Handbook of Renaissance Meteorology*, 3.3, 'Miscellaneous Fiery Impressions'; for 'impression' v. also Empson, *Seven Types of Ambiguity*, 2nd edn., 1947, pp. 166-7.

9. *Poems*, ed. Donaldson, p. 97.

10. *Elegies and Songs and Sonnets*, ed. Gardner, p. 81.

11. v. Duncan-Jones (*I.A. Richards: Essays in His Honor*), p. 216; Berthoff (1970), pp. 84-6; Stocker (1986), pp. 275-6.

12. v. Berthoff (1970), p. 215; Duncan-Jones (*I.A. Richards: Essays in His Honor*), p. 215 n. 3.

13. The paraphrase of Fulgentius, *De expositione Virgilianae continentia* (1589) is from D.C. Allen, *Mysteriously Meant*, The Johns Hopkins Press, Baltimore and London, 1970, p. 138.

14. Duncan-Jones mentions *Arcadia* (*I.A. Richards: Essays in His Honor* p. 215); cf. *The Countesse of Pembrokes Arcadia* ed. Feuillerat, I.i. and II.vii.

15. *Pericles*, ed. F.D. Hoeniger, Arden Shakespeare, London and NY, 1963, p. 159: v. Allardyce Nicoll, 'Shakespeare and the Court Masque', *Shakespeare Jahrbuch*, 94, 1958, pp. 51-62.

16. St Ambrose, *Apol. post. pro David*, cap. 3, cit. Quarles, *Emblemes*, London, 1635, III. xi, p. 167.

17. *Areopagitica* (*CPW*, II, ed. Ernest Sirluck, 1959, p. 527).

18. For Petrarchism and *The Unfortunate Lover* v. Legouis (1968), p. 71; Palmer (*Eng. Misc.* 1973-4), pp. 32-3; Wilcher (1985), p. 37; Anne Ferry, *All in War with Time*, Harvard U.P., Cambridge, Mass., and London, pp. 230-33.

19. v. Bradbrook and Lloyd Thomas (1940), p. 29 n. 1; J. Max Patrick, 'Marvell's "The Unfortunate Lover" ', *Explicator*, 20, 1961-2, no. 65: and especially Colie (1970), pp. 110-113.

20. cf. Otto van Veen, *Amorvm Emblemata*, Antwerp, 1608: the first engraving is of Venus and Cupid in triumph surrounded by transfixed humans, animals, fish, fowl, and insects.

21. cf. Inigo Jones's 'A Storm and Tempest' design for the first scene of Davenant's *Salmacida Spolia* (Stephen Orgel and Roy Strong edd., *Inigo Jones: The Theatre of the Stuart Court*, London and Berkeley, LA, 1973, II. 742-3).

22. Stocker argues convincingly for a significant relationship between *Salmacida Spolia* and *The Unfortunate Lover* (1986, pp. 264-6 and 268-80).

23. Palmer (*Eng. Misc.* 1973-4, p. 37) and Røstvig (Friedenreich ed. *Tercentenary Essays*, 1977, p. 254) draw attention to Bruno's motto *Mors et Vita*.

24. According to Duncan-Jones (*I.A. Richards: Essays in His Honor*), p. 219. The

classical sources are *Odyssey* IV. 499–511 and *Aeneid* I. 39–45.

25. cf. *The Definition of Love*, ll. 31–2.
26. For comparisons with Blake v. Long (1984), pp. 17–18; for Promethean reading v. R.B. Hinman, 'The Apotheosis of Faust: Poetry and New Philosophy in the Seventeenth Century' (Malcolm Bradbury and D.J. Palmer edd. *Metaphysical Poetry*, Stratford-upon-Avon Studies 11. London, 1970), p. 171.
27. v. Berthoff (1970), p. 81 n. 9; Duncan-Jones (*I.A. Richards: Essays in His Honor*), pp. 220–1; but also v. Long (1984), pp. 229–30 n. 13.
28. *Poems*, ed. Wilkinson, *Dialogue. Lucasta, Alexis*, p. 42; cit. Margoliouth/Legouis I. 256.
29. v. Schwenger (*MLQ*, 1974), pp. 364–7.
30. v. Berthoff (1970), p. 82.
31. Ecclus. 49: 1 (v. Duncan-Jones, Margoliouth/Legouis I. 256); Patterson (1978, pp. 24–5) and Stocker (1986, pp. 283–4, 292, 298–9) extend the allusion with reference to Charles I.
32. *Poems*, ed. Martin, *Steps to the Temple*, p. 106.
33. 'Story': v. Margoliouth/Legouis I. 256: Craze suggests that 'Story' = epitaph (1979, p. 112).
34. v. Patterson (1978), pp. 23–4.
35. For the best discussion of the 'gentle reader' vis-à-vis *The Unfortunate Lover* v. Duncan-Jones (*I.A. Richards: Essays in His Honor*), pp. 221–2.

The Gallery

36. Political and literary allusions suggest a date for both lyrics *c.* 1649.
37. But for the significance of time in *The Gallery* v. Toliver (1965), pp. 173–4 and 'Marvell's Songs and Pictorial Exhibits' (Friedenreich ed. *Tercentenary Essays*, 1977, pp. 105–20), p. 113; also v. Thomas Clayton, ' "It is Marvel He Outdwells His Hour" ' (*Tercentenary Essays*, pp. 46–75), pp. 62–4.
38. v. Friedman (1970), p. 40; Wilcher (1985), p. 25.
39. *FQ* III. i. 34–8.
40. Charles H. Hinnant points out the relevant change of taste between the Tudor/Jacobean period and the Caroline in 'Marvell's Gallery of Art', *RenQ*, 24, 1971, pp. 26–37 (29).
41. v. Frances A. Yates, *The Art of Memory*, London, 1966, chapters 1 and 2: for Simonides v. pp. 1–4 and pp. 26–30.
42. Colie (1970), p. 107.
43. *FQ* II. ix. 50.
44. For the tradition v. Jean H. Hagstrum, *The Sister Arts*, Univ. of Chicago Press, Chicago, Illinois, 1958, Part I: for Marino and Marvell v. pp. 114–17.
45. v. Hagstrum, *Sister Arts*, pp. 102–4; J.V. Mirollo, *The Poet of the Marvelous: Giambattista Marino*, Columbia U.P., NY and London, 1963, pp. 46–51; Stephen Warman, 'The Subject-Matter and Treatment of Marino's Images', *Studi Secenteschi*, X, 1969, Biblioteca dell' 'Archivum Romanicum', ser. 1, vol. 106, Florence, 1970, pp. 57–131.
46. v. Margoliouth/Legouis I. 256; v. also Craze (1979), pp. 117–18.
47. For a detailed discussion of *The Gallery* in this light v. Hinnant (*RenQ*, 1971), pp. 26–37.
48. v. Marino, *La Galeria*, 2nd impression, Venice, 1620, pp. 14, 19, 49.

49. Fuller, *The Profane State*, 1648, V. i. 'The Harlot', p. 344: cf. V. iii, 'The Witch', p. 352, for anti-female prejudice.
50. For vulture iconology v. Hinnant (*RenQ*, 1971), p. 33.
51. Hinnant explains the unusual sleeping Aurora by assimilation with Sleeping Venus (*RenQ*, 1971), pp. 31-2.
52. v. Hagstrum, *Sister Arts*, pp. 116-17.
53. cf. Carew, *Ingratefull beauty threatned* (*Poems*, 1640, p. 28).
54. Donne, *The Dreame*, l.8 (*Elegies and Songs and Sonnets*, ed. Gardner, p. 80).
55. *The Poems of William Habington*, ed. Kenneth Allott, Liverpool U.P., Liverpool and London, 1948, p. 15; Waller, *Poems &c*, 1645, p. 65.
56. It is also interesting that there are five portraits in all: Robert Fludd holds that five is the best number for a memory group, and that there should be one principal image (v. Yates, *Art of Memory*, p. 326).
57. v. Winifred Nowottny's discussion of the *da capo* ending in *The Language Poets Use*, Athlone Press, London, 1962, pp. 95-6.
58. For the name Clora/Chloris and her description v. Hinnant (*RenQ*, 1971, p. 36), who cites Ovid, *Fasti* V. 183ff., 359; and *FQ* II. iii. 30.
59. *A Hue and Cry after Fair Amoret*, l.8 (*Complete Works of William Congreve*, ed. M. Summers, 1923, iv. 74).
60. cf. Jonson's song *Still to be neat, still to be dressed* (*Epicoene* I. i. 91-102; *Poems*, ed. Donaldson, 1975, pp. 351-2): cit. Winny ed. *Some Poems*, p. 112.
61. For Clora/nature identification v. Warnke (*SEL*, 1965), pp. 24-5; Toliver (1965), p. 177.

The Fair Singer

62. *Ars Amatoria*, III. 315-16.
63. v. Finney, *Musical Backgrounds*, chapter IV, 'Music and Neoplatonic Love', pp. 76-101: Finney cites the Ovid reference (n. 62 above) on p. 91.
64. v. Friedman (1970), pp. 44-5; Berthoff (1970), pp. 115-6.
65. *Poems*, ed. Wilkinson, 2nd edn., 1953, pp. 25-6.
66. For the literal effect of the singer's breath v. Finney, *Musical Backgrounds*, p. 93 and pp. 97-8.
67. v. Colie (1970), pp. 99-100; Carey (Patrides ed. *Approaches*, 1978), p. 142.
68. For a comparative study including this judgment v. Leishman (1966), pp. 49-58.
69. *Poems*, ed. Donaldson, p. 145.
70. v. Klause (1983), p. 172 n. 53.

Mourning

71. *Two Songs at the Marriage of the Lord Fauconberg and the Lady Mary Cromwell*, First Song, l.1 (Margoliouth/Legouis I. 125).
72. Margoliouth/Legouis I. 56; McQueen/Rockwell, pp. 30, 31.
73. v. Summers cit. Colie (1970), p. 21; Colie herself compares and contrasts *Mourning* and *Eyes and Tears* (p. 126): v. also Wilcher (1985), pp. 13-24.
74. For wordplay v. Paul Delany, 'Marvell's "Mourning"', *MLQ*, 33, 1972, pp. 30-6 (31-2). Delany, Craze (1979, p. 66) and Wilcher (1985, p. 21) comment on the controlled effect.

75. *Hamlet*, I. ii. 76.
76. Colie notes both possible links (1970, p. 100 and p. 131).
77. v. Delany (*MLQ*, 1972), p. 32.
78. v. Ricks (Patrides ed. *Approaches*, 1978), pp. 112-13: cf. Spenser, *FQ* III. xi. 31. For the Danae myth as an allegory of the mercenary nature of women v. Thomas Wilson, *The Arte of Rhetorique*, London, 1553, Fol. 104.
79. v. Leishman (1966), pp. 42-3 for Latin and neo-Latin precedents.
80. This might provide a tentative link with the political subtext of *The Unfortunate Lover*: for *Donatives* v. Margoliouth/Legouis I. 257.
81. For the significance of pearls v. Delany (*MLQ*, 1972), p. 35. Duncan-Jones compares Herbert's image of diving 'In tears like seas', *Marie Magdalene*, ll. 10-12 (Margoliouth/Legouis I. 257); Leishman (1966, p. 45) compares Sir Henry Wotton's pearl-diver in 'A Description of the Countreys Recreations'.
82. For wordplay v. Nowottny, *The Language Poets Use*, pp. 157-8.
83. The phrase is Nowottny's (*The Language Poets Use*, p. 158). For further comments on the ending v. Alvarez, *School of Donne*, pp. 118-9; Delany (*MLQ*, 1972), pp. 35-6; Wilcher (1985), pp. 22-23.
84. v. *UAH*, XIV-XV: cf. Colie (1970), p. 101.

Daphnis and Chloe

85. Leishman (1966, pp. 124-6) notes the formal similarity of Carew's *Separation of Lovers*.
86. But contrast Friedman (1970), pp. 114-19 (115-16).
87. For the abstention/fruition dilemma v. Gransden (*Ariel*, 1970), pp. 91-2.
88. For the connection with *Daphnis and Chloe* attributed to Longus v. Legouis (1968), p. 29; Wilcher (1985), p. 77. Nevo briefly touches on the Daphnis/Leander parallel (*SEL*, 1965, p. 16).
89. v. Colie (1970, pp. 46-7) and Long (1984, pp. 27-8) on Daphnis' histrionics.
90. v. Wilcher (1985), pp. 80-1.
91. Source suggested by Duncan-Jones, cit. Leishman (1966), pp. 121-2: text from *The Works of Sir John Suckling: The Plays*, ed. L.A. Beaurline, Oxford, 1971, pp. 65-6.
92. cf. Friedman (1970), p. 118; Long (1984), p. 28.
93. v. note on the textual emendation in Margoliouth/Legouis I. 258.
94. For comments on Chloe's exclusion v. Colie (1970), p. 47; Donno (Friedenreich ed. *Tercentenary Essays*, 1977), p. 40; Long (1984), pp. 28-9.
95. For the significance of 'Phlogis' v. Margoliouth/Legouis I. 258.
96. *The Poems of Jonathan Swift*, ed. Harold Williams, 2nd edn., Oxford, 1958, I. 120.
97. For the Thomason tract connection v. L.N. Wall (Margoliouth/Legouis I. 258). For 'Lawes' as laws of nature v. Donno ed. *Complete Poems*, p. 230; contested by Craze (1979, p. 42). v. also Nevo on art and nature (*SEL*, 1965, p. 17).
98. e.g. Gransden (*Ariel*, 1970), p. 92; Long (1984), p. 29.

Part II, section iii: *The Definition of Love*

1. v. Frank Kermode, 'Definitions of Love', *RES*, n.s.7, 1956, pp. 183–5 (184).
2. v. Angela G. Dorenkamp, 'Marvell's Geometry of Love', *ELN*, 9, 1971–2, pp. 111–15 (111); Carey (Patrides ed. *Approaches*, 1978), p. 138.
3. v. Kermode (*RES*, 1956), p. 184; Maren-Sofie Røstvig, 'Images of Perfection' (Earl Miner ed. *Seventeenth-Century Imagery*, Univ. of California Press, Berkeley, LA and London, 1971), pp. 1–24 (16). For kinds of definition involved v. B.J. Sokol. 'The *Symposium*, Two Kinds of "Definition", and Marvell's "The Definition of Love" ', *N&Q*, 233, 1988, pp. 169–70.
4. *Remarks Upon a Late Disingenuous Discourse*, 1678 (Grosart ed. *Prose Works*, IV. 183) cit. Toliver (1965), p. 54 n. 1: Toliver also compares Milton's *Art of Logic* I.xxx (*CPW* VIII, ed. Maurice Kelly, 1982, pp. 310–11).
5. v. Marjorie Hope Nicholson, *The Breaking of the Circle*, rev. edn., 1960, Columbia U.P., NY, Oxford, London, p. 64; Dennis Davison, 'Marvell's "The Definition of Love" ', *RES*, n.s.6, 1955, pp. 141–6 (Davison modifies the geometric link, pp. 143–5); Colie (1970), p. 59; Dorenkamp (*ELN*, 1971–2), pp. 111–15. For Hobbes quotation v. *Leviathan*, ed. C.B. Macpherson, Penguin Books, Harmondsworth, 1968, p. 105.
6. Included in *Elizabethan Lyrics*, ed. Norman Ault, London, 1986 (first pubd. 1925, rev. edn. 1949), p. 154 and pp. 178–9. For logical and lyrical 'definitions' v. Tuve, *Elizabethan and Metaphysical Imagery*, II. xi. 2 (pp. 299–309).
7. Crispin de Passe the Elder, *Thronus Cupidinis*, 3rd edn., Amsterdam, 1620 (Universiteits-Bibliotheek Amsterdam, 1968), sigs.L2^r–L3^r, 'Qui veut sçavoir Amour & sa nature'.
8. Sokol (*N&Q*, 1988, p. 169) relates the poem directly to the *Symposium*; v. also Hyman (1964), pp. 53–9.
9. v. *Dialoghi d'Amore*, tr. Friedeberg-Seeley and Barnes, pp. 329–31.
10. v. Berthoff (1970), pp. 88–110; King (1977), pp. 89–100. Both ingeniously attempt to get round the difficulty of 'never meet.'
11. *Religio Medici* II. vi (*Works*, ed. Geoffrey Keynes, London, 1964, first pubd. 1928, I. 79): cit. Røstvig (Miner ed. *Seventeenth-Century Imagery*), p. 16.
12. *De Rerum Natura* IV. 1105–11, cit. Harold Love, The Critical Forum, *EiC*, 27, 1977, pp. 374–5 (374).
13. For circle and androgyne v. Røstvig (Miner ed. *Seventeenth-Century Imagery*), pp. 16–17; for 'penetration' v. E.B. Greenwood, 'Marvell's Impossible Love', *EiC*, 27, 1977, pp. 100–109 (a reading challenged by Love, pp. 374–5). Sokol contrasts Marvellian 'damaged or endangered spheres' with Platonic 'undamaged spheres' (*N&Q*, 1988, p. 170).
14. v. Douglas Bush, *English Literature in the Earlier Seventeenth Century 1600–1660*, Oxford, 2nd rev. edn., 1962, p. 172: for comparison/contrast v. Berthoff (1970), pp. 93–4.
15. *Works*, ed. Feuillerat, I. 174.
16. *Poems*, ed. Waller, 1905, pp. 130–1: v. Margoliouth/Legouis I. 260: for comparison/contrast v. Friedman (1970), p. 183; Berthoff (1970), p. 93 and pp. 104–5.
17. *Poems*, ed. Waller, 1905, pp. 81–2.
18. Preface to *Astrophil and Stella*, 1591: 'The argument cruell chastitie, the Prologue hope, the Epilogue dispaire' (v. *The Poems of Sir Philip Sidney*, ed. William A.

Ringler Jr., Oxford, 1962, p. xlix). Craze does deduce 'a temporal sequence' from hope to despair, disregarding the force of the metaphor 'begotten' (1979, p. 87).

19. v. Friedman (1970), p. 195 n. 80: Greenwood (*EiC*, 1977), pp. 106–7.
20. v. Bradbrook and Lloyd Thomas (1940), pp. 45–6 n. 1: v. also Davison (*RES*, 1955), p. 142; John Coolidge, 'Marvell and Horace' *MP*, 63, 1965–6, pp. 111–20 (114); Kitty Datta, 'Marvell's Prose and Poetry: More Notes', *MP*, 63, 1965–6, pp. 319–21. The quotation is from *Odes of Horace*, tr. Michie, pp. 80–1.
21. The text is taken from the English version of *Iconologia*, London, 1709, p. 56. For the Renaissance view of the Fates v. Starnes and Talbert, *Classical Myth and Legend in Renaissance Dictionaries*, pp. 340–86.
22. *RT II*, p. 230: v. Smith's note, p. 379. v. also Isabel G. MacCaffrey, 'Some Notes on Marvell's Poetry, Suggested by a Reading of His Prose', *MP*, 61, 1964, pp. 261–9 (265); Datta (*MP*, 1965–6), pp. 319–21; Carey's objection to MacCaffrey (introd. to *Critical Anthology*, 1969, pp. 20–1); Berthoff (1970), pp. 219–20.
23. *RT*, p. 54; Juvenal, Satire X. 365–6 (Marvell has 'but' for 'we' in l.365).
24. On conjunctions v. Colie (1970), pp. 91–2.
25. e.g. Davison (*RES*, 1955), pp. 143–5; Dean Morgan Schmitter and P. Legouis, 'The Cartography of "The Definition of Love" ', *RES*, n.s. 12, 1961, pp. 49–54.
26. v. *OED*, 'Planisphere' (1636 edn. of *Exercises*): cit. Margoliouth/Legouis I. 260; Leishman (1966), p. 69 n. 1.
27. v. Berthoff (1970), p. 101 n. 30.
28. From *LXXX Sermons* (1640): v. *Sermons*, edd. Simpson and Potter, VI. 59 and VII. 69. Legouis cites the second example, and suggests that Donne's 'crush' may have prompted Marvell's 'cramp'd' (*RES*, 1961, p. 54).
29. For this context applied to *The Definition of Love* v. Stocker (1986), pp. 231–3.
30. cf. Shakespeare, *Othello*, III. iii. 92–3: 'and when I love thee not,/Chaos is come again'; also Donne, *A Nocturnall upon S. Lucies Day*, ll. 24–6.
31. v. Leishman (1966), pp. 69–70; Ferry, *All in War with Time*, pp. 242–9; A.J. Smith, 'Marvell's metaphysical wit' (Patrides ed. *Approaches*, 1978, pp. 56–86), p. 61; Sharrock (*English*, 1979), p. 36; Wilcher (1985), pp. 47–8.
32. v. F.W. Bateson's editorial rider to Greenwood, 'Marvell's Impossible Love' and James Turner's riposte (*EiC*, 27, 1977, pp. 109–11 and p. 377).
33. cf. Shakespeare, *Measure for Measure*, ed. J.W. Lever, Arden Shakespeare, London and Harvard U.P., Cambridge, Mass., 1965, IV. iii. 156 and editor's note p. 119. Craze cites *The Winter's Tale*, I. ii. 289 (1979, p. 85); v. also Margoliouth/Legouis I. 260.
34. Davison (*RES*, 1955, pp. 145–6) connects *The Definition of Love* specifically with the Platonic love cult of the Cavaliers: Berthoff dissents (1970, pp. 94–5).
35. cf. Rajan's reading (Patrides ed. *Approaches*, 1978), pp. 163–4.

The Match

36. Klause discusses the two poems in terms of their parallelism (1983, p. 62).
37. v. Berthoff (1970), p. 131.
38. v. Carey (Patrides ed. *Approaches*, 1978), p. 145.
39. But v. Hodge (1978), pp. 91–2.
40. *Britannia's Pastorals*, 1613, Song 2, p. 27.
41. *Epistolae Ho-Elianae*, London, 1645, Sect. 4, Letter XIV, p. 19.

42. Joshua Poole, *The English Parnassus*, London, 1657, pp. 249–58; *Hero and Leander*, Sestiad I, ll. 45–50 (*Poems*, ed. Maclure, pp. 7–8).
43. cf. Godfrey Goodman, *The Fall of Man, or, the Corruption of Nature*, London, 1616 (v. p. 365 ff.). Klause reads an indictment of Nature, or Nature's Lord, into the poem (1983, p. 72).
44. The male lover allots his Love an extra stanza, so that the match is conventionally unequal, 4: 5. cf. Cornelius Agrippa on 2: 3 'an odd number is the Male and the even the Female' (*Of Occult Philosophy*, tr. J.F., 1651, p. 188, cit. Gardner ed. *Donne: Elegies and Songs and Sonnets*, p. 220).
45. cf. Norford (*ELH*, 1974), pp. 63–4.
46. Hodge gives the conception more credit, but even he finds *The Match* an interesting failure (1978, p. 92).
47. For Cowley parallels v. Margoliouth/Legouis I. 261: for parallels from Donne and Lord Herbert v. Friedman (1970), p. 87 n. 9.
48. cf. Colie (1970), pp. 124–5.

Part II, section iv: *The Picture of little T.C. in a Prospect of Flowers*

1. v. *OED*, 'prospect': I. 3,5; II, 7,8. Many readings emphasise the temporal prospect e.g. Joseph H. Summers, 'Marvell's "Nature"', *ELH*, 20, 1953, pp. 121–35 (130–4); Stocker (1986), pp. 134–5.
2. For comparison/contrast with Maria in *UAH* v. Toliver (1965), p. 170; Friedman (1970), p. 176 and pp. 243–4.
3. v. H.M. Margoliouth, 'Andrew Marvell: Some Biographical Points', *MLR*, 17, 1922, pp. 351–61 (359–60).
4. v. E.E. Duncan-Jones, *TLS*, 30 October, 1953 (p. 693). The phrase is also used by Carew in *Upon the King's Sickness*, l.37 and *Coelum Britannicum*, 3rd Song, l.1 (*Poems*, 1640, p. 60 and p. 256): v. Margoliouth/Legouis I. 261; Craze (1979), pp. 262–3. For a possible link with Edward Benlowes's *Theophila* (1652), v. E.E. Duncan-Jones, 'Benlowes, Marvell, and the Divine Casimire: A Note', *HLQ*, 20, 1956–7, pp. 183–4.
5. cf. Herrick, 'Here she lies, a pretty bud' (*Upon a child that dyed*) and the two epitaphs entitled *Upon a Child* (*Poetical Works*, ed. L.C. Martin, Oxford, 1956, pp. 123, 69, 224). Milton's *On the Death of a Fair Infant* (not printed till 1673) uses comparable flower imagery. cf. Jonson's epitaphs for children including *On My First Daughter* (*Poems*, ed. Donaldson, p. 16).
6. Henry James, *The Awkward Age*, New York Edition 9, NY, 1963 (first pubd. 1908), II. iv. 91.
7. For golden-age interpretation v. Patrick Cullen, 'Imitation and Metamorphosis: The Golden-Age Eclogue in Spenser, Milton, and Marvell', *PMLA*, 84, 1969, pp. 1559–70 (1568–70); P. Legouis' reply and Cullen's subsequent modification, *PMLA*, 86, 1971, pp. 275–7, 480–1, and 1030–1. v. also Gransden (*Ariel*, 1970), p. 83; Long (1984), p. 6. For 'golden' in a Sidneian sense v. A.E. Dyson and Julian Lovelock, 'Serpent in Eden: Marvell's "The Picture of Little T.C. in a Prospect of Flowers"', *CS*, 5, 1972, pp. 261–5 (262).
8. For the play-element, and little T.C. as representative of human intellect, v.

Warnke (*SEL*, 1965), pp. 26-8.

9. v. Kermode's note (ed. *Selected Poetry*, p. 93).

10. v. *Valerius Terminus: Of the Interpretation of Nature* (*The Philosophical Works of Francis Bacon*, repr. from Ellis and Spedding, ed. John M. Robertson, NY, 1970, first pubd. 1905, p. 188): cit. Fowler ed. *PL*, 1971, p. 415, note on VIII. 343-56.

11. Carey (Patrides ed. *Approaches*, 1978), p. 136.

12. *The Mower against Gardens*, ll. 35-6.

13. Dyson and Lovelock note the 'words of struggle and choice' (*CS*, 1972) p. 262.

14. Summers uses the terms 'alienation' and 'superiority' as well as 'delight' (*ELH*, 1953), p. 131.

15. v. note 4 above: Patterson juxtaposes T.C. and O.C. (1978, p. 53).

16. For the connection with Petrarch's *Trionfi* v. Alastair Fowler, *Triumphal Forms*, Cambridge, 1970, p. 78.

17. For the possible force of 'chaster' v. Dyson and Lovelock (*CS*, 1972), p. 263.

18. e.g. Toliver (1965), pp. 168-9; King (1977), pp. 104-5.

19. *UAH*, LXXXX-LXXXXIII.

20. Summers (*ELH*, 1953), p. 133.

21. For 'Enemy of Man' as Satan v. Peter Berek, 'The Voices of Marvell's Lyrics', *MLQ*, 32, 1971, pp. 143-57 (154-5); Friedenreich (Friedenreich ed. *Tercentenary Essays*, 1977), p. 160.

22. Leishman's phrase: v. his survey of the motif (1966), pp. 166-88 (167).

23. *To my young Lady Lucy Sidney*, *Poems*, 1645, pp. 24-5: cit. Leishman (1966), p. 175.

24. v. Bradbrook and Lloyd Thomas (1940), p. 51; E.M.W. Tillyard, *Poetry, Direct and Oblique*, 1964, p. 25; Wallerstein, *Studies in Seventeenth-Century Poetic*, pp. 175-6; Berthoff (1970), p. 126; Friedman (1970), p. 177; Craze (1979), p. 264. v. also Stocker who glosses *umbra* 'the classical image for the *vita otiosa*' (1986, p. 136).

25. According to John Aubrey (*Aubrey's Brief Lives*, ed. Oliver Lawson Dick, 2nd edn., London, 1950, p. 20).

26. For comment on the construction v. Carey (Patrides ed. *Approaches*, 1978), pp. 151-2; Craze (1979), p. 265.

27. For the possibility/impossibility of the injunction v. Summers (*ELH*, 1953), pp. 132-3; Toliver (1965), p. 170.

28. *UAH*, LXXXVI-LXXXVIII; LXXXXIV-LXXXXVI.

29. For attitudes to 'reform' coupled with *The Mower against Gardens* v. Friedman (1970), p. 178; Klause (1983), p. 73 and p. 175 n. 95; Wilcher (1985), p. 93.

30. The phrases are from Jeremy Taylor (v. passage quoted on pp. 142-3 of text); and Keats, *Ode on Melancholy*, l.21 (*Poems*, ed. H.W. Garrod, 2nd edn., Oxford, 1958, p. 275). Bruce King gives an alternative explanation of the flowers in 'Marvell's Tulip', *N&Q*, 214, 1969, p. 100. My own reading is closer to Summers (*ELH*, 1953), p. 132.

31. v. Cullen (*PMLA*, 1969), p. 1569; King reads the whole poem allegorically (1977, pp. 101-9); v. also Stocker (1986), pp. 134-5.

32. Fanshawe's translation of Guarini: v. *A Critical Edition of Sir Richard Fanshawe's 1647 Translation of Giovanni Battista Guarini's "Il Pastor Fido"*, edd. Walter F. Staton Jr. and William E. Simeone, Oxford, 1964, p. 126, IV. ix. 4199-4202 (4202).

33. v. Colie (1970), pp. 53-4.

34. v. Friedman (1970), p. 179; Dyson and Lovelock (*CS*, 1972, pp. 264-5) offer

alternative responses to the 'shock' ending. cf. Summers (*ELH*, 1953), pp. 133–4.

35. For infant mortality v. Antonia Fraser, *The Weaker Vessel: Woman's Lot in Seventeenth-Century England*, London, 1985 (first pubd. 1984), pp. 80–4: for family history v. n. 3 above. Unlike most critics, Craze assumes that Marvell would probably have been ignorant of the earlier T.C.'s existence (1979, p. 266).

36. cf. Matthew's eating the forbidden fruit and its effects in Bunyan, *The Pilgrim's Progress: The Second Part* (*Grace Abounding and The Pilgrim's Progress*), ed. Roger Sharrock, Oxford/London, 1966, pp. 297–8 and 327–8): for a parallel literal account v. Richard Baxter, *Reliquiae Baxterianae*, London, 1696, pp. 2–3.

Part II, section v: *The Mower Poems*

1. Critics who treat the Mower poems as a group on grounds similar to mine include Toliver (1965), pp. 103–12; Creaser (*EiC*, 1970), pp. 403–23; Wilcher (1985), pp. 89–105. Colie dissents (1970, p. 30). v. also Cullen, *Spenser, Marvell, and Renaissance Pastoral*, pp. 183–4 n. 1.

The Mower against Gardens

2. cf. Time in Spenser's Garden of Adonis (*FQ* III. vi. 39).

3. For England as garden v. Shakespeare, *Richard II*, III. iv. 43–7 and *UAH*, XLI; for woman as garden v. Thomas Campion, *There is a garden in her face* (*Elizabethan Lyrics*, ed. Ault, pp. 486–7); for poem as garden v. Sir William Alexander, *Anacrisis*, [?] 1634 *Critical Essays of the Seventeenth Century*, ed. J.E. Spingarn, Oxford, 1957, first pubd. 1908, I. 182; the mind as garden is the basis of the *hortus mentis* tradition.

4. *Sir William Temple upon the Gardens of Epicurus*, ed. A.F. Sieveking, London, 1908, p. 21.

5. The title is Adolphus Speed's (v. *Adam out of Eden*, London, 1659, 'To the Reader'): cf. Cowley, *Essays, in Verse and Prose*, 'Of Agriculture' and 'The Garden' (*Essays* etc., ed. Waller, 1906, p. 403 and pp. 422–3); John Evelyn, *Kalendarium Hortense*, London, 1664, Introduction, p. 55. v. also Nicholas A. Salerno, 'Andrew Marvell and the *Furor Hortensis*', *SEL*, 8, 1968 pp. 103–20.

6. v. Montague, *Miscellanea Spiritualia*, London, 1648, pp. 377–8; Thomas Vaughan, *Magia Adamica* (*Works*, ed. Rudrum, 1984, p. 158).

7. v. Marcia E. Allentuck, 'Marvell's Pool of Air', *MLN*, 74, 1959, pp. 587–9; Kitty Datta suggests that the phrase may have reached Marvell through James Howell, *Instructions for Forreine Travell*, London, 1642, p. 170, in 'Marvell and Wotton: A Reconsideration', *RES*, n. s. 19, 1968, pp. 403–5 (403).

8. v. Margoliouth/Legouis I. 262: v. also *Encyclopedia Britannica*, 1971, 22, 'Tulip'.

9. Cowley, *Beauty*, l. 22 (*Poems*, ed. Waller, 1905, p. 116); Taylor. *A Discourse of the Nature, Offices and Measures of Friendship*, London, 1657, pp. 39–40.

10. Shirley, *Poems* &c., London, 1646, pp. 69–70 (69).

11. Browne, Dedication to *The Garden of Cyrus*, 1658, (*Works*, ed. Keynes, 1964, I. 176). Colie cites the first quotation (1970), p. 161.

12. Lipsius, *A Discourse of Constancy: In Two Books (De constantia)*, tr. R.G., London, 1654, II. iii. 78, 79.

13. Evelyn, *Kalendarium Hortense*, Introduction, p. 55: for the practical and contemplative benefits of horticulture cf. Ralph Austen, *A Treatise of Frvit-trees . . . Together with The Spirituall use of an Orchard*, Oxford, 1653, A Preface to the Reader.

14. John Parkinson, *Paradisi in Sole Paradisus Terrestris*, London, 1629, pp. 364–6: v. Margoliouth/Legouis I. 262.

15. v. Kermode ed. *Selected Poetry*, pp. xix; Craze (1979), p. 135.

16. e.g. Randolph, *Upon love fondly refus'd for Conscience sake, Poems*, 1640, pp. 114–16 (115), cit. Frank Kermode, 'Two Notes on Marvell', *N&Q*, 197, 1952, pp. 136–8 (136–7) and Leishman (1966), pp. 132–3. cf. Wye Saltonstall, *Picturae Loguentes*, 2nd edn., London, 1635, no. 29, 'A Gardiner', sigs. F11^r–F12^v (F12^v); Milton, *CPW*, IV, ed. Don M. Wolfe, 1966, i. 566.

17. For grafting v. Kermode ed. *Selected Poetry*, p. xvi–xviii; Leishman, following E.E. Duncan-Jones (1966, pp. 134–6); J.C. Calderhead, 'The Cherry and the Laurel', *N&Q*, 212, 1967, pp. 337–9; Nicholas A. Salerno, 'Andrew Marvell and the Grafter's Art', *EA*, 21, 1968, 125–32, challenged by Robert Wilcher, 'Marvell's Cherry: A Reply to Mr Salerno', *EA*, 23, 1970, pp. 406–9; Carey (Patrides ed. *Approaches*, 1978), pp. 148–9 and pp. 153–4 n. 7.

18. Kermode makes this explicit equation (*Selected Poetry*, p. xix): v. also Swardson, *Poetry and the Fountain of Light*, pp. 95–6.

19. For political/economic readings of the poem v. Hill, *Puritanism and Revolution*, pp. 348–50; Bruce King, ' "The Mower against Gardens" and the Levellers', *HLQ*, 33, 1969–70, pp. 237–42; McKeon (*YES*, 1983), pp. 60–1.

20. v. James Turner, *The Politics of Landscape*, Oxford, 1979, p. 162.

21. Selden, *Table-Talk* (1689), Temple Classics ed. Israel Gollancz, London, n.d., p. 97. cf. John Aubrey on fairies, *Remaines of Gentilisme and Judaisme*, ed. James Britten, Publications of the Folk-Lore Society IV, London, 1881, pp. 29–30, 102, 125–6; Richard Corbett, *The Faeryes Farewell, Poems*, ed. J.A.W. Bennett and H.R. Trevor-Roper, Oxford, 1955, pp. 49–52. Keith Thomas surveys the subject in *Religion and the Decline of Magic*, Harmondsworth, 1978 (first pubd. 1971), 19. iv, pp. 724–34.

22. v. Berthoff (1970), p. 141 n. 23.

23. v. Hunt (1978), p. 44; also ' "Loose Nature" and the "Garden Square": the gardenist background for Marvell's poetry' (Patrides ed. *Approaches*, 1978, pp. 331–51).

24. *A Discourse of Constancy*, p. 77.

Damon the Mower

25. For comment on the mower as protagonist v. Margoliouth/Legouis I. 263–4; Cullen, *Spenser, Marvell, and Renaissance Pastoral*, pp. 189–90 n. 3; Friedman (1970), pp. 120–1. For varying attitudes to Damon v. inter al., Creaser (*EiC*, 1970), pp. 406–13; Berek (*MLQ*, 1971), pp. 147–51; David Kalstone, 'Marvell and the Fictions of Pastoral', *ELR*, 4, 1974, pp. 174–88 (175–83); Elaine H. Baruch, 'Themes and Counter-themes in "Damon the Mower" ', *CL*, 26, 1974, pp. 242–59.

26. *Picturae Loguentes*, sigs. G10^v–G12^r: quoted passages on G10^v, G11^v, G12^r respectively.

27. *A Gorgeous Gallery of Gallant Inventions*, 1578 (*Elizabethan Lyrics*, ed. Ault,

pp. 78-9). Contrast 1.4 with *The Mower to the Glo-Worms*, ll. 5-8.

28. *Aurelian Townshend's Poems and Masks*, ed. E.K. Chambers, Oxford, 1912, pp. 6-7 (6).

29. v. Eclogue II. 8-13. For Virgil and *Damon the Mower* v. Kalstone (*ELR*, 1974), pp. 176-83; Paul Alpers, 'Convening and Convention in Pastoral Poetry', *NLH*, 14, 1982-3, pp. 277-304 (287-97).

30. v. Cowley, *The Grashopper, Anacreontiques* (*Poems*, ed. Waller, 1905, p. 57): for the grasshopper in literary tradition v. Allen, *Image and Meaning*, pp. 154-8; Kitty Scoular, *Natural Magic*, Oxford, 1965, pp. 108-12. For the frog v. Theocritus, Idyll X. 52-3.

31. cf. Milton, Arcades, ll. 96-7.

32. *Twicknam Garden*, l.9 (*Elegies and Songs and Sonnets*, ed. Gardner, p. 83). For Marvell's snake v. Nevo (*SEL*, 1965), p. 19; Creaser (*EiC*, 1970), p. 406; Baruch (*CL*, 1974), p. 246.

33. I follow the emendation 'mads' (Bodl. MS. Eng. poet. d. 49) instead of the Folio 'made' (v. Macdonald ed. *Poems*, p. 172).

34. v. Leishman (1966), pp. 80-2, 137-8, 153, 190, 224-37, 244.

35. e.g. Carew, *Song, A beautifull Mistris* (*Poems*, 1640, p. 9); Henry Lawes, *Ayres and Dialogues. The First Booke*, p. 15, *Gaze not on Swanns*; Cleveland, *Upon Phillis walking in a morning before Sun-rising* (*Poems*, ed. Morris and Withington, p. 15).

36. *Clorinda and Damon*, ll. 9-19: Friedman also notes the parallel (1970, pp. 131-2).

37. v. Margoliouth/Legouis I. 264.

38. For meaning of gifts v. Friedman (1970), p. 132 and p. 145 n. 52; Baruch (*CL*, 1974), pp. 248-50: Kalstone emphasises the Cyclops parallel (*ELR*, 1974, pp. 181-2).

39. For the importance of the Fall in the Mower poems v. Barbara Everett's seminal article 'Marvell's "The Mower's Song"', *CQ*, 4, 1962, pp. 219-24: Tayler, *Nature and Art in Renaissance Literature*, pp. 157-62; Creaser (*EiC*, 1970), pp. 405-13; Carol Gilbertson, '"Many *Miltons* in this one Man": Marvell's Mower Poems and *Paradise Lost*', *Milton Studies*, 22, 1986, pp. 151-72. For a dissenting view v. Cullen, *Spenser, Marvell, and Renaissance Pastoral*, pp. 183-4.

40. v. Margoliouth/Legouis I. 264.

41. Baruch comments on the poem's time-scheme (*CL* 1974, pp. 248, 253).

42. v. Leishman (1966), pp. 139-40.

43. For the pun v. Friedman (1970), pp. 133-4 and pp. 145-6 n. 54.

44. Cullen compares *FQ* VI. x (*Spenser, Marvell, and Renaissance Pastoral*, p. 188); v. also Alpers (*NLH*, 1982-3), p. 295.

45. For the significance of thistles and/or iron v. Friedman (1970), p. 146 n. 56; King (1977), p. 128; Wilcher (1985), pp. 98-9.

46. cf. Colin Clout in Spenser's 'Januarye' Eclogue, *The Shepheardes Calender*, ll. 43-6. v. also Cullen on *The Mower's Song* (*Spenser, Marvell, and Renaissance Pastoral*, p. 195).

47. v. for example Geoffrey H. Hartman, 'Marvell, St. Paul, and the Body of Hope', *ELH*, 31, 1964, pp. 175-94 (189-90); Carey (Patrides ed. *Approaches*, 1978), pp. 142-3.

48. v. Erwin Panofsky, 'Et in Arcadia Ego: Poussin and the Elegiac Tradition' (*Meaning in the Visual Arts*, NY, 1957, pp. 295-320). Time's sickle as a castration symbol may also be of interest for *Damon the Mower* (v. Panofsky, *Studies in Iconology*, p. 74).

49. v. Margoliouth/Legouis I. 265.

50. v. Kalstone (*ELR*, 1974), p. 182.

The Mower to the Glo-Worms

51. Henry Vaughan's phrase: 'Christs Nativity', l.18 (*Poems*, ed. Martin, 1957, p. 442).
52. For glow-worms in literary tradition v. Scoular, *Natural Magic*, pp. 103–8 (Pliny cited p. 103).
53. *Pseudodoxia Epidemica*, III.xxvii. 12 (*Works*, ed. Keynes, 1964, II 262–3).
54. Shakespeare, *Julius Caesar*, II. ii. 30–1 (ed. T.S. Dorsch, Arden Shakespeare, London, and Harvard U.P., Cambridge, Mass., 1955, p. 52).
55. Isaiah 40: 6–8. A number of critics comment on the relevance of this passage to the Mower poems.
56. Milton's phrase: *PL*, XII. 313 (ed. Fowler, p. 624).
57. *Select Discourses*, 1660, I (*Cambridge Platonists*, ed. Patrides, p. 131).
58. *Poetical Works*, ed. Martin, 1956, p. 217. Scoular cites this among other examples (*Natural Magic*, p. 107).
59. *XXV Sermons*, 1653, p. 170 (*The Golden Grove: Selected Passages from the Sermons and Writings of Jeremy Taylor*, ed. Logan Pearsall Smith, Oxford, 1930, repr. 1955, p. 175).

The Mower's Song

60. v. Everett (*CQ*, 1962), p. 223.
61. Bacon, *The Advancement of Learning*, I (*Works*, edd. Spedding et al., 1870, III. 287).
62. v. Ripa, *Iconologia*, 1709, p. 72, fig. 287, Speranza: Hope, 'A young Woman clad in green, crown'd with a Garland of Flowers'. cf. p. 23, fig. 92, Diletto: Delight, a boy in green. 'The Green signifies the *Vivacity* and *Delightfulness* of green Meadows to the *Sight*'.
63. e.g. Wilcher (1985), p. 102.
64. Tayler notes the pun 'luxuriant' (*Nature and Art in Renaissance Literature*, p. 156).
65. For 'gawdy' v. King (1977), p. 141; Craze (1979), p. 153.
66. e.g. Henry Howard, Earl of Surrey, 'The soote season' (*Poems*, ed. Emrys Jones, Oxford, 1964, Clarendon Medieval and Tudor Series, p. 2); Samuel Daniel, 'Now each creature joys the other' (*Elizabethan Lyrics*, ed. Ault, pp. 157–8); Donne, *Twicknam Garden* (*Elegies and Songs and Sonnets*, ed. Gardner, pp. 83–4).
67. v. Cullen, *Spenser, Marvell, and Renaissance Pastoral*, p. 195.
68. For effect of refrain v. Margoliouth/Legouis I. 266.
69. cf. Henry Vaughan, *Corruption*, ll. 15–16 (*Works*, ed. Martin, 1957, p. 440). Toliver compares Adam (1965, p. 111); Chernaik compares Milton's Satan (1983, p. 26).
70. For apocalyptic readings v. Hartman (*ELH*, 1964), pp. 190–2; Stocker (1986), pp. 234–40: I do not find in the poem the idea of renovation which seems essential to this interpretation.
71. v. note 26 above.

Ametas and Thestylis making Hay-Ropes

72. v. Carey (Patrides ed. *Approaches*, 1978), p. 138: for poem's strategy v. also Cullen, *Spenser, Marvell, and Renaissance Pastoral*, pp. 198-200.
73. v. Winny's note (*Some Poems*, p. 95). Winny compares *UAH*, LIV: the name Thestylis recurs in *UAH*, LI.
74. Shakespeare, *The Winter's Tale*, IV. iii. 11-12 (ed. J.H.P. Pafford, Arden Shakespeare, London, and Harvard U.P., Cambridge, Mass., 1963, p. 80).

Part III

1. Donno ed. *Critical Heritage* (1978), index and p. 14.
2. p. 99: cit. Carey ed. *Critical Anthology* (1969), p. 25.
3. Cowley's phrases: v. 'Of Agriculture', *Essays, in Verse and Prose (Essays* etc., ed. Waller, 1906, p. 401).
4. v. Toliver (Friedenreich ed. *Tercentenary Essays*, 1977), pp. 109-10.

Part III, section i: *Musicks Empire*

1. *Timaeus* 47. D., tr. by R.G. Bury, Loeb Classical Library, London and NY, 1929, p. 109. cf. Plotinus, *Enneads*, tr. by Stephen MacKenna, 4th edn., rev. B.S. Page, London, 1956, I. iii. 1, p. 37.
2. For history of musical ideas v. Leo Spitzer, 'Classical and Christian Ideas of World Harmony', *Traditio*, 2, 1944, pp. 409-64, and 3, 1945, pp. 307-64; Finney, *Musical Backgrounds*; Hollander, *Untuning of the Sky;* Joscelyn Godwin, *Harmonies of Heaven and Earth: The Spiritual Dimension of Music from Antiquity to the Avant-Garde*, London, 1987.
3. v. Ficino, cit. Finney, *Musical Backgrounds*, passim: e.g. *Commentary*, tr. Jayne, I. iv: text, p. 40; translation, p. 130.
4. *Poems*, ed. Robert Krueger, Oxford, 1975, pp. 237-8 (237).
5. Finney, *Musical Backgrounds*, p. 52.
6. v. *Republic*, III. x (tr. by P. Shorey, Loeb Classical Library, London and NY, 1930, I. 246-9).
7. Charles Butler, *The Principles of Musik*, London, 1636, I. i. 1-2, 'Of the Moodes'.
8. *Religio Medici*, II. 9 (*Works*, ed. Keynes, I. 84).
9. *Sermons*, London, 1637, pp. 22-3. For Church music controversy v. Finney, *Musical Backgrounds*, chap. III; Hollander, *Untuning of the Sky*, pp. 245-66.
10. cf. Toliver (Friedenreich ed. *Tercentenary Essays*, 1977), pp. 107-11.
11. e.g. Hollander, 'Marvell's Commonwealth and "The Empire of the Ear" ', (*Untuning of the Sky*, pp. 299-315); Jonathan Goldberg, 'The Typology of "Musicks Empire" ', *TSLL*, 13, 1971-2, pp. 421-30.
12. *Sermons*, ed. Potter and Simpson, 1955, II. 170 (no. 2 in *XXVI Sermons*). Goldberg cites part of this passage in parallel to *Musicks Empire*, st. VI (*TSLL*, 1971-2, p. 429).

13. *Complete Shorter Poems*, ed. Carey, 1971, pp. 161-5 (164). For discussion of Milton's poem v. Spitzer (*Traditio*, 1945), pp. 336-40; James Hutton, 'Some English Poems in Praise of Music', *Eng. Misc.*, 2, 1951, pp. 1-63 (47-50); Finney, *Musical Backgrounds*, chap. VIII; Hollander, *Untuning of the Sky*, pp. 323-31.

14. cf. Hollander, *Untuning of the Sky*, p. 311.

15. For world as organ v. Athanasius Kircher, *Mvsvrgia Vniversalis*, Rome, 1650, II. x. 1, illustration opposite p. 366; Finney, *Musical Backgrounds*, pp. 13-17 and p. 240 n. 25. For world as lute v. *Du Bartas His Deuine Weekes and Workes*, tr. Sylvester, 1613, p. 256; Finney, pp. 12-13.

16. v. Goldberg (*TSLL*, 1971-2, p. 424) citing I Corinthians 13: 1. A.J.N. Wilson proposes an alternative classical allusion in 'Andrew Marvell: *Upon the Hill and Grove at Bill-borow* and *Musicks Empire*', *JRLB*, 51, 1968-9, pp. 453-82 (472-4).

17. Spitzer (*Traditio*, 1945), p. 312.

18. For Jubal connotations v. Goldberg (*TSLL*, 1971-2), pp. 424-5; King (1977), p. 147. For pagan parallels v. Ralegh, *History of the World*, ed. Patrides, 1971, p. 150; Wilson (*JRLB*, 1968-9), pp. 475-7.

19. Cowley, 'The Garden', st. 3, *Essays, in Verse and Prose* (*Essays* etc., ed. Waller, 1906, p. 423).

20. v. Goldberg (*TSLL*, 1971-2), pp. 425-6; King (1977), pp. 147-8.

21. v. *PL*, XI. 558-63 and 607-12: Fowler annotates 556ff. with ref. to *Musicks Empire* (1971 edn., p. 593). (The likely date of *Musicks Empire* is, however, long before the publication of *PL*.)

22. *The Wel-Tvned Cymbal:* quotations on pp. 24, 28, 25, respectively.

23. Hollander regards it as 'almost completely... secular' (*Untuning of the Sky*, p. 312); King regards it as a type of Jerusalem (1977, p. 148).

24. Leishman, however, considers performers to be 'unexorcisable' (1966, p. 220).

25. Wilson compares Roman colonies (*JRLB*, 1968-9, pp. 478-9).

26. v. Hollander, *Untuning of the Sky*, pp. 34-5; King (1977), p. 149.

27. Wilson (*JRLB*, 1968-9), pp. 481-2: for Moses allusion v. also Hollander, *Untuning of the Sky*, pp. 313-14; Goldberg (*TSLL*, 1971-2), pp. 428-9; King (1977), p. 150. Wilson and Hollander comment on the etymology of Muse/music/mosaic.

28. Craze discovered the *Gondibert* source and stresses its importance for the Fairfax connection (1979, pp. 256-7); but he does not investigate all the possible similarities.

29. Sir William D'Avenant, *Gondibert: An Heroick Poem*, London, 1651, p. 126: subsequent quotations are on pp. 133, 137, 138 respectively.

30. v. Goldberg (*TSLL*, 1971-2), pp. 429-30; King (1977), pp. 151-3.

31. v. Margoliouth/Legouis I. 266-7.

32. v. Hollander, *Untuning of the Sky*, p. 314.

33. v. Sprigge, *Anglia Rediviva*, London, 1647, sig.*B2, p. 9 and pp. 321-3; May, *A Breviary of the History of the Parliament of England*, 1655 (Francis Maseres ed. *Select Tracts relating to the Civil Wars in England*, London, 1826, I. 66).

34. ed. Brian Fairfax, London, 1699: Fairfax's affection for the Psalms ('Heavens Hallelujahs') is evident from 'Imployments of my Solitude' (Bodl. MS. Fairfax 40).

35. v. *Short Memorials*, sig.K1ʳ.

36. *Defensio Secunda, A Second Defence* (*CPW*, IV. i, ed. Don M. Wolfe, 1966, tr. by Helen North, p. 669).

37. v. Donald A. Roberts, notes on *A Second Defence* (*CPW*, IV. i. 669-70): cf. Patterson on the Fairfax poems (1978, pp. 95-110).

Part III, section ii: *The Garden*

1. e.g. Harry Berger Jr., 'Marvell's "Garden": Still Another Interpretation', *MLQ*, 28, 1967, pp. 285–304; J.H. Summers, 'Reading Marvell's "Garden" ', *CentR*, 13, 1969, pp. 18–37 (repr. in *The Heirs of Donne and Jonson*, London, 1970, chap. V). Klause reads it as self-parody (1983, pp. 112–16).
2. For relation between *The Garden* and *Hortus* v. A.H. King, 'Some Notes on Andrew Marvell's Garden', *ES*, 20, 1938, pp. 118–21; Carl E. Bain, 'The Latin Poetry of Andrew Marvell', *PQ*, 38, 1959, pp. 436–49 (438–43); William A. McQueen, 'The Missing Stanzas in Marvell's *Hortus*', *PQ*, 44, 1965, pp. 173–9; George Williamson, 'Marvell's "Hortus" and "Garden" ' (*Milton & Others*, London, 1965, pp. 140–9); Colie (1970), pp. 153–4.
3. For translation of *Hortus* v. McQueen/Rockwell, pp. 23–5.
4. However both McQueen (*PQ*, 1965, p. 176) and Long (1984, p. 127) emphasise the direct polarity of *Hortus*.
5. v. Toliver (1965), p. 141.
6. cf. *FQ*, III. vi. 49, 'laying his sad darts/Aside'. The reading of Bodl. MS.Eng. poet. d.49 makes the assignment of trees clearer.
7. For numerology v. Stocker (1986), p. 247; for classical rhetoric v. J.E. Siemon, 'Generic Limits in Marvell's "Garden" ', *PLL*, 8, 1972, pp. 261–72.
8. Thomas Vaughan, *Anthroposophia Theomagica*, 1650 (*Works*, ed. Rudrum, p. 66; v. also pp. 76–9).
9. For varying structural divisions v. Craze (1979), p. 168; Berger (*MLQ*, 1967), p. 288ff; Summers, *Heirs of Donne and Jonson*, pp. 139–40.
10. v. Thomas Vaughan, *Works*, ed. Rudrum, p. 68.
11. Wilcher notes a potential distinction between 'motives' and 'activities' (1985, p. 132).
12. cf. Summers, *Heirs of Donne and Jonson*, p. 142.
13. For wordplay v. Colie (1970), pp. 147–8; Friedman (1970), pp. 150–1.
14. *Ode. Upon Liberty*, st. 6, *Essays, in Verse and Prose* (*Essays* etc., ed. Waller, 1906, p. 391).
15. Critics who adopt the 'naive speaker' reading to a greater or lesser extent include Berger, Summers, Colie, Klause: Carol Marks Sicherman calls him 'an amusing fanatic' in 'The Mocking Voices of Donne and Marvell', *BuR*, 17, 1969, ii, pp. 32–46 (45); Siemon assesses the 'naive' reading (*PLL*, 1972, pp. 262, 271–2).
16. *alma*: v. King (*ES*, 1938), p. 119.
17. Patrides contends that these presences prove st. VIII a delusion: v. ' "Till prepared for longer flight": The sublunar poetry of Andrew Marvell' (Patrides ed. *Approaches*, 1978, pp. 31–55), p. 51. But surely allegory and myth are distinct from a flesh-and-blood 'Mate'?
18. Sidney, 'O sweet woods', l.42 (*Poems*, ed. Ringler, 1962, pp. 68–9).
19. v. *A Masque Presented at Ludlow Castle* [*Comus*], ll. 628–40 (*Complete Shorter Poems*, ed. Carey, 1971, pp. 206–8).
20. *pace* Norford, who defines passion as 'the emotional form of action' (*ELH*, 1974, p. 62), and Stocker, who identifies 'love and activism' (1986, p. 241). Others emphasise the retreat from love: v. W.R. Orwen, 'Andrew Marvell's "The Garden" ', *N&Q*, 191, 1946, pp. 247–9; Poggioli, *Oaten Flute*, p. 175.
21. v. Maren-Sofie Røstvig, 'Andrew Marvell's "The Garden": A Hermetic Poem', *ES*, 1959, pp. 65–76 (70–2), also *The Happy Man*, Oslo, 1954, rev. edn.,

Norwegian Universities Press, 1962, I. iv; J.C. Maxwell, 'Two Notes on Marvell's Language', *N&Q*, 213, 1968, p. 377; Margoliouth/Legouis I. 267.

22. For 'delicious' v. Milton Klonsky, 'A Guide through the Garden', *SeR*, 58, 1950, pp. 16-35 (20); Summers, *Heirs of Donne and Jonson*, p. 144; Friedman (1970), p. 155; Kalstone (*ELR*, 1974), p. 184.

23. For pastoral hyperbole v. notes 34 and 35 on '*Damon the Mower*': the glow-worm is Thomas Stanley's contribution (*Poems*, 1651, pp. 5-6, *The Gloworme*).

24. v. D.C. Allen, 'Symbolic Colour in the Literature of the English Renaissance', *PQ*, 15, 1936, pp. 81-92 (85-6); Kermode, 'Green in Marvell' (*N&Q*, 1952), pp. 137-8; Colie (1970), p. 158 n. 36.

25. More: v. *Cambridge Platonists*, ed. Patrides, p. 266; Browne: v. *Works*, ed. Keynes, 1964, I. 217.

26. v. Colie (1970), p. 159.

27. st. 1 (*The Mistress, Poems*, ed. Waller, 1905, p. 140). For Marvell and Cowley v. Carey (Patrides ed. *Approaches*, 1978), p. 137: Allan Pritchard, in 'Marvell's "The Garden": A Restoration Poem?' *SEL*, 23, 1983, pp. 371-88, uses Cowley and other parallels to support redating.

28. Orwen exemplifies the 'disappointed lover' reading (*N&Q*, 1946, pp. 247-9). For heat/retreat wordplay v. King (*ES*, 1938), p. 119; Frank Kermode, 'The Argument of Marvell's "Garden" ', *EiC*, 2, 1952, pp. 225-41 (234); Colie (1970), p. 160: Legouis is more sceptical (Margoliouth/Legouis I. 267).

29. v. Ovid, *Metamorphoses*, I. 452-567; 689-712.

30. v. Kermode (*EiC*, 1952), pp. 234-5.

31. e.g. Berger (*MLQ*, 1967), p. 292; Summers, *Heirs of Donne and Jonson*, pp. 146-7; Colie (1970), pp. 159-60. The same argument applies *a fortiori* to st. VIII.

32. v. Bradbrook and Lloyd Thomas (1940), p. 60.

33. ll. 3-4: McQueen/Rockwell, pp. 42-3.

34. For symbolism v. M.C. Bradbrook and M.G. Lloyd Thomas, 'Marvell and the Concept of Metamorphosis', *The Criterion*, 18, 1938-9, pp. 236-54 (239): Kermode argues that symbolism confuses the issue (*EiC*, 1952, p. 234); but v. Summers, *Heirs of Donne and Jonson*, p. 146. For analogues v. Christine Rees, 'The Metamorphosis of Daphne in Sixteenth- and Seventeenth-Century English Poetry', *MLR*, 66, 1971, pp. 251-63.

35. v. Ovid, *Metamorphoses*, I. 553-6.

36. *Religio Medici*, II. 9 (*Works* ed. Keynes, 1964, I. 83): Stocker also cites Browne (1986, p. 241).

37. *Publick Employment and an Active Life prefer'd to Solitude*, London, 1667, p. 31. For similar ridicule of wishful thinking about alternatives to human sex, v. Wilson, *Arte of Rhetorique*, 1553, Fol. 33.

38. *The Historie of the World. Commonly called, The Natvrall Historie of C. Plinivs Secvndvs*, tr. by Philemon Holland, London, 1601, V. xvii, p. 101.

39. Leishman supports the emendation (1966, p. 295), but it is not adopted in Margoliouth/Legouis: Craze rejects it for reasons with which I am in entire agreement (1979, pp. 174-5).

40. *pace* Summers, *Heirs of Donne and Jonson*, pp. 149-50.

41. cf. Sharrock, 'a personal vision of the good life' (*English*, 1979, p. 26).

42. v. Legouis (1968), p. 45. For symbolism taken to extremes, and a corrective, v. John McChesney's note and Don A. Keister's reply (*Explicator*, 10, 1951-2, nos. 4 and 24).

43. *To my mother Mrs. Anne Cokain*, 1658 (*The Poems of Sir Aston Cokayne*, ed.

Richard Morton, Hamilton, Ontario, 1977, p. 244).

44. v. Margoliouth/Legouis I. 268 (Duncan-Jones and Wall); Winny ed. *Some Poems*, p. 125; Jonson, *Poems*, ed. Donaldson (p. 89 and note); Hodge (1978), pp. 87–8; Rajan (Patrides ed. *Approaches*, 1978), p. 166. v. also Tayler, *Nature and Art in Renaissance Literature*, p. 167.

45. v. Klonsky, 'ripe round feminine forms' (*SeR*, 1950, p. 21); Harold Wendell Smith, 'a sort of giant fleshy orchid, deliciously hostile', 'Cowley, Marvell and the Second Temple'. *Scrutiny*, 19, 1952-3, pp. 184–205 (190); Anthony Hecht, 'a species of physical rape', 'Shades of Keats and Marvell', *HR*, 15, 1962-3, pp. 50–71 (53); Berger, 'tropical and sinister... animated with siren purpose' (*MLQ*, 1967, p. 289); Summers, 'pleasantly aggressive' (*Heirs of Donne and Jonson*, p. 148). But for counter-argument v. John N. Serio, 'Andrew Marvell's "The Garden": An Anagogic Reading', *OUR*, 12, 1970, pp. 68–76 (73-4).

46. The original Fall reading proposed by William Empson (*Some Versions of Pastoral*, London, 1935, pp. 131-2) has been adopted, contested, or modified by various commentators: e.g. King (*ES*, 1938), p. 120; Kermode (*EiC*, 1952), pp. 235–6; Colie (1970). pp. 162-3; Legouis (Margoliouth/Legouis I. 268). Empson replies to his critics and constructs an entertaining fresh scenario in 'Natural Magic and Populism in Marvell's Poetry' (Brett ed. *Essays*, 1979, pp. 42-6).

47. v. Carey (Patrides ed. *Approaches*, 1978), pp. 151-2.

48. v. L.W. Hyman, 'Marvell's "Garden" ', *ELH*, 25, 1958, pp. 13–22; Røstvig (*ES*, 1959), p. 73.

49. v. Empson, *Some Versions of Pastoral*, pp. 124-5 and Brett ed. *Essays*, 1979, pp. 44-5; Kermode (*EiC*, 1952), pp. 236-7; P. Legouis, 'Marvell and the New Critics', *RES*, n.s.8, 1957, pp. 382-9 (382-3) and Margoliouth/Legouis I. 268; Summers, *Heirs of Donne and Jonson*, p. 149; Rajan (Patrides ed. *Approaches*, 1978), p. 166 and pp. 172-3 n. 20.

50. cit. and tr. Leishman (1966), p. 312: v. also Emson, *Some Versions of Pastoral*, p. 125. For comment on textual variant v. Lord ed. *Complete Poetry*, p. 49.

51. v. Leishman (1966), p. 313; Margoliouth/Legouis I. 268.

52. *Ode. Of Wit*, st. 8 (*Poems*, ed. Waller, 1905, p. 18).

53. e.g. Wallerstein, Klonsky, Hyman, Røstvig, Toliver, Friedman, Colie. For an alternative Stoic reading of the poem v. T. Katharine Thomason, 'The Stoic Ground of Marvell's "Garden" ', *TSLL*, 24, 1982, pp. 222-41. For a Cartesian reading v. Daniel Stempel, '*The Garden:* Marvell's Cartesian Ecstasy', *JHI*, 28, 1967, pp. 99-114.

54. Bacon, *The Advancement of Learning:* for this and the following quotations v. *Works*, edd. Spedding et al., 1870, III. 287, 395, 343-4 respectively.

55. For terminology v. Margoliouth/Legouis I. 268-9; Empson, *Some Versions of Pastoral*, p. 126; Walton, *Metaphysical to Augustan*, pp. 134-5; Stempel (*JHI*, 1967), pp. 109-10; William Leigh Godshalk, 'Marvell's *Garden* and the Theologians', *SP*, 66, 1969, pp. 639-53 (648-9); Berthoff (1970), pp. 149-51; Long (1984), p. 128.

56. Gerard Manley Hopkins, *God's Grandeur*, l.10 (*Gerard Manley Hopkins*, ed. Catherine Phillips, Oxford/NY, 1986, p. 128).

57. v. King (*ES*, 1938), p. 121: cf. *UAH*, l.645 (Margoliouth/Legouis I. 291).

58. *The Spirituall Use of an Orchard*, 1653, A Preface to the Reader.

59. v. Bradbrook and Lloyd Thomas (*The Criterion*, 1938-9), p. 241; Serio (*OUR*, 1970), p. 75.

60. *Phaedrus* 250, cit. Hyman (*ELH*, 1958), p. 20; Kermode (*EiC*, 1952), pp. 239–40; Maren-Sofie Røstvig, 'Benlowes, Marvell, and the Divine Casimire', *HLQ*, 18, 1954–5, pp. 13–35 (29–30); Stocker (1986), pp. 247–8.

61. *Emblemes*, 1635, V.x, pp. 281–2: cit. Dennis Davison, 'Notes on Marvell's "The Garden" ', *N&Q*, 211, 1966, pp. 25–6 (26).

62. For former reading v. Poggioli, *Oaten Flute*, pp. 177–8; Klause (1983), pp. 114–5: for latter reading v. Røstvig (*HLQ*, 1954–5), pp. 29–30, and note 89 below. Chernaik uses the illuminating phrase 'mimesis of ecstasy' (1983, p. 37). v. also Friedman (1970), pp. 169–70.

63. For significance of 'various Light' v. Friedman (1970), p. 171; Stocker (1986), p. 248. Stempel comments on *lumen naturale* (*JHI*, 1967), p. 112; Dale Herron distinguishes between *lux* and *lumen*, 'Marvell's "Garden" and the Landscape of Poetry', *JEGP*, 73, 1974, pp. 328–37 (335). For contemporary imagery of Light cf. Cowley, *Hymn. To light* (*Poems*, ed. Waller, 1905, pp. 444–7); Milton, *PL*, III. 1–55 (ed. Fowler, 1971, pp. 141–6).

64. *PL*, IV. 286 (ed. Fowler, 1971, p. 212).

65. ll. 35–40: for the connection v. Joseph A. Wittreich Jr., following Hyman, 'Perplexing the explanation: Marvell's "On Mr Milton's *Paradise Lost*" ' (Patrides ed. *Approaches*, 1978, pp. 280–305), p. 299; Stocker (1986), pp. 248–9.

66. For time in *The Garden* v. Ellrodt, *Les Poètes Métaphysiques Anglais*, II. iii. 118–9.

67. For former attitude v. Leishman (1966), pp. 307–8: Miner disapproves (*Metaphysical Mode from Donne to Cowley*, pp. 89–91).

68. *The First Anniversarie: An Anatomy of the World*, l. 99 and ll. 105–7 (*John Donne: The Epithalamions Anniversaries and Epicedes*, ed. W. Milgate, Oxford, 1978, pp. 24, 25).

69. e.g. Summers, *Heirs of Donne and Jonson*, pp. 151–2; Stocker (1986), p. 251: Siemon questions whether the blasphemy appears unconscious or deliberate (*PLL*, 1972, pp. 270–1). v. also Colie (1970), pp. 166–7.

70. Summers, *Heirs of Donne and Jonson*, p. 151.

71. v. Kermode (*EiC*, 1952), p. 241; Legouis (*RES*, 1957), p. 387; Hecht (*HR*, 1962–3), pp. 55–6.

72. Donne, *Devotions*, XVII. Meditation.

73. *A Moral Essay, preferring Solitude to Publick Employment*, Edinburgh, 1665, p.[40].

74. *Of Solitude*, st.7, *Essays, in Verse and Prose* (*Essays* etc., ed. Waller, 1906, p. 396): also cit. Leishman (1966), p. 306.

75. *Publick Employment and an Active Life prefer'd to Solitude*, 1667, p. 58.

76. v. *Hermes Mercurius Trismegistus his Divine Pymander*, tr. Everard, 1657, II. 27, 29, 37, pp. 25–7.

77. v. Wallerstein, *Studies in Seventeenth-Century Poetic*, pp. 333–4; Hyman (*ELH*, 1958), pp. 13–22; Røstvig (*ES*, 1959), pp. 65–76: contested by Legouis (Margoliouth/Legouis I. 270).

78. Cleveland, *Clievelandi Vindiciae*, London, 1677, pp. 25–6. For a more serious analogy v. Spenser, *FQ*, III. xii. 46 (1590 edn.: v. *FQ*, ed. Hamilton, 1980, p. 421 and note): also v. Browne, *Britannia's Pastorals*, 1613, I. iii. 53.

79. *Poems*, 1640, pp. 129–30.

80. v. Berger (*MLQ*, 1967), pp. 300–1; Friedenreich (Friedenreich ed. *Tercentenary Essays*, 1977), p. 174.

81. v. *PL*, VIII. 352–451 (ed. Fowler, 1971, pp. 416–20).

82. *The Doctrine and Discipline of Divorce*, I, Preface and chap. ii (*CPW*, II, ed. Sirluck, 1959, p. 235 and pp. 245-7).

83. The quoted phrase is Wilcher's (1985, p. 140); v. also Stocker (1986), p. 251.

84. v. above pp. 141-4: for horticulturist background of *The Garden*: v. also Salerno (*SEL*, 1968), pp. 103-20; Margaret Ann Carpenter, 'Marvell's "Garden" ', *SEL*, 10, 1970, pp. 155-69.

85. Saltonstall, *Picturae Loquentes*, no. 29, sigs. F11^r, F12^r.

86. v. Friedman (1970), pp. 173-4: for symmetry of first and last stanzas v. Hyman (*ELH*, 1958), p. 22; Siemon (*PLL*, 1972), p. 269.

87. *Du Bartas his Deuine Weekes and Workes*, tr. Sylvester, 1613, 'Eden', p. 217.

88. *XCVI. Sermons*, London, 1629, Sermons of the Resurrection, preached on Easter-day, Sermon xiv, Easter-day 1620, pp. 538-9. I owe this reference to Miss Rosemary Syfret.

89. For religious interpretations v. Stewart, *Enclosed Garden*, chap. V; King (1977), chap. 15: for religious/poetic reading v. Stocker (1986), pp. 240-56.

90. v. Margoliouth/Legouis I. 270-1.

91. Sidney's 'zodiac' of the poet's wit (*Apology for Poetry*) is cited by Berger (*MLQ*, 1967, p. 303) and Stocker (1986, p. 254): for *The Garden* and poetry v. also Herron (*JEGP*, 1974), pp. 328-37.

92. v. Margoliouth/Legouis I. 271.

93. For emphasis on transience v. Summers, *Heirs of Donne and Jonson*, p. 153; Klause (1983), p. 115.

94. v. Stocker (1986), pp. 252-3.

95. *Odes*, IV. ii. 27-36 (tr. Michie, 1967, pp. 214-15): v. Margoliouth/Legouis I. 271; John M. Potter, 'Another Porker in the Garden of Epicurus: Marvell's "Hortus" and "The Garden" ', *SEL*, 11, 1971, pp. 137-51 (147-8).

Index